DOING
MANAGEMENT
RESEARCH

DOING
MANAGEMENT
RESEARCH

A COMPREHENSIVE GUIDE

Raymond-Alain Thiétart et al.

Translated by Samantha Wauchope

SAGE Publications
London • Thousand Oaks • New Delhi

First published in English in 2001

Originally published in French as *Méthodes de Recherche en Management* by Dunod, Paris

© Dunod 1999

Work published with financial support from the French Ministry of Culture – Centre National du Livre and the University Paris-Dauphine

 SAGE Publications Ltd
6 Bonhill Street
London EC2A 4PU

SAGE Publications Inc
2455 Teller Road
Thousand Oaks, California 91320

SAGE Publications India Pvt Ltd
32, M-Block Market
Greater Kailash - I
New Delhi 110 048

British Library Cataloguing in Publication data

A catalogue record for this book is available from the British Library

ISBN 0 7619 6516 5
ISBN 0 7619 6517 3 (pbk)

Library of Congress control number available.

Typeset by SIVA Math Setters, Chennai, India
Printed in Great Britain by The Cromwell Press Ltd, Trowbridge, Wiltshire

CONTENTS

LIST OF AUTHORS

Florence Allard-Poesi — Maître de conférences, University of Paris XII-Val-de-Marne

Jacques Angot — Research Fellow, University of Paris-Dauphine

Philippe Baumard — Professor, IAE Aix en Provence

Sandra Charreire — Maître de conférences, University of Paris XII-Val-de-Marne

Carole Donada — Professor, Essec, Paris

Florence Durieux — Maître de conférences, University of Paris-Dauphine

Sylvie Ehlinger — Maître de conférences, University of Cergy-Pontoise

Bernard Forgues — Professor, University of Paris XII-Val-de-Marne

Martine Girod-Séville — Professor, University of Le Mans

Carole Drucker-Godard — Research Fellow, University of Paris X-Nanterre

Corinne Grenier — Professor, École supérieure de commerce, Troyes

Jérôme Ibert — Maître de conférences, University of Paris XII-Val-de-Marne

Emmanuel Josserand — Maître de conférences, University of Paris-Dauphine

Christine Maréchal — Research Fellow, University of Paris-Dauphine

Ababacar Mbengue — Professor, University of Reims

Patricia Milano — Maître de conférences, University of Paris-St. Denis

Véronique Perret — Maître de conférences, University of Cergy-Pontoise

Isabelle Royer — Maître de conférences, University of Paris-Dauphine

Raymond-Alain Thiétart — Professor, University of Paris-Dauphine and Essec

Isabelle Vandangeon-Derumez — Maître de conférences, University of Paris XII-Val-de-Marne

Jean-Marc Xuereb — Professor, Essec, Paris

Philippe Zarlowski — Professor, Essec, Paris

INTRODUCTION

R.A. Thiétart

Management is an extremely broad area of research. From the sixteenth-century Italian word *maneggiare*, meaning to control and train with care and skill, management can be defined as the way we guide, direct, structure and develop an organization. It touches on all organizational and decision-making aspects that underlie the functioning of the organization.

Management is less concerned with establishing procedures, whether legal, social or fiscal, than it is with motivating groups of men and women to work together towards a specified collective action. Management defines the operating conditions of the social entity – the enterprise, administration or institution – so that each member can contribute his or her best to the collective effort. Management is applicable to all levels of the organization. It can encompass the division of roles in a production plant, the formalization of a company's strategic orientation or the development and operationalization of measures to provide incentives and to evaluate performances. In short, the principal problem of management is discovering how to make social groups live together so that together they can produce more than the simple sum of their individual expertise. The role of management is thus immense, as it conditions the success and the good functioning of a great number of companies and organizations. It is also a complex role, concerned as it is with the human condition and all its cognitive contradictions – we do not all see the same thing, nor do we see things in the same way, depending on our individual representations of the world. We are similarly fraught with emotional contradictions, their origins often submerged deep within our subconscious.

Management, through its reach and its breadth, offers the researcher an inexhaustible mine of questions, from the most concrete to the most esoteric. These questions vary, too, according to their subject, aims and the research approach adopted. The subject of a research question might be a study of *content* (for example, describing the features of an organization that encourage its members to be innovative) or an analysis of a *process* (such as finding out how decisions are taken during times of crisis). Aims include to *describe*, to *explain*, to *predict*, or to *establish a norm*. For example, a question might aim to describe organizational learning, or to explain how the memory of an organization functions (to understand the mechanisms that take this beyond the memory of individual actors, so that it is the organization itself that remembers). Other questions might aim to predict the outcome of a strategy (by revealing determinant or influential factors), or to establish norms to ensure an organization runs smoothly (which comes down to an inventory of recommended courses of action). Finally, research questions can change according to the approach adopted. The approach might, for example, consist of *constructing* a new theory of incentives; of *testing* propositions about what motivates companies to diversify; of *classifying*, through empirical observation, ways companies work together to coordinate their activities; of *advancing a new concept* of organizational knowledge, or *representing*, through empirical investigation, the practical experience of post-acquisition management.

These three kinds of questions – which vary according to the subject, aim, and method – can be combined in numerous ways. For example, a researcher might want to study a process, both to understand it and to use it as the basis for elaborating a new theory or adapting an existing one. She might also study this same process in order to describe it, to add to the knowledge the scientific community has of it. Or she could direct her efforts at analyzing its content, deriving hypotheses from existing theories with the aim of comparing them with empirical reality. A research question is thus never limited to a subject without an aim or an approach, or to a single aim alone. A research question involves the combination of a subject (what to study), a purpose (why, for what end) and a process (how to proceed).

The richness of the field is not limited to research questions. The diversity of the theoretical foundations and methodologies that researchers can draw from adds an additional degree of complexity to this combination. As in every new science, multiple paradigms coexist, diverse techniques are employed, numerous theories are developed and utilized. This prodigality is both fortuitous and a handicap for management research. It is fortuitous in that untrammeled imagination coexists alongside the sometimes dry, but necessary, strictness of well-established procedures. Out of this diversity, too, new avenues can open: innovative concepts, different operating styles that are sources of progress. It is a handicap, because the best coexists with the worst. False prophets can take refuge behind the pretext of the breadth of the field, and the necessity to adapt their research approach to the problems at hand.

Finally, management research is characterized by a paradox. This paradox is intimately connected to the very nature of the subject. Management is a living social subject in which the practical experience of those caught up in it confer legitimacy and rights. Because of its amplitude, management science is the business of everyone, not just of researchers. Everyone is an expert on it, and talks about it, sometimes with great competence. Management science is seen as requiring more than specific research. It is a matter that concerns the whole community and its legitimacy! And there we find ourselves trapped in a recursive loop, where management research loses its social meaning because of the very fact of its importance. Research, in losing its legitimacy in the eyes of the very people who practice it, remains then all too often limited to closed circles of the initiated. It frequently ignores those whom it is supposed to serve.

We must strive to break this circle: to sort out the wheat from the chaff, to legitimize and make visible work that is often confidential, to find a happy medium between the extremes of inward looking research and research that is more practical but with reduced scope. Only works characterized by a real effort to pursue relevance, importance and precision can achieve these ends. Such works already exist, and have for several years – they show us the path we can follow. Management research must capitalize on these.

No one can claim ownership of the truth, however, and the diversity of research to date proves this. Researchers will always lean towards one approach rather than another; according to their experience, their training, their beliefs and their values. Where in the past we emphasized their differences, new research in management is moving towards reconciling seemingly contradictory schools of thought. We bring practical knowledge and theoretical knowledge together – in action research, for example – and establish connections between positivist and constructivist epistemologies, which we previously sought to demarcate. Even qualitative and quantitative processes are being used in parallel, in research methods incorporating triangulation. Dogmatism seems to be retreating in favor of approaches that are grounded in real problems rather than in arbitrary structures. This is good! This is genuine progress!

Research feeds on multiple experiences. From these can emerge a better understanding of the organizational phenomena we wish to study. This statement can shock proponents of positivist approaches, who prefer to pursue a process of refutation. But a diversity of approaches, without rejecting any one of them *a priori*, is a source of richness and discovery in a field still far from being as formalized as that of other sciences. Moreover, because of its breadth, it is understandable, even desirable, that management research should draw from varied methodologies and epistemological paradigms – methodologies dictated by the nature of the objects studied and influenced by cultural traditions, and epistemological paradigms often influenced by researchers' own beliefs.

There are two principal models of research in management. The first is the dominant American model; characterized by a quantitative, deductive approach, strongly emphasizing structured methods and confined to research questions deliberately restricted for purposes of control and precision. The aim is, as in 'normal' sciences, to compare theory with fact. One consequence can be a disproportionate emphasis on technique to the detriment of content. The second model is the European, which is more qualitative. It is inductive, often described as approximate, where method is only incidental and there is no real effort to accumulate. The aim is to explain a problem in its context: globally and in terms of its dynamics. Attention is given to meaning more than method, which is often regarded as secondary.

This apparent split has its roots in the respective research traditions of the two continents. Europe has a long tradition of research in the social sciences and has been strongly influenced by works on bureaucracy, political processes and the teachings of Weber, Marx and Piaget, brought up to date by Crozier, Hickson and Mayntz. The postmodernist movement of Derrida and Lyotard and the structuralism of Giddens have recently added to this panorama. This tradition places the emphasis on challenging major existing schemata and accepted schools of thought, and on seeking a global, holistic understanding of phenomena. The process is more in line with Carnap's logic of gradual confirmation than Popper's logic of refutation. The strong influence of these sometimes very old ways of thought shows up in the way in which management research is conducted: more qualitative, more inductive!

In America, the behaviorist tradition proliferates. It still influences the manner in which research is carried out today. This tradition is one of positivist theories and principles taken from normal sciences. Laws exist, and the researcher's task is to discover them. This is done through a step-by-step accumulation of knowledge, in the context of a logic of refutation. Although criticized in Europe as being reductionist, even simplistic, this type of research has provided important results and opened new avenues on both theoretical and empirical levels. I will just mention here its contribution to areas of institutional economy, incentives, evolutionism and resources, to illustrate some recent examples of the value of such work. Of course, remarkable exceptions to this tradition exist in America, and it would be a mistake to think that all American research is quantitative and based purely on deductive logic. Examples to the contrary are numerous, as is shown by the influential contributions of writers such as Perrow, Weick, Whyte or Mintzberg, Pfeffer, Starbuck and Van Mannen.

Beyond the disputes of cliques and the opposition, sometimes sterile, between schools of thought, the problem remains of knowing how to study management. What questions should researchers ask when they want to explore a management problem? And what is management? Is it a practical activity or a science, an objective reality or a collection of representations? Does it have an objective subject, or is its subject, even more so than for other fields, an elusive phenomenon that constantly slips away from the observer? Do we apprehend reality in management or are we part of its construction? How do we broach a research question? Can we establish a definitive investigative procedure, one that is thorough and convincing? What tools do we have to describe and understand what we observe? And how are we to observe? Must we choose a specific research procedure or can we mix different styles? These are some of the questions that researchers must ask themselves when they explore management problems and seek to discover their meaning. Yet the ultimate goal of our research must never be forgotten: to explain and to help actors who are confronted with concrete management problems.

It is the aim of this book to get researchers to ask themselves these questions, and to offer them some possible answers. *Doing Management Research* is the result of an intellectual adventure which has lasted for three years. The goal was to write a work covering the principal aspects of management research, less from a theoretical angle than from one based on the practical difficulties that confront researchers during their investigations. We did not set out to rework what has already been done by talented authors – we are not providing a collection of techniques or a toolbox for researchers to use. In writing this book our intention was to put ourselves in the researcher's shoes from the outset; from the moment he or she takes an idea and wants to investigate it.

In doing this, however, we have had to stress the circularity and the recursive nature of the investigative process. It is very rare, in fact, for a researcher to be able to follow a plan to the letter, without anything going wrong. More often, the process has to be adjusted regularly, in line with contingencies that arise along the way. An observational field might dry up prematurely, or an analysis technique could turn out to be unsatisfactory when put into practice. Observation conditions within an organization can change, casting doubts on original methodological choices. Much more so than in other fields (such as physical sciences), management research is undertaken in an atmosphere of uncertainty, in which the researcher has very imperfect control of the observational field. In fact, it is only after its complexity and unexpected aspects have been revealed that the researcher can find a way through this tangle. Good research depends on coherence and relevance, and the quality of the circular dialectic of aims, method and analysis. This is not to suggest we should reject the idea that there are defined stages to be followed if we are to conduct research well. However, we need to accept the fact that, once drawn up, a research plan is not immutable. It can evolve, and choices made initially can be later reviewed, in line with events that crop up along the way. At the same time, when we do make adjustments, these too must be done meticulously, and always with an eye to their coherence. Typical of research in management, where the context is difficult to control, alteration of one part of the epistemological/methodological construction can have multiple repercussions. The importance of this must be recognized. Researchers must demonstrate a certain opportunism when faced with the fluctuating reality of organizations.

This work is the fruit of the collective labor of academics, professors, lecturers and researchers, in colleges and universities, who over the past three years have sought to answer the numerous questions a researcher faces in the course of a research project. We have had to rethink our initial design for the work, which was at first visualized as seamless, without beginning or end. Instead we have yielded to a reconstructed logic, that of an ideal research project. The chapters follow, for practical reasons, a linear plan. Nonetheless, they are linked one to another within a vast network, in which each element influences and is influenced by all of the composite parts. The spirit of the work may seem paradoxical, in that it questions the ideal of management research. But this ideal does not exist in absolute terms, except in the thoroughness and the conviction of the discursive reproduction of the completed work. A relative ideal, a contextualized ideal, is presented and placed in perspective along the following lines.

The work is constructed so as to answer the questions a researcher poses before, during and after the research process. Each chapter has been written to be at once independent and interdependent: independent in their treatment of a given subject; interdependent in that the directions they suggest are dependent on researchers' epistemologies and the methodological choices they have made. (To emphasize the circular aspect of the research process, the work was initially envisaged as being cylindrical in form, and without pagination. As you see, the idea was abandoned. What would you think if you were holding a 'cylind-book' or a 'book-linder' in your hands? Without bringing up the problems of storage in a flat briefcase or on a shelf!)

The decision was therefore made to assemble the chapters in a 'logical' manner. We begin with the epistemological questions researchers might ask at the beginning of their investigations, and finish by looking at how researchers write up their work and communicate their results. The book comprises four parts: Conception, Implementation, Analysis and Publication and communication. The first part, Conception, covers the big questions preliminary to the work of research. It invites researchers to question the nature of the reality (constructed or given) to be explained, and to define what they propose to study (the research problem, or question) and the purpose of their research (to test or to construct). Questions about the type of approach to adopt (qualitative or quantitative) and the aspect to focus on (process or content) are discussed here. The second part, Implementation, takes us to the core of the research: the methodology. We look at the research design, choosing a field of investigation, selecting measuring instruments, collecting data, and validating observations. The third part, Analysis, is more technical. It presents tools researchers can use to find meaning in the mass of information they collect. We explore causal, longitudinal and process analyses; classification methods, comparison analyses and analyzing social networks, discourses and representations. These are the methods and analyses most commonly used in management research. The fourth and final part of the book, Publication and communication, brings us to the transmission of the knowledge we have created. We discuss why research has to be communicated in an appropriate form, and how to find networks in which it will be appreciated. These four parts, though, should not be seen as a preordained sequence, beyond which there is no salvation. Earlier phases are often challenged in the course of the research, to adapt to contingencies that arise along the way. We envision these parts more as a temporary structure, enabling meaning to be given to the presentation as a whole. Readers are free to read the book in a sequential manner, from the first page through to the last, or to skip parts as they feel fit. Or they might go directly to a particular chapter, if they wish to go into more depth on a specific point.

Each part is subdivided into chapters. The chapters of Parts I and II follow a conventional order. In a research study, however, it is not unusual to have to constantly move back and forth among the elements dealt with in these chapters. Methodological choices can be contradictory to epistemological orientations taken very much further back. In Parts III and IV, the order of the chapters is not important, as they deal with specific techniques and with general advice.

The first part of the book Conception, sets out the epistemological choices researchers must make, along with choices about the orientation of their research. In Chapter 1, 'Epistemological foundations', Martine Girod-Séville and Véronique Perret address questions about the status of scientific knowledge, how it is developed and what is its worth. While these questions may seem to be very much preliminary to research, they are, in fact, at the heart of every investigation. Researchers' pre-existing ideas of what scientific knowledge is influence the way they see 'reality', and this in turn influences the methods they will use to understand, explain, describe or predict. After questioning the nature of scientific knowledge, we then turn to focus a little more on what the researcher wants to do. The second chapter, 'Constructing the research problem', by Florence Allard-Poesi and Christine Maréchal, looks at how researchers construct the research problem (research question) through which they will explore reality – the question they are endeavoring to respond to, and which will guide the entire research process. In Chapter 3, 'Exploring and testing', Sandra Charreire and Florence Durieux explain how the research process unfolds. Researchers must decide whether they want to compare an existing theory with reality, to use reality to elaborate a new theoretical construction, or to develop a theoretical construction and compare this with empirical observations. There are no right or wrong answers. What matters is that the process they decide to follow is congruent with other choices they have already made. In Chapter 4, 'What approach with which data', Philippe Baumard and Jérôme Ibert show that determining the approach and data to use is one of the essential choices researchers are confronted with. They show how the aims of the research (to describe, explain, predict or to establish a norm) and the data and approach (qualitative and quantitative) that will achieve these aims are all connected. In the fifth chapter, 'Researching content and researching process', Corinne Grenier and Emmanuel Josserand present two major directions research can take. Whereas content-based research proposes a static analysis based on the nature of the subject under study, process-based research is a dynamic analysis in terms of flux. Grenier and Josserand argue that it is more the formulation of the research question and the choice of method than the nature of the research itself that dictates the difference between these two approaches. This chapter closes the first part of the work.

In the second part of the book, Implementation, we move to more practical aspects of the research process. The chapters here answer researchers' questions about what steps to follow, what type of observations to make and how to make them, and how to establish the validity of results. Essential to any study, the concrete exercise of carrying out research depends on these issues. This part commences with the sixth chapter; 'Research design' by Isabelle Royer and Philippe Zarlowski. By design, they mean interconnecting the different stages of a research project. These stages include establishing a research question, reviewing relevant literature, collecting and analyzing data, and presenting final results. The chapter looks at the relationship between epistemological positioning and methodology, and between research design and the maturity of the scientific knowledge in a given domain. It shows how a research design is constructed, and how this can evolve over the course of the research. In Chapter 7, 'Linking concepts and data', by Jacques Angot and Patricia Milano, we are at the heart of the implementation process. The chapter discusses how we can link empirical knowledge with theoretical. The understanding researchers have of the empirical world depends not only on the degree of knowledge they have of the theoretical world, but also on epistemological positioning. In practice, our epistemological positioning tends to influence the way we measure what we observe. In Chapter 8, 'Sampling', Isabelle Royer and Philippe Zarlowski review how to select elements from which to collect data – how to put together a sample. Samples can be composed of a large number of individual items, as is the case in studies requiring a quantitative treatment, or they can be made up of fewer items, as for in-depth case study analyses. The chapter considers a number of selection methods and explains possible biases. Chapter 9, 'Data collection and managing the data source' by Jérôme Ibert, Philippe Baumard, Carole Donada and Jean-Marc Xuereb, presents the different instruments researchers can use to collect primary and secondary data, both qualitative and quantitative. Data collection is a crucial stage in the research project: data constitutes the basic material of the research. The chapter emphasizes the importance of the relationship between the subject (the data source) and the researcher. Chapter 10, 'Validity and reliability', is the last chapter of Implementation. Carole Drucker-Godard, Sylvie Ehlinger and Corinne Grenier consider the problem of knowing whether a description accurately represents the phenomenon studied (validity), and whether the same phenomenon would be similarly observed at different times or by other observers (reliability). They explore several types of validity – construct validity, measurement validity and internal and external validity – and discuss ways to improve the reliability of both quantitative and qualitative research.

With Analysis, the third part of the book, we move into the more technical aspects of research. Here we find the toolbox. Chapter 11, 'Comparison tests' by Ababacar Mbengue, tackles questions of choosing and applying statistical comparison tests. Mbengue reiterates the importance of acknowledging the hypotheses underlying the use of a test. Without this, test results cannot have any meaning. He establishes a general distinction between parametric and non-parametric tests, and sets out the most commonly used tests in relation to the questions management researchers ask. In Chapter 12, 'Causal analysis and modeling', Ababacar Mbengue and Isabelle Vandangeon-Derumez describe how to build and test causal relationships between variables. They remind us that to testing causal relationships we must first construct a causal model. Mbengue and Vandangeon-Derumez present causal modeling as a four-stage process: the researcher must first specify the phenomenon to be modeled; then identify its concepts and variables; then describe the relationships between these concepts and variables; and, finally, test the model. The thirteenth chapter, 'Classifying and structuring' by Ababacar Mbengue and Carole Donada, looks at techniques researchers can use to organize and simplify large amounts of data. Classification methods enable us to break up a body of data comprising a great number of different objects into a small number of organized classes of identical or similar objects. Structuring methods allow us to discover the factors or dimensions that form the internal structure of a data set. Chapter 14, 'Analyzing social networks' by Jacques Angot and Emmanuel Josserand presents the methods researchers can use to study relationships between individual analysis units. These could include relations between individual actors within an organization, the links between the departments making up the organization or the relations that exist between it and other organizations. These methods can equally well be used to identify individuals or units that play a particular role, or to better understand relationships of power and communication. In Chapter 15, 'Longitudinal analyses' by Bernard Forgues and Isabelle Vandangeon-Derumez, we move into the area of studying phenomena over the course of time. Longitudinal studies are becoming more and more frequent in management research, as researchers try to understand the dynamics of organizational phenomena. The chapter describes and explains a broad range of analysis methods, both quantitative (event analysis, sequential methods and cohort analysis) and qualitative (chronological matrix, analysis of cycles and phases).

Chapter 16, 'Analyzing representations and discourse' by Florence Allard-Poesi, Carole Drucker-Godard and Sylvie Ehlinger, shows us how to dissect, classify and analyze information contained in a document, a communication or a discourse. Researchers in management have to make sense of a considerable mass of verbal and written data. Nevertheless, only two main types of methods of doing so are particularly developed in the chapter: content analysis and cognitive mapping.

The fourth part of this work, Publication and communication, takes us into an area that might seem inconsequential when compared to the epistemological and methodological considerations of the first three parts. Yet by communicating our knowledge, disseminating the results of our research, transmitting the fruits of our labor to a network of researchers, we ensure that the work we accomplish does not remain just an exercise, certainly inspiring, but limited to one individual or to a small group of the initiated. In Chapter 17, 'Writing up the research', Bernard Forgues outlines the various ways our research can be communicated to others. He explains the conventions to be observed in a research article, and gives us advice on issues from writing up a study to how to present our research and its results. Forgues emphasizes the importance of this phase, explaining that it enables meaning to be given to the completed work, which must be understood as a stage in a social process. In Chapter 18, 'The research environment', Jean-Marc Xuereb suggests ways researchers can control their own context; from choosing a thesis advisor to building up a network of peers and contacts. He discusses how researchers can profit from professional associations, through which they can disseminate their work.

With this chapter we complete the work. As you can readily appreciate, the variety of subjects tackled reflects the scope of the knowledge a researcher in management needs to have. All the same, a distinction must be made between recurrent knowledge, which must be mastered whatever the type of research (Parts I, II and IV), and knowledge that is mobilized in accordance with the problem at hand (Part III). Choices have had to be made in each chapter. An informed reader might be disappointed by the degree of development of certain areas covered. This was a purposeful decision. We did not set out to compete with other specialized works, but to remind researchers of the questions they must ask themselves, and to direct them towards possible responses to these questions from which they can draw inspiration. Whenever a more technical discussion may be required, we have referred readers to more specialized works. Four or five basic works are suggested at the end of each chapter, to provide readers who want to study a subject in greater depth with a starting point.

The adventure of writing *Doing Management Research* is now ended. This has been a fine project in which each one of us has given something of his or her experience with research. The book is in fact a testimony to those who practice daily what they write about. It is not a collage of the experiences of others, but very much a collective construction. It is up to the reader now to take the reins, in the hope that this book will help him or her to contribute to research in management.

PART I

CONCEPTION

This first part of the present work invites readers to question the nature and the purpose of the research they wish to undertake. The explicit and implicit choices they make will be affected by the type of research they want to do and the way they want to do it. One important question researchers must answer concerns their conception of the reality of the management phenomena they wish to study. If this is an objective reality, they will need to develop and choose appropriate measuring instruments to study it. But it may be a constructed reality, its existence dependent on the subjectivity of the researcher – an elusive reality that transforms and slips out of our grasp just as we think we are drawing close to it. After answering this first question, the subject of their research must be defined: what they are setting out to study. But here again, the answer is not as simple as we might wish. We show that the research subject is constructed and not, except artificially, given. It fluctuates, reacts and is contingent upon the conception of the research process and how this process unfolds. Once the subject has been defined, researchers are faced with the choice as to what they want to achieve. There are two main directions to take. The first consists of constructing a new theoretical framework from, among other things, their observations. The second is to test a theory; to compare it with empirical observations. Researchers will also have to decide on an approach, either qualitative or quantitative, or perhaps a mixture of the two, and on the type of data they will need to collect: decisions that must be congruent with the aim of their research. Finally, researchers have to decide how they will attack their research question: whether to study content (a state) or to study a process (a dynamics). The methodologies used will differ according to the choices they have already made. It is vital for researchers to give careful consideration, and as early as possible, to these questions of the nature, the aim and the type of research they want to undertake, and the empirical sources available to them or which they wish to use.

1

EPISTEMOLOGICAL FOUNDATIONS

Martine Girod-Séville and Véronique Perret

Outline

All research work is based on a certain vision of the world, employs a methodology, and proposes results aimed at predicting, prescribing, understanding or explaining. By recognizing these epistemological presuppositions, researchers can control their research approach, increase the validity of their results and ensure that the knowledge they produce is cumulative.

This chapter aims to help the researcher conduct this epistemological reflection, by providing the tools needed to answer the following three questions: How is knowledge generated? What is the nature of the produced knowledge? What is the value and status of this knowledge? In answering these questions, inspiration may be drawn from the three major epistemological paradigms usually identified with organizational science: the positivist, the interpretativist, and the constructivist paradigms. From this researchers can evaluate the scientific validity of their statements and reflect on the epistemological validity and legitimacy of their work. Consideration of such questions can help researchers to elaborate their own positions in relation to the epistemological pluralism present in organizational science.

Epistemology is the study of knowledge, and so of science: the study of its nature, its validity and value, its methods and its scope. Epistemological questioning is vital to serious research, as through it researchers can establish the validity and legitimacy of their work. All research is based on a certain vision of the world, uses a certain method and proposes results aimed at predicting, prescribing, understanding, constructing or explaining. Recognizing that they have these presuppositions allows researchers to control their research approach, to increase the validity of the knowledge produced and to make this knowledge cumulative. Epistemology is, therefore, consubstantial with all research.

In this chapter, we invite researchers wanting to establish the legitimacy of their work to examine their research approach by posing the following three questions:

What is the nature of the knowledge we can generate through our research?
Before we can embark on a quest for new knowledge, we have to ascertain
clearly what it is we are looking for. Will such knowledge be objective? Will
it be an accurate representation of a reality that exists independently of our
experience or understanding of it? Or will it be our particular interpretation of
reality? Is such knowledge a construction of reality? We encourage researchers
to question their vision of the social world – to consider the relationship
between subject and object.

How can we generate scientific knowledge?   Are we to generate new knowledge through a process of explanation, understanding or construction? In asking this we are questioning the path we take to gain knowledge.

What is the value and status of this knowledge?   Is the knowledge we generate
scientific or non-scientific? How can we assess this? How can we verify and
corroborate our new knowledge? Is it credible and transferable? Is it intelligible
and appropriate? Through questioning these criteria we can evaluate the knowledge we produce.

    To answer these questions, researchers can draw inspiration from the three
major paradigms that representing the main epistemological streams in
organizational science: the positivist, interpretativist and constructivist paradigms. According to Kuhn (1970), paradigms are models, intellectual frameworks or frames of reference, with which researchers in organizational science
can affiliate themselves. The positivist paradigm is dominant in organizational science. However, there has always been a conflict between positivism
and interpretativism, which defends the particularity of human sciences in
general, and organizational science in particular. Constructivism, meanwhile,
is becoming increasingly influential among researchers working in organizational science.

    Constructivism and interpretativism share several assumptions about the
nature of reality. However, they differ in the particular ideas they express about
the process of creating knowledge and the criteria with which to validate
research. As we will see further on, the aim of positivism is to explain reality,
whereas interpretativism seeks, above all, to understand it and constructivism
essentially constructs it. The answers given to different epistemological questions by each of the paradigms are summarized in Table 1.1.

    In the rest of this chapter we will concentrate on explaining the different
positions taken by each of the paradigms *vis-à-vis* the nature of the knowledge
produced, the path taken to obtain that knowledge and the criteria used to validate the knowledge. This discussion will lead on to an inquiry into the existence of epistemological pluralism, which we will look into further in the final
part of the chapter.

SECTION 1   WHAT IS KNOWLEDGE?

Before we can give due thought to the question of what knowledge is, we must
first consider the related question of the nature of reality. Does reality exist

Table 1.1   *Epistemological positions of the positivist, interpretativist and constructivist paradigms*

Epistemological questions	Paradigms		
	Positivism	Interpretativism	Constructivism
Status of knowledge	**Ontological hypothesis:** The knowledge object has its own essence	**Phenomenological hypothesis:** The essence of the object is multiple (interpretativism), cannot be attained (moderate constructivism) or does not exist (radical constructivism)	
	Independence of subject and object	Dependence of subject and object	
Nature of 'reality'	**Determinist hypothesis:** The world is made up of necessities	**Intentionalist hypothesis** The world is made up of possibilities	
How is knowledge generated?	**Discovery**	**Interpretation**	**Construction**
	The research question is formulated in terms of 'for what reasons ...'	The research question is formulated in terms of 'what motivates actors to ...'	The research question is formulated in terms of 'to what ends does ...'
	Privileged status of explanation	Privileged status of understanding	Privileged status of construction
What is the value of knowledge? (Validity criteria)	Degree of confirmation Refutability Logical consistency	Credibility Transferability Dependability Confirmability	Adequacy 'Teachability'

independently of the observer, or is our perception of reality subjective. What part of 'reality' can we know?

1. A Positivist Understanding of Reality

For positivists, reality exists in itself. It has an objective essence, which researchers must seek to discover. The object (reality) and the subject that is observing or testing it are independent of each other. The social or material world is thus external to individual cognition – as Burrell and Morgan put it (1979: 4): 'Whether or not we label and perceive these structures, the realists maintain, they still exist as empirical entities.' This independence between object and subject has allowed positivists to propound the principle of objectivity, according to which a subject's observation of an external object does not alter the nature of that object. This principle is defined by Popper (1972: 109): 'Knowledge in this objective sense is totally independent of anybody's claim to know; it is also independent of anybody's belief, or disposition to assent; or to assert, or to act. Knowledge in the objective sense is knowledge without a knowing subject.' The principle of the objectivity of knowledge raises various problems when it is applied in the social sciences. Can a person be his or her own object? Can a subject really observe its object without altering the nature of that object? Faced with these different questions, positivist researchers will exteriorize the object they are observing. Durkheim (1982) thus exteriorizes social events, which he considers as 'things'. He maintains that 'things' contrast with ideas in the same way as our knowledge of what is exterior to us contrasts with our knowledge of what is interior. For Durkheim, 'things' encompasses all that which the mind can only understand if we move outside our own subjectivity by means of observation and testing.

In organizational science, this principle can be interpreted as follows. Positivist researchers examining the development of organizational structures will take the view that structure depends on a technical and organizational reality that is independent of themselves or those overseeing it. The knowledge produced by the researcher observing this reality (or reconstructing the cause-and-effect chain of structural events) can lead to the development of an objective knowledge of organizational structure.

In postulating the essence of reality and, as a consequence, subject–object independence, positivists accept that reality has its own immutable and quasi-invariable laws. A universal order exists, which imposes itself on everything: individual order is subordinate to social order, social order is subordinate to 'vital' order and 'vital' order is subordinate to material order. Human beings are subject to this order. They are products of an environment that conditions them, and their world is made up of necessities. Freedom is restricted by invariable laws, as in a determinist vision of the social world. The Durkheimian notion of social constraint is a good illustration of the link between the principle of external reality and that of determinism. For Durkheim (1982), the notion of social constraint implies that collective ways of acting or thinking have a reality apart from the individuals who constantly comply with them. The individual finds them already shaped and, in Durkheim's (1982) view, he or she cannot then act as if they do not exist, or as if they are other than what they are.

Consequently, the knowledge produced by positivists is objective and a-contextual – in that it relates to revising existing laws and to an immutable reality that is external to the individual and independent of the context of interactions between actors.

2. A Subjective Reality?

In the rival interpretativist and constructivist paradigms, reality has a more precarious status. According to these paradigms, reality remains unknowable because it is impossible to reach it directly. *Radical constructivism* declares that 'reality' does not exist, but is invented, and great caution must be used when using the term (Glasersfeld, 1984). *Moderate constructivists* do not attempt to answer this question. They neither reject nor accept the hypothesis that reality exists in itself. The important thing for them is that this reality will never be independent of the mind, of the consciousness of the person observing or testing it. For interpretativists, 'there are multiple constructed realities that can be studied only holistically; inquiry into these multiple realities will inevitably diverge (each inquiry raises more questions than it answers) so that prediction and control are unlikely outcomes although some level of understanding (*verstehen*) can be achieved' (Lincoln and Guba, 1985: 37). Consequently, for constructivists and interpretativists, 'reality' (the object) is dependent on the observer (the subject). It is apprehended by the action of the subject who experiences it. We can therefore talk about a phenomenological hypothesis, as opposed to the ontological hypothesis developed by the positivists. The phenomenological hypothesis is based on the idea that a phenomenon is the internal manifestation of that which enters our consciousness. Reality cannot be known objectively – to seek objective knowledge of reality is utopian. One can only represent it, that is, construct it.

Subject–object interdependence and the rebuttal of the postulate that reality is objective and has its own essence has led interpretativist and constructivist researchers to redefine the nature of the social world.

For interpretativists and constructivists, the social world is made up of interpretations. These interpretations are constructed through actors' 'interactions, in contexts that will always have their own peculiarities. Interactions among actors, which enable development of an intersubjectively shared meaning, are at the root of the social construction of reality' (Berger and Luckman, 1966).

The Social Construction of Reality

Sociological interest in questions of 'reality' and 'knowledge' is thus initially justified by the fact of their social relativity. What is 'real' to a Tibetan monk may not be 'real' to an American businessman. The 'knowledge' of the criminal differs from the 'knowledge' of the criminologist. It follows that specific agglomerations of 'reality' and 'knowledge' pertain to specific social contexts, and that these relationships will have to be included in an adequate sociological analysis of these contexts ... A 'sociology of knowledge' will have to deal not only with the empirical variety of 'knowledge' in human societies, but also with the processes by which any body of 'knowledge' comes to be socially established as 'reality' ... And insofar as all human 'knowledge' is developed, transmitted and maintained in social situations, the sociology of knowledge must seek to understand the processes by which this is done in such a way that a taken-for-granted 'reality' congeals for the man in the street. In other words, we contend that *the sociology of knowledge is concerned with the analysis of the social construction of reality* ... Society is indeed built up by activity that expresses subjective meaning. It is precisely the dual character of society in terms of objective facticity *and* subjective meaning that makes its *'reality sui generis'*. The central question for sociological theory can then be put as follows: How is it possible that subjective meanings become objective facticities? How is it possible that human activity should produce a world of things? In other words, an adequate understanding of the *'reality sui generis'* of society requires an inquiry into the manner in which this reality is constructed.

(Extracts from Berger and Luckmann, 1966: 3, 18)

The self-fulfilling prophecies of Watzlawick (1984) are a good illustration of the way actors can themselves construct the social world. A self-fulfilling prophecy is a prediction that verifies itself. According to Watzlawick (1984), it is a supposition that, simply by its existence, leads the stated predicted event to occur and confirms its own accuracy. The prediction proves to be accurate, not because the chain of cause and effect has been explained, nor by referring to laws of an external reality, but because of our understanding, at a particular moment, of the interactions among actors. From this, the succession of subsequent interactions is easy to foresee. Consequently, according to Watzlawick (1984), the degree to which we can predict behavior is linked not to a determinism external to the actors, but to the actors' submission to imprisonment in an endless game that they themselves have created. In self-fulfilling prophecy, the emphasis is on interaction and the determining role of the actors in constructing reality. Such prophecies depend heavily on context. They can only be made once we understand the context of the interaction – an understanding through which we are able to learn the rules of the game.

Consequently, interpretativists and constructivists consider that individuals create their environments by their own thoughts and actions, guided by their goals. In this world where everything is possible and nothing is determined, and in which we are free to make our own choices, it has become necessary to reject determinism in favor of the intentionalist hypothesis. The knowledge produced in this way will be subjective and contextual, which has numerous research implications, as Lincoln and Guba emphasize in the case of the interpretativist paradigm.

The Interpretativist Paradigm and its Research Implications

One characteristic of operational inquiry, natural setting, can be justified by its logical dependence on the axioms that undergird the paradigm. The naturalist elects to carry out research in the natural setting or context of the entity for which study is proposed because naturalistic ontology suggests that realities are wholes that cannot be understood in isolation from their contexts, nor can they be fragmented for separate study of the parts; because of the belief that the very act of observation influences what is seen, and so the research interaction should take place with the entity-in-context for fullest understanding; because of the belief that context is crucial in deciding whether or not a finding may have meaning in some other context as well; because of the belief in complex mutual shaping rather than linear causation, which suggests that the phenomenon must be studied in its full-scale influence (force) field; and because contextual value structures are at least partly determinative of what will be found.

(Lincoln and Guba, 1985: 39)

To sum up, the nature of the knowledge that we can hope to produce will depend on our assumptions about the nature of reality, of the subject–object relationship and the social world we envisage (see Table 1.2).

These elements (nature of reality, nature of the subject–object link, vision of the social world) constitute reference points for researchers wishing to define the epistemological position of their research.

Table 1.3, constructed on the basis of work by Smircich (1983) and Schultz and Hatch (1996), shows clearly that the nature of the knowledge produced in

Table 1.2 *Assumptions underlying the nature of the knowledge produced*

	Nature of knowledge produced	Nature of reality	Nature of subject–object relationship	Vision of social world
Positivism	A-contextual, objective	Ontological hypothesis	Independence	Determined
Interpretavism and constructivism	Subjective, Contextual	Phenomenological hypothesis	Interdependence	Intentional

the field of organizational culture depends on the researcher's assumptions about the nature of the social world.

Their understanding of the nature of the knowable reality and the social world will indicate the path researchers must take to obtain knowledge. In a positivist framework, researchers seek to discover the laws imposed on actors. In an interpretativist framework, they seek to understand how actors construct the meaning they give to social reality. In a constructivist framework, researchers contribute to the actors' construction of social reality.

SECTION 2   GENERATING NEW KNOWLEDGE

1. Explaining Reality

By accepting the assumptions of objectivity, the ontology of reality and the determinism of the social world, positivists commit themselves to the search for external reality and the mechanisms that condition it. The positive ideal would be to find a universal law that explains reality and reveals objective truth.

Even the most traditional positivists recognize that this ideal remains utopian (Comte, 1844, 1988). However, they maintain that an understanding of the laws that govern reality is a prerequisite for generating new knowledge. Scientific progress is thus characterized by a reduction in the number of laws as links are established between them. The key idea behind this vision is that these laws exist even if they cannot all be discovered.

The positivist vision of reality leans towards explanatory research, to answer the question 'for what reasons'. Such research seeks constant concomitance among phenomena, and tries to reconstruct chains of cause and effect. In the example of organizational structure, the positivist researcher tries to reconstruct the causes of structural events, so as to determine the laws that, independently of the actors involved, have governed organizational reality.

The causal approach accounts for a social fact by relating it to another social fact external to the individuals involved. It leads researchers to examine the economic, political and technical reasons for the fact's presence. As the positivist paradigm has evolved, it has detached itself from pure causal

Table 1.3 *Two notions of culture*

	Culture from a positivist viewpoint – an instrumental vision of culture	Culture from an interpretativist viewpoint – a metaphorical vision of culture
Vision of social world	**Predefined and universal** The social world has an objective, independent existence that imposes itself on human beings (Smircich, 1983). Therefore, similar levels and functions of culture are documented in all organizations (Schultz and Hatch, 1996).	**Emergent and specific** The social or organizational world exists only as a pattern of symbolic relationships and meanings sustained through the continued processes of human interaction (Smircich, 1983). Therefore, opportunities for creation of meaning are unique to each cultural context (Schultz and Hatch, 1996).
Conception of organizational culture	**Organizations have a culture** Organizations are seen as social instruments that produce goods and services, and, as a by-product, they also produce distinctive cultural artifacts such as rituals, legends, and ceremonies (Smircich, 1983).	**Organization is a culture** Organizations are to be understood as cultures. This paradigm promotes a view of organizations as expressive forms, manifestations of human consciousness (Smircich, 1983).
Research questions on organizational culture	Language, symbols, myths, stories, and rituals are taken as cultural artifacts. The interest is the search for predictable means for organizational control and improved means for organization management. Because all research in this paradigm has these basic purposes, the issue of causality is of critical importance. Researchers ask 'What do organizations accomplish?' and 'How may they accomplish it more efficiently?' (Smircich, 1983).	Language, symbols, myths, stories, and rituals are taken as generative processes that yield and shape meanings and that are fundamental to the very existence of organization. Researchers ask 'How is organization accomplished?' and 'What does it mean to be organized?' (Smircich, 1983).

(Cont.)

Table 1.3 (Contd.)

	Culture from a positivist viewpoint – an instrumental vision of culture	Culture from an interpretativist viewpoint – a metaphorical vision of culture
Mode of analysis	**Categorical** Identification of cultural elements and discovering the causal relations between them. Analysis is conducted by filling in predefined variables and mapping the causal relations between them. The culture is often added to the list of explanatory organizational variables such as strategy, technology and environment (Schultz and Hatch, 1996).	**Associative** Reading meanings and exploring the associations between them. Interpretativists explore the active creation of meaning and the ways in which meanings are associated in organizations. In this mode of analysis, particular cultural themes, images and metaphors emerge. Exploring and describing the rich character of cultural themes, images, and metaphors depends upon the researcher's ability to make and use associations (Schultz and Hatch, 1996).

research. It now recognizes more than simply linear causality (one cause – one effect), and accepts the possibility of multiple or circular causality. It is therefore possible to take a positivist position without implying that all laws through which we can explain reality are laws of linear causality. Nevertheless, in generating new knowledge, the positivist paradigm still follows a path determined largely by the idea that knowable reality has its own meaning, and that this meaning does not necessarily depend on a researcher's personal beliefs.

2. Interpreting Reality

Interpretavism calls the possibility of uncovering causal links into question, because 'all entities are in a state of mutual simultaneous shaping, so that it is impossible to distinguish causes from effects' (Lincoln and Guba, 1985: 38). The process of creating knowledge therefore involves understanding the meaning actors give to reality – rather than explaining reality, interpretativists try to understand it through actors' interpretations. This process must take account of actors' intentions, motivation, expectations, motives and beliefs – which all relate more to practice than to facts. Thus, unlike positivists, interpretativists draw a clear distinction between understanding and explaining.

Positivists make no such differentiation between understanding and explaining; the second, by necessity, encompasses the first. Explanation implies understanding. Nevertheless, this is not an understanding that emanates from the meaning actors give to their actions.

The privileged status that interpretativists accord to understanding is based on the concept of *verstehen* (understanding) developed by Max Weber. This concept unites the two levels of understanding on which the knowledge creation process is based. On one level, *verstehen* is the process by which individuals are led, in their daily lives, to interpret and understand their world. On another level, and in a more restrictive sense, *verstehen* is the process by which researchers interpret the subjective meanings behind the behavior of the individuals they are studying (Lee, 1991).

Understanding, or interpreting, behavior must by necessity involve inquiring into local meanings (localized in time and place) that actors give to their behavior. In the case of organizational structure, interpretativist researchers will be drawn towards contextualized research to analyze the daily functioning of an organization. This involves carrying out field studies, which favor direct observation and on-site interviews.

3. Constructing Reality

Constructivists share this research approach as far as understanding is concerned, but with two essential differences. Whereas for interpretativists the process of understanding consists above all of 'revealing' the reality of the actors studied, constructivism sees the process of understanding as contributing to constructing that reality. Reality is thus constructed by the act of knowing, rather than being given by an objective perception of the world (Le Moigne, 1995). According to this hypothesis, the path we take when we generate knowledge is constructed as we go along. This conception of knowledge construction is strongly present in the works of Piaget (1970), for whom knowledge is as much a process as a result. Moreover, for constructivists, the process of understanding is linked to the aim of the researcher's knowledge project. In this there is a teleological hypothesis, which advances the notion that all human activity involves a predetermined purpose or design. The process of building up knowledge therefore has to take account of subjective intentions or purpose. Le Moigne (1995) emphasizes that, in comparison with positivism, the different constructivist epistemologies enable researchers to recognize a knowledge project, rather than a knowledge object that is separate from its investigator. To understand in terms of purposes or plausible goals becomes the aim of scientific research.

The answers given by the positivist, interpretativist and constructivist paradigms to the first two epistemological questions (the nature of the knowledge our research produces and the path we take to produce it) will have strong implications on the value of this knowledge. The third section of this chapter deals with the status and validity of knowledge.

SECTION 3   VALIDITY CRITERIA

Researchers can evaluate the knowledge they produce by using different criteria of validity. Each of the epistemologies we are looking at – the positivist, the interpretativist and the constructivist – incorporate a number of validity criteria.

1. Positivist Validity Criteria

For positivism, specific criteria enable researchers to distinguish clearly between scientific and non-scientific knowledge. These criteria have evolved along with positivism, and have moved from 'verification' to 'degree of confirmation' and 'degree of refutation'.

1.1 Verification

Early positivists applied the principle of 'verification': a proposition is either analytical or synthetic, and is either true by virtue of its own definition or, in certain situations, by virtue of practical experience. A synthetic proposition has meaning if, and only if, it can be verified empirically (Blaug, 1992). Verification obliges researchers to assure the truth of their statements through empirical verification.

1.2 Degree of confirmation

As positivism has evolved, other criteria have supplanted verification. The term 'degree of confirmation' refers to the probabilistic logic proposed by Carnap. The logic of confirmation calls the certainty of truth into question. It is based on the idea that we cannot say that a proposition is universally true, but only that it is probable. We can never be sure that it is true in every case and in all circumstances. Consequently, we can only confirm it against experience, or by drawing on the results of other theories – but we will not be able to establish its truth as certain (Hempel, 1964). Carnap's (1962) vision of science can be summed up as follows: All theories are impossible to prove, but they present different degrees of probability. Scientific honesty consists of only stating theories that are highly probable, or simply specifying for each scientific theory the factors that support it and the theory's probability in light of these factors. A theory can be probable – in fact Carnap replaces the notion of proof by degree of probability. Researchers who subscribe to Carnap's probabilistic logic are compelled to evaluate the degree of probability with which their statements are confirmed.

1.3 Refutation

According to Popper's principle of 'refutation', we can never maintain that a theory is true, but we can say it is not true – that is, that it has been refuted. The following example is a good illustration. To the question 'Are all swans white?' the only answer that is scientifically acceptable is 'No'. However many white swans we have observed, we do not have the right to infer that all swans are white. Observing a single black swan is sufficient to refute this conclusion.

A theory that has not been refuted is then a theory that is provisionally corroborated. The term 'corroboration' is important for Popper, who draws a clear distinction between it and 'confirmation':

> By the degree of corroboration of a theory I mean a concise report evaluating the state (at a certain time *t*) of the critical discussion of a theory, with respect to the way it solves its problems; its degree of testability; the severity of the tests it has undergone; and the way it has stood up to these tests ... The main purpose of the formulae that I proposed as definition of the degree of corroboration was to show that, in many cases, the more improbable (improbable in the sense of the calculus of probability) hypothesis is preferable.

> (Popper, 1972: 18)

According to this principle, a theory is scientific if it is refutable – that is, if it accepts that certain results may invalidate it. However, any theory that cannot be refuted is not scientific. This includes psychoanalysis (for example, the Freudian hypothesis of the subconscious) and Marxism, along with other theories that remain valid whatever observations are made about them. Popper insists on the asymmetry of verification and invalidation. For him, there is no logic of proof, but a logic of refutation, and argues that, consequently, we must construct our scientific propositions from hypotheses that can be refuted.

1.4 Logical consistency

Finally, in assessing the validity of research, positivism only recognizes as scientific those methods that respect formal logic (deductive logic). This idea is referred to as 'logical consistency'. One test for logical consistency is to show that all of a theory's propositions are related to one another by the rules of formal logic, or are logically deducible from the same set of premises (Lee, 1991). Positivism refuses to consider inductive logic as scientific. It argues that the only logic that enables us to reproduce reality objectively is deductive logic.

Inductive logic enables us to move from particular observations to general statements. Deductive logic, on the other hand, uses true premises and the rules of formal inference to establish the truth-value of a proposition (or its non-refutation). These two types of logic will be examined in greater depth in Chapter 3.

2. Interpretativist Validity Criteria

Interpretativists and constructivists both question the primacy of deductive logic, and the specific and universal character of the validity criteria proposed by positivists. For interpretativists, validity criteria are criteria of trustworthiness. Lincoln and Guba (1985) identify these as credibility, transferability, dependability and confirmability.

Credibility

> How can one establish confidence in the 'truth' of the findings of a particular inquiry for the subjects with which and the context in which the inquiry was carried out? When we consider the assumption of multiple constructed realities, there is no ultimate benchmark to which one can turn for justification – whether in principle or by a technical adjustment via the falsification principle. Reality is now a multiple set of mental constructions ... To demonstrate 'truth value' we must show that the reconstructions that have been arrived at via the inquiry are credible to the constructors of the original multiple realities ... The implementation of the credibility criterion becomes a twofold task: first, to carry out the inquiry in such a way that the probability that the findings will be found to be credible is enhanced, and, second, to demonstrate the credibility of the findings by having them approved by the constructors of the multiple realities being studied.
>
> (Lincoln and Guba, 1985: 295–6)

Transferability

> How can one determine the extent to which the findings of a particular inquiry have applicability in other contexts or with other subjects? Interpretativists make the assumption that at best only working hypotheses may be abstracted, the transferability of which is an empirical matter, depending on the degree of similarity between sending and receiving contexts. Transferability inferences cannot be made by an investigator who knows only the sending context.
>
> (Lincoln and Guba, 1985: 297)

Dependability

> How can one determine whether the findings of an inquiry would be repeated if the inquiry were replicated with the same (or similar) subjects in the same (or similar) context? In the conventional paradigm, for this criterion there must be something tangible and unchanging 'out there' that can serve as a benchmark if the idea of replication is to make sense. An interpretativist sees reliability as part of a larger set of factors that are associated with the observed changes. Dependability takes into account both factors of instability and factors of phenomenal or design induced change.
>
> (Lincoln and Guba, 1985: 299)

Confirmability

> How can we establish the degree to which the findings of an inquiry are determined by the subjects and conditions of the inquiry and not by the biases, motivations, interests, or perspectives of the inquirer? An interpretativist prefers a qualitative definition of this criterion. This definition removes the emphasis from the investigator (it is no longer his or her objectivity that is at stake) and places it where, as it seems to the investigator, it ought more logically to be: on the data themselves. The issue is no longer the investigator's characteristics but the characteristics of the data: are they or are they not confirmable?
>
> (Lincoln and Guba, 1985: 300)

3. Constructivist Validity Criteria

Constructivists question the classic criteria proposed by positivists. They contest the verification–refutation alternative, saying verification is illusory and refutation inadequate. It is illusory, they say, to devise a scientific process using verification criteria when one's vision of the world is based on phenomenological and intentionalist hypotheses. It is inadequate to devise a scientific process using refutability criteria when one defends the constructed and transforming nature of research projects in disciplines such as organizational science.

In constructivism, criteria for validating knowledge are still very much a topic of debate. However, while constructivist epistemology refuses to acknowledge any single validity criterion, certain authors propose sources for validating knowledge. We will present two of them here; the adequation (or suitability) criterion proposed by Glasersfeld (1984), and the 'teachability' criterion defended by Le Moigne (1995).

Adequation   Glasersfeld (1984), who is considered a radical constructivist, holds that knowledge is valid when it fits a given situation. He illustrates this principle using the metaphor of a key. A key fits if it opens the lock it is supposed to open. Here, suitability refers to a capacity: that of the key and not of the lock. Thanks to professional burglars, we are only too well aware that many keys cut very differently from our own may nonetheless open our door!

Teachability   The criteria relating to teachable knowledge can be expressed in terms of reproducibility, intelligibility, and constructibility. In Le Moigne's (1995) view, it is no longer enough for model-makers to demonstrate knowledge. They have to show that this knowledge is both constructible and reproducible, and therefore intelligible. It is important for modelers to be scrupulous about explaining their aims when constructing teachable knowledge.

The validity criteria applied by constructivists do not impose a single method of constructing knowledge, but are able to accept and defend a multiplicity of methods. Constructivists do not see deductive reasoning as the only valid reasoning method, accepting too other methods such as analogy and metaphor.

SECTION 4   A PLURALITY OF PARADIGMS

In this section we look at the researcher's position in relation to the paradigms presented earlier. We discuss whether researchers have to choose between paradigms, or whether, to the contrary, they have a degree of freedom to tailor their own position. To answer these questions, researchers need to think about the position they wish to adopt in relation to the problem of paradigm incommensurability. According to McKinley and Mone (1998: 170) incommensurability can be defined 'as occurring when there are logically or normatively incompatible schools of thought, and no consensually acknowledged reference system exists for deciding between them'.

The coexistence of positivist, interpretativist and constructivist paradigms in works in organizational science may be seen as either a sign of the immaturity of this science, or as an opportunity for researchers working within this discipline. Kuhn (1970) holds that the presence of a single paradigm characterizes normal science, while the coexistence of different paradigms can be symptomatic of periods of scientific revolution. However, researchers in organizational theory tend to see plurality as an opportunity, and approach this plurality using a number of standpoints or strategies. On the basis of work done by Scherer (1998), we can point to three main positions possible. In the view of certain authors (Burrell and Morgan, 1979; Jackson and Carter, 1991), who advocate isolationism, a researcher must choose one of the paradigms and stick to it. Others (Lee, 1991; Pfeffer, 1993; Donaldson, 1997), who advocate integration, say we should direct our efforts towards seeking a common standard. For those who advocate a multi-paradigm approach (Weaver and Gioia, 1994; Schultz and Hatch, 1996), dialogue between paradigms is possible and even desirable.

Isolationists argue that the different paradigms that exist within organizational theory cannot be reconciled – that no dialogue is possible between them, and should not even be attempted. 'There is no common measure among paradigms of inquiry, so that representatives of opposed paradigms live in different worlds, hold mutually exclusive beliefs, use different vocabularies, etc.' (Weaver and Gioia, 1994: 565). Here, the fragmentation of organizational science can be explained in part by the fact that researchers voluntarily adopt a particular paradigm – in the view of Burrell and Morgan (1979), adopting a paradigm is a veritable act of faith.

Many authors insist that integration and the establishment of a reference paradigm is the only guarantee of true scientific progress (Pfeffer, 1993; Lee, 1991; Donaldson, 1997). They argue that consensus about a paradigm is a precondition for the development of organizational science, and that fragmentation is an obstacle to this. Lee (1991) proposes an integrated framework that reconciles the three levels of understanding: a subjective understanding, an interpretive understanding and a positivist understanding. Donaldson (1997), meanwhile, proposes a reintegration of frameworks under the hegemony of a positivist paradigm.

It is often said that much research in organizational science borrows elements from different paradigms, thus obtaining what could be called a mixed epistemological position. Miles and Huberman (1984a) give an example of a moderate positivist position.

An example of moderate positivism

It is good for researchers to make their preferences clear. All too often, the reader has to intuit whether the author is, for example, operating from the standpoint of a logical positivist, a symbolic interactionist, or a social phenomenologist. These people all look differently at the world of social affairs and social science. We think of ourselves as logical positivists who recognize and try to atone for the limitations of that approach. Soft-nosed logical positivism, maybe … We believe that social phenomena exist not only in the mind but also in the objective world – and that there are some lawful and reasonably stable relationships to be found among them. In part, of course, these phenomena exist objectively in the world because people construe them in common or agreed-upon ways, so those perceptions are crucial in understanding why social behavior takes the form it does. Still, even if people do not themselves apprehend the same analytical constructs as those derived by researchers, this does not make such constructs invalid or contrived. Given our belief in social regularities, there is a corollary: Our task is to express them as precisely as possible, attending to their range and generality and to the local and historical contingencies under which they occur.

(Miles and Huberman, 1984a: 19)

Advocates of the multi-paradigm perspective maintain, meanwhile, that dialogue between paradigms is not only possible but necessary to advance our understanding of social phenomena. Weaver and Gioia state that.

> A successful multi-paradigm perspective must explain how different theoretical approaches might be related, but must do so (a) while preserving genuine multiplicity (e.g. the relatedness does not involve the reduction of one approach to another) and, (b), without uncritically embracing the disunifying paradigms paradigm (i.e. the increasingly entrenched view of organizational inquiry that – by appealing to the incommensurability thesis – purports unalterably to divide the field into mutually exclusive and contradictory metatheoretical camps).
>
> (Weaver and Gioia, 1994: 566)

According to this perspective, works that propose different methodologies enable dialogue between paradigms. For instance, Hassard (1991) considered the case of Britain's Fire Brigade from the standpoint of the four paradigms identified by Burrell and Morgan (1979). Similarly, Schultz and Hatch (1996) presented a new multi-paradigm strategy based on an interplay between paradigms. By examining research into organizational culture, Schultz and Hatch revealed connections and contrasts between paradigms, and thus provided a foundation for new interpretations of culture.

CONCLUSION

We hope this chapter will help researchers to answer the epistemological questions their research raises. We hope too that it persuades them to examine the nature of the reality they hope to apprehend, the relationship they have with their research subject, the ways in which they might approach knowledge production, and the criteria through which they can evaluate the knowledge they produce. Epistemological questioning should lead researchers to:

- understand the presuppositions on which their research rests
- explain the implications of their choices so as to master their research.

It is vital researchers conduct this kind of epistemological reflection and critically examine the knowledge they produce. Such self-questioning also opens up the possibility of constructive epistemological debate between researchers, which is indispensable to the production of cumulative knowledge.

The issues we have discussed in this chapter also raise questions at a methodological level. Several other chapters in this work, and Chapters 2 and 3 in particular, will elaborate on the methodological consequences of the different epistemological choices researchers make. Chapter 2, for example, shows to what extent the way in which we construct our research question is dependent on the epistemological presuppositions underlying the research itself.

FURTHER READING

Le Moigne, J.L., *Les épistémologies constructivistes*, Collection Que Sais-je? no. 2969, Paris: Presses Universitaires de France, 1995.

Lincoln, Y. and Guba, E., *Naturalistic Inquiry*, Beverley Hills, CA: Sage, 1985.

Popper, K., *The Logic of Scientific Discovery*, London: Hutchinson, 1977.

2

CONSTRUCTING THE RESEARCH PROBLEM

Florence Allard-Poesi and Christine Maréchal

Outline

'What am I looking for?' The research problem is the objective of a study – it is the general question the researcher is trying to answer. Inasmuch as it expresses and crystallizes the research's knowledge target, the subject of the inquiry is necessarily a key element in the whole research process. It provides guidelines by which researchers can question the aspects of reality they have decided to study, or can develop an understanding of the reality.

This chapter provides the researcher with some techniques to assist in elaborating the research problem. It begins by defining what is meant by a research problem, and shows how this signification can differ according to the investigator's epistemological assumptions. It then proposes different methods by which a research problem may be constructed, and presents a number of possible approaches to take. Finally, using examples, it illustrates the recursive nature of, and some of the difficulties involved in, the process of constructing the research problem.

The research problem is the general question the researcher is trying to respond to, or the objective of a study. In a way, it is the answer to the question 'What am I looking for?' The research problem is relatively broad and general, distinguishing it from other 'questions' that are in fact more precise and practical renderings of this essential objective. As this research objective is formulated as a question, it is clearly different from other research elements that do not necessarily involve a logic of inquiry: theoretical elements (concepts, models, theories), methodological elements (measurement tools, scales, management tools) or empirical elements (facts, events). Two examples of research problems are given below.

Example: Two research problems

1 Cossette and Audet (1992)

Working from a critical examination of the notion of representation in research into organizations, Cossette and Audet set out to 'elaborate a method of mapping the representations held by managers within organizations.'

2 Allison (1971)

Allison's study was an attempt to understand how the United States government took the decision to blockade during the Cuban missile crisis.

The research problem is a key element of the research process: it translates and crystallizes the researcher's knowledge project, his or her objective. It is through the research problem that researchers study aspects of the reality they hope to discover, or attempt to develop an understanding of that reality.

To know what we are looking for seems to be a prerequisite for any research work. As Northrop (1959) puts it, 'Science does not begin with facts or hypotheses but with a specific problem'. In accordance, a lot of textbooks assume that researchers always start from a defined problematic: a general question to which they want to respond. But the problems that we address as researchers are not simply handed to us by the world about us. We invent them, we construct them – whatever our knowledge goal may be. The process of constructing a research problem is then *itself* an integral part of the research process, a step that is all the more decisive as it constitutes the foundation on which everything else is to be built.

Traditionally, too, the processes of constructing the architecture and the methodology of a research project – the research design – are seen to be guided by the research problem. But these mapping-out stages can *themselves* influence the initial definition of the problematic at hand. They can lead to alterations in the research problem. In fact, it is not unusual for researchers to recognize that the concepts contained in their initial research problem are insufficient or poorly defined when they try to put them into practice, or after an in-depth reading of related works (see Figure 2.1).

Constructing the research problem is an essential step that can serve to guide the research process and the methodological choices made within it. At

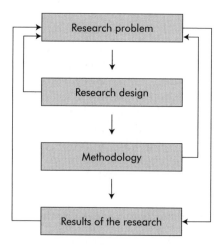

Figure 2.1   *Construction of the research problem as an essential part of the research process*

the same time, however, consideration of the research process and associated methodological choices can itself influence how the research problem will be constructed (see the following example for an illustration of this recursive aspect of constructing the research problem).

Constructing the research problem, a circular process

In her work into the cognitive approach of the organization, Allard-Poesi (1998) investigates causal mapping – the graphical representation of a person's causal beliefs about a particular domain. Her initial objective was to understand what a collective causal map in organizations actually is and how it emerges from the individual causal maps of its members, which supposedly vary greatly. A review of existent works on causal maps revealed that the notion of cognitive map is used in reference to very different methodologies, and involves differing and even contradictory constructs and visions of cognition. It seemed, in fact, more pertinent to consider a causal map as a tool for apprehending the representations held by members of an organization than as a theoretical construct in itself. This thinking led Allard-Poesi to redefine her question by way of the notion of representation. Her research problem became '*What does collective representation in organizations consist of, and how does it emerge from the differing representations held by organizational members?*' By redefining her research problem in this way, Allard-Poesi was able to open up her theoretical framework, which had initially been centered on the cognitive approach of the organization. She was able to reconsider her research design, notably by taking a more socio-cognitive approach.

Constructing one's research problem appears then to be a recursive process, with no set rules. It is without doubt the moment in which the researcher's skills are really put to the test: skills in areas of intuition, precision, realism and imagination.

SECTION 1   WHAT IS A RESEARCH PROBLEM?

1. A Question Expressing a Knowledge Project

To construct a research problem is to elaborate a question or problematic through which the researcher will construct or discover reality. The question produced links or examines theoretical, methodological or empirical elements.

The theoretical elements of the research problem may be concepts (collective representation, change, learning, collective knowledge or cognitive schemes, for example), explicative or descriptive models of phenomena (for instance, innovation processes in an unstable environment or learning processes in groups) or theories (such as Festinger's theory of cognitive dissonance). Some authors place particular emphasis on the primacy of the question's theoretical dimension. However, in our opinion, we can also construct a research problem by linking or examining theoretical elements, empirical elements or methodological elements. For example, empirical elements could be a decision taken by a board of directors, a result such as the performance of a business, or facts or events; methodological elements could include the method of cognitive mapping, a scale for measuring a concept or a method to support decision-making processes.

A theoretical, empirical or methodological element does not, in itself, constitute a research problem. To take up our first examples, neither 'the Cuban missile crisis' nor 'a method of constructing the representations held by managers' constitute in themselves a research problem. They are not questions through which we can construct or discover reality. However, examining these elements or the links between them can enable the creation or discovery of reality, and therefore does constitute a research problem. So, 'How can we move beyond the limits of cognitive mapping to elicit the representations held by managers?' or 'How was the decision made to blockade during the Cuban crisis?' do constitute research problems.

Examining facts, theoretical or methodological elements, or the links between them enables a researcher to discover or create other theoretical or methodological elements or even other facts. For instance, researchers may hope their work will encourage managers to reflect more about their vision of company strategy. In this case, they will design research that will create facts and arouse reactions that will modify social reality (Cossette and Audet, 1992). The question the researcher formulates therefore indirectly expresses the type of contribution the research will make: a contribution that is for the most part theoretical, methodological or empirical. In this way, we can talk of different types of research problem (see following examples).

Example: Different types of research problems

1 'What does a collective representation in an organization consist of, what is its nature and its constituent elements, and how does it emerge from the supposedly differing representations held by its members?' This research problem principally links concepts, and may be considered as theoretical.
2 'How can we move beyond the limits of cognitive mapping in eliciting the representations held by managers?' In this case, the research problem would be described as methodological.
3 'How can we accelerate the process of change in company X?' The research problem here is empirical (the plans for change at X). The contribution may be both methodological (creating a tool to assist change) and empirical (speeding up change in company X).

The theoretical, methodological or empirical elements that are created or discovered by the researcher (and which constitute the research's major contribution) will enable reality to be explained, predicted, understood or changed. In this way the research will meet the ultimate goals of management science.

To sum up, constructing a research problem consists of formulating a question linking theoretical, empirical or methodological elements, a question which will enable the creation or discovery of other theoretical, empirical or methodological elements that will explain, predict, understand or change reality (see Figure 2.2).

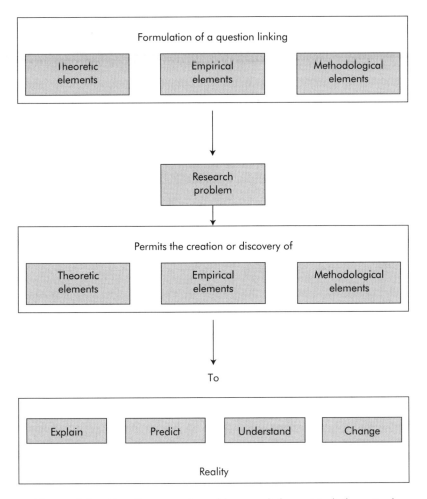

Figure 2.2   *How the research problem can link empirical, theoretical and methodological elements*

2. Different Research Problems for Different Knowledge Goals

A knowledge goal assumes a different signification according to the researcher's epistemological assumptions. The type of knowledge researchers seek, and that of their research problem, will differ depending on whether they hold a positivist, interpretative or constructivist vision of reality.

For a positivist researcher, the research problem consists principally of examining facts so as to discover the underlying structure of reality. For an interpretative researcher, it is a matter of understanding a phenomenon from

Table 2.1   *Research problems and epistemological approach*

Assumptions	Positivist	Interpretativist	Constructivist
Nature of reality: Subject–object relationship	Ontology Independence	Phenomenology Interaction	Phenomenology Interaction
Research goal	Discover and explain the structure of reality	Understand the significations people attach to social reality, and their motivations and intentions (verstehen)	Propose a reality constructed by the researcher
Validity of knowledge	Consistency with facts	Consistency with experience	Usefulness/ suitability in relation to a project
Origin of knowledge	Observation of reality	Empathy	Construction
Nature of the research problem	Examination of the facts	Development of an inside understanding of a phenomenon	Development of a knowledge project
Origin of the research problem	Identification of theoretical inadequacies for explaining or predicting reality	Immersion in the phenomenon studied	Need to transform the knowledge proposed
Position of the research problem in the research process	Exterior to the research process Guides the research process	Interior to the research process Unfolds as part of the research process	Interior to the research process Guides and unfolds within the research process
References	Anderson (1983); Kerlinger (1973)	Hirschman (1986); Hudson and Ozanne (1988); Lincoln and Guba (1985)	Le Moigne (1995); Von Glaserfeld (1987)

the inside in an effort to understand the significations people attach to reality, as well as their motivations and intentions. Finally, for constructivist researchers, constructing a research problem consists of elaborating a knowledge project which they will endeavor to satisfy by means of their research.

These three different epistemological perspectives are based on different visions of reality and on the researcher's relationship with that reality. Consequently, they each attribute a different origin and role to the research problem, and give it a different position in the research process.

The research problem and, therefore, the process by which it is formulated will differ according to the type of knowledge a researcher wishes to produce.

The relationship between the epistemological assumptions of the researcher and the type of research problem they will tend to produce is presented in Table 2.1. The categories presented here can only be indicative and theoretical. Their inclusion is intended to provide pointers that researchers can use in identifying their presuppositions, rather than to suggest they are essential considerations in the construction of a research problem. Most research problems in management sciences are in fact rooted in these different perspectives.

However, once a research problem has been temporarily defined during the research process, it is useful to try to understand the assumptions underlying it, in order to fully appreciate their implications for the research design and results.

2.1 A positivist approach

Positivists consider that reality has its own essence, independently of what individuals perceive – this is what we call an ontological hypothesis. Furthermore, this reality is governed by universal laws: real causes exist and causality is the rule of nature – the determinist hypothesis. To understand reality, we must then try to explain it, to discover the simple and systematic associations between variables underlying a phenomenon (Kerlinger, 1973).

From the positivist viewpoint, then, the research problem consists essentially of examining facts. Researchers construct their research problem by identifying inadequacies or inconsistencies in existing theories, or between theories and facts (Landry, 1995). The results of the research will be aimed at resolving

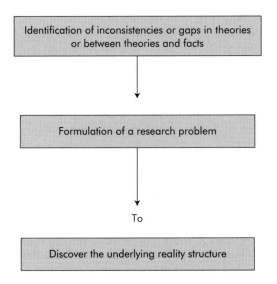

Figure 2.3   *Origins of the research problem and knowledge goal in the positivist research approach*

or correcting these inadequacies or inconsistencies so as to improve our knowledge about the underlying structure of reality (see Figure 2.3).

The nature of the knowledge sought and of the research problem in the positivist epistemology imply that, in the research process, the research problem should be external to scientific activity. Ideally, the research problem is independent of the process that led the researcher to pose it. The research problem then serves as a guide to the elaboration of the architecture and methodology of the research.

2.2 An interpretativist approach

For interpretativists, reality is essentially mental and perceived – the phenomenological hypothesis – and the researcher and the subjects studied interact with each other – the hypothesis of interactivity (Hudson and Ozanne, 1988). In accordance with these hypotheses, interpretativists' knowledge goal is not to discover reality and the laws underlying it, but to develop an understanding (*verstehen*) of social realities. This means developing an understanding of the culturally shared meanings, the intentions and motives of those involved in creating these social realities, and the context in which these constructions are taking place (Hudson and Ozanne, 1988; Schwandt, 1994).

In this perspective, the research process is not directed by an external knowledge goal (as in the positivist research approach), but consists of developing an understanding of the social reality experienced by the subjects of the study. The research problem, therefore, does not involve examining facts to discover their underlying structure, but understanding a phenomenon from the viewpoint of the individuals involved in its creation – in accordance with their own language, representations, motives and intentions (Hudson and Ozanne, 1988; Hirschman, 1986).

The research problem thus unfolds from researcher's immersion in the phenomenon he or she wishes to study (efforts to initiate change in a university, for example). By immersing him or herself in the context, the researcher will be able to develop an inside understanding of the social realities he or she studies. In particular, the researcher will recognize and grasp the participant's problems, motives and meanings (for instance, what meanings actors attach to the university president's efforts to initiate change, and how they react to them).

Here, constructing a research problem does not equate to elaborating a general theoretical problematic that will guide the research process, with the ultimate aim of explaining or predicting reality. The researcher begins from an interest in a phenomenon, and then decides to develop an inside understanding of it. The specific research problem emerges as this understanding develops. Although interpretativists may enter their research setting with some prior knowledge of it, and a general plan, they do not work from established guidelines or strict research protocols. They seek instead to constantly adapt to the changing environment, and to develop empathy for its members (Hudson and Ozanne, 1988). From the interpretative perspective, this is the only way to understand the social realities that people create and experience (Lincoln

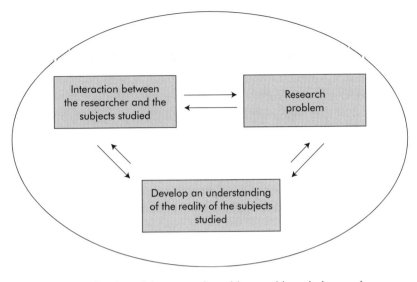

Figure 2.4   *Origins of the research problem and knowledge goal in the interpretative research approach*

and Guba, 1985). The research problem will then take its final form semi-concomitantly with the outcome of the research, when researchers have developed an interpretation of the social reality they have observed or in which they have participated (see Figure 2.4).

This is, of course, a somewhat simplistic and extreme vision of interpretativism. Researchers often begin with a broadly defined research problem that will guide their observations (see Silverman, 1993, for example). This is, however, difficult to assess as most interpretative research, published in American journals at least, are presented in the standard academic format: The research problem is announced in the introduction to the article, and often positioned in relation to existing theories and debates, which can give the mistaken impression that the researchers have clearly defined their research problem before beginning their empirical investigation, as in the positivist approach.

2.3 A constructivist research approach

For the constructivists, knowledge and reality are created by the mind. There is no unique real world that pre-exists independently from human mental activity and language: all observation depends on its observer – including data, laws of nature and external objects (Segal, 1990: 21). In this perspective, 'reality is pluralistic – i.e. it can be expressed by a different symbol and language system – but also plastic – i.e. it is shaped to fit the purposeful acts of intentional human agents' (Schwandt, 1994: 125). The knowledge sought by constructivists is therefore contextual and relative, and above all instrumental and

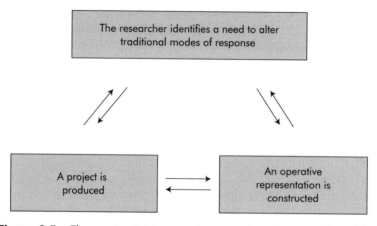

Figure 2.5   *The constructivist research approach to the research problem*

goal-oriented (Le Moigne, 1995). Constructivist researchers construct their own reality, starting from and drawing on their own experience in the context 'in which they act' (Von Glaserfeld, 1988: 30). The dynamics and the goal of the knowledge construction are always linked to the intentions and the motives of the researcher, who experiments, acts and seeks to know. Eventually, the knowledge constructed should serve the researcher's contingent goals: it must be operational. It will then be evaluated according to whether it has fulfilled the researcher's objectives or not – that is, according to a criterion of appropriateness (Le Moigne, 1995).

From this perspective, constructing the research problem is to design a goal-oriented project. This project originates in the identification of a need to alter traditional responses to a given context – to change accepted modes of action or of thought. The construction of the research problem takes place gradually as the researcher develops his or her own experience of the research. The project is in fact continually redefined as the researcher interacts with the reality studied (Le Moigne, 1995). Because of this conjectural aspect of the constructivist process of constructing knowledge, the research problem only appears after the researcher has enacted a clear vision of the project and has stabilized his or her own construction of reality.

Thus, as in the interpretative research approach, the constructivist's research problem is only fully elaborated at the end of the research process. In the constructivist research approach, however, the process of constructing the research problem is guided by the researcher's initial knowledge project (see Figure 2.5). The researcher's subjectivity and purposefulness are then intrinsic to the constructivist project. This intentional dimension of the constructivist research approach departs from the interpretative one. The interpretative research process is not aimed at transforming reality and knowledge and does not take into account the goal-oriented nature of knowledge.

The type of research problem produced, and the process used to construct it, will vary depending on the nature of the knowledge sought and the underlying vision of reality. As we pointed out earlier, the categories we have presented are representative only. If a researcher does not strongly support a particular epistemological view from the outset, he or she could construct a research problem by working from different starting points. In such a process, it is unlikely that the researcher will follow a linear and pre-established dynamics.

SECTION 2   CONSTRUCTING THE RESEARCH PROBLEM

1. Point of Departure

Researchers can use different points of departure to elaborate their research problem. Concepts, theories, theoretical models relating to the phenomenon they wish to study, methodological approaches or tools, facts observed within organizations, a field-study opportunity, a general theme of interest, or a combination of these may be used. Studying a well-known research problem using a new methodological approach, using an existing theory to study a new phenomenon or re-examining theories (in light of the problems encountered by managers, for example) are all possible routes to take in elaborating a research problem.

1.1 Concepts, theories and theoretical models

Reading over published research works with a critical eye can reveal conceptual contradictions, gaps or inadequacies within the body of theoretical knowledge on a given subject. Strange constructs, theoretical inadequacies in some models, contradictory positions among researchers, heterogeneous research designs, concepts or study contexts, are all openings and, therefore, opportunities for constructing a research problem.

A large number of researchers have used the insufficiencies of existing theories (see the following example) or a comparison of two contradictory theoretical frameworks as starting points in constructing their research problems. In this connection, articles synthesizing the current state of a theme or a particular concept are often useful bases on which to construct a research problem.

Example: Starting from existing theories

Steers (1975) reviews 17 multivariate models of organizational effectiveness. Organizational effectiveness is defined as the efficiency with which an organization acquires and uses its resources within a given environment. The author compares these models along four dimensions: primary evaluation criteria, nature – descriptive versus normative – generalizability and derivation – and synthesizes their inadequacies. His analysis starts from the observation that the concept of organizational effectiveness is rarely defined in existent literature, even when it is expressly referred to. While the author does not himself explicitly choose a new perspective from which to study organizational effectiveness, his remarks and observations on the dimensions of the concept are still angles from which to elaborate new research problems.

For example, following on from Steer's work, one could think of introducing a social dimension in the concept of organizational effectiveness, a dimension that is often overshadowed in theoretical works. The research could thus aim to answer the following question: *'What is the social dimension of organizational effectiveness?'*

Detecting inadequacies or contradictions in theories or in definitions of existing concepts is one useful method for starting research. Using a theory or theoretical perspective to study phenomena other than those to which it has until now been applied can also form an interesting basis on which to elaborate research problems (see the following example). Finally, we can simply choose to test certain theoretical principles that have already been advanced, but have not yet been convincingly tested.

Example: Using an existing theoretical perspective to study a new phenomenon

Tracy (1993) proposed to use the living systems theory developed by Miller (1978) for studying organizational behavior and management. He focused his analysis on usual organizational topics and phenomena – in particular, organizational structure – to which the living systems theory has already been applied, and proposed a synthesis of this research. In this article, Tracy outlines the general precepts of the theory and then details its underlying assumptions and theoretical implications. The article offers a good introduction for those interested in constructing a research problem using this theoretical framework.

From Tracy's work, one could envisage studying organizational configurations using the living systems theory. This theory proposes in fact a typology of the subsystems involved in the organization of living systems, identifies the properties and the role of actors and suggests how to regulate the system transversally. The initial research question could be: *'How can the specialization of skills be managed within organizations?'* The research goal would be to construct a typology of company configurations according to the organizational goals and environment – that is, using the living systems theory.

1.2 Starting from a methodology

While, at the moment, most research problems in management science seem to find their genesis in theoretical and conceptual thinking, the methodological approaches or tools used can also constitute interesting starting points for elaborating a research problem. Two possibilities are here available to the researcher. First, the research problem may consist of examining existing methods or methodological approaches, identifying their limits and attempting to propose new ones (see following example). One could propose a new scale for measuring performance, or a new method to analyze discourse, or to support decision-making, for example.

Example: Using a methodology

Eden et al. (1983) set out to design a method to support strategic decision-making in groups. Two assumptions underlie this research project: first, that creating consensus in a group while taking into account the particularities of its members' individual visions is difficult and, second, that traditional group decision-making methods rely on formal approaches. The research goal, therefore, was to design a decision-making method that accounted for potential differences in managers' representations of their problems, and that would facilitate consensus and creative resolution of strategic problems. The method they proposed used cognitive mapping techniques (see Chapter 16). Through cognitive mapping, managers' representations are elicited and then aggregated. These aggregates are then discussed in groups, which enables the strategic problems encountered to be resolved creatively.

The other possible route is to use a new method or a new methodological approach to tackle a theoretical research problem that has already been the subject of other research. In this case, however, researchers should be careful to justify from the start the research problem they are studying (drawing on one of the configurations described in the previous section). Moreover, any method used implies a certain number of constraints that will, to a certain extent, limit the investigation. Many methods, for instance, fall within a given epistemological tradition or involve particular theoretical assumptions that are not necessarily made explicit. It is then very useful to pay attention to such considerations before deciding upon a particular research method. Researchers should weigh up all restraints inherent in the method used, and should evaluate their implications at a theoretical level.

Example: Tackling a classic research problem through a new method

Barr et al. (1992) began their research with the following question: 'Why is it that, in the same environment, and whatever the quality and expertise of their management teams, certain companies are able to adapt and renew themselves while others cannot – and decline inexorably?' Considering the limitations of classic theoretical frameworks, the authors chose to study the problem of organizational renewal from a cognitive perspective. They developed and analyzed organizational cognitive maps of two companies and then linked their conclusions to organizational learning theory.

1.3 Starting from a concrete problem

Companies' difficulties and managers' questions are favorite starting points for research in management. A research problem constructed on this basis ensures interest in the project from a managerial point of view. However, we need to make sure that, eventually, we also find a theoretical perspective on which the research problem and design will both rely.

1.4 Starting from a research setting

Some researchers begin their investigations with a research setting already in mind. This is very often the case when companies enter into research agreements: the researcher and the company agree on a relatively general research topic, for which precise modalities then have to be defined. In such a situation, the construction of a research problem will often be influenced by managerial considerations.

In the case of particularly inductive research, for example, when an interpretative approach is used (see Gioia and Chittipeddi, 1991), researchers often start with a very broad question in mind and a research setting in which to carry out their enquiry. Their research problem will only truly emerge as they gain a clearer understanding of the context (see Section 1). There are, however, disadvantages in setting off on a field study without a specific research problem (see Section 2.2).

1.5 Starting from an area of interest

Finally, many researchers will naturally be drawn towards studying a particular theme. However, interest in a particular domain does not constitute a 'question' as such. The theme the researcher is interested in must then be refined, clarified and tested according to theories, methodologies, managerial interests or possible fieldwork opportunities, so as to elaborate a research problem as such. Researchers might look for any theoretical gaps in the chosen domain, review the concepts most frequently invoked and the methods most often used, or question whether other concepts or methods may be relevant; or identify managers' preoccupations. Researchers have to consider what they can bring to the subject, and what field opportunities are available to them.

2. 'Good' Research Problems

Beyond the various starting points mentioned previously, there are no recipes for defining a good research problem, nor any 'ideal' routes to take. On top of this, as we have seen, researchers subscribing to different epistemological paradigms will not define a 'good research problem' in the same way. We can, nevertheless, try to provide researchers with some useful guidelines, and warn them against possible pitfalls to be aware of when defining their research problem.

2.1 Delimiting the research problem

Be precise and be clear   Researchers should always endeavor to give themselves as precise and concise a research problem as possible. In other words, the way the research problem is formulated should not lend itself to multiple interpretations (Quivy and Van Campenhoudt, 1988). For example, the question *'What impact do organizational changes have on the everyday life of employees?'* is too vague. What are we to understand by 'organizational changes'? Does this mean structural change? Changes in the company's strategy? Changes in the decision-making process? We would advise this researcher to put his or her research problem to a small group of people, and to invite them individually to indicate what they understand it to mean. The research problem will be all the more precise when interpretations of it converge and correspond to the author's intention.

Having a precise research problem does not mean, however, that the field of analysis involved is restricted. The problem may necessitate a vast amount of empirical or theoretical investigation. Having a precise research problem simply means that its formulation is univocal. In this perspective, researchers are advised to avoid problems that are too long or confused, which prevent a clear understanding of the researcher's objective and intention. In short, the research problem must be formulated sufficiently clearly to ground and direct the researcher's project.

Be feasible   In the second place, novice researchers or researchers with limited time and resources should endeavor to give themselves a relatively narrow research problem:

> As I tell my students, your aim should be to say 'a lot about a little problem'. This means avoiding the temptation to say 'a little about a lot'. Precisely because the topic is so wide-ranging, one can flit from one aspect to another without being forced to refine and test each piece of analysis.
>
> (Silverman, 1993: 3)

If a research problem is too broad, researchers risk finding themselves with a mass of theoretical information or empirical data (if they have already started their fieldwork) which quickly becomes unmanageable and which will make defining the research problem even more difficult ('What am I going to do with all that?'). In other words, the research problem must be realistic and feasible, i.e. in keeping with the researcher's resources in terms of personality, time and finances. This dimension is less problematic when researchers have significant time and human resources at their disposal (see Gioia and Chittipeddi, 1991).

In short, a relatively limited and clear research problem prevents the researcher from falling into the trap of what Silverman (1993) calls 'tourism'. Here, Silverman is referring to research that begins in the observational field, without any precisely defined goals, theories or hypotheses, and focuses on social events and activities that appear to be new and different. There is a danger here of overvaluing cultural or subcultural differences and forgetting the common points and similarities between the culture being studied and that to which one belongs. For instance, a researcher who is interested in managers' work and restricts his or her attention to their more spectacular interventions would be forgetting aspects that are no less interesting and instructive – for example, the daily and routine aspects of the manager's work.

Be practical   As their theoretical or empirical investigative work proceeds, researchers can clarify and narrow down their research problem. If they are initially interested in a particular domain (organizational learning for instance), they may formulate a fairly broad initial question ('What variables favor organizational learning?'). They may then limit this question to a particular domain ('What variables favor organizational learning during the strategic planning process?') and/or specify the conceptual framework they are interested in ('What cognitive or structural variables favor organizational learning during the strategic planning process?'). Through this narrowing down, the theoretical and empirical investigation will be guided and then easier to conduct.

Conversely, one should avoid confining oneself to a very narrow research problem. If the problem involves conditions that are too difficult to meet, the possibilities for empirical investigation may be greatly reduced. Similarly, if researchers focus too soon on a specific question, they may shut themselves off from many research opportunities that might well have broadened the scope of their research problem. They also risk limiting their understanding of the context in which the phenomenon studied is taking place. Finally, if researchers limit their research problem too much when it has been little studied, they may have only few theoretical and methodological elements to draw on when beginning their fieldwork. They will then have to carry out an exploratory theoretical work to redefine their initial research problem.

In sum, it appears difficult to strike a balance between a too large research problem that is impossible to contain, and a too limited research problem that shuts off study opportunities. This is one of the major difficulties researchers will confront when starting out on a research project.

2.2 Recognizing the assumptions underlying a research problem

Scientific Goal   Beyond the qualities of clarity and feasibility, the research problem must possess qualities of 'relevance'. Quivy and Van Campenhoudt (1988) define 'relevance' as the general mode and intention – explicative, normative, moral or philosophical – underlying a research problem. A research problem is 'relevant' if its underlying intention is understanding or explaining reality (which are the overriding goals of science). 'Do bosses exploit workers?' 'Is work flexibility socially fair?' 'What are the organization's aims?' are questions that translate moral (in the case of the first two) and philosophical intentions (in the case of the last one). But in our opinion, the principal aim of the social sciences is not to make moral judgements about the functioning of organizations – even if a moral or political concern may inspire a research problem (Parker, 1993; 1994). The social sciences lack sufficient methods to answer philosophical problems – even if philosophical thinking, through epistemology in particular, is essential to the development of these disciplines. In sum, a research problem must translate into a knowledge project, whether comprehensive, explicative or predictive.

Underlying values and assumptions   While a research problem should not have a 'moral' or 'political' intention, researchers must be aware of and question its underlying values and assumptions (others than the epistemological assumptions we have mentioned earlier in this chapter). For example, and it is particularly true in management sciences, some research problems are stamped with the idea that research enables humanity to progress and the organization's efficiency to be improved. For instance, the research problem 'how can we improve organizational learning?' conceals the assumption that organizational learning improves the organization's efficiency or the employees' well-being. But is it necessarily so?

Because of the strong influence of trends in managerial and economic thinking, one must be particularly wary of concepts and notions that contain the idea of progress or improvement in efficiency in management science – in relation, for instance, to culture, change, consensus or communication. But, as Silverman (1993: 5) puts it, 'an uncritical belief in "progress" is an unacceptable basis for scientific research'. In our opinion, researchers should question the assumptions and values underlying their research problem and that will influence their research design and methodology and, therefore, their research results and implications. To return to our initial example, why should we assume that organizations must learn, that they must have a 'strong' culture, that the environment changes more quickly today than before, or that shared meanings and consensus in the organization improve its functioning and efficiency? Are these assumptions based on some reality? Or are they the expression of our current values and ways of thinking: new imperatives that replace those of the scientific work organizations of the 1920s?

Silverman (1993) here calls researchers to use a historical, cultural and political sensitivity in order to detect the interests and motivations behind their research problem and to understand how and why these 'problems' emerge. Why is there more interest in, and therefore more research problems about, organizational learning today? What does this sudden interest in 'environmental issues' mean? Such questions can help us to understand how and why these new 'realities' emerge. They also encourage us to look critically at the way we formulate our research problems, thus freeing ourselves from some taken-for-granted beliefs about organizations.

3. Constructing a Research Problem: Illustrations

Given the difficulties outlined above, constructing a research problem is rarely a matter of taking just one of the routes we have presented. It is often a case of moving back and forth between theoretical and empirical steps. A general research problem stemming from an initial review of existent literature may prove flawed when the concepts it relies on are operationalized or may be too broad to investigate with limited means and resources. In the following, we present two examples of paths taken by researchers in constructing a research problem. These different experiences are not presented as model examples. To the contrary, they are intended to show the diversity of processes that may be followed and the difficulties that may be encountered when constructing a research problem.

A linear dynamic   A research problem can emerge clearly and quite quickly after research has begun. As the example described below shows, combining two theoretical approaches (the evolutionist theory and the theory of non-linear dynamic systems) to analyze a relatively classic phenomenon (the management of innovation) enables one to compose an original research problem relatively early in the research process.

Example: A question resulting from the confrontation between two theoretical fields

My research question was directly inspired by my training. As a graduate in pure mathematics, I sought to use my theoretical knowledge to gain a better understanding of organizations. My thesis was based on studying the evolution dynamics of a group of innovation projects. I started from chaos theory, with which I was familiar, and I chose to apply it to the management of innovation principally because it appealed to me. While reviewing related work on the subject, I noticed that innovations were rarely studied at the level of a population, and that their evolution dynamics was non-linear. I then thought of using evolutionary theory to build a model of the laws underlying the evolution of this population. I discovered that parametric models were potentially chaotic. This drew my ideas together and I had my research problem: *'How does a population of innovation projects live and die?'* Once I had posed my research problem, my research work consisted of testing this conceptual framework.

A recursive dynamics   While the process followed in the previous example seemed to unfold without great difficulty, the construction of a research problem is often less linear. A lot of research begins on ill-defined theoretical and methodological bases. The difficulties will be all the greater if the researcher chooses to work from an original or little-known epistemological perspective. The following example illustrates a more treacherous route. This young researcher was initially interested in the process of knowledge capitalization within an organization. After theoretical reflection on the subject, she redefined her research problem and focused on the collective construction of knowledge. Her research problem then seemed to be clear enough: *'How does collective knowledge construct itself within organizations?'* This redefinition led her to conduct new theoretical investigations, but she has had trouble developing an empirical vision of her research problem. Her choice of constructivism as her epistemological position has numerous implications in the construction of her research problem. After an initial exploratory empirical phase, she now feels that synthesizing her initial observations will enable her to specify the practical terms of her research problem.

Example: A research problem resulting from theoretical reflection in the constructivist perspective

I began my thesis in December and I've already taken three months to arrive at a satisfactory research problem. When I first started on my thesis, I wanted to study the process of knowledge capitalization within organizations. This is an important managerial problem that interests many companies. However, I quickly reached my first impasse: firstly, a thesis had already been written on a closely related subject, and secondly, it seemed important to me to tackle the problem of knowledge construction before that of its capitalization.

Over the following three months, I read through published works with a new research problem in mind. I wanted to know how knowledge was collectively constructed and to understand its dynamics within organizations. This is a subject that had never really been dealt with at the level at which I wished to study it, that of working groups. I skimmed through some writings on knowledge in different domains and eventually took the direction of an American model of social psychology. However, I found it difficult to integrate this very heterogeneous reading material in the way I had hoped.

Over the summer I found a company that was interested in my research, and I had to begin to actively put together an initial conceptual framework (very perfunctory to start with) and to delve into epistemological and methodological considerations. However, I didn't know how to observe knowledge construction and was not really sure which information to collect. I opted for a very inductive process.

After around three months of fieldwork, I have neither completely resolved these methodological questions nor really defined my epistemological position. I am now synthesizing my first field results, which I hope will enable me to clarify these points and specify my research problem.

Finally   These two 'stories' are, of course, far from being comparable. They reflect different states of advancement in the research process (the research has been completed in the first example, but is ongoing in the second). However, they illustrate some of the difficulties researchers can come up against when they are trying to construct their research problem. In addition to the difficulties engendered by theoretical investigation and by drafting an initial broad research problem, researchers often meet instrumentation problems or empirical constraints that can lead them to redefine their research problem (see Chapter 7). These difficulties are even greater when a field opportunity presents itself or when the researcher seeks to define his or her epistemological position. Then it is a question of 'making the best with what you have'. A researcher might, for example, conduct an initial exploratory study (as in the two examples cited above) and specify the research problem once he or she has developed an initial 'understanding' of the phenomenon studied. Alternatively, the researcher may prefer to wait until he or she has resolved his or her methodological or epistemological problems. We strongly advise researchers who encounter such difficulties to discuss them with their colleagues. The questions they will ask and the efforts at clarification the researcher will be pushed to make will serve as leads, openings and sources of inspiration and structuring that will help to construct a research problem.

CONCLUSION

We have tried to show, and to illustrate, the diversity of approaches and processes that can be used when constructing a research problem, while underlining the difficulties and traps that pepper this process. Research is a lengthy, difficult and demanding work. However, it is above all about finding or creating one's own questions, giving oneself a project and committing oneself, all of which doubtless renders this process at once so harrowing, yet so fascinating.

The research problem thus constructed can comprise different types of question: 'What?' 'How?' 'Why?' 'Who?' 'Where?' 'When?' 'Is it?' These questions can relate to very different realities – depending on the approach taken and where the researcher's epistemological sympathies lie. It is, therefore, advisable to specify, beyond the objective one has set oneself, the general direction the research will take. The following chapter is aimed at helping researchers to do just this.

FURTHER READING

Blaug, M., *The Methodology of Economics: Or How Economics Explain*, Cambridge: Cambridge Surveys of Economic Literature, 1992.

Hudson, L. and Ozanne, J.L., 'Alternative Ways of Seeking Knowledge in Consumer Research', *Journal of Consumer Research*, 14, 1988: 508–21.

Kerlinger, Fred N., *The Foundation of Behavioral Research*, New York: Holt Rinehart and Winston, 1973.

Knorr-Cetina, K.D., *The Manufacture of Knowledge: An Essay on the Constructivist and Contextual Nature of Science*, New York: Pergamon, 1981.

Landry, M., 'A Note on the Concept of "Problem"', *Organization Studies*, 16 (2), 1995: 315–43.

Lincoln, Y.S. and Guba, E.G., *Naturalistic Inquiry*, Beverley Hills, CA: Sage, 1985.

Silverman, D., *Interpreting Qualitative Data, Methods for Analysing Talk, Text, and Interaction*, London: Sage, 1993.

3

EXPLORING AND TESTING

Sandra Charreire and Florence Durieux

Outline

This chapter aims to answer the question 'How do I inquire?', by presenting the two processes central to the construction of knowledge: exploration and testing. Exploration is the process through which the researcher seeks to formulate innovative theoretical propositions, while testing appraises the reality of theoretical conjecture. The first section of the chapter presents the logical processes – deduction and induction – on which exploration and testing depend. The second section discusses three possible methods of exploration (theoretical, empirical and hybrid). In the third section the classic hypothetico-deductive testing method is presented. We conclude by examining how exploration and testing can be reconciled within the overall research design.

The two preceding chapters have addressed questions of epistemological choices and deciding upon a research question. The object of this chapter is to answer the question, 'How do I inquire?' The chapter explains the two processes central to the construction of knowledge: exploration and testing. Exploration is the process through which the researcher seeks to formulate innovative theoretical propositions, while testing appraises the reality of theoretical conjecture. Exploration and testing take place in a transitional phase of the research process; after the definition of the research question, but ahead of the collection and processing of data – and before final choices are made concerning methodological design.

Exploration and testing are both fundamental to management research, and draw upon epistemological debates over both how scientific knowledge is generated, and the status of the knowledge produced (see Chapter 1). A researcher's epistemological positioning will affect the choices he or she makes; whether to test or to explore. Whereas the process of testing resolutely places research within the positivist paradigm, the process of exploration has no particular association with any single paradigm. Indeed, the 'explorative' researcher might endorse paradigms as different from each other as, for example, positivism, constructivism or interpretativism.

SECTION 1   THEORETICAL BACKGROUND

Exploration and testing are two processes through which we construct knowledge. To explore in management consists of discovering, or looking further into, a structure or a way of functioning in order to satisfy two broad objectives: the quest for explanation (and prediction) and the quest for comprehension. Through exploration, researchers satisfy their initial intentions: to propose innovative theoretical results – to create new theoretical links between concepts, or to integrate new concepts into a given theoretical field. Testing is the set of operations by which we assess the reality of one or more theoretical elements. Testing is also used to evaluate the significance of hypotheses, models or theories to a given explanation.

The dichotomy (exploration and test) we suggest in this chapter is justified by the different types of logic that are characteristic of these two processes. To explore, the researcher adopts an approach that is either inductive or abductive, or both – whereas testing calls for a deductive method.

1. Logical Principles

1.1 Deduction

By definition, deduction is characterized by the fact that, if the hypotheses formulated initially (premises) are true, then the conclusion that follows logically from these premises must necessarily be true.

> **Example: A classic deduction: the syllogism of Socrates**
>
> 1 All men are mortal.
> 2 Socrates is a man.
> 3 Socrates is mortal.
>
> In this example of deductive logic, (1) and (2) are the premises and (3) the conclusion. It is not possible that (3) is false once (1) and (2) are accepted as true. Schematically this argument follows the following logic: every A is B, C is A, therefore C is B. (See also Chapter 1)

We should not, however, limit deduction to the type of syllogism evoked in the above example. In fact, logicians make a distinction between formal and constructive deduction. Formal deduction is an argument or an inference – a logical operation by which one concludes the necessary consequence of one or several propositions – that consists of moving from the implicit to the explicit, the most usual form being the syllogism. Although formal deduction involves valid logical reasoning, it is sterile insofar as the conclusion does not enable us to learn a new fact. The conclusion is already presupposed in the premises; consequently the argument is tautological. Constructive deduction, on the other hand, while also leading to a necessary conclusion, makes a contribution to our knowledge. The conclusion is a *demonstration* – composed not only of the contents of the premises, but also of the logic by which one shows that one circumstance is the consequence of another.

Deductive logic thus underpins the hypothetico-deductive method. This consists of elaborating one or more general hypotheses, and then comparing them against a particular reality in order to assess the validity of the hypotheses formulated initially.

1.2 Induction and abduction

Induction, in logic, usually means to assert the truth of a general proposition by considering particular cases that support it. Mill (1843: 26) defines it as 'the operation of discovering and proving general propositions ... by which we infer that what we know to be true in a particular case or cases, will be true in all cases which resemble the former in certain assignable respects'. Induction is called summative (or complete) if it proceeds through an enumeration of all cases that its conclusion is valid for. Induction is called ampliative (or incomplete) if its conclusion goes beyond its premises. That is, the conclusion is not a logical consequence of the premises. Ampliative induction is thus an inconclusive argument.

The Principle of Induction

If a great number of A have been observed in very varied circumstances, and if one then observes that all of the As without exception have the property B, then all As have the property B ... Let us suppose, for example, that I have observed a great number of ravens in extremely varied circumstances; having noted that all those observed so far have been black, I conclude from this: 'All ravens are black'. It is a perfectly legitimate inductive inference. But this logic does not offer any guarantee that the next raven that I observe will not be pink.

(Chalmers, 1976: 25)

This argument illustrates the principle of induction. Researchers in management, however, frequently explore complex contexts; drawing from them a large number of observations of a variety of natures which are at first ambiguous. They will then attempt to structure their observations so as to derive meaning from them. In the social sciences, the aim is not really to produce universal laws, but rather to propose new theoretical conceptualizations that are valid and robust, and are thought through in minute detail. It is said, then, that the researcher proceeds by abduction (a term employed in particular by Eco, 1990) or by adduction (term used by Blaug, 1992).

The Abduction Process

Abduction is an inferential process (in other words, a hypothesis) which is opposed to deduction, because deduction starts from a rule, considers a case of this rule and automatically infers a necessary result:
   Let's (re)consider the abduction about the white beans. I find a fistful of beans on the table. On the table too is a sack. What tells me that I need to connect the beans

on the table with the sack? I could ask myself whether the beans came from the sack, whether someone brought them there and then left. If I focus my attention on the sack (and why on that sack?) it is because in my head a sort of plausibility appears, such as 'It is logical that the beans came from the sack'. But there is nothing which guarantees me that my hypothesis is the right one.

There are three levels of abduction. On the first level, the Result is strange and unexplainable, but the Rule already exists somewhere, perhaps inside the same field of problems, and one just must find it, and find it to be the most probable. On the second level, the Rule is difficult to identify. It exists elsewhere, and one must believe that it could be extended to this field of phenomena. On the third level, the Rule does not exist, and one must invent it: this is the case of Copernicus, who decides that the universe must not be heliocentric for reasons of symmetry.

(Eco, 1990: 158–9)

Thus induction is a logical inference which confers on a discovery an *a priori* constancy (that is, gives it the status of law), whereas abduction confers on it an explanatory status which then needs to be tested further if it is to be tightened into a rule or a law.

By applying an abductive method, the researcher in management can use analogy and metaphor to account for observed phenomena, or to illustrate or explain propositions. The aim is to use the comparison as an aid in deriving meaning. An analogy is an expression of a relationship or a similarity between several different elements. Consequently, to argue analogically involves drawing connections and noting resemblances (so long as these indicate some sort of relationship). The researcher proceeds then by association, through familial links between observed phenomena. Metaphors are transfers by analogical substitution – a metaphor is a figure of speech by which we give a new signification to a name or a word, in order to suggest some similarity. The metaphor is thus relevant only as far as the comparison at hand; it can be described as an abridged comparison.

In management, recourse to analogical reasoning or metaphor is common when researchers choose to construct knowledge through exploration. Pentland (1995) establishes a relationship between the structures and processes of grammatical models and the structure characteristics of an organizational environment along with the corresponding processes likely to be produced within it. Using metaphor as a transfer by analogical substitution, Pentland demonstrates to what extent the 'grammatical metaphor' can be useful in understanding organizational processes.

In his work *Images of Organization*, Morgan (1986) discusses using metaphor as an aid in analyzing organizations. Morgan sees metaphor as a tool with which to decode and to understand. He argues that metaphorical analysis is an effective way of dealing with organizational complexity. Morgan raises the metaphorical process to the status of legitimate research device. He distinguishes several metaphorical conceptions of the organization: in particular as a

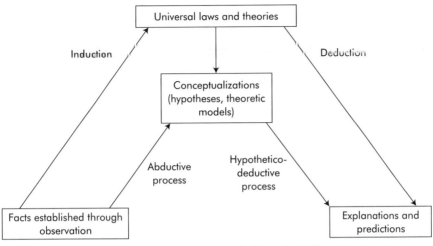

Source: Adapted from Chalmers (1976)

Figure 3.1 *Logical processes and scientific knowledge*

machine, an organism, a brain and a culture. The choice of which metaphorical vision to borrow influences the meaning produced.

1.3 Constructing knowledge

Although so far we have differentiated between induction and deduction, used respectively for exploration and testing, these two logics are complementary when it comes to the *construction* of scientific knowledge (see Figure 3.1).

It is traditionally considered that deductive reasoning moves from the general to the particular, and inductive from the particular to the general. For Blaug (1992) however, induction and deduction are distinguished by the character – demonstrative or not – of the inferences formed. The conclusions of inductive or abductive reasoning are not demonstrations. They represent relationships that, through the thoroughness with which they have been established, have achieved the status of valid propositions. These propositions are not, however, certain – as those elaborated through deduction can be. They are regarded as inconclusive, or uncertain, inferences.

Yet 'certain' and 'uncertain' inferences are both integral to the process of constructing new knowledge. From our observations, we can be led to infer the existence of laws (through induction – an uncertain inference) or, more reasonably, conceptualizations: explanations or conjectures (through abduction – again uncertain). These laws or conceptualizations might then be used as premises, and be subjected to tests. By testing them we might hopefully develop inferences of which we are certain (through deduction). In this way, researchers are able to advance explanatory and/or predictive conclusions.

2. Theoretical Elements

Exploration can often lead researchers to formulate one or more temporary working hypotheses. These hypotheses may in turn be used as the basis of further reflection, or in structuring a cohesive body of observations. But while the final result of the exploration process (using an abductive approach) takes the form of hypotheses, models, or theories, these constitute the starting point of the testing process (in which deduction is employed). It is from these theoretical elements that the researcher will try to find an answer to the question he or she posed initially.

2.1 Hypotheses

In everyday usage, a hypothesis is a conjecture about why, when, or how an event occurs. It is a supposition about the behavior of different phenomena or about the relationships that may exist between them. One proposes, as a hypothesis, that a particular phenomenon is an antecedent or a consequent of, or is invariably concomitant to, other given phenomena. Developed through theoretical reflection, drawing on the prior knowledge the researcher has of the phenomena being studied, hypotheses are actually the relationships we establish between our theoretical concepts.

> A concept refers to certain characteristics or phenomena that can be grouped together. Alternatively, a concept represents similarities in otherwise diverse phenomena … Concepts are located in the world of thought … are abstracted forms and do not reflect objects in their entirety but comprehend only a few aspects of objects.
>
> (Zaltman et al., 1973: 22–3)

When we map out a hypothesis, we explain the logic of the relations that link the concepts involved (see Figure 3.2). From the moment it has been formulated, the hypothesis replaces the initial research question, and takes the form of a provisional answer.

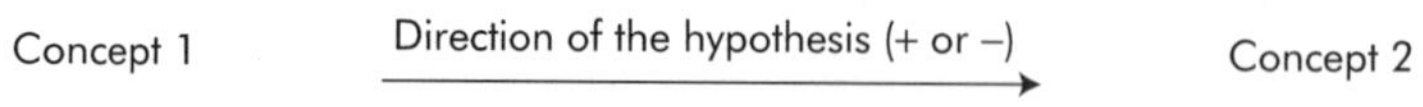

Concept 1   Direction of the hypothesis (+ or –) ————→   Concept 2

Figure 3.2   *Schematic representation of a hypothesis*

If the direction of the hypothesis is positive, the more Concept 1 is present, the stronger Concept 2 will be; if the direction is negative, then the presence of Concept 1 will lessen the presence of Concept 2.

Like the research subject, a research hypothesis should have certain specific properties. First, the hypothesis should be expressed in observable form. To assess its value as an answer to the research question, it needs to be weighed against experimental and observational data. It should therefore indicate the type of observations that must be collected, as well as the relationships that must be established between these observations in order to verify to what extent the hypothesis is confirmed (or not) by facts.

For example, let us consider the following hypothesis: 'There are as many readings of a text as there are readers of it.' Here we have an expression that cannot be operationalized, and which therefore cannot constitute an acceptable research hypothesis in the sense we have outlined. In reading a text we acquire a mental image which will always lose something when it is verbalized. The concept of protocol sentences is generally applied in such a case, but this can still only partly account for the results of the reading.

On the other hand, a hypothesis such as 'Organizations with interorganizational linkages should show a lower failure rate than comparable organizations without such linkages' (Miner et al., 1990: 691) indicates the kind of observations we need to have access to if we are to assess its legitimacy. The researcher is led to identify the existence or not of interorganizational links and the suspension or not of the organization's activities. The hypothesis can be represented by the diagram in Figure 3.3.

Existence of interorganizational links $\xrightarrow{\quad + \quad}$ Low failure rate

Figure 3.3   *Representation of the interorganizational linkages hypothesis*

Second, hypotheses should not be relationships based on social prejudices or stereotypes. For example, the hypothesis that 'absenteeism increases with an increase in the number of women in a company' leads to a distorted view of social reality. Ideological expressions cannot be treated as hypotheses.

In practice, it is rare for researchers to restrict themselves to only one hypothesis. The researcher is most often led to work out a body of hypotheses, which must be coherent and logically consistent. It is only then that we have the form of a model.

2.2 Models

There are many definitions of the term 'model'. According to Kaplan (1964: 263): 'We say that any system A is a model of system B if the study of A is useful for the understanding of B without regard to any direct or indirect causal connection between A and B.'

In the social sciences, a model is a schematic illustration of physical or cognitive relationships among its elements. In practice, a 'model' is a simplified representation of a process or a system that is designed to explain and/or simulate a real situation. The model is then schematic, in that the number of parameters it incorporates is sufficiently limited that they can be readily explained and manipulated.

The subject–model relationship is by nature subjective. In other words, the model does not aim to account for every aspect of the subject, nor even every aspect of any one possible approach to the subject (see Figure 3.4).

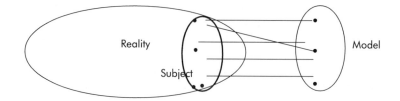

Figure 3.4   *Relationship between a model and reality*

2.3 Theories

In broad terms, a theory can be said to be a body of knowledge, which forms a system, on a particular subject or in a particular field. But this definition is of limited use in practice. That said, as authors continue to formalize more precisely what they mean by theory, the number of definitions of the term continues to increase. Zaltman, et al. (1973) note ten different definitions, all of which have one point in common: theories are sets of interconnected propositions. Ambiguity or confusion between the terms 'theory' and 'model' is not uncommon.

It is not the aim of the present chapter to settle this debate. We will use the term here with the definition suggested by Bunge (1967: 387):

> Theory designates a system of hypotheses. A set of scientific hypotheses is a scientific theory if and only if it refers to a given factual subject matter and every member of the set is either an initial assumption (axiom, subsidiary assumption, or datum) or a logical consequence of one or more initial assumptions.

To be more precise, we can adopt the vocabulary of Lakatos (1974), and say that a theory is a system made up of a 'core' and a 'protective belt' (see Figure 3.5). The core includes the basic hypotheses that underlie the theory, those which are required – they can be neither rejected nor modified. In other words, the core cannot be modified by methodological decision. It is surrounded by the protective belt, which contains explicit auxiliary hypotheses that supplement those of the core, along with observations and descriptions of initial conditions (Chalmers, 1976).

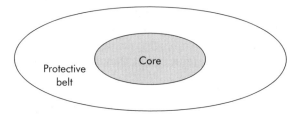

Figure 3.5   *Schematic representation of a theory*

Researchers in management do not deal with laws or universal theories. Instead they construct or test theories that are generally qualified as substantive. It is important to distinguish the claims of such substantive theories from those of more universal theories. Glaser and Strauss (1967) make a distinction between substantive and formal theories: a substantive theory is a theoretical development in direct relation to an empirical domain, whereas a formal theory relates to a conceptual domain.

A concept of inclusion exists between these two levels of theories. A formal theory usually incorporates several substantive theories that have been developed in different or comparable empirical fields. While formal theories are more 'universal' than substantive theories, which are 'rooted' in a context, a formal theory generally evolves from the successive integration of several substantive theories (Glaser and Strauss, 1967).

In the above discussion we have looked at the two types of logic that underlie the two processes we employ in constructing knowledge (exploration and testing). We have also considered the theoretical elements key to these logical processes.

SECTION 2   EXPLORATION

In management research, empirical methods – various forms of observation, interviews, investigations, simulations or quasi-experimentation, or a combination of various techniques (multi-methods) – are used more frequently to explore and to develop new theoretical constructs than in testing them (Snow and Thomas, 1994). While the exploration process itself does not presuppose a choice of either a qualitative or a quantitative methodological design, qualitative methodologies are more commonly employed, being more efficient as far as the finality of the research is concerned (see Chapter 4). Similarly, exploration does not limit the epistemological choices available to the researcher – who can explore from either a positivist or a constructivist perspective, for example.

1. Theoretical Exploration

Theoretical exploration consists in developing a connection between two or more theoretical fields that have not been linked previously in other works. These fields or disciplines do not have to be totally circumscribed by the researcher, however. In fact, researchers can only focus on a limited area of a field or discipline – that which seems to be the most relevant to their research subject.

The researcher will select and employ a certain number of theoretical elements in each of the fields (or disciplines) studied, and in so doing will delimit the conceptual framework of the research. Exploration is carried out at the level of the newly established connections between the fields or disciplines under study. At this point results are expected either to complete, or round off, an incomplete explanation, or to advance another understanding altogether.

Example: Grammatical models and organizational processes

Pentland (1995) explores theoretically the possible usefulness of the grammatical metaphor to describe and conceptualize organizational processes in an original way. Drawing on writings in both organizational theory and linguistics, Pentland establishes a parallel between grammatical and organizational processes by making analogies between these two distinct disciplines. He shows how grammatical models represent an opportunity for management research because they constitute a new way to describe sequences of actions that are characteristic of organizational processes. By relating culture, institutional structures and coordination techniques to actions, routines and possible organizational processes, he shows the strong explicative power grammatical models hold for research in management. The principal interest of such models (and of Pentland's theoretical exploration) lies in the explicit connection between the structural characteristics of a context and the organizational processes possible in that context.

Theoretical exploration necessitates an inductive method, which may lead researchers to propose analogies between a number of theoretic fields. The exploration must, though, remain relevant to the field in which they are working.

2. Empirical Exploration

The empirical method involves exploring a phenomenon from a *tabula rasa* (clean slate) starting point – putting aside all prior knowledge we have of the subject at hand. This method theoretically enables a researcher to develop 'anew' – and independently – existing knowledge about a subject. Empirical exploration employs a purely inductive logical method, which favors, in theory, the development of new inferences.

In practice, this method is not used in management in the strict *tabula rasa* sense. Its applicability to such research is limited. Researchers cannot throw off their prior understandings and beliefs entirely. They cannot see all there is to be seen, but only that which they know how to see. Researchers' personalities, previous experience, and even the way their minds are structured, all influence their perception.

Our observations, even the most unchecked, are guided by what we are *able* to see and by what we are *prepared* to see. It is very difficult, even utopian, to argue that we can truly make a clean slate of our knowledge. We cannot hope to carry out research with the eyes of a newborn baby, with no *a priori* assumptions about the world. Even the paradigm selected comes into question here. Rather than representing a thought-out choice, this may say more about the personality of the researcher, and his or her aspirations or natural affinities.

Empirical exploration remains useful, however, when researchers investigate little-known, or even totally unknown, phenomena. Inductive inferences are appropriate when there is no available base of potentially useful knowledge, as they permit researchers to make sense of observations of which they know nothing about.

An ethnologist who discovers a hitherto unknown people can employ an empirical explorative method to determine the rules of their society, and to try to understand their language and beliefs. If, however, studies have already been made of a people, or it is known that links exist between them and known civilizations, the ethnologist will have little to gain by employing such a method. To do so would in all likelihood amount to 'reinventing the wheel' – a lot of time could be spent on exploring phenomena about which much is already known. Miles and Huberman (1984a) warn researchers in management who are eager to rid themselves of the scientific knowledge at their disposal against precisely such a situation.

In management, ethnographic methods make it possible to explore little-known phenomena without having to establish a rigid conceptual framework from the outset. This leaves the researcher the possibility of discovering new links or different explanations. These methods are based on the principle of the researcher's immersion in the context.

Example: Initiating change in an organization

Gioia and Chittipeddi (1991) carried out a two-and-a-half-year-long ethnographic study looking at how change was initiated within an organization; in this case an American university. The results of this interpretative search were twofold. An initial analysis highlighted four phases in the process of the initiation of change – envisioning, signaling, revisioning and energizing. Two underlying logics (sense-making and sense-giving) then explained this process, and these played a part in the creation, by the actors, of the new organizational order.

The authors proposed a new conceptual framework (sense-making and sense-giving) to understand the process of the initiation of change. This emerged from a second analysis carried out in the light of the four phases identified in the first analysis. Their theoretical framework thus sprang directly from their data – Gioia and Chittipeddi had not constructed an initial theoretical framework, which would have guided not only their data collection but also their analysis. Instead they followed a methodological design that was very close to ethnographic methods (participant and neutral observation, a long immersion in a context). The technique of narrating journalistically what they observed enabled the first result to emerge (the identification of four phases of the process). The authors made a conscious effort to center their research on inductive reasoning; they even sought to avoid the premature formulation of hypotheses, which they would then have been tempted to test. The second level of analysis aims at conceptualization; a study of the 'history' of this change, from a theoretical perspective.

As empirical exploration is not molded around an initial conceptual framework, it is in a sense a 'back-to-front' research method in comparison to traditional research in management (in which an initial theoretical design guides and influences the exploration).

3. Hybrid Exploration

Hybrid exploration consists in continually shifting between observations and theoretical knowledge throughout the research process. The researcher begins by putting forward concepts to which the literature relevant to the subject of the research is progressively integrated. This theoretical knowledge will be used in making sense of the empirical observations collected in the course of the research. In this sense the method is deductive.

Hybrid exploration is a method that permits the researcher to enrich or expand upon existent knowledge of a subject. Such research tends towards a strong theoretical realism, and the production of theoretical constructs firmly rooted in the facts at hand (Glaser and Strauss, 1967).

The problem of contextualization usually arises at some time during the explorative process. Although there is nothing to oblige researchers to test the results of their explorations, many authors (in particular, Glaser and Strauss) encourage researchers to formulate their new theoretical frameworks in such a way that they can be tested. In other words, although the new conceptualization they have produced relates to the particular environment they studied, it has hopefully emerged through a strict and systematic approach (methodological design) which the researcher should be able to explain and justify. It may then be tested in other similar or comparable contexts. It is, however, advisable to take certain precautions when putting a produced theoretical element to the test in contexts other than that from which it originally emerged. Most importantly, the researcher must clearly define the *a priori* typology of the context in which it applies.

SECTION 3   TESTING

Testing is, as we have noted, a process by which a theoretical element is assessed in a real situation. While researchers are free to employ qualitative or quantitative methodological designs to test their propositions, quantitative methods are more frequently used to serve the logic of the testing process.

1. Testing a Hypothesis

When a hypothesis is subjected to a test, it is considered in line with a reality that serves as a reference. It is therefore indispensable to demonstrate, from the outset, how a researcher can determine whether a hypothesis is acceptable or not with regard to a particular reality.

1.1 Is the hypothesis acceptable?

At no moment during the test does the researcher invent. Testing is a matter of finding actual results. All the same, the results of a test should not be taken as true or false in the absolute, but only in relation to the conceptual framework of the test and the specific experimental conditions. A favorable result from this 'comparison with reality' – which could be seen as a confirmation of the hypothesis – does not, in fact, constitute decisive proof. It is only a temporarily convincing corroboration. The force with which a hypothesis is corroborated by a given body of facts depends on a variety of factors. Hempel (1966) proposes four corroboration criteria: quantity, diversity, precision and simplicity.

Of these four criteria, simplicity appears to be the most subjective. Popper (1977) argues that the simpler of two hypotheses is the one that has the greatest empirical content. For him, the simplest hypothesis is that which would be easiest to establish as false. While it is true that we cannot prove a hypothesis decisively, it is also true that a single contradictory case is all that is required to show it to be false.

We can push this argument even further by asking whether this credibility can be quantified. If we propose a hypothesis *h*, with a body of terms *k*, it is possible to calculate the degree of credibility of *h* relative to *k* – expressed as $C(h,k)$. Carnap (1960) designed a general method to define what he called the 'degree of confirmation' of a hypothesis in relation to a given body of evidence – as long as both the hypothesis and the evidence are expressed in the same formalized language. Carnap's concept satisfies all the principles of the theory of probability, and draws on the principles of probabilistic acceptability.

For our purposes here, and in the interests of clarity, we will focus on the essential criteria of an acceptable hypothesis: can it be refuted?

1.2 The hypothetico-deductive method

In practical terms, when researchers undertake to test a hypothesis, a model, or a theory, they generally use the hypothetico-deductive method.

Figure 3.6 (Anderson, 1983) illustrates how the hypothetico-deductive method is used to test hypotheses from a theory's 'protective belt'.

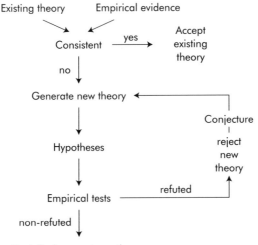

Figure 3.6   *The hypothetico-deductive method applied to the testing of a theory (Anderson, 1983: 28)*

More precisely, this process can be broken down into four basic steps:

1 We determine which concepts will enable us to respond to our research question. To do so, we must identify, through extensive reference to previous works, the hypotheses, models, or theories that correspond to our subject.
2 We observe in what ways the hypotheses, models or theories do not entirely, or perfectly, account for our reality.
3 We determine new hypotheses, models or theories.
4 We implement a testing phase which will enable us to refute, or not, the hypotheses, models or theories.

Example: An illustration of the hypothetico-deductive method

To explain the hypothetico-deductive method more clearly, we will look at how Miner et al. (1990) approached the following research question: 'What is the role of interorganizational linkages in organizational transformations and the failure rate of organizations?'

On the basis of existing works, the authors proposed five independent hypotheses. To simplify matters we will present only one of these here.

(*h*) : Organizations with interorganizational linkages should show a lower failure rate than comparable organizations without such linkages.

We saw in Figure 3.3 that this hypothesis can be illustrated.

The authors proposed to operationalize these concepts by measuring the following variables:

interorganizational linkages → affiliation with political party
failure → permanent cessation of a newspaper's publication

Choosing to study the population of Finnish newspapers from 1771 to 1963, the authors used a means comparison test to differentiate the relative weights of linked and non-linked organizations. The results of this test led to the non-refutation of the postulated hypothesis.

In general, it is rare for research to focus on a single hypothesis. For this reason it is important to know how to test a set of hypotheses.

2. Testing a Model

We have seen that a model can take many forms. We will consider here one particular form of model: the realization of a system of logically connected hypotheses (see Figure 3.7).

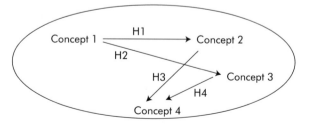

Figure 3.7   *Schematic representation of a model*

Before we begin, we should explain that to test a theory, which we have defined (following Lakatos [1974]) as a core surrounded by a protective ring, is to test a hypothesis or a body of hypotheses that belong to the protective ring. That is, to test a theory is to test either a single hypothesis or a model.

The first step in testing such a model is to break down the relationships within it into simple hypotheses, which we can then test one by one. We then arrive at one of the following situations:

- None of the hypotheses are refuted (the model is tentatively accepted).
- Some hypotheses are refuted (the model tentatively accepted in part).
- All the hypotheses are refuted (the model is rejected).

Yet this method is insufficient, although it can provide a useful cursory approach to a complex model. Testing hypotheses should not be confused with testing a model. To test a model involves more than just testing, one by one, the hypotheses of which it is constituted. Reducing a model to juxtaposed hypotheses does not always allow the researcher to take account of the interactions – synergies, moderations and mediations – that operate between them. There are, however, specific ways to test a model as a whole – using structural equations, for example.

The principle of refutability that applies to hypotheses applies equally to models. Models may be rejected (or not rejected) at a given time and in given circumstances. In other words, to test a model comes down to judging the quality, or the representiveness, of it as a simulation of reality. If it is poor, the model is rejected. In the case of the model not being rejected, it can then be said to constitute a useful simulation tool with which to predict the studied phenomenon.

3. Testing Rival Theoretical Elements

We often find ourselves in a situation in which there are a number of rival theories or models. If a researcher is to base his or her work, at least to some extent, on one particular theory or model, he or she must first test each rival theory or model to ascertain how it contributes to understanding the phenomenon under study. The testing method is essentially the same for models and theories.

Faced with competing theories or models, the researcher has to consider how they are to be evaluated and how he or she is to choose between them. This is an epistemological debate, which draws on questions of the status of science itself. It is not our intention to take up a position on this debate here. We will simply propose that a preference for one theory or model above others is neither the result of the justification, through scientific experimentation, of the terms of which the theory or model is made up of, nor is it a logical reduction of the theory or model to experimental findings.

Popper (1977) suggests we should retain the theory or the model that 'defends itself the most'. That is, the one which seems to be the more representative of reality. In practice, researchers may be led to provisionally accept different models that may serve the needs of their research. To choose between these, Dodd (1968) proposes a hierarchical list of 24 evaluation criteria, which we can group into four categories: formal, semantic, methodological and epistemological. The researcher can evaluate the quality of each model according to these criteria.

Put simply, one way open to the researcher is to test each model individually, using the same testing method, and then to compare the quality to which each represents reality. The researcher compares the deviations observed between values obtained from the model and real values. The model that deviates least from reality is then taken as being 'more representative of reality' than the others. It is this model that the researcher will finally retain.

CONCLUSION

Exploration and testing are processes central to the construction of knowledge. In this chapter we have explained the two logical processes they are based on – induction and abduction – and defined the nature of the theoretical elements employed. But although we have presented exploration and testing separately here, this is not to suggest that these two processes are mutually exclusive. A researcher may well decide only to explore, or only to test. That said, researchers are very often led to reconcile the two processes. A researcher may, for example, start from an exploration based on observing empirical facts, and from this propose a conjectural explanation that he or she will then test against reality. This is what we call the experimental method (Mill, 1843).

Another possibility is for a researcher to start from a theory, and then select certain hypotheses that can be tested in a real situation. If one or more hypotheses are not corroborated, the researcher may then propose new hypotheses based on new observations. The researcher may proceed to test these newly ventured hypotheses. We can see here how exploring and testing may follow on from one another within a research project, neither having any necessary precedence over the other.

Example: Researching organizational memory using a combined deductive/abductive approach

A researcher studying organizational memory structured her project around an approach that was at first deductive, then abductive. She began by establishing ten propositions (hypotheses) relative to the functioning of organizational memory. These ten propositions were the result of theoretical exploration of the literature in two distinct fields (cognitive science and management science). This revealed two conceptions of how organizational memory functions: the symbolic approach and the connectionist. Then, and by adopting deductive reasoning, she tested the propositions by applying a 'Popperian' refutation logic – comparing them with the 'reality' of a case study of the French nuclear power system.

In the second phase of her study, the researcher decided to explore the case empirically, basing her work on the method proposed by Glaser and Strauss (1967), with the aim of developing a substantive theory of the way in which organizational memory functions. She used the abductive method to elicit, from her case study data, the theoretical device that she was finally to propose. From this second phase she was able to infer that organizational memory functions through the interaction of two memories: one official and explicit, the other clandestine and more implicit.

The above example illustrates the recursive relationship between exploring and testing, and shows how different explorative methods may be employed within a single study (in this case, theoretical exploration to establish the set of ten propositions, then empirical exploration to develop the substantive theory proposed). It also illustrates how inductive and deductive inferences work together when we produce knowledge in management.

FURTHER READING

Chalmers, A.F., *What is this Thing Called Science? An Assessment of the Nature and Status of Science and its Methods*, St Lucia: University of Queensland Press, 1976.

Eco, U., *The Limits of Interpretation (Advances in Semiotics)*, Bloomington, IN: Indiana University Press, 1990.

Glaser, B.G. and Strauss, A.L., *The Discovery of Grounded Theory: Strategies for Qualitative Research*, New York: Aldine De Gruyter, 1967.

Miles, M.B. and Huberman, M.A., *Analysing Qualitative Data: A Source Book for New Methods*, Beverly Hills, CA: Sage, 1979.

Popper, K.R., *The Logic of Scientific Discovery*, London: Hutchinson, 1977.

4

WHAT APPROACH WITH WHICH DATA?

Philippe Baumard and Jérôme Ibert

Outline

In this chapter we look at the choices open to researchers when determining what kind of empirical data their research requires, and how to approach its collection and analysis. We begin by showing that all data is a representation: data collection is a process of discovery and invention that requires an epistemological position on the part of the researcher. Data is also subjective, as its source can react to the observing researcher-collector. We distinguish between primary and secondary data, and evaluate data in terms of its validity, accessibility and flexibility, as well as from the perspective of its collection and analysis. The distinction between qualitative and quantitative approaches in relation to the nature of the data, the orientation of the study, the objective or subjective character of the results obtained and the flexibility of the study are then evaluated. Finally, the possibility of a combined approach – both qualitative and quantitative – is considered, using either a sequential process or a triangulation.

One of the fundamental choices researchers have to make is to determine what approach and what type of data are most suitable to their research question. This choice is very much a double-edged question. On the one hand is the objective being pursued: to explore, construct, test, to improve what is known, to discover what is not. On the other is the existing situation: that which is available and accessible, that which has already been done, that which is feasible and that which is not. The existent must itself be considered in terms of both aspects: data (which can be primary or secondary) and approach (which can be qualitative or quantitative). In making these choices the researcher is in fact seeking to reconcile three essential research elements: purpose, approach and data.

Arising very early on in the research process, the orchestration of these choices is costly not only because they engage the researcher in a long-term commitment, but also because many of their implicit dimensions are irreversible. In this chapter we try to give readers the means to make these choices, by pointing out the possible incompatibilities of certain approaches and certain data and, above all, by estimating the cost of each decision in terms of time, of the impact the decision will have on the research and of its reversibility.

SECTION 1 CHOOSING DATA

1. What Is 'Data'?

'Data' is conventionally seen as forming the premises of theories. Researchers seek out and gather information – data – which can then be processed, using methodical instrumentation, to produce results and to improve on or to replace existing theories. However, two unstated and questionable propositions are hidden behind this commonsense understanding of data. The first is that data precedes theory. The second, arising from the first, is that data exists independently of researchers, who simply 'find' it and 'compile' it in order to impose their processes on it. The grammar of research only endorses such assumptions, as we conventionally distinguish between the phases of collecting, processing and analyzing data. It is as if, quite naturally, items of data were objects existing independently from their collection, processing and analysis. It is obvious that this proposition is both false and true. It is false because data does not precede theory, but is at once the medium and the continuing purpose for it. We use data just as much as we produce it, whether at the start of our theoretical reflection or closer to its completion.

Data is both a repository for and a source of theorization. Above all, the datum is a premise; a statement in the mathematical sense, or an accepted proposition. Its acceptance can be stated openly or implicitly – information can be presented in such a way that it implicitly carries the status of truth. This acceptance is essentially a convention that enables researchers to construct and to test propositions. The fact that this convention might be true or false, in a general sense, has no bearing on its scientific truth. By its acceptance, 'data' is given the status of assertions that allow researchers to continue their work without having to struggle over the truth value of the statements they make. Data frees researchers from having to believe in each proposition they put forward. It allows them to put ontological questions aside, or at least to relegate them to the background, so that they can operationalize their research process.

1.1 Data as a representation

Individual data items are accepted representations of a reality that we are not able to grasp empirically (through the senses) or theoretically (through abstract thought). The main reason for this is that reality cannot be reduced to a smaller part capable of expressing it in its entirety. The fact of having 'lived through' a reality does not mean that one possesses that reality, but more that one has grasped certain aspects of it to a greater or a lesser degree of intensity. The metaphor of a car accident can help us here to more fully understand this paradox. Anyone can 'describe' an accident, to differing degrees of exactitude, but to those who have lived through it there is an additional dimension that cannot be expressed. Two people who have survived the same car accident will have two different experiences of this single event, which can be considered as a shared reality. Their shared experience of the same event will have produced two distinct sets of data; sets that differ from each other, and differ even more from the description of the event by a person who did not experience it.

One could easily argue against the validity of this example by suggesting that qualitative data – that is, built up from accounts, descriptions and transcriptions of experiences – makes these differences obvious. However, the quantitative or qualitative nature of the data does not fundamentally change the problem. If we ask the two people involved in the accident to evaluate on scales of 1 to 5 the various sensations they had felt during the accident, we would still end up with different perceptions of the same reality. This could mean that (a) the reality of the accident was different for the two participants, or that (b) translation of a single reality by two different actors, by means of scales, can give different results. In both cases, the researcher will have integrated the 'data'; that is, he or she will have accepted that one or the other means of representing the phenomenon (using scales, or anecdotal) is a suitable method of constructing data. Thus the status of 'data' is partly left to the free choice of the researcher. A researcher could consider an event that can be directly observed can itself constitute a datum, without the intermediary of instruments to transform stimuli into codes or numbers (for example, via categorization or the use of scales). A second way of compiling data is needed when researchers confront phenomena that are not directly observable, such as attitudes, in which case they have to rely on the use of instruments to transform these phenomena into a set of measurements. A common example is the use of a scale, through which actors can qualify their attitudes. This instrument can nevertheless be equally well applied to observable phenomena, such as behavior, in which case a third data compilation method is required (see Figure 4.1).

Even the transcription of an administrative committee meeting is simply a set of representations. Data-representations enable us to maintain a correspondence between an empirical reality and a system of symbols, and vice versa

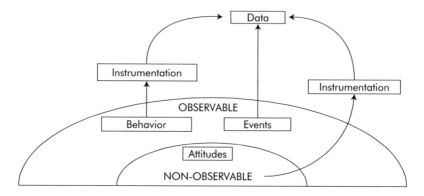

Figure 4.1   *Three ways of compiling a database*

(Stablein, 1996: 514). Other researchers' case studies can be used as 'data', for example. These case studies are representations, which can be compared to others collected, assembled or constructed by the researcher in pursuing the research question; although, whereas representations taken from earlier case studies form part of the research's database, other types of representations belong to the system of symbols that enables theorization. From this we can see that while all data is a representation, every representation is not necessarily a datum (ibid.). Whether a representation is to be considered as a datum or not has more to do with the researcher's epistemological position than any particular research methodology.

The scientific method traditionally accepts that the empirical world exists externally to the researcher, and that the researcher's aim is to 'discover' it (Lakatos, 1965). This objective world is then immune to any subjective differences in the researchers who observe and record it. In studying the structure of scientific revolutions, Kuhn (1970) has, however, been able to show that scientific paradigms are sets of beliefs shared by communities of researchers, and that the data items used by researchers in defending or promoting their paradigm are 'conceptions': representations arising from the intersubjectivity of researchers sharing these beliefs.

1.2 Data and the researcher's epistemological position

Data is at once a 'discovery' and an 'invention'. When a dichotomy is established between these facets, discovery and invention, a bias can be introduced into the construction of theory. Researchers who, in an effort to maintain absolute objectivity, decide to limit data to 'discoveries' can, by deliberately avoiding a part of the data they consider to be too subjective, limit the creative part of their research. At the other extreme, a researcher who takes the position that there is no such thing as objective data, no reality beyond the interaction between the researcher and his or her sources – that observed reality is only an invention – risks blocking the progress of the research in paradoxical impasses, where 'all is false, all is true'.

The compilation of data (its discovery-invention) is in fact a task involving evaluation, selection and choices that have important implications for the outcome of the research. Moreover, this process will signify the epistemological position of the research. A recognizable emphasis on the epistemological positioning of researchers runs throughout this book, as this is a question that cannot be evaded. Epistemological positioning is not a choice that is made once and held for the entire research process. The process of compiling research data is part of a continual movement back and forth between theory and its empirical foundations. Each time they move between the two, the question of what constitutes a datum returns researchers to the related issue of their epistemological position. Without this constant questioning, though, there is a risk of finding epistemological contradictions in the completed work: 'constructivist' research that treats data in a positivist manner or, vice versa, 'positivist' research that regards intersubjective representations as objective realities.

1.3 The subjectivity of data due to the reactivity of its source

The term 'data' is misleading. It implies the pre-existence, or the objective existence, external to the researcher, of a collection of facts and formal knowledge available and ready to be used. In fact, nothing is less objectively available than a datum. Data can be produced through an observer–observed relationship. When subjects are aware that their behavior is being observed, their attitudes are being evaluated, or events they are involved in are being studied, they become 'reactive' data-sources in the process of compiling a database (Webb et al., 1966).

Although the reactivity of the source can easily be shown in the context of collecting primary data in qualitative studies, it is not exclusively connected to that context. The fact that the data comes from a primary (firsthand) source or a secondary one (secondhand) is not a sufficiently discriminating criterion in terms of source reactivity. Researchers can collect behavioral data directly through non-participant observation without the subjects observed being aware of this observation and able to influence the data by reacting to it. On the other hand, organizational actors who give researchers access to secondary internal data, or reports or documents, can in fact intervene in the process of compiling the database. This intervention may be just as much through information they have highlighted as through information they have omitted or concealed. While it is usual, and quite rightly so, to emphasize the reactivity of primary data sources, secondary data is not exempt from this type of phenomenon.

The methodological approach to data, quantitative or qualitative, is not a satisfactory way to delimit situations of interactivity of data sources. Data collected through questionnaires or in-depth interviews can be affected by the withholding of information: the direction the data takes is in a sense that desired by the subjects who form its source. Whatever the approach, quantitative or qualitative, researchers are constrained to qualify and to maintain careful control over their presence during the stages of data collection and data processing (see Chapter 9).

The determining question is perhaps the following: 'Is the data affected by the reactivity of its source to the observant researcher?' In other words, it is useful to distinguish data obtained 'obstrusively' (with the subject-sources aware of its collection), from that obtained 'unobstrusively' (unknown to the subject-sources). Data collected 'unobstrusively' can be used to complement or to 'tie together' data that has been collected in an 'obstrusive' way, and is therefore marked by a certain subjectivity. This subjectivity may be due to the distortion induced by the subjects' perceptual filters (Starbuck and Milliken, 1988) or to the selectivity of their memory. Data that has been collected 'unobstrusively' can also be useful when interpreting contradictions within data obtained from reactive sources (Webb et al., 1966; Webb and Weick, 1979).

2. Using Primary and Secondary Data

2.1 When to privilege primary or secondary data

If data is a representation, are researchers bound to creating their own system of representations – their own data – or can they be satisfied with available representations? Is theorization based on secondary data only of a lesser scientific standing than that which is 'grounded' in the field by the researcher himself or herself? In fact, many researchers in the social sciences tend to reply in the affirmative, sharply criticizing their colleagues who 'theorize' from other researchers' data. Thus it is very often supposed that researchers cannot theorize from case studies that they have not conducted personally in the field.

But, although quite common, such a judgement is a received idea, and can be counterproductive (Webb and Weick, 1979: 652). In his 1993 article 'The collapse of sense-making in organizations: the Mann Gulch disaster', Weick uses Maclean's *Young Men and Fire* (1992) as a secondary source. Maclean's book draws on archival documents, interviews and observations to describe the deaths of 13 firemen in a fire, the magnitude of which had been tragically underestimated. Weick's theorization was an important contribution to the organizational sciences, although he did not experience the events at first hand. It is certainly necessary to put such experiences into perspective. The theorization that Weick refines in his article is the fruit of many months of research, and Maclean's book can be seen as just one piece in a work that is much broader and much more progressive in its scope.

We would not advise an inexperienced researcher to take on this kind of research without having first acquired, through fieldwork, a good understanding of data and how it is compiled. In this regard, collecting primary data gives researchers the opportunity to experience directly the 'reality' that they have chosen to study.

To sum up, the choice between using primary or secondary data should be brought down to a few fundamental dimensions: the ontological status of the data, its possible impact on the internal and external validity of the project, and its accessibility and flexibility.

Received ideas about primary data   Weick's theorization on the fire at Mann Gulch, and the acclaim his article has received, testify to the received ideas a scientific audience can hold on the standing of research according to the kind of data on which it is based. It is a great temptation to yield to ideology and to limit oneself to using primary data only, even when appropriate data is already available, out of a concern to conform to the audience's expectations. The foremost received idea about primary data concerns its ontological status. There is a tendency to accord greater truth-value to research based on primary data. The argument is that the author has 'witnessed' the phenomena with his or her own eyes. But this 'Doubting Thomas' syndrome can give rise to excessive confidence in actors' statements, and can lead researchers to produce theories that are not properly developed, precisely because they have not sufficiently distanced themselves from the field. Similarly, primary data is generally considered to be a superior source of internal validity, because the researcher will have established a system of data collection suited to the project and the empirical reality being studied. This belief in a superior internal validity arises from the fact that the researcher, in collecting or producing the data, is assumed to have eliminated rival explanations by allowing for them and monitoring for other possible causes. However, the relative liberty researchers have in instigating such controls, and the relative opacity they can generate in their instrumentation, does temper such a belief. The excessive confidence that stems from this autonomy in data production can, on the contrary, induce the researcher to be satisfied with weak outlines and to ignore important explanatory or intermediary variables.

On the other hand, it is usual to attribute to primary data a negative effect on the external validity of the research. Because the researcher will have been the only one to have 'interacted' with 'his' or 'her' empirical reality, a research work that is based solely on primary data can kindle doubt in its audience. But such doubt is unfounded, and represents a received idea that usually leads researchers to 'compensate' for their primary data with an excess of ad hoc secondary data. This secondary data is often introduced to cement the external validity of the research, when researchers realize that they are to some degree 'out on a limb'.

Primary data is also often thought to be difficult to access, although very flexible. This is not always the case! But because researchers tend to think they cannot gain access to the primary data they need, they often give priority to available secondary data, whereas the project may warrant particular instrumentation and the production of specific data. Similarly, too much confidence in the supposed 'flexibility' of primary data can lead researchers to become bogged down in fieldwork which can turn out to be much less flexible than the literature would suggest. Actors can resist the efforts of the researcher, play token roles, or give the responses that they feel will please the researcher – and so continually, albeit in good faith, bias the study.

Received ideas about secondary data   Secondary data is also the object of a certain number of received ideas regarding its ontological status, its impact on internal or external validity, and its accessibility and flexibility. The most persistent of these undoubtedly concerns secondary data's ontological standing. Because it is formalized and published, secondary data often comes to be attributed with an exaggerated status of 'truth'. Its objectivity is taken at face value, and its reliability is considered equivalent to that of the publication in which it appears. Thus greater integrity is accorded to information from a recognized and accepted source than to information from lesser-known sources, without even questioning the conditions of production of these different sets of data. This phenomenon is accentuated by the use of electronic media that supplies data in directly exploitable formats. Formalization of data in a ready-to-use format can lead researchers to take the validity of this data, which they are manipulating, for granted.

Similar received ideas exist about the impact secondary data has on the research's internal validity. The apparently strict organization of available data can suggest that it would be easier to control the internal validity of research based on it. However, as Stablein reminds us (1996: 516), internal validity should be demonstrated through the validity of the constructs it uses, that is, by clarifying and justifying the connections between the construct and the operational procedure through which it is manipulated – although Podsakoff and Dalton (1987) found that only 4.48 per cent of authors provided proof of the validity of their constructs in the published articles they examined. The formalization of secondary data can thus be wrongly assimilated to an intrinsic soundness. This last received idea leads researchers to believe their research will somehow be made secure by the use of secondary data. But, by attributing an *a priori* degree of confidence to the secondary data they manipulate, researchers are in fact simply externalizing (by passing this responsibility to others) the risks connected to the internal validity of their work.

The same shortcomings apply to the use of secondary data to increase the validity of results and their generalization. External validity is also conditioned by the validity of the work the secondary data has been drawn from.

The greater accessibility of secondary data is another disputable received idea. Such a belief can give researchers an impression of the completeness of their research, convinced they have had access to all available data. The apparent ease of accessing secondary data can lead researchers either to be quickly inundated with too much data, or to be too confident that they have 'gone over the whole question'.

Parallel to this is the common acceptance that secondary data is fairly inflexible (thus making such data difficult to manipulate), which can in turn cause researchers to believe that secondary data must be more reliable than primary data. This is, however, a naïve belief – as the fact that secondary data is fixed and formalized does not in any way signify that the phenomena it describes are similarly fixed and formalized. In other words, the use of secondary data can bring with it greater exposure to a maturation effect (see Chapter 10).

We have pointed out the potential dangers of choosing which data is most appropriate to a study on the basis of received ideas about the different qualities of primary and secondary data. It is fallacious to build a research project based on qualities supposed to be intrinsic to these two types of data. The use of primary or secondary data does bring with it a certain number of constraints in the research process, although these are mainly logistic. The fact that data is primary or secondary entails specific precautions in the collection and analysis stages.

2.2 Constraints inherent to primary or secondary data

Collection constraints   Primary data poses significant collection problems. To begin with, the researcher has to gain access to the field, then to maintain this field – that is, to preserve this access and regulate the interaction with respondents – whether the primary data is to be collected through surveys or interviews, or through direct observation (see Chapter 9). The use of primary data therefore necessitates the mastery of a complex system of interaction with the field. Poor handling of this can have consequences for the entire project. Conversely, the use of secondary data enables the researcher to limit this inter-action with the field, but offers less scope in compiling a database appropriate to the research question. This task can be long and laborious. Often the collabora-tion of actors who can authorize access to certain external databases or can guide researchers in finding their way through the organization's archives is required.

Analysis constraints   Similarly, primary and secondary data each entail speci-fic analysis difficulties. Distortions in an analysis can arise at different levels according to whether the data is primary or secondary.

The use of primary data essentially poses problems of controlling the inter-pretations that are developed from this data. Researchers are in effect 'defendant and jury', insofar as they themselves gather the data that they will later analyze. Researchers may sometimes implicitly pursue their model or their construct both when collecting their data (an instrumentation bias) and when analyzing it (by failing to eliminate other possible causes, or by focusing on the desired construct).

The analysis of secondary data involves another kind of constraint. If researchers are confronted with secondary data that is partial, ambiguous or contradictory, they can rarely go back to the source to complete or to clarify it. The researcher is in effect forced to question either people quoted in the archives, or those who collected the data. That is, they are compelled to collect primary data ad hoc. This is a costly process, and access to the individuals con-cerned is only possible in exceptional cases.

2.3 Combining primary and secondary data

Primary and secondary data are complementary at all stages of the research process. If primary data is incomplete, it can be supplemented by secondary data, for example historical, so as to better understand the background of an event, or to weigh the case study against information that is external to it. Conversely, research that is initially based on secondary data (for example, a statistical database on direct foreign investments) could be usefully backed up by primary data (such as interviews with investors). The major difficulty encountered here is that the researcher has to evaluate his or her own database. Researchers may realize during data analysis that their database was inadequate, which would then entail a return to the data collection phase, whether the data required is primary or secondary (see Figure 4.2).

SECTION 2   CHOOSING AN APPROACH: QUALITATIVE OR QUANTITATIVE?

Researchers have to decide what type of approach they want to use to collect and to analyze their data. In other words, how they are going to tackle the

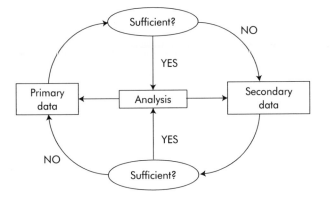

Figure 4.2   *Using both primary and secondary data*

empirical side of their research. We begin this section by examining what distinguishes a qualitative from a quantitative approach. We then show how these two approaches can be complementary.

1. Qualitative and Quantitative Approaches

It is conventional in research to make a distinction between the qualitative and the quantitative. However this distinction is both equivocal and ambiguous.[1] The distinction is equivocal as it is based on a multiplicity of criteria. In consulting works on research methodology we find, in sections discussing the distinction between qualitative and quantitative, references to 'qualitative or quantitative data' (Downey and Ireland, 1979; Glaser and Strauss, 1967; Miles, 1979; Miles and Huberman, 1984b; Silverman, 1993); to quantitative and qualitative variables (Evrard et al., 1993; Lambin, 1990), and to 'qualitative methods' (Jick, 1979; Silverman, 1993; Van Maanen, 1979). The distinction between qualitative and quantitative is, moreover, ambiguous because none of these criteria allow for an absolute distinction between the qualitative and the quantitative approach. We will turn now to a critical examination of the various criteria involved: the nature of the data, the orientation of the research, the objective or subjective character of the results obtained and the flexibility of the research.

As data collection methods, which are among the distinguishing characteristics of both qualitative and quantitative approaches, are discussed at length in another chapter in this book (Chapter 9), we will restrict our discussion here to other distinguishing characteristics.

1.1 The qualitative/quantitative distinction and the nature of our data

Does the distinction between qualitative and quantitative go back to the very nature of a researcher's data?

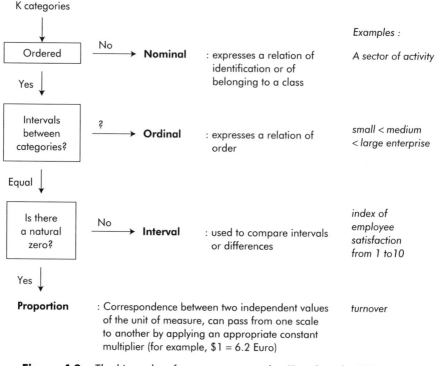

Figure 4.3   *The hierarchy of measurement scales (Evard et al., 1993: 276)*

Many authors distinguish between qualitative and quantitative data. For Miles and Huberman (1984b), qualitative data corresponds to words rather than figures. Similarly, Yin (1989: 88) explains that 'numerical data' provides quantitative information, while 'non-numerical data' furnishes information that is clearly of a qualitative nature. All the same, the nature of the data does not necessarily impose an identical method of processing it. The researcher can very well carry out, for example, a statistical and consequently quantitative analysis of nominal variables.

According to Evrard et al. (1993: 35), qualitative data corresponds to variables measured on nominal and ordinal (non-metric) scales, while quantitative data is collected using interval scales and proportion scales. These scales can be arranged hierarchically according to the quality of their mathematical properties. As shown in Figure 4.3, this hierarchy goes from a nominal scale, the weakest one from a mathematical point of view, to the proportional scale, the best of the measurement scales.

As Figure 4.3 shows, measuring variables on nominal scales allows us to establish relationships of identification or of belonging of a class. The fact that these classes may be identified by numbers (a department number, for example, or an arbitrarily chosen number) does not in any way change their properties. The one statistical calculation permitted is that of frequency.

Often a classification can be obtained using variables measured on ordinal scales, but the origin of the scale remains arbitrary. If the intervals between categories are unequal, statistical calculations are limited to measures of position (median, quartiles, deciles …). Arithmetical calculations cannot be performed with this data. Once the intervals between categories become equal, however, we can speak of interval scales. More statistical calculations can be carried out on variables measured on this type of scale, as here we move into data said to be 'quantitative', or to 'metric' scales, for which we can compare intervals and determine ratios of differences or distances. Means and standard deviations can be calculated, however, zero is defined arbitrarily.

The best-known example of an interval scale is that used to measure temperature. We know that 0 degrees on the Celsius scale, the freezing point of water, corresponds to 32 degrees on the Fahrenheit scale. We can convert a data item from one scale to another by a positive linear transformation ($y = ax + b$, where $a > 0$). However, if there is no natural zero, relationships cannot be established between absolute quantities. For example, it is misleading to say that 'yesterday was half as hot as today', when we mean that 'the temperature was 50 per cent less in degrees Fahrenheit than today'. If the two temperatures are converted into Celsius, it will be seen that 'half as hot' is not correct. The arbitrary choice of zero on the measuring scale has an effect on the relationship between the two measurements.

Where a natural zero exists, we come to proportional scales. Common examples include measurements of money, length or weight. This kind of data is therefore the richest in terms of the possible statistical calculations that can be operated on it, since the researcher will be able to analyze relationships in terms of absolute values of variables such as wage levels or company seniority.

The different aspects of qualitative and quantitative data that we have considered in this chapter clearly show that the nature of the collected data does not dictate the employment of a qualitative or a quantitative research approach. To choose between a qualitative or a quantitative approach we have to evaluate other criteria.

1.2 The qualitative/quantitative distinction in relation to the orientation of the research: to construct or to test

Research in management is characterized by two main preoccupations: constructing and testing theoretical objects. When researchers direct their work towards verification, they have a clear and definite idea of what they are looking for. On the other hand, if they are carrying out explorative research, typified by theoretical construction, researchers are often far less sure of what they may find (see Chapter 3).

It is conventional to correlate investigation with a qualitative approach and verification with a quantitative. Silverman, for example, distinguishes between two 'schools' in the social sciences, one oriented towards the quantitative testing of theories, and the other directed at qualitatively developing theories (1993: 21). Once again, however, we find that this association is a received idea – researchers can equally well adopt a quantitative or a qualitative approach whether they are constructing or testing (see Chapter 3). 'There is no fundamental clash between the purposes and capacities of qualitative and quantitative methods or data ... Each form of data is useful for both verification and generation of theory' (Glaser and Strauss, 1967: 17–18).

We should point out here, though, that researchers rarely choose a qualitative approach with the sole intention of testing a theory. This choice is generally accompanied by a fairly definite orientation towards construction. This tendency can be explained by the cost, particularly in time, of using a qualitative approach just to test a theory. If the test turns out to be positive, the researcher will have no choice but to test it again – by conducting another data collection and analysis process. The qualitative approach in effect locks the researcher into a process of falsification, as the only aim can be to refute the theory and not to validate it in any way.

The qualitative approach is not designed to evaluate to what extent one can generalize from an existing theory. In his discussion of the case study, which he positions within the qualitative method, Stake argues that 'by counter-example, the case study invites a modification of the generalization' (1995: 8). This modification involves a construction. The limitation of qualitative approaches lies in the fact that such studies are necessarily carried out within a fairly delimited context. Although a researcher can increase the external validity of a qualitative study by including several contexts in the analysis, in accordance with a replication logic (see Chapter 10), the limitations of the qualitative approach in terms of generalization lead us to attribute more external validity to quantitative approaches. Conversely, the qualitative approach gives a greater guarantee of the internal validity of results. Rival explanations of the phenomenon being studied are often far easier to evaluate than they are when a quantitative approach is taken, as researchers are in a better position to cross-check their data. The qualitative approach also increases the researcher's ability to describe a complex social system (Marshall and Rossman, 1989).

The choice between a qualitative and a quantitative approach therefore seems to be dictated primarily in terms of each approach's effectiveness in relation to the orientation of the research; that is, whether one is constructing or testing.

Guarantees of internal and external validity should be considered in parallel, whatever type of research is being carried out. But in order to choose between a qualitative and a quantitative approach, researchers have to decide on the priority they will give to the quality of causal links between variables, or to the generalization of their results. Of course, it would be ideal to assure the greatest validity in results by employing both of these approaches together.

1.3 Qualitative/quantitative research for objective/ subjective results

It is generally acknowledged that quantitative approaches offer a greater assurance of objectivity than do qualitative approaches. The necessary strictness and precision of statistical techniques argue for this view. It is, then, not surprising that the quantitative approach is grounded in the positivist paradigm (Silverman, 1993).

While the objective or subjective nature of research results is often seen as forming a divisive line between qualitative and quantitative approaches, there are in fact several areas of possible subjectivity in management research, depending on the particular type of qualitative approach taken. A number of proponents of the qualitative approach have also discussed ways of reducing the subjectivity historically attributed to this research tradition.

According to Erickson (1986), the most distinctive feature of qualitative investigation is its emphasis on interpretation – not simply that of the researcher but, more importantly, that of the individuals who are studied. This emphasis is comparable to that of ethnographic research, which seeks 'to reconstruct the categories used by subjects to conceptualize their own experience and world view' (Goetz and LeCompte, 1981: 54). Other writers, however, emphasize the subjectivity of the researcher more than that of the subjects. According to Stake (1995), researchers must position themselves as interpreters of the field they are studying, even if their own interpretation may be more labored than that of the research subjects. In fact, the qualitative approach allows for both the subjectivity of the researcher and that of the subjects at the same time. It offers an opportunity to confront multiple realities, for it 'exposes more directly the nature of the transaction between investigator and respondent (or object) and hence makes easier an assessment of the extent to which the phenomenon is described in terms of (is biased by) the investigator's own posture' (Lincoln and Guba, 1985: 40).

However, the qualitative approach does not rule out an epistemological posture of objectivity of the research with regard to the world that it is studying. This criterion of objectivity can be seen as an 'intersubjective agreement'. 'If multiple observers can agree on a phenomenon, their collective judgment can be said to be objective' (Lincoln and Guba, 1985: 292). Some proponents of the qualitative approach, notably Glaser and Strauss (1967), have developed a positivist conception of it. For Miles and Huberman (1984b) while the source of social phenomena may be in the minds of the subjects, these phenomena also exist in the real world. These authors argue for an amended positivism, advocating the construction of a logical chain of evidence and proof to increase the objectivity of results.

To sum up, data collection and analysis must remain consistent with an explicit epistemological position on the part of the researcher. Although the qualitative approach allows the researcher to introduce a subjectivity that is incompatible with the quantitative approach, it should not, however, be limited to a constructivist epistemology.

1.4 The qualitative/quantitative distinction in relation to the flexibility of the study

The question of the flexibility available to the researcher in conducting his or her research project is another crucial factor to consider in choosing whether to use a qualitative or a quantitative approach.

When a qualitative approach is used, the research question can be changed midway, so that the results are truly drawn from the field (Stake, 1995). It is obviously difficult to modify the research question during the more rigid process that is required by the quantitative approach, taking into account the cost that such a modification would entail. With the qualitative approach, too, the researcher usually has the advantage of greater flexibility in collecting data, whereas the quantitative approach usually involves a stricter schedule. Another problem is that once a questionnaire has been administered to a large sample of a population, it can be difficult to assess new rival explanations without taking the research program back to the draft stage.

2. Combined Approaches: Using Sequential Processes and Triangulation Strategies

One way researchers can exploit the complementary nature of qualitative and quantitative approaches is by using a sequential process:

> Findings from exploratory qualitative studies may ... provide a starting point for further quantitative or qualitative work. In multi-method projects, group discussions and in-depth interviews are frequently used in piloting to clarify concepts and to devise and calibrate instrumentation for inclusion in structured questionnaires.
>
> (Walker, 1985: 20)

The qualitative approach can in this way constitute a necessary and remunerative stage in an essentially quantitative study. Given the considerable degree of irreversibility inherent to the quantitative approach, the success of such a research project very much depends on the researcher taking necessary precautions along the way.

Another practical way researchers can combine qualitative and quantitative approaches is by means of a triangulation. This involves using the two approaches simultaneously to take advantage of their respective qualities. 'The achievements of useful hypothetically realistic constructs in a science requires multiple methods focused on the diagnosis of the same construct from independent points of observation through a kind of triangulation' (Campbell and Fiske, 1959: 81). The idea is to consider a formalized problem by formalizing along two complementary axes. The differential effect can then provide invaluable information for the researcher. Triangulation strategies aim to improve the precision of both measurement and description.

Triangulation allows the research design to be put to the test, by ensuring that findings are not just a reflection of the methodology used (Bouchard, 1976). This does not simply mean commingling the two types of data and methods. Using complementary data does not of itself constitute a triangulation, but a natural action used in the majority of research projects (Downey and Ireland, 1979). It is a mistake to think that the 'qualitative' researcher does not make use of quantitative data, or that he or she is somehow opposed to measurement (Miles, 1979). The fact that a researcher uses a symbolic numerical system or a symbolic verbal system to translate an observed reality does not necessarily define the type of approach they are using. In their manual on qualitative analysis, for example, Miles and Huberman (1984b) suggest counting data items to highlight recurrence, for the reason that figures are more economical and easier to manipulate than are words, as well as having greater visibility in terms of trends.

The combination of qualitative and quantitative approaches, that is, their complementary and dialectical use, enables researchers to institute a dialogue distinguishing between what is observed (the subject of the research) and the two ways of symbolizing it:

> Qualitative methods represent a mixture of the rational, serendipitous, and intuitive in which the personal experiences of the organizational researcher are often key events to be understood and analyzed as data. Qualitative investigators tend also to describe the unfolding of social processes rather than the social structures that are often the focus of quantitative researchers.
>
> (Van Maanen, 1979: 520)

Triangulation allows the researcher to benefit from the advantages of the two approaches, counterbalancing the defects of one approach with the qualities of the other (Jick, 1979).

CONCLUSION

Coordinating data, approaches and aims is essential to any successful research process. The researcher's choices are, however, partly determined by factors that are external to the aims of the research. Time restrictions can lead researchers to make compromises (in terms of internal and external validity) in their desire to produce results. By focusing on the most accessible units of analysis, researchers are often led to revise their ambitions and adapt their research questions. They might reduce their sample sizes, give preference to exemplary populations when constructing theory or test only a part of the theories originally envisaged. On the other hand, researchers can also be led to adopt a more systematic and more ambitious process, making use of a triangulation both of methods and data.

Between these two extremes there are a variety of other ways researchers can coordinate data, approaches and aims. We have not discussed all the possibilities in this regard here as, to ensure that this issue is approached realistically, we felt it was more pertinent to point out certain incompatibilities.

Researchers are generally very concerned about their 'contribution to the literature'. This expression implies that the essential thing for a research work is to produce new results. But there is another contribution that management research can make which should not be ignored, and does not exclude making a contribution to the literature. Researchers can bring innovations to the coordination of data, approaches and aims. We hope this chapter has demonstrated the importance of recognizing and questioning received ideas about the different types of data we work with, and the scope of the different possible approaches. In closing, it seems to us to be more constructive to bear in mind the complementarity, rather than the opposition, of different types of data and the different approaches that permit their collection and analysis.

NOTE

1 The difference between ambiguity and equivocality has been defined by Weick (1979: 180).

FURTHER READING

Campbell, D.T. and Fiske, D.W., 'Convergent and Discriminent Validation by the Multitrait-Multimethod Matrix', *Psychological Bulletin*, 56, 1959: 81–105.

Jick, T.D., 'Mixing Qualitative and Quantitative Methods: Triangulation in action', *Administrative Science Quarterly*, 24, 1979: 602–11.

Lincoln, Y.S. and Guba, E.G., *Naturalistic Inquiry*, Beverly Hills, CA: Sage, 1985.

Miles, A.M. and Huberman, A.M., *Analysing Qualitative Data: A Source Book for New Methods*. Beverly Hills, CA: Sage, 1984.

5

RESEARCHING CONTENT AND RESEARCHING PROCESS

Corinne Grenier and Emmanuel Josserand

Outline

In this chapter we consider two possible ways of studying a phenomenon: by conducting research into either its content or its process. Whereas to study a phenomenon's content is to investigate its composition, a study of its process attempts to explain the phenomenon's behavior through time.

Both of these approaches are given a detailed presentation in the first two sections. The third section provides researchers with a more discriminating conception. It explains how these two approaches can be mutually enriching when used in parallel, but acknowledges that, finally, it is their conception of reality together with the state of current literature on a phenomenon that will direct researchers towards researching content, researching process, or a combined study.

Understanding a research question requires making a certain number of choices. We will examine here two ways of studying the same management phenomenon: researchers can choose between content-based study and process-based study.

The many different definitions found in books and articles describing these two options all focus on the following elements:

1 Content-based research proposes an analysis based on the nature of the subject under study. It seeks to learn what it is composed of.
2 Process-based research, on the other hand, analyzes the phenomenon in terms of its 'flux'. It aims to reveal its behavior over time, and to apprehend its evolution. Such studies are sometimes known as dynamic or longitudinal.

One of the objectives of this chapter is to show that most management subjects can be apprehended in terms of either dimension: content or process. The main difference between these two types of research lies essentially in the formulation of the research question and the methodology chosen. Table 5.1 illustrates the differences between these two ways of approaching a research

Table 5.1 *Different ways of studying the same phenomenon*

	Content-based research	Process-based research
Controlling interorganizational networks	How can the control exercised by some companies over others within a network be explained?	How are interorganizational agreements reached, and how do they evolve over time?
	Research based on the content of the network may consist of describing the connections between companies belonging to the same network. Taking this description as a starting point, one is then able to classify the members in terms of their position within the network.	In order to understand what drives the members of a network, attention can be focused on the process of exchanges, by looking at the way in which collective action is formed and transformed over time.
	It is possible to explain in this way why some units have greater control than others over exchanges within the network.	Research then consists of reconstituting the process of interaction between units, describing the chain of events and the evolution of the relationships between these units.
Organizational memory	What is organizational memory made of, and by what means is it archived?	How is organizational memory formed and transformed?
	In order to understand organizational memory, an inventory of the various means of stocking collective knowledge – archives, databanks, structure – can be made.	An organization's memory can be understood as a flow of knowledge that is conveyed among the members who constitute the organization.
	The body of knowledge contained in procedures, data banks or in tacit rules provide an indication of the collective memory that stems from the aggregation of individual memories.	The different phases of transforming knowledge are studied: its acquisition, retention and storage, and its restoration or its loss. Acquiring new knowledge from other individuals is via our interaction, or through working together.

topic, using two different studies – of interorganizational network control and of organizational memory – as examples.

The distinction we are making here between content and process may seem to be radical. Yet it is frequently used to structure the field of management research. These two types of research correspond to two traditional schools of thought, which disagree over two essential criteria: the nature of 'time' itself, and how research takes time into account. Even excepting these criteria, however, the two schools of thought do not merge into a harmonious whole in terms of ideas and practice. The very diversity that makes them so valuable is also what makes them difficult to present clearly. We will not attempt to make an exhaustive rendering of their diversity here, but we will give examples using such different themes as organizational structure, innovation, strategic development, team work or change, in order to provide readers with a broad range of content- and process-based research.

SECTION 1   CONTENT-BASED RESEARCH

Researchers carry out content-based research in order to reveal the composition of the object under study. There are many reasons why a researcher may want to carry out this type of research. Nevertheless, this elementary, broad definition of content-based research hides the tremendous diversity to be found within studies of this type. This suggests that content-based research does not form a homogenous body of work.

1. Why Choose Content-based Research?

A cross-section or a video still of an object that we wish to study are two possible metaphors for understanding the purpose of content-based research. The idea is to describe something statically, as it appears at a given point in time. Time is only taken into account implicitly, and the study is not concerned with the object's evolution. Content-based research reveals the existence or coexistence of a certain number of elements rather than the manner in which the object evolves over time. As we will see further on, this does not mean that the temporal dynamics of the object under study are ignored; an object's temporal dynamics may be used to explain it, or be included as an element of the object's context. Temporal dynamics do not, however, directly enter the field of content-based research.

Two types of content-based research can be distinguished. They differ in terms both of the methods used and the types of questions they deal with. The first consists in describing the subject of the research in order to understand it better. The goal of research pursued in this way is not to explain the object under study in the sense of causality research, but rather to describe it. The purpose of the description is to improve one's understanding of the object under study. The idea is to go beyond the object's perceived complexity. The second type of content-based research aims to show and to explain the causal links between the variables the object is composed of. The researcher attempts to delineate the causes or consequences of a given situation.

More precisely, researchers may be confronted with a new problematic for which little or no empirical material or theoretical research exists. In a situation like this, it seems appropriate to devote a certain effort to describing the object under study. This is the case, for example, when new practices appear or when researchers study an aspect that has not yet been empirically studied in any depth. Bailyn et al. (1997) describe an intervention technique aimed at harmonizing the needs of individuals and the goals of the organization.

Example: Descriptive content research on the 'dual agenda' method

Bailyn et al. (1997) describe a method of resolving the opposition between individuals' goals and the organization's objectives. From the theoretical and empirical observation of the difficulties many employees have in reconciling their private lives and their commitment to a company, the authors describe several situations in which they were able, within the framework of action research, to identify the contents of this method, and thus to define the manner in which to proceed. Their method consists of carrying out group interviews with a double goal. These interviews should encourage actors to consider how the way in which they organize their work affects their private lives. This increases the group's awareness of the ways in which conflicts between their professional and their private lives affects their performance at work. The discussion is then oriented towards identifying 'leverage points' that may help reduce these conflicts.

These interviews should result in concrete suggestions, which can then be tested by the enterprise. The authors call this process a 'dual agenda'. By explaining in detail the way they proceeded in several different companies, they contribute to a better understanding of the articulation between professional and personal agendas, and add to our knowledge of a new technique.

It can also be rewarding to look into methods belonging to another domain or culture. Japanese management techniques and their practical applications in American companies have, for example, inspired a large number of empirical and conceptual studies. The simple act of describing the successful way that Japanese companies have been run and drawing implications this may have on managing western companies was a contribution in and of itself. It then becomes possible to consider the difficulties that arise in adapting techniques from different cultures. This type of descriptive content-based research is illustrated by the following example.

Example: Descriptive content-based research into adapting Japanese-style teamwork to the USA

Cutcher-Gershenfeld et al. (1994) studied the adaptation of different levels of Japanese-style teamwork to American-Japanese joint ventures in the USA. This study was part of a larger research program analyzing the exchange of American and Japanese managerial techniques. Its purpose is to understand teamwork better: its organization, the context in which it is used and the difficulties encountered in its application. The study looked at eight joint ventures, and included 150 individual and 75 group interviews. Three types of teamwork were detected, and these were described along with the contexts in which they appear.

The 'lean production' system optimizes the production process but reduces workers' autonomy. The 'social-technical' system is based on a high level of worker autonomy, although this autonomy can turn out to be costly. The third system, 'off-line teams', resolves specific problems but cannot be applied to daily operations.

Description can thus be a first approach; an improvement in our understanding of a phenomenon that until now was relatively unexplored by the scientific community. The purpose is essentially exploratory. But a major challenge for all researchers is to demonstrate the advantages of their work clearly. Insofar as the researcher is simply describing a phenomenon without being able to indicate its causes, it is absolutely essential to insist upon the theoretical and managerial advantages gained by carrying out the description. This empirical work is also indispensable before explicatory content-based research can be done. It is only with an in-depth knowledge of the elements that make up a phenomenon that researchers can attempt to understand the causal links that develop among these elements and which, in the end, determine the form of the phenomenon under study.

2. Troubleshooting Content-based Research

Research questions, as well as the tools and methods employed, will differ depending on whether the researcher's goal is to describe or to explain the object of the content-based research.

In carrying out content-based research, the researcher aims to reveal the composition of a variable under study, either descriptively or explicatively. Problems may be encountered in the following areas:

1 Researchers should pay particular attention to carefully defining the object they are studying. For example, a researcher wishing to learn about the structure of an organization should specify if he or she intends to study the firm's formal structure, as it might appear in an organizational chart, or include its informal structure as well. In the latter case, the research may bring to light intangible elements of this informal structure. The researcher must clearly formulate the research question relative to either the organization's formal structure, or both the formal and informal dimensions of the structure.

2 This general problem raises a second one, relative to the theoretical or empirical models that researchers may employ in order to understand the object of a study. With the exception of exploratory research on an item that has been little studied in management research, a wealth of theoretical models exists with which to describe or explain phenomena. The questions formulated and methodologies used will vary depending on whether the researcher intends to analyze an item's content on the basis of theory, or from empirical data.

3 Researchers must pay particular attention to carefully defining their level of analysis. By defining their level of analysis, researchers may decide they need to refine their study, to study their research object in greater or lesser depth. For example, a researcher who wants to use description to compare

the structure of different companies (to look at the functions and organization of their structural elements) should specify ahead to what level he or she wants to take this description. Such a study could include the various departments represented on the organizational chart and the liaisons between them, the services making up each department and the liaisons between them, or go as far as the individuals making up and working in each service. The choice of the level of decomposition and description will depend above all on the purpose of the research, but also on the material available.

2.1 Principal problems in content-descriptive research

We will present here two possible approaches out of the many available for this type of research. The first approach consists in breaking down, or 'decomposing' the object under study into a certain number of elementary characteristics. The second approach is more global and aims to better apprehend the object as a whole (identification of its form), rather than to break it into parts. In most cases, however, researchers will need to employ both approaches simultaneously, without making such a sharp distinction between them.

How is descriptive content-based research done through decomposition? One type of descriptive research aims in particular at improving understanding through decomposing the object. The research then follows the classic Cartesian process. In this situation, the corresponding research question is: what is the object under study made up of? What are its elements? Mintzberg's 1973 study of the activities of company directors illustrates this type of process.

> **Example: Researching the activities of company directors**
>
> One example of descriptive content analysis is Mintzberg's (1973) study of the activities of company directors. Mintzberg wanted to describe directors' actual activities, the way they use their time. The methodology he selected can be broken into three stages. Data was first collected on meetings scheduled over a one-month period, on the organization the manager was part of and on the directors themselves. Then came a period of structured observation. The researcher observed the directors in action. Each event was coded according to various criteria. In order to avoid an overly restrictive coding, the criteria were not determined by analyzing existing literature but were established during and after the observation process. The study followed five experienced company presidents for a period of one week each. This research, proceeding through decomposition only, enabled the identification of ten key roles around which directors structure their time (for example, negotiator, intermediary, source of information or company spokesperson). It challenged Fayol's classic vision of directors wielding tight control over all elements of their organization.

The object under analysis might be one of many things: organizational structure, an individual's cognitive map, the composition of a group or a decision-making process. In all cases, the goal is to find the elements that compose the studied object. A structure is broken down into subunits, a cognitive map into concepts, a group into individuals, a process into its constitutive elements. The links and relations between the elements also form part of what we are aiming to describe. The methodologies used can be extremely diverse. They can include, for example, network analysis (see Chapter 14), discourse and representation analysis (see Chapter 16). Analysis of social networks effectively enables us to understand an organization through decomposing it; by breaking it down to the level of individuals and the ties existing between them. We can also attempt to understand a firm's cohesion by studying the ties between individuals who belong to its constitutive units. By the same token, discourse and representation analyses enable concepts and the links between them to emerge by decomposing the discourses or representations in question. In this manner, one can, for example, try to discover the directors' principal preoccupations by analyzing interviews on how they run their companies. Analyzing discourse and representations can, among other things, enable us to identify the recurrent themes in these interviews and to reveal key concepts.

How is descriptive content-based research achieved through identifying forms? A second type of descriptive content-based research aims to go beyond decomposition in order to apprehend the research subject as a whole; instead of decomposing it, researchers identify forms. In this case, the researcher's goal is to underline the interdependence of the elements that make up the research subject. The essential point of these theories is to demonstrate that the properties of a form can be of greater importance than the properties of each element the form is comprised of. For example, no single strategic decision determines a firm's competitiveness, which is determined rather by the coherence of strategy with environmental structure and conditions. What matters most is that these three interdependent elements constitute a balanced form.

The logic of form research is used by a number of different schools of thought in management research (who ascribe to theories similar to that of gestalt). The configurational approach can be found among these schools of thought, and is very popular in management research. It concerns such varied domains as strategic groups, organizational configurations, strategy categories, and leadership and management styles. The general principle is to study an object by gathering observations into categories – homogenous groups that facilitate our apprehension of reality. Each category is represented by what can be called a configuration or an ideal type. Elements can then be characterized by their similarity to the configuration of the category. Through the use of configurations, researchers introduce a certain amount of order into the complexity of discrete, discontinuous and heterogeneous observations. Each category acts as a sort of benchmark, allowing researchers to work on their contents more precisely. To do this, researchers adopt two distinct approaches: taxonomy uses empirical data to establish the configurations; whereas typology uses a theoretical approach.

Establishing a taxonomy involves an empirical and inductive classification process. It can call upon statistical techniques known as classification and structuration (see Chapter 13). Research into strategic groups, for example, usually uses this type of statistical tool to describe the competitive situation within a given industry (Ketchen et al., 1993). Taxonomies improve our understanding of the industry analyzed, by allowing us to generate strategic maps. A taxonomy can also be the result of a qualitative approach. An example is Goold and Campbell's (1987) study, in which the objective was to highlight different management styles.

Example: Goold and Campbell's (1987) taxonomy of management styles

Goold and Campbell (1987) wanted to examine the role of the head office in large companies, and the way it which it affects peripheral units. From an analysis of existing research, they identified two principal areas in which the head office (the center) was active: determining strategy (or planning influence) and monitoring performance (or central influence). The empirical part of the research was made up of 16 case studies. For each case, 5 to 20 interviews with central management were carried out. These were supplemented by direct observation of certain meetings and by collecting information on formal elements. The data enabled an evaluation of the planning influence and the central influence exercised by central management in each firm studied. The combination of these two influences allowed the authors to define 'management styles'. Eight 'management styles', that is, eight configurations composed of various combinations of the two types of influence, were established in this way. The authors deduced normative implications from their research. They found that the three of the eight styles stood out, in that they were better able to balance the major tensions within the organizations. These were the styles known as financial control, strategic control and strategic planning.

The second mode of classification is typology. Typology has a conceptual foundation: unlike taxonomies, typologies are not born of empirical research. They can be the result of an analysis of existing research or of the researcher's accumulated experience. Mintzberg (1980) identifies, for example, five distinct organizational configurations (simple structure, mechanical bureaucracy, professional bureaucracy, divisional form and 'adhocracy'), obtained by combining a firm's different components. Research into organizational structure often calls upon this configurational approach.

The fundamental problem researchers are confronted with when they attempt to define forms is linked to the difficulties involved in establishing boundaries between the forms identified. As we indicated above, each configuration corresponds to an ideal type. Even when these ideal types are precisely defined, organizational reality never matches them perfectly. The question is then what status researchers should give the configurations defined by management research. Another question concerns taxonomies in particular, for which the classification method used has a determinant effect on the configurations obtained. Researchers must be able to justify with precision the choices they are inevitably called upon to make.

2.2 Principal problems in content-explanatory research

This type of research often uses the hypothetical-deductive approach combined with a quantitative method.

Using a hypothetical-deductive method to explain content　This is the most frequently used approach in management research. A certain number of hypotheses are formulated in relation to causal links between variables known as explicative and explained. These links between variables are then tested and interpreted to establish the existence of causality (see Chapter 12). The aim is to explain the variance of the dependent variable, and to understand why it is in a given state. The contingency school has inspired a great amount of explicative content research. The idea of contingency corresponds to a firm's need to constantly adapt to its environment if it is to survive. Govindarajan's (1988) research follows this line of reasoning.

Example: A contingent approach at the level of the operational unit

Govindarajan (1988) studied the administrative mechanisms governing the relations between general management and the operational units of diverse groups. He observed that different strategies are adopted in operational units depending on their local context. The question of what type of supervision mechanisms should be adopted is then posed. Starting from a review of existing research, the author formulated a series of hypotheses on the supervision mechanisms best suited to a given strategy. The hypotheses were of the following type: 'for an operational unit employing a strategy of cost-domination, reinforcing the importance of achieving goals is associated with high performance'. Data on supervision mechanisms and operational unit performance were collected by questionnaire from 121 unit managers in 24 companies. The hypotheses were then tested by performing a multiple-regression analysis. The research demonstrated the necessity of adapting supervision mechanisms to the strategy adopted by each individual operational unit.

Explicative content research often calls upon the results of descriptive content studies. These studies provide the concepts or configurations required to formulate hypotheses as well as the operationalization of research variables.

Other possibilities for explicative content research　Quantitative hypothetical-deductive research has dominated research management for a long time. It aims for high external validity and encourages an accumulation of knowledge. Still, it presents two limitations. First, the use of numeric data often requires proxy variables to be defined, which transforms reality. Second, the rigid framework of the hypothetical-deductive process can impede the emergence of new ideas.

Other possibilities do exist. Researchers can use a qualitative process, and rediscover all the subtlety of the reality studied. This does not exclude the formulation of propositions, which are then confronted with reality via case studies. Researchers may also use an inductive process; in this case causal links emerge directly through fieldwork. Tellis and Golder's (1996) study illustrates the possibility of revealing causal links through an inductive and qualitative approach.

Example: An inductive and qualitative approach to finding causality

Tellis and Golder (1996) observed that the pioneer advantage innovators have only rarely translates into a dominant situation in the middle term. They then set out to establish what caused certain pioneers to maintain their dominant position. In order to achieve this, Tellis and Golder used a historical reconstitution method, which allowed them to study the positions of firms in some 50 product categories. They triangulated their study by analyzing both documents from the period studied (1,500 periodicals and 275 books) and data gathered directly from experts. They were therefore able to reveal determinants which had not been perceptible to actors in the sector itself. The authors identified five factors that conditioned high performance: a vision of the existing mass market based on an innovative idea, managerial perseverance, allocation of sufficient financial resources, continual innovation and synergy.

SECTION 2   PROCESS-BASED RESEARCH

Let us go back to the metaphor of video. If content-based research is comparable to hitting the pause button, then the film is rolling again in process-based research. The time dimension is placed at the heart of the managerial issues studied. That which researchers intend to describe and understand (for example, decision-making or strategic changes in organizations) is operationalized in the form of a variable whose evolution, transformation or change is being studied. The dynamic and temporal aspects are primordial here.

Beyond this general characteristic in relation to evolution, process-based studies do not form a homogenous body of research. On the contrary, they are extremely diverse from both a theoretical and a methodological point of view (Pettigrew, 1992).

1. Why Choose Process-based Research?

1.1 The goals of process-based research

Process-based research describes and analyzes the way in which a variable evolves over time (Van de Ven, 1992). For example, a researcher's goal may be to analyze how a strategic decision is taken within an organization, to understand how an idea takes shape and turns into strategic innovation or to grasp how the firm acquires knowledge.

In order to study 'how', researchers may need to reveal the evolutionary path of the variables over time (Monge, 1990). In this way, they can measure a variable's time span (how long it is present for), periodicity (is the observed variable's behavior stable over time or not?) or else its evolutionary trend (is it decreasing or increasing over time?).

But studying a process should go beyond that. Reconstituting the evolution of a variable should lead to revealing the different 'time intervals' that make up its process and articulate its evolution over time (Pettigrew, 1992). The process then appears as the sequence of change of an organizational variable (Miller and Friesen, 1982). Thus process-based research enables researchers to identify and articulate intervals such as sequences, cycles or phases that describe a variable's behavior over time (refer to Chapter 15 in this book for definitions of the terms sequence, cycle and phase). One delicate task consists of naming these intervals, in order to explain the process under study in as precise and helpful a way as possible. For example, Miller and Friesen (1982) suggested a momentum-revolution model to explain change in organizations. The terms 'momentum' and 'revolution' are explicit. The first describes a long period of steady, continuous evolution within an organization, while the second applies to an (often brief) period of radical upheaval.

Finally, process-based research may aim to describe or explain the studied object's evolution over time.

1.2 Descriptive and explanatory process-based research

Descriptive process-based research   Describing a process leads a researcher to pay particular attention to the elements the process is composed of, as well as their order and sequence over time. Observing its constitutive variables is here central to a processual analysis with a descriptive purpose.

Three main (and complementary) goals can explain why researchers carry out descriptive process-based research.

The first goal is to develop an in-depth description over time of the object under study. The value of this description is based on the value of the collected data and the identification of dimensions or subvariables that will be useful in understanding the process. A researcher can thus demonstrate regularity – patterns or configurations – in the process, and identify and name the sequences and phases it is composed of.

Describing the process itself, as studies about organizational change (Pettigrew, 1992) encourage us to do, can be another goal of process-based research of a descriptive nature. Historical studies of the structural and strategic development of organizations (Chandler, 1962) also serve this purpose. The environment is taken into account not to explain how a phenomenon came about but rather to situate it in the context of the collected information.

Finally, researchers may wish to compare two or more observed processes. In this way, in his work on decision-making processes, Nutt (1984) compared 78 processes to find patterns and identify different temporal developments within the decision-making process. The work of Mintzberg et al. (1976) on non-structured decision-making processes corresponds to the same research objective.

> ### Example: How is decision-making structured over time?
> ### (Mintzberg et al., 1976)
>
> Using a study of 25 decision-making processes, the authors break the processes' temporal development down according to the activities it is composed of. They present a very general model combining three phases: identifying, developing and selecting. This model can be articulated seven different ways, depending on the nature of the solution adopted.

Explanatory process-based research   The goal of analyzing a process can be to explain the phenomenon observed – to explain how a variable (the object under study) evolves over time, relative to the evolution of other variables. In this case, researchers attempt to answer the following question: 'Would an evolution or modification of variable X be related to or necessarily imply a modification of variable Y?'

**Example: How did Intel decide to abandon
the computer memory sector? (Burgelman, 1994)**

Burgelman wanted to understand the decision-making process whereby, in the mid-1980s, the Intel firm stopped researching and producing computer memory in order to concentrate only on microprocessors. The author began by investigating the evolution and dynamics of the variable 'the process of deciding to leave an industrial sector'. He wanted to describe this variable, and to understand its evolution particularly in terms of the skills that distinguish Intel from the competition. Strategic and industrial analysis calls for researchers to understand the distinctive competencies a firm has that may provide sources of advantage over the competition in the firm's economic sector. Burgelman followed the evolution of these competencies in the field of electronic components (microprocessors and memory chips) over the period studied. The author tried to understand how a sector's evolution can influence a firm's decision to leave it. Burgelman's work is based on a logic of co-evolution. An organization's strategy (the decision to abandon an industrial sector) appears as the result of a co-evolution between an external, sector variable (a sector's competitive advantages) and an internal, organizational variable (the firm's unique skills). Only process-based research allows for perception of the dynamic of this co-evolution.

2. Conducting Process-based Research

Let us look at the main stages of process-based research through the following example. While this example illustrates a possible modus operandi for researchers wishing to describe or explain the phenomena they are studying, it should not be taken as *the* model to follow. Researchers may have very good reasons for adopting a different research design. This example does provide, however, an interesting illustration of what a process-based study can be. By setting forth the main steps in the research process, it enables us to enumerate the main problems researchers are likely to encounter.

2.1 How is process-based research conducted?

The example, based on the work of Van de Ven and his team of researchers (Van de Ven et al., 1989), illustrates descriptive process research.

**Example: How do innovations appear and develop within
an organization? (Van de Ven et al., 1989; Van de Ven
and Poole, 1990) – a descriptive process-based study**

Van de Ven and his team wished to describe very concretely 'the temporal order and the sequential steps involved when innovative ideas are transformed and implemented into concrete reality' (Van de Ven and Poole, 1990: 313). A major research program was launched at three different sites. Data collection and analysis were articulated around the four main steps described below.

The first step in the research process was to specify the study's process variable (the innovative process, or the birth, transformation and implementation of new ideas into reality).

The second step was to clearly define the period of observation and the observation sample.

The third step consisted in defining the core concepts, or subvariables, which would permit the researchers to observe the evolution of the 'innovation' variable. Five core concepts were defined – actors, ideas, transactions, context and results. These core concepts demonstrated the manner in which the authors defined the innovative process in these organizations. Through them, the researchers were able to follow and characterize the 'innovation' variable over time. The authors broke down the observed history of an innovation into its critical incidents, and described and studied each incident from the perspective of the five core concepts. Each incident was the subject of a binary analysis. The five core concepts were coded 0 or 1, depending on whether the actors, ideas, transactions, context or results of the innovation changed over time or not. This breakdown and encoding of the innovation's history over time was based on the principles of sequential process analysis.

The fourth, and final, step consisted of classifying critical incidents and determining phases of the processes, which enabled researchers to follow the development of these innovation processes over time.

Through their research, the authors were able to describe how an innovation process unfolds within an organization, by breaking the longitudinal history down into phases and describing each phase in terms of the evolution of the variables 'ideas', 'actors', 'transactions', 'context' and 'results'.

The type of research described above results in reconstructing history over time and permits us to 'describe' what happened.

2.2 The main stages of process-based research

The study presented above demonstrates the following principal stages:

1 The researcher breaks down the process variable he or she is studying into core concepts (or subvariables). This first decomposition stage permits the researcher to become familiar with the process under study, and to follow its evolution through its constitutive elements. The researcher is at this point confronted with the problem of how to decompose the process variable.

2 Once the process variable has been decomposed, the researcher will study and describe the research subject over time. The researcher will follow its evolution through the different dimensions of the concepts that make up its process. During this essential stage, researchers may have some difficulty in delimiting the process under study. This delimitation is, above all, temporal. The researcher is confronted with the problem of deciding when the phenomenon being studied actually begins and ends. The question of delimitation must then be seen in terms of the subject of the research. Researchers who wish to observe, for example, the decision-making process within organizations, will soon realize that *the* decision whose development they intended to track turns out to be inextricably bound up with other, concomitant decisions (Langley et al., 1995). The researcher has to

decide how to isolate the single phenomenon under observation from a myriad of other phenomena, as the firm is functioning and changing throughout the observation period. The question of delimitation must therefore be considered in terms of both the internal and external contexts in which the process is taking place. Researchers are faced with the ticklish problem of needing to take several contexts into account (on several levels of analysis: personal, organizational and environmental), and of having to absorb a tremendous amount of data relative to actors, the organization and its external environment.

3   The researcher will need to identify the critical incidents, and analyze and classify them in order to reveal the temporal intervals affecting the process's development. The researcher will then be confronted with another problem – that of having to articulate the identified 'intervals' over time, relative to each other. These intervals will often appear to overlap to the point that it can be extremely difficult to separate them from one another, or they may follow one after another in exceedingly variable ways, depending on the organizations studied. The studied process may follow an evolution that may be, to a greater or a lesser extent, anarchic, non-linear or complex.

3. Troubleshooting Process-based Research

Three principal problems confronted in process studies are in the areas of: (a) recognizing, and then decomposing the process variable to be studied; (b) delimiting the process under study, and (c) arranging temporal intervals over time (that is, reconstituting the studied chronology).

3.1 Decomposing the process variable

The process variable will remain abstract if it is not broken down into the elements (or subvariables) that participate in its development over time. The essential problem is that of deciding which elements should be included. Within the framework of purely inductive reasoning (Glaser and Strauss, 1967), researchers use empirical data to reveal 'sensitive concepts' – concepts that give meaning to (or make sense of) the information that has been collected – and the different dimensions they may take. With other methodologies (partially inductive or deductive), the researcher will draw on existing work as well as empirical data to construct a conceptual framework that will integrate all the constitutive subvariables of the studied variable.

Most process studies are based on generally accepted codification systems for longitudinal studies. These codification systems are not themselves dependent on the contents of the study – they define the chief domains within which the codes should be established empirically. Miles and Huberman (1984a) propose several codings.

Codification Systems for Decomposing Process Variables
(Miles and Huberman, 1984a)

Miles and Huberman propose two methods of codification to decompose the process variable and study its evolution over time.

1. The process variable can be decomposed in terms of:
   - (a) acts (short-term actions, taking place over a few seconds, minutes or hours)
   - (b) activities (longer-term actions: days, weeks, months – representing elements that are more significant to an individual's commitment)
   - (c) signification (participants' verbal productions, which define and orient action)
   - (d) participation (holistic involvement or adaptation to a situation or setting)
   - (e) relations (interrelations between several actors considered simultaneously)
   - (f) settings (the different settings of the study, considered as a single unit of analysis).

2. The process variable can also be decomposed in terms of (adapted):
   - (a) setting/context (general information about the environment)
   - (b) the definition of the situation (how the context of the themes is defined)
   - (c) perspectives (modes of thought, orientations)
   - (d) manners of perceiving people and objects (greater detail than perspectives)
   - (e) activities (types of behavior which appear frequently)
   - (f) events (specific activities)
   - (g) strategies (ways of accomplishing goals)
   - (h) social structures and relations (official networks).

A researcher may not wish to decompose the process variable in such a detailed manner, preferring to adopt a more general coding. For instance, in their study of the decision-making process, Mintzberg et al. (1976) decided to decompose the 23 processes they studied solely in terms of different activities (which they called routines). By this coding they identify seven different modes of decision-making.

Researchers generally articulate their codification of the processes they study around the following three generic concepts: the actors involved, the activities taking place and contextual elements. Using this as a broad framework, researchers may choose to focus particularly on one of the three categories, depending on their subject's particularities or the objective of their study.

3.2 Delimiting a process in time

The question of delimitation is twofold; it is posed both in terms of time and in terms of the subject and context of the study.

Process-based research aims to describe and analyze the evolution of a variable across time – to describe what happens between a given point in time (T) and a later point (T + n). But it is not always easy for researchers to establish the starting point and the end point of a phenomenon. Organizations are constantly in flux: making decisions, moving, hesitating, deciding, going forward then questioning the idea, etc. The decision to proceed with a structural change may be preceded by a long maturation period, the beginning of which is often hard to identify. Key actors may begin to discuss the idea of 'change' informally among themselves, before addressing the firm's executive management in an equally informal manner, and before a single word has ever been written about such an important issue. Can ideas discussed among staff members at the beginning of the process of structural change be taken into account, or are we dealing with nothing more than the usual exchange of ideas and opinions which we all express at our place of work? This question of temporal delimitation is important for two reasons. First, it obliges researchers to decide when to begin collecting data. Second, the way in which the beginning of the process is defined can influence our interpretation of the process itself.

Example: How the way a process is delimited in time can influence its analysis

In studying a change in a firm's strategic vision, seemingly initiated by a new actor, defining the beginning of change before or after that actor's arrival at the firm may lead to different analyses of the process. In the first case (situating the beginning of the change of vision before the actor's arrival), explaining the process depends less on an actor-based logic and more on a systems-based logic, related to the organization itself (the organization is viewed as a system, itself made up of different systems). Whereas, in the second case (situating the beginning of the change of vision after the actor's arrival), the process is explained on the basis of the actor's capacity to induce the emergence of new representations and a new vision within the organization (Gioia and Chittipeddi, 1991).

To address this issue, Hickson et al. (1986) recommend following a process 'from the first deliberate action that initiates movement towards a decision (when, for example the subject is discussed at a meeting or a report is requested) until it has been approved (when the decision and its application are made official)' (Hickson et al., 1986: 100). Researchers may also form their own opinion based on interviews with organizational actors in which a reconstruction of the process may be solicited. Finally, we recommend that researchers do not hesitate to go as far back as possible into the organization's past and to collect even seemingly out-of-date data. A good knowledge of the firm's past can allow researchers to judge whether a simple, informal announcement might indeed indicate the beginning of a process, or if it is no more than a common remark for the firm in question.

Delimiting a process in time poses one other major problem. Time is a relative concept. An individual's time frame may be quite different from that of an organization. The more closely we study daily events the more likely we are to notice change. Conversely, the more we study an event as a whole, going back to its origins, the more likely we are to perceive continuity (Van de Ven and Poole, 1990: 316). There are no hard and fast rules defining the 'right' level to observe a process from. To compensate for this, it is often recommended to adopt an observation perspective including multiple levels of analysis. In this way, an organization's evolution can be studied alongside the actions taken by key actors within it.

3.3 Arranging temporal intervals

The time intervals that make up the process of a variable will usually emerge through studying the variable's evolution.

Before arranging these intervals logically, researchers may run into difficulty in deciding how many intervals are applicable to their processual model. Hannan and Freeman's (1977) ecological model, for example, is based on three phases (variation, selection, and retention) while Miller and Friesen's (1980) model of organizational change is constructed around just two phases (momentum–revolution). Other models are based on a more detailed evolution of the process studied. Pounds (1969), for instance, constructed his processual model of the emergence and resolution of strategic problems within an organization around eight phases:

1 Choosing a resolution model.
2 Comparing it to the actual situation.
3 Identifying the differences.
4 Selecting a particular difference.
5 Considering alternative operators (solvers).
6 Evaluating the consequences of the choice of operators (solvers).
7 Choosing a particular operator (solver).
8 Putting the chosen operator (solver) into action in order to resolve the strategic problem.

Studies seem to waver between a low number of intervals, which make it easier to comprehend the pace of a process, and a larger number of intervals, enabling a more detailed explanation. The question of how many intervals should be used in building a processual model remains largely up to the researchers' judgement. It will depend on the level of detail the researcher intends to give in describing the temporal arrangement of the studied process.

Once the time intervals have been identified, the researcher is confronted with the problem of their articulation over time. The researcher must consider whether these time intervals follow one another or whether they overlap, with a second appearing before the first is really over. Different models of processual development have been presented in organizational literature.

**Five Models for Describing a Process's Development
over Time (Langley et al., 1995)**

Langley and her colleagues present five basic models that permit us to describe how a process develops over time, or how the different time intervals of which the process is made up of are linked.

The first model is known as 'sequential' and hinges on the sequence of phases over time. Each phase is clearly identified and separated from the previous one and the one that follows it. The sequences never overlap.

The second model is known as 'anarchic' and has no apparent development structure. The different time intervals follow on from each other, overlap, and clash, finally resulting in what the authors call a 'garbage can' process.

The third model is known as 'iterative' and is a mixture of sequential evolution and anarchic development. The process is able to evolve steadily until the moment an unexpected events occur, or an internal conflict arises about the way the process is being conducted, which introduces a break in the development of the process. The actors involved in the process will tend to repeat the same operations until a solution is found which enables them to start the next phase of the process.

In addition to these three models, which seek to describe the development of a single object, the authors also identified two processes that account for the development of a group of objects, taken globally.

A fourth 'convergence' model describes how several objects (for example, several decisions) are linked over time and gradually converge towards a single object (that is, a single decision). The convergence model describes a process by gradually reducing the variety of objects as time goes on. The process is no longer guided by a clear diagnostic or target, but by the idea that successive approximate solutions come to light gradually. Little by little, the process evolves towards a single solution.

This contrasts with the fifth 'inspiration' model, in which convergence towards a single solution occurs via successive stages (and no longer gradually). The central idea in this model is that development is no longer steady, but is broken at certain key moments of its history, when certain solutions are discarded and others are clearly identified and accepted.

Models of management processes abound in management literature. Such work provides researchers with representations of different 'types' of evolution that the process they intend studying may follow over time. Researchers may decide to adopt a particular model before starting their research, or they may attempt to use their data to establish a model. This choice will be dependent on whether the researcher adopts an inductive or deductive position in conducting the research (see Chapter 3).

SECTION 3   POSITIONING RESEARCH

The first two sections of this chapter contrasted content-based research with process-based research. The aim of the third section is to enable researchers to measure the consequences of their choices and clearly position their research. We encourage researchers to be aware that the two approaches, one based on content and one on process, are mutually enriching, and that they both contribute to the study of the same object.

1. Combining Content and Process

The boundary between process and content is often difficult to pinpoint, as the two types of analysis complement each other. It is often just as difficult to study content without taking into account its structuring over time as to study a process without knowing its composition.

1.1 How processes can enrich content-based research

Processes can be integrated into descriptive, content-based analysis in two ways. On the one hand, the configuration hinges on a certain number of dimensions that include in most cases some processes. On the other hand, approaches that use decomposition can reveal the processes underlying the object being studied, without going into detail about the different stages involved.

We can, for example, define an organizational configuration according to the strategies it adopts, its company structures or the monitoring and planning processes it employs. We could also include here the variable 'the strategy formulation process'. This process can be centralized to a varying degree. When we describe a process of strategy formulation as 'very centralized', we use the process without reference to the sequence of stages that make it up. The researcher refers to existing works that have already categorized the process. As the example below illustrates, the process can then be considered as a 'category of concepts' (Van de Ven, 1992).

> ### Example: How processes can enrich descriptive content-based research
>
> The example provided by Bartlett and Goshal (1989) is explicit on this subject. The authors present a new organizational configuration for transnational companies that have a presence in several countries. They construct a model of the ideal transnational organization using organizational innovations they have observed during studies conducted in several companies. Their model of the transnational organization does not really exist, but is inspired by the authors' empirical work. It is based on certain managerial innovations, including new ways of managing coordination or innovation processes. For example, the authors propose additions to classic global and local innovation processes. They suggest systematically spreading local innovations, and introducing a coordinated process of global innovation, combining the efforts of the most competent subsidiaries. The logic of these processes is described, but not their dynamics. Although Bartlett and Goshal refer to process categories, they do not describe them in detail.

Processes enrich explicative, content-based research in the same way. Processes can first be used – and therefore operationalized – as constructs, and measured as fixed entities (variables), whose attributes can range from low to high on numerical scales. For example, when Govindarajan (1988) studies the appropriateness of a decision-making process in particular environmental conditions, the process itself is not studied. It is simply taken into account through a certain number of proxy variables that enable researchers to define the degree of centralization of decision-making.

Explicative content-based research can also use processes to explain the results it produces. Often, in fact, the data collected is not able to show the existence of causality links, but rather the simultaneous presence of two or more phenomena. So, in a hypothetico-deductive model, it is the formulation of the hypothesis that raises the correlation to the level of a causality link. Proving the hypothesis often involves processual logic. The process is integrated as an element that explains the causal relationship between independent and dependent variables (Van de Ven, 1992). This approach is illustrated by the following example.

Example: Using process to prove a causal relationship

We can refer back to Govindarajan's (1988) study of the central mechanisms governing the relations between general management and the operational units of diverse groups. Govindarajan uses a process-based explanation to prove that decentralization has a positive influence on the performance of a unit facing environmental uncertainty. In fact, a centralized company faced with environmental uncertainty sees its centralizing process paralyzed by the need to deal with the many exceptions that arise in subunits which do not have decision-making power. Very quickly, management is no longer able to arbitrate effectively between the subunits. The weak performance of companies that adopt centralized structures in an uncertain environment can be explained by a process of progressive paralysis in decision-making. Although Govindarajan provides a process-based explanation of the result, the process is simply mentioned and not studied directly.

1.2 How content enriches process-based research

Following the evolution of this variable involves decomposing it into elements such as actors (internal and external), methods of action and elements supporting action. This decomposition corresponds to a reflection on content. Before conducting a process-based study, one therefore needs to use content-based research to discover the categories that constitute a process. For example, Hickson et al. (1986) concentrated on identifying the different variables that make up a decision-making process (these variables relate to the progression of the process, and any ruptures in this progression, to the actors and to the stakes of the decision). They were able to identify and categorize several types of decision-making processes in terms of the state of the variables they are composed of.

Content also enriches our knowledge of a process in another way. Processual analysis can consist of studying the way an object develops over time between a state (1) and a state (2). It is important for researchers to have a precise understanding of both states (1) and (2) so the progression between them can be established. Content-based research enables us to obtain precise knowledge about these states.

2. Research Strategy: Choosing to Research a Process, Content or Both?

Beyond their mutual enrichment, process-based and content-based research are linked in another way. Together they enable researchers to grasp the reality of an object. The position researchers choose to adopt depends both on their knowledge of the object being studied and the nature of the object.

2.1 Choosing between process and content

As Table 5.1 illustrates, the choice between research into process and research into content is not based on the object that is being studied. Researchers need to combine the two approaches if they are to improve their knowledge about a particular object. Let us return to the metaphor of cinema and photography. Cinema is but a succession of fixed images. However, it is precisely this succession of fixed images which enables us to visualize the evolution over time of the object being studied. Weick (1979) expresses a similar idea when he says that the organizational process and the consequences of this process are in reality inseparable – they are interchangeable notions. Weick argues that the same things are involved, and that we can call them either organization or an organizational process, according to the length of time we spend observing them. Watching a collectivity for a longer period creates the impression that the organization process is under way. Looking at it for shorter periods will suggest that an organization exists (Weick, 1979: 16).

In making these choices, researchers must take into account not only their personal aspirations and the constraints linked to the data available, but also how much is known about the object they intend to study. Knowing the current state of play in relation to a particular object allows a researcher to choose an approach that enriches existing knowledge. If an object has already been studied closely from the angle of its content, researchers may need to supplement their knowledge with process-based research (and vice versa). For example, the notion of a life cycle naturally calls for processual research centered on revealing the successive stages that make up the life cycle. However, once the major phases have been identified and corroborated by several convergent research projects, work can then be done on the content of each of these phases to increase our understanding of the subject. When this work has been carried out, fresh processual research is then called for, which can help researchers to better understand the way the phases link up. Researchers must therefore be capable of choosing between a content- or process-based position so as to shed new light on the subject with a view to building up our knowledge.

Establishing cumulative knowledge is very much dependent on new practices emerging within organizations. These practices raise new questions and alter research needs, as much for content-based research as for process-based work. It is clearly very important for researchers to consider the type of research they have chosen. They could, for example, pose the following question: 'Are the results of my research relevant to the practices which will be in operation when they are published?'

2.2 Towards a mixed approach?

Given that the two approaches overlap, certain works seek to integrate content- and process-based research (Jauch, 1983; Jemison, 1981). Researchers who advocate content-based study will tend to pose questions in terms of dynamics. In fact, the way of tackling one of the main questions in strategic management – 'why certain firms succeed while others fail?' – has evolved to the point that it now tends to incorporate a processual and dynamic dimension (Porter, 1991). Certainly, a firm's success depends partly on striking a balance between strategic and environmental choices, but we must be able to assess this balance over time, because it is constructed over time. Conversely, the school of process-based study attaches great importance to understanding the 'content' of the phenomena being studied (Itami and Numagami, 1992). Process-based analysis should not be considered as incompatible with content-based analysis, since all decision taken within an organization, and all organizational systems, are but the result of a succession of states, stages and dynamics. The 'why' of strategic choices, the 'what' of a strategic decision and the 'how' of such decisions complement each other (Chakravarthy and Doz, 1992).

The following discussion of Honda's success illustrates the necessity of combining the two approaches if we wish to understand certain management phenomena. When analyzing the 'Honda case', it seems a risky research strategy to choose to focus exclusively on either process or content. Such an approach may permit researchers to concentrate their efforts, but they risk grasping only a part of the phenomenon being studied.

The Success of Honda: An Explanation via Content or Process

Content and process are at the center of a famous controversy over the success of Honda in the American market. The traditionally accepted explanation is one based on content – the BCG logic of research into the effects of experience and economies of scale is used. An alternative explanation hinges on a process-based approach, and longitudinally retraces the commercial actions taken by Honda representatives to create the market, first in California, then in the rest of the USA. This controversy seems now to have closed with an enriching 'gentleman's agreement', which argues clearly in favor of an integrative approach.

(Mintzberg et al., 1996)

CONCLUSION

Management researchers can position themselves on one of the three quadrants synthesized in Table 5.2. Research may be content-based, in which case time

Table 5.2 *Positioning in management research*

		Importance of content in the research	
		Slight	Great
Importance of time in the research	Slight	—	Content-based research
	Great	Process-based research	Mixed research

and evolution over time are considered to be of secondary importance. Such work only allows the researcher to come to a better understanding of the object being studied, or the causal relationships between the different elements it is made up of. Conversely, research may focus essentially on process. The central aim of such work is to follow the evolution over time of the object being studied. A researcher's knowledge of the content of the phenomenon is used only through the different elements it is composed of (actors, activities, contextual elements). Finally, it may be necessary or enriching to adopt a mixed approach. Here, researchers pay equally close attention to the content as to the process of the object they are studying.

The central question is the importance that is placed on time. This question is posed independently of the object being studied – researchers cannot adopt a valid position without understanding that all objects can be analysed on the basis of either their content or their process. Researchers must also be aware of the necessary complementarity of the two analyses. There is no content-based analysis which does not give rise to reflection on process, and vice versa. It may well be more judicious at times, taking into account the state of our knowledge of an object, to adopt one type of research or another to study a particular object.

It is clear that the researcher's disposition, experience and intuition all have an equally important role to play. The choice may also be restricted by the amount of data available, or by limited access to the field of study. This naturally brings to mind the various methodological constraints (including the available tools and the collection and processing of data) which all investigation involves.

FURTHER READING

Abbott, A., 'A Primer on Sequence Methods', *Organization Science*, 1 (4), 1990: 375–92.

Meyer, A., Tsui, A. and Hinings, C., 'Configurational Approaches to Organizational Analysis', *Academy of Management Journal*, 36 (6), 1993: 1175–95.

Miller, D. and Friesen, P., 'The Longitudinal Analysis of Organizations: A Methodological Perspective', *Management Science*, 28 (9), 1982: 1013–34.

Monge, P., 'Theoretical and Analytical Issues in Studying Organizational Processes', *Organization Science*, 1 (4), 1990: 406–30.

Van de Ven, A., 'Suggestions for Studying Strategy Process: A Research Note', *Strategic Management Journal*, 1 (3), 1992, summer special issue: 169–88.

PART II

IMPLEMENTATION

The chapters in this part look at the more practical aspects of research. Once a researcher has established the foundations of the work, and made the conceptual choices discussed in the first part of this book, the question arises of the procedure to take. The following chapters answer questions about what steps to follow, what and how to observe and how to establish the validity of results. They help prepare the concrete exercise of carrying out research. First, the researcher must define the different stages of the research project. These stages include establishing a research question, reviewing relevant literature, collecting and analyzing data, and presenting final results. One should always keep in mind, however, that neither the content nor the sequence of these stages is arbitrary or rigid. The design can evolve over the course of the research, as the researcher comes up against unforeseen difficulties or unexpected events. Once the plan has been established, the researcher must determine how the connection between the empirical realm and the theoretical is to be made. Theoretical concepts have to be translated into practical terms in order to measure what is observed (how this translation will be achieved will of course depend on the epistemological positioning the researcher has adopted). The researcher then has to select which elements to collect data from. We discuss the choice and the composition of samples – from samples comprising a large number of individual items to smaller samples containing only a limited number of items. Selecting an appropriate sampling method is further complicated by the numerous potential biases that must be taken into account. We then move on to the phase of collecting data in the field. This is a crucial stage, as the data collected is the raw material on which the research is based. Finally, we address questions of validity and reliability. This is a matter of evaluating whether the phenomenon studied is faithfully reproduced (validity) and whether it would be represented in a similar manner by other observers or at other times (reliability).

6

RESEARCH DESIGN

Isabelle Royer and Philippe Zarlowski

Outline

This chapter looks at the process of drawing up an initial research design, and at the evolution of this design over the course of the research.

The emergence of new paradigms in the social sciences has generated two types of epistemological debate. The first controversy is over the relationship between epistemological positioning and methodology; the second, over the relationship between research design and the maturity of the scientific knowledge in a given domain. These questions are presented in the first section of this chapter, along with their repercussions on research design.

The second section invites the researcher to consider the first mapping out of the research design as itself a defined stage of the research process. A way of approaching this initial design process is proposed, and some suggestions are given to limit possible mistakes. The final section illustrates the potential for an initial design to evolve during the research process.

The research design[1] is the framework through which the various components of a research project are brought together: research question, literature review, data, analysis and results. According to Grunow (1995), it is a crucial element of any empirical research project, whatever the research question and the chosen methodological point of view.

However, many research designs prove to be inadequate. As a reviewer for *Administrative Science Quarterly* and the *Academy of Management Journal*, Daft (1995) noted that he had to reject a large number of articles, and 20 per cent for this very reason. Grunow (1995), in a study of more than 300 examples of empirical research, both published and unpublished, noted that only 20 per cent presented no design problems. Grunow explained these design flaws by the general absence of strict determinist links between the various components of the research. Nevertheless, that does not mean that any arbitrary combination of research elements may be used (Grunow, 1995). Obviously, there is not one single 'correct' design appropriate to a research problem. Several designs are possible. While some are more attractive or original than others, certain designs can definitely be deemed 'poor'.

In general, the quality of a design is partly a question of the overall logic of the research approach taken, and partly of how coherent its various components are. Apart from these two major principles, there are no precise rules. Bartunek et al. (1993) contend that qualitative and quantitative methods may both be used to solve the same problem. Neither is there a strict relationship between methodology and the level or type of analysis used. The level of analysis (individuals, groups, organizations or interorganizational) bears no relation to the type of approach used. In fact, no particular method appears indisputably superior to another in absolute terms. As McCall and Bobko (1990) argue, the most important aspect to consider in choosing a method is not the method in itself but what it is able to reveal of a particular problem.

This chapter is not, therefore, going to provide a set of rules for constructing a successful research design. It will merely make some suggestions about how to approach this process, and what questions researchers should ask themselves.

SECTION 1   EPISTEMOLOGY AND RESEARCH DESIGN

Before we present in detail the debate over the implications the epistemological positioning of a research project may have on its design, we will briefly mention the evolution of research approaches that has brought about this debate. The related question of the degree of maturity of knowledge in a field of study and the type of design that is appropriate will be the subject of the third part of this section.

1. Research Approaches in the Social Sciences

Approaches to research in the social sciences evolved significantly over the course of the twentieth century. Until the 1950s, these were primarily centered on the positivist paradigm of Comte, based on the postulate of the objectivity of reality (see Chapter 1). This concept of research is represented by the scientific method that is today presented in most textbooks (see Figure 6.1). According to this approach:

> Scientific investigations begin in the free and unprejudiced observation of facts, proceed by inductive inference to the formulation of universal laws about these facts, and finally arrive by further induction at statements of still wider generality known as theories; both laws and theories are ultimately checked for their truth content by comparing their empirical consequences with all the observed facts, including those with which they began.
>
> (Blaug, 1992: 4)

According to this positivist paradigm, theories are accepted if they correspond to reality – understood through empirical observation – and are rejected if they do not. The test phase is dominated by surveys, followed by statistical analysis (Ackroyd, 1996).

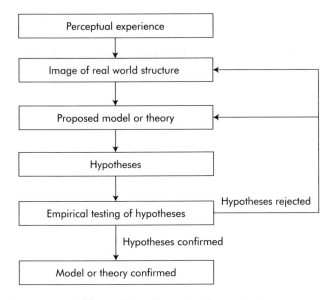

Figure 6.1   *The scientific method*

New perspectives developed in the philosophy of science from the early 1950s. Within the positivist paradigm, new perceptions suggested a modification of the status of theories and the scientific method, and the hypothetico-deductive model was adopted. According to this model (Popper, 1977) explained, a theory cannot be confirmed but only corroborated (or temporarily accepted). In terms of method, this new perception meant that hypotheses had to be formulated in such a way as to be refutable, or 'falsifiable'. It prohibited the development of ad hoc or auxiliary hypotheses, unless they increased the degree to which the system could be refuted. Other paradigms appeared alongside these concepts: in particular, constructivism and the interpretative paradigm. According to these new paradigms, there is not one sole reality – which would be possible to apprehend, however imperfectly – but multiple realities; the product of individual or collective mental constructions that are likely to evolve over the course of time (Guba and Lincoln, 1994).

During this period, along with a lot of activity in philosophy of science, new research approaches were promoted in both the constructivist and the interpretative paradigms. The majority, such as grounded theory in the positivist paradigm and participatory action research in the constructivist paradigm, were qualitative. The increased use of new approaches was coupled with an attempt to formalize both the approaches themselves and the data collection and analysis methods employed. Researchers today have a vast choice of options available through which to approach the question they have chosen to study (Hitt et al., 1998).

We do not propose to detail all of these many and varied methods and approaches here. Nevertheless, by way of illustration, we will present a simplified version of certain generic research approaches: ethnography, grounded theory and experimentation (see Table 6.1).

Table 6.1 Three research approaches

Approach	Experimentation	Ethnography	Grounded theory
Main objective	Testing causal relationships	Describing, explaining or understanding a particular social phenomenon in its natural setting	Constructing an explanatory theory about a social phenomenon based on the identification of regularities
Method	Hypotheses testing: often carried out in a laboratory, on small, homogeneous samples	In-depth case study analysis	Multiple case studies
Data collection	Rigorously controlled data collection procedure, through an experimental design in which explanatory factors vary while others remain constant, so as to isolate their impact on the dependent variable	Flexible process in which the research question and the collected information may both evolve. Principal method: continuous observation of the phenomenon within its context. Secondary methods: all types	Iterative process with interaction between data, analysis and theory. Methods used: interviews plus many other methods, particularly the use of written material and observation
Analysis	Quantitative analysis, particularly analysis of variance	Primarily qualitative analysis	Qualitative analysis and additional use of quantitative analysis
Bibliography	Campbell and Stanley (1966); Cook and Campbell (1979); Spector (1981)	Atkinson and Hammersley (1994); Jorgensen (1989); Reeves Sanday (1983); Van Maanen (1983b)	Glaser and Strauss (1967); Strauss and Corbin (1990; 1994)

2. The Influence of Paradigm on Design

Many writers contend that epistemological positioning will have a decisive influence over the design a researcher will be able to implement. Pure positivism, for example, accepts only the scientific method (based on using quantitative data to test hypotheses) as likely to produce truly scientific knowledge. Constructivists, on the other hand, will maintain that the study of individuals and their institutions requires specific methods that differ from those inherited from the natural sciences. These positions have often led to the two approaches being seen as antithetic – and to qualitative approaches being considered as an alternative to quantitative positivist approaches.

Without going into further detail on the various elements of this debate, we will merely mention here that the relationship between research design and epistemological positioning is by no means simple, and that the association of qualitative methods and constructivism on the one hand and quantitative methods and positivism on the other represents an oversimplification of this relationship.

According to Van Maanen (1983a), although qualitative approaches are more likely to be guided by constructivist logic, that does not preclude them being carried out according to positivistic scientific logic. According to Yin (1990), a case study can be used to test a theory. This qualitative procedure then clearly fits in with the positivist 'falsification' approach of Popper.

In more general terms, research approaches are not systematically attached to a particular paradigm. Ethnography, for example, is used by proponents of both paradigms (Atkinson and Hammersley, 1994; Reeves Sanday, 1983). Ethnography may be used by a researcher who wishes to understand a reality through an interpretative process, or by a positivist wishing to describe reality, to discover an explanatory theory, or to test a theory (Reeves Sanday, 1983).

At the level of data collection and analysis, the links between paradigm and methods are even more tenuous. Ackroyd (1996) considers that, once established, methods no longer belong to the discipline or the paradigm in which they were engendered, but rather become procedures whose use is left to the discretion of the researcher. In this respect, the association of qualitative methods and constructivism, and of quantitative methods and positivism, seems outdated. As we saw with research approaches, the choice of qualitative data collection or analysis methods is not the prerogative of one particular paradigm. Similarly, whereas qualitative methods are dominant in the constructivist and interpretative paradigms, quantitative methods are not excluded. They can notably permit additional information to be made available (Atkinson and Hammersley, 1994; Guba and Lincoln, 1994; Morse, 1994). Certain authors go so far as to encourage the simultaneous or sequential use of qualitative and quantitative methods to study a particular question, in accordance with the principle of triangulation (Jick, 1979). When the results obtained by the different methods converge, the methods reinforce each other and concur, increasing the validity of the research.

There is no simple link between a researcher's epistemological positioning and any particular research approach. The range of designs that can be implemented proves to be even wider than a restricted appreciation of the relation between epistemology and methodology would suggest. It is not just the method in itself, but the way it is applied and the objective it serves that indicate the epistemological positioning of research. However, the overall coherence of the research project is paramount, and choices made in constructing a design should not compromise this coherence. Several writers feel that the researcher's chosen epistemological position should always be made clear for this reason (Denzin and Lincoln, 1994; Grunow, 1995; Otley and Berry, 1994).

3. 'Maturity' of Knowledge

The debate over epistemological positioning and its impact on research design is echoed in a second controversy; over the degree of 'maturity' of knowledge in a given field and the type of design that can be used.

If we accept a traditional conception of scientific research, a relationship should indeed exist between these two elements. According to the normative model, the research process should begin with exploratory studies, to be followed by more 'rigorous' approaches: experiments and surveys. Exploratory studies are designed to encourage the emergence of theories, and to identify new concepts or new explanatory variables in fields in which knowledge is as yet poorly developed. Hypotheses and models are formulated at this stage, which must then be tested within a 'stricter' methodological framework. Exploratory studies use 'small' samples, and this presents two significant deficiencies with regard to the requirements of the scientific method. First, the rules of statistical inference prohibit researchers from generalizing from their results: the samples are too small and not sufficiently representative. Moreover, such exploratory studies do not permit researchers to sufficiently isolate the effect of a variable by controlling other potentially influential variables. Therefore, according to this normative model of scientific progress, we can only increase our knowledge by testing hypotheses using 'rigorous' research approaches based on quantitative data (Camerer, 1985). This model also implies that it would be inappropriate to carry out experimental or quantitative studies in a relatively unexplored field, since they must be preceded by case studies.

Alongside this research tradition, which is still widely endorsed, are rival models that do not confine qualitative approaches to the proposal of theories and quantitative approaches to the testing of them. According to these models, explanatory theories can emerge from a purely descriptive correlation study of quantitative data, or even from observations made within an experimental design. Case studies can also be used to test existing theories or to increase their scope to include other contexts.

Some researchers question the sequential aspect of the progression of research work: exploring reality before testing hypotheses. According to Schwenk (1982), it is possible to follow two different approaches – case studies and laboratory experiments – concurrently, from the same initial conceptual work; at least for research questions where the influence of the context is not decisive, and therefore where laboratory experimentation is possible.

SECTION 2   PLANNING THE RESEARCH

The design stage often results in a proposal stating the approach the researcher will follow and the essential methodological choices he or she has made (the data collection and analysis methods he or she will use, and the observational field). These choices should always be justified in line with the research question. Although such formalization is not essential at this stage, it will be required when it comes to publishing research results. It is important to keep in mind, however, that the structure of the completed research will be evaluated, not that of the initial design. The structure conceived during the design stage can evolve during the research, as opportunities or difficulties are encountered along the way.

Notwithstanding, it is definitely not recommended that researchers omit the design stage. The design guides the course of the research and helps avoid at least some of the obstacles that can crop up in latter stages of the research. Researchers can come up against an impasse, or at least a snarl, at late stages of their research that stem from preceding stages – in which case they can be very difficult to resolve (Selltiz et al., 1976). When such problems are serious and appear late in the piece, they can waste time and demand further effort that might have been avoided. They can even appear insurmountable and halt the research entirely. For example, when a researcher, after collecting data through 300 completed questionnaires, realizes they were not given to the right people in the first place, data collection will probably have to start all over again. More forethought at the design stage would probably have made it possible to avoid this type of incident. Many problems can stem from a defective or unsatisfactory research design. Experimental results can in some cases be unusable because of the omission of a control variable. Often, the only solution is to start the experiment again. A thorough knowledge of the literature or the research field may help to avoid such an oversight. Statistical results may not be significant if the sample used is too small. At best the researcher will be able to increase the size of the sample, but if that is not possible, the research may have to be redirected towards another application. A good preliminary knowledge of the selected statistical method's application conditions generally makes it possible to determine the number of observations that will be required. A detailed design, presenting the general procedure and justifying the research components selected, will help to avoid this type of error. Planning the research and putting together an initial design should definitely be seen as a distinct and important stage of the research.

1. When to Construct a Research Design

The design stage usually comes after defining the research question and before beginning data collection (see Figure 6.2). Constructing a research design consists of defining the means necessary to answer the research question: selecting data collection and analysis methods and determining data types and sources (including details of sample composition and size). This is why it is useful to

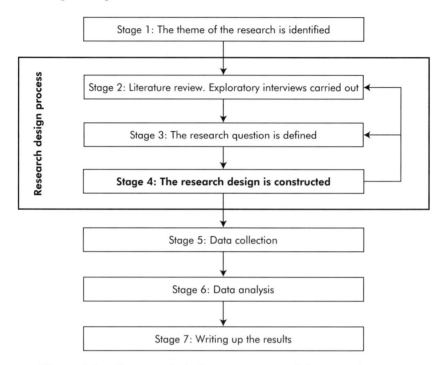

Figure 6.2   *The research design stage as part of the research process*

define the research question beforehand – even if the formulation is still a little unclear, one should at least know what one wishes to study. Of course, within the framework of constructivist or inductive approaches, the research question cannot be specified during the design stage. In this case, only the topic is defined during the development of the design: the research question is built up progressively as data is collected and analyzed (see Chapter 2).

Moreover, we recommend establishing a coherent research design before moving on to the data collection. To start collecting data without knowing how it is to be analysed entails the risk of it being inapplicable. This can also lead to the researcher wasting an observation field that can be difficult to replace, especially if the phenomena under study are sensitive or out of the ordinary.

Within the framework of a doctoral dissertation, construction of a research design begins only after some months of reading and exploratory work – through which a research question is formulated. Depending on the approach chosen, these activities may take on very different forms. A researcher might carry out an exhaustive literature review as part of a hypothetico-deductive approach – leading to a conceptual framework. But a more cursory reading involving a small number of works only might be more applicable to an inductive approach. Whichever approach is chosen, constructing a research design is generally a lengthy process. Simple logical deduction is rarely enough on its own. Instead, a process of trial and error is entered upon, which continues until the researcher is satisfied that he or she has come up with a complete, coherent, and potentially feasible design. This process often requires new reading, in particular on the general approach chosen, but also on data analysis methods and data collection and sampling techniques. Similarly, further exploration is often required, in particular to find an accessible observation field and to evaluate the feasibility of the intended data collection process. For case studies, for example, a researcher might at this stage make preliminary contact with a manager of the organization chosen: not simply to gain access to the observation field, but also to specify which sources of information are available and authorized. It is also a good time to ensure that the chosen means of data collection is acceptable to all concerned.

Constructing a design is also a way to improve the precision or the formulation both of the research question and of the theoretical references (Grunow, 1995). Putting the research into a practical perspective makes it easier to estimate its feasibility. For example it can lead to a researcher restricting or limiting the research question if it appears too broad to be handled in its entirety. By questioning methodological choices and the types of results that might stem from them, researchers can often identify inaccuracies, even omissions, in their design concept. Such revelations can return researchers to the literature, to supplement theoretical references that have proved unsatisfactory. Consequently, research design construction is an ongoing process (see Figure 6.2). It will require more or less time depending on the approach chosen, on the level of preliminary methodological knowledge, and on the difficulties encountered by the researcher in finding an appropriate field. The precision and detail of this initial design will depend on the strictness of the research approach. For example, a research design in which the researcher intends to build-up an interpretation of a phenomenon via an in-depth case study could be limited to an outline comprising the research topic, the general approach, the choice of field and the generic data collection and analysis methods that will be used. By definition, this approach leaves great scope for flexibility, allowing new elements to emerge. But a project in which the validity of the results is closely related to the precision and control of the system will require a far more detailed design.

2. How to Construct a Research Design

Morse (1994) suggests using the normal procedure backwards, that is, to start by imagining what one might find. Imagining the expected or even the desired result often makes it possible to refine a research question and to determine appropriate research methods. Similarly, it is preferable to select analysis techniques before defining the data collection process in detail, as each technique has its restrictions in terms of the type of data required as well as the appropriate mode of collection.

2.1 Data analysis

A great number of data analysis methods are available, both quantitative and qualitative. Each has its own goals (comparing, structuring, classifying, describing, etc.) and sheds light on different aspects of the problem in question. The choice of analysis method depends on the research question and the type of result desired. As we have already indicated, no method is superior to another in absolute terms. The complexity of the analysis is not a guarantee of a better quality of research. Indeed, complex analysis methods are not necessarily the best adapted to the research question. Daft (1995) warns researchers that statistics are no substitute for clearly defining concepts, and that highly sophisticated statistical processing can distance the data from reality to such a point that the results become difficult to interpret.

Each analysis method depends on hypotheses that limit its conditions of use. Each one brings its own restrictions concerning the nature of the data, the number of observations necessary, or the probability distribution of these observations. Choosing an analysis method requires a perfect understanding of its conditions, so that the researcher can detect in advance any factors that could make it unusable within the framework of his or her research. It is advantageous to consider various methods before making a definitive choice. Not only can this help to identify a more appropriate method than the one initially envisaged, but it is also a good way to clarify different methods' conditions of use and to understand their limits.

By identifying a method's limitations beforehand, researchers can consider using a second, complementary, method from the outset, to compensate for any deficiencies of the primary method and to reinforce research results. In this case, researchers must always ensure the two methods are compatible, and take account of the particular requirements of each one.

Choosing a Method

Is the method appropriate to my research question?
Will the method enable me to arrive at the desired *type* of result?
What are the conditions of use of this method?
What are the limitations or the weaknesses of this method?
What other methods could be appropriate to my research question?
Is the method better than these other methods? If so, why?
What skills does this method require?
Do I possess these skills or can I acquire them?
Would the use of an additional method improve the analysis?
If yes, is this second method compatible with the first?

Analysis methods are not limited to those traditionally used in management research. It is more than possible to use a technique borrowed from another discipline. A new method can generate new knowledge, or extend knowledge to a wider field. However, importing methods is by no means easy (Bartunek et al., 1993). The researcher has to evaluate whether the method is adaptable to the new context: this requires a detailed understanding of its limits and underlying assumptions.

2.2 Data collection

Data collection can be divided into four principal components: the type of data collected; the data collection method used; the nature of both the observation field and the sample; and data sources. Each of these components must be appropriate to the research question and the data analysis method selected – that is, research question, data collection and data analysis must be coherent. The feasibility of these choices must also be taken into account.

Identifying the data needed to investigate a research question presupposes that the researcher has a good idea about what theories are likely to explain the phenomenon. This seems obvious for research destined to test hypotheses using data collected through questionnaires, but can also be useful when a researcher uses an inductive procedure to explore a phenomenon. Yin (1990) argues that encouraging a researcher to begin collecting data too early in a case study is the worst piece of advice one can give. Even for exploratory research, the relevance of the data, just like the choice of participants or of observation sites, depends to an extent on researchers' prior familiarity with the phenomena they study. However, the other extreme is to refrain from starting data collection on the pretext that doubts remain. Since the main contribution of exploratory study is in gaining new insights, this presupposes that the existing literature cannot explain everything beforehand.

The data collection method used should enable the researcher to collect all information needed to answer the research question. Once again, many methods are possible: close-ended questionnaires, observation, verbal protocols, unstructured interviews, etc. Some are better adapted than others to the collection of a given type of information, and all of them have their limitations. An inadequate data collection method can also invalidate the whole research. For example, a closed-mail questionnaire using a random sample of managers is unsuitable for research that proposes to study a subtle and intangible decision-making process (Daft, 1995). Sometimes several data collection methods can be used to increase the validity of the data. For example, *ex post* interviews are likely to prove insufficient to reconstruct a chronological path of actions because of divergence in participants' recollections. In this case, documents might be collected to supplement the data gathered from interviews or to validate it, according to the principle of triangulation.

Researchers should always ensure that the observational field can answer the research question. The size and the composition of the sample should also be determined during the design construction phase. It is useful to verify that the sample size is sufficient to implement the analysis method. At this stage, too, the researcher should define the structure of the sample (or samples) as this will affect the validity of research.

Data sources should also be taken into account when constructing a research design. In survey research, answers can differ greatly according to the respondent. There are particular biases associated with the hierarchical or functional position of respondents. For example, in a study of the characteristics of management control systems, a questionnaire sent to the heads of a large company might provide information about the company's formal structure. This source, though, would probably be insufficient if the researcher wanted to know how managers used this structure, and whether they were satisfied with it. Researchers should always ensure their respondents can provide the information they are seeking. Similarly, when using secondary data, researchers should question its adequacy. Identical wording can hide different realities, according to who constructed the data and how it was collected. In the case of data collected over a period of time, the researcher could also question whether the definition and the data collection method did not change as time went on. For example, an apparent drop in a company's workforce may reflect a downsizing or a change in the definition of workforce, which may no longer include certain workers such as temporary labor.

Data Collection

Nature of the data
- What information do I need to respond to the research question?
- Is the type of data adapted to the data analysis method?

Data collection method
- Is the data collection method suitable to the research question?
- Does it allow me to collect the data I need?

Observational field and sample/s
- Does the field enable me to answer the research question?
- Is the sample size sufficient for the analysis I wish to carry out?
- Does the composition of the sample pose problems in terms of research validity?

Data sources
- Will the respondent(s) be able to give me all the information I need?
- Are there other possible respondents?
- If so, have I chosen the best ones? If so, would it be relevant to question the other respondents?
- Does the secondary data correspond to what I am looking for?
- Are there other possible sources and, if so, are they better?
- Is it possible for me to improve the data before processing it?

Feasibility
- Do I consider the cost and duration of the data collection acceptable?
- Do I need someone to help me collect my data?
- Does the data collection method require particular training?
- If so, do I know how to do it, or can I learn how?
- Are my observational field and my subjects accessible? If so, for how long will this be the case?
- Is the data collection method acceptable for the field and the subjects under observation (in terms of form, duration, etc.)?

Contrary to other research components, choices concerning data collection are not dictated solely by a need for coherence. Data collection often raises practical problems that result in revising the ideal guidelines the researcher had already established. Any research design is consequently a compromise between theoretical and practical considerations (Suchman, in Miller, 1991). It is therefore recommended at this stage to take account of the feasibility of the design in addition to its coherence.

Researchers should ensure the duration of the data collection phase is reasonable, and that they have enough funds to complete it. If, for example, a research question requires 40 case studies, the researcher should plan for a long period of investigation. Researchers can use assistants but, if funds are not sufficient, it would be better to revise the research design, or to reduce the scope of the research question. Similarly, in researching cultural differences, translation or travelling costs can be prohibitory, and lead the researcher to limit the number of countries under study.

Many other feasibility difficulties also exist. For example, the administration of a questionnaire in an organization often requires obtaining permission (Selltiz et al., 1976). Very often, a study of an ongoing product development requires a contract of confidentiality with the company. Researchers should always evaluate whether the observational field is accessible, and estimate the consequences of possible constraints imposed by the field on the research. They should also decide whether the data collection system will be tolerated by the subjects under observation. For example, it is not easy to convince a busy executive to agree to be closely observed for an entire day to record the time given over to various activities (reading of strategic reports, meetings, telephone calls, etc.). Similarly, executives do not necessarily agree to filling out daily questionnaires detailing all the people they met in the course of their work. In general, access to the field is easier when the members of the organization are interested in the results.

In an attempt to anticipate these various feasibility problems, Selltiz et al. (1976) strongly advise meeting other researchers who have worked in similar or close fields, to question them on the problems they may have faced, or even the pleasant surprises they had. Another suggestion is to explore the field beforehand, which could help to identify and resolve certain difficulties.

2.3 Expected results

The reiterative and recursive process involved in constructing a coherent design can very easily drift off course. It can produce a design in which the three elements (data collection, data processing and the expected result) may be perfectly coherent among themselves, whereas the expected result no longer answers the research question formulated at the outset. At this stage it is useful to evaluate once again whether the result will be coherent with the original research question. If they diverge, it may be more profitable to reformulate the question, or even to return to the stage of reviewing the literature, rather than recommencing to construct a new design to respond to the initial question. Modifying the research question at this stage does not cast doubts on the hypothetico-deductive principles of hypothesis testing, as data collection has not yet been carried out.

Researchers can also, at this stage, reassess the contribution they expect their work to make to their research domain. When hypothetico-deductive approaches are used, the answer to this question is known as soon as the research question is defined. Nevertheless, since the development of the design can lead to the question being reduced or altered, it may still be useful to question the expected contribution. It would obviously be a pity to realize at the end of the research that the results add little or nothing to the existing knowledge in the domain (Selltiz et al., 1976).

Expected Results

- Will the expected results answer the research question?
- Will these results correspond to the literature?
- What is the expected contribution of the research in the domain I have chosen?
- To what extent could my results be generalized?

As researchers have many data collection and analysis methods at their disposal, a wide variety of designs are open to them – from those that follow a standard approach to far more complex solutions. It is therefore up to the individual researcher to put together a research design that can effectively answer the question he or she has chosen to consider.

SECTION 3   EVOLUTION OF A DESIGN

Although the relevance and coherence of the initial research design have a direct influence on the quality of later research stages, this design is by no means inalterable. Problems and opportunities will arise as the research progresses, which can have an effect on the design. Meyer (1992) illustrates such evolution. His research design evolved following an event that occurred during data collection. Meyer was carrying out interviews in hospitals in the San Francisco area when doctors in the area began a general strike. This social action gave him the opportunity to turn his research into a quasi-experiment, which he did.

This section looks at a number of ways in which a design can evolve during the course of the research. We explore how to incorporate flexibility into a research approach, and how this can enable positive developments to take place as opportunities arise.

1. Design Flexibility

Thus far we have presented the various stages of research in sequential order, underlining their interdependence. It is this very interdependence which necessitates a coherent research design, with certain choices having a real effect on the later stages of research (Selltiz et al., 1976). However, this sequentiality is limited to the level of a general overview of the research process. In practice, research stages rarely follow a strictly linear progression: the research process does not unfold as a well-ordered sequence, where no stage can start before the preceding one is finished (Daft, 1983; Selltiz et al., 1976). Stages overlap, are postponed or put forward, repeated or refined according to the exigencies and opportunities of the research environment. The boundaries between them tend to become fuzzy. Two consecutive stages can share common elements, which can sometimes be dealt with simultaneously. According to Selltiz et al. (1976), in practice, research is a process in which the different components – reviewing existing works, data collection, data analysis, etc. – are undertaken simultaneously, with the researcher focusing more on one or another of these activities as time passes.

The literature review is a perfect example of this. Whatever the type of design, this referral to existing works continues throughout the entire research process. Background literature is often essential for analysis and interpretation. Further reading, or rereading past works, makes it possible to refine the interpretation of the results and even to formulate new interpretations. Moreover, since the results of the research are not necessarily those expected, analysis can lead to a refocusing of the literature review. A researcher may decide to voluntarily exclude some works he or she had included. Conversely, additional bibliographical research may need to be carried out, to explain new aspects of the question being studied. This can lead to including a group of works which, voluntarily or not, had not been explored in the beginning.

Therefore, while it is generally accepted that reading is a precondition to relevant research, it is never done once and for all. Researchers turn back to the literature frequently throughout the whole research process, the final occasion being when writing the conclusions of the research.

Some research approaches are, by nature, more iterative and more flexible than others. Generally speaking, it is frequent in case studies to acquire additional data once the analysis has begun. Several factors may justify this return to the field. A need for additional data, intended to cross-check or increase the accuracy of existing information, may appear during data analysis. Researchers can also decide to suspend data collection. Researchers can reach saturation point during the data collection phase – they may feel the need to take a step back from the field. As described by Morse (1994), it is often advisable to stop data collection and begin data analysis at this point. The principle of flexibility is at the heart of certain approaches, such as grounded theory (Glaser and Strauss, 1967) where each new unit of observation is selected according to the results of analyses carried out in the preceding units. In this procedure, data collection and data analysis are carried out almost simultaneously, with frequent returns to the literature in an attempt to explain new facts that have been observed. These many iterations often result in refining the research question, and sometimes in redefining it entirely, according to observations and the opportunities that arise.

Experimentation, on the contrary, is a more sequential process. The data analysis phase begins only when all the data has been collected. Moreover, this data collection method is quite inflexible. An experiment cannot be modified while it is being carried out. Indeed, that would cast doubt on the very principle of control that constitutes the basis of the method. If difficulties arise, the researcher can simply stop the experiment in progress and start another. Between these extremes, investigation by questionnaire is not very flexible or evolving, but it is sometimes possible, should difficulties occur, to supplement missing information by calling back the respondent, or increasing a sample with a second series of inquiries. Thus, even within the framework of research based on stricter procedures, a return to the data collection stage remains possible after the beginning of data analysis.

2. Problem Areas

Whichever the approach, various problems can emerge during research, be it during pre-tests, data collection or data analysis. These problems do not necessarily imply the need to change the initial design, and it is advisable to estimate their impact before undertaking a modification of the research design. However, in the event of significant problems, a modification of the design can be necessary – even several modifications, depending on the difficulties encountered.

2.1 Pre-tests and pilot cases

The research process generally includes activities that seldom appear in proposed methodologies (Selltiz et al., 1976). Fitting in between the stages of design and data collection, pre-tests and pilot cases aim to assess the feasibility of the research through evaluating the reliability and validity of the data collection tools used, be they quantitative or qualitative. While carrying out a pre-test is invaluable for research based on a very rigid design, such as experimentation, evaluating the data collection system through pre-tests can be useful for any type of design.

Questionnaires can be 'pre-tested' on a small sample population, mainly to check that the wording of the questions is not ambiguous. Experimental stimuli can be similarly tested, and designs based on multiple case studies can include a preliminary stage, in which a pilot case study is carried out. This is often chosen by the researcher on the basis of favorable access conditions, and will be used to assess both the proposed data collection procedures and the type of data needed to address the research question. For a single case study, the data collection system can be pre-tested at the beginning of the collection phase. For example, researchers may try to evaluate their influence on the phenomenon under study, or test different ways of carrying out interviews.

The impact of pre-tests or pilot cases on a research project varies according to what the researcher is trying to test and the problems that are revealed. In many cases, this evaluation of the data collection system leads to reformulating or modifying the questionnaire or interview guide, without having any effect on the design. However, pre-tests and pilot cases can also reveal more fundamental problems, likely to lead to a stage of 'reconceptualization': new hypotheses may be defined, which will then need to be tested, or the research question itself might need to be modified. Pre-testing can even lead researchers to alter their research approach completely. A case study might be substituted for a survey if the pre-test revealed complex processes that could not be captured through a questionnaire.

2.2 Difficulties encountered during data collection

Interviewing, observing actors within an organization, or collecting documents are relatively flexible data collection methods. For example, a researcher can easily modify the course of an interview to explore a new topic raised by the respondent. If necessary, it is often possible to return to a respondent for additional information. Similarly, the method used to sort information is likely to undergo modifications during the collection process. But while collecting qualitative data is more flexible than collecting quantitative data, access to the field may be more difficult. Unexpected events during data collection can have an effect on the site chosen for the investigation – perhaps even completely calling it into question. A change in management, a modification in organizational structures, a transfer of personnel, a merger or an acquisition, or a change in shareholder structure are all likely to modify the context under study. The disturbances these events can cause may make access conditions more difficult. Respondents' availability might decrease, and key respondents might even leave the organization. In some cases, the field may become irrelevant because of such changes, especially when it had been selected according to very precise criteria that have since disappeared.

Researchers can also find their access denied following a change in a key informant or an alteration in the management team. For example, the new managers might consider the study (approved by the previous team) inopportune. While such a case is fortunately rare, many other obstacles are likely to slow down a research project, or create specific problems of validity and reliability. Research requiring a historical approach can come up against difficulties in gathering enough data, perhaps due to the loss of documents or the destruction of archival data.

Problems of confidentiality can also arise, both outside and within the organization being studied (Ryan et al., 1991). For example, as the design evolves, the researcher may unexpectedly need to access a different department of the company. This access could be refused for reasons of confidentiality. The researcher may obtain information that would prove embarrassing for certain participants if revealed. The planned data validation procedure might then have to be modified. For example, the researcher may have planned to provide all interviewees with a summary of the information collected from each other interviewee. Such a procedure of data validation will have to be abandoned if problems of confidentiality arise.

Difficulties arise during data collection with less flexible research approaches too, using questionnaires or experiments – even if all precautions have been taken during the pre-test stage. Samples may be too small if the response rate is lower than expected or the database ill adapted. Measurement problems may not be detected during the pre-test phase, for example, because of a bias in the sample used for the pre-test. Indeed, pre-tests are sometimes carried out on a convenient sample whose elements are chosen because of their accessibility. Consequently, they can be somewhat removed from the characteristics of the population as a whole.

Selltiz et al. (1976) suggest several solutions to solve field problems. However, before deciding to modify the design, the researcher should evaluate the potential impact of the problems. If the research cannot be carried out under the 'ideal' conditions that had been defined initially, the difference between the ideal and the real conditions do not necessarily question the research validity. One solution is to carry out only minor modifications to the design, if any, and to specify the limits of the research. When problems are more significant, some parts of the research must be redone. This can be expensive, including in psychological terms, since the researcher has to abandon part of the work. One possibility is to find a new field in which to carry out the research. Another solution involves modifying the research design. One question can be investigated through different research approaches. For example, faced with difficulties of access to the field, research on behavior, initially based on observing actors in their organizational environment, could sometimes be reoriented towards an experimental design.

Problems encountered during data collection are not necessarily insurmountable. The research design can often be adapted, without abandoning the initial subject, even if in some cases an entirely new design has to be formulated.

2.3 Difficulties encountered during data analysis

Whatever approach is adopted, obstacles can appear during the analysis phase. These obstacles will often ultimately enrich the initial design as new elements – new data collection processes or new analyses – are included, to increase the reliability of the results or improve their interpretation.

Analysis and interpretation difficulties are frequent with qualitative research approaches. These may lead researchers to return to the field, using, for example, different data collection methods to supplement information they already have. Such new data might be analysed in the same way as the previously collected data, or it might be processed apart from the previous data. If an ethnographic approach is used, for example, a questionnaire could complement data collected by observation.

A researcher may find it impossible to formulate satisfactory conclusions from the analysed data. In a hypotheses-testing approach, survey or databases results may lack of significance, especially when the sample is too small. In this case, the conclusions will be unclear. If sample size cannot be increased, one solution is to apply another data analysis method to replace or complement those already carried out. In a hypothetico-deductive approach, the data collected may lead to rejecting the majority of, or even all, the hypotheses tested. This result constitutes in itself a contribution to the research. However, the contribution will be improved if this leads the researcher to propose a new theoretical framework (Daft, 1995). Comparing research results with existing literature, in particular in other domains, can help researchers to formulate new hypotheses and adapt the conceptual framework they use. These new proposals, which have enriched the research, may be tested later by other researchers. A qualitative approach can also produce new hypotheses. For example, research initially centered on testing hypotheses that have been deduced from existing models could be supplemented by an in-depth case study.

Obstacles confronted during the analysis stage can often result in modifying the initial research design. While this generally consists of adjusting or adding to the design, sometimes it will have to be abandoned entirely. This is the case, for example, when an ethnographic approach is replaced by an experimentation.

3. General Design Process

While an initial design can hopefully pinpoint uncertain areas, in order to avoid the emergence of problems in later stages of the research, this does not guarantee that difficulties will not arise requiring either adjustments or even more significant modifications to the design. Yet design evolution is not necessarily due to difficulties occurring during the course of research. As we saw at the beginning of this third section, this evolution can be the result of iterations and flexibility inherent to the approach. It can also be the result of opportunities arising at various stages of the research. Collected data, a first data analysis, a comment from a colleague, a new reading or an opportunity to access a new field are all means of bringing forward new ideas, hypotheses or explanatory or comprehensive models. These may lead researchers to reconsider the analysis framework, to modify the research question or even to give up the initial approach in favor of a new one that they now consider more relevant.

Constructing the final research design is an evolutionary process. It generally includes an amount of looping back and repeating stages, both when putting together the initial design and later on in the research (see Figure 6.3).

The actual construction of a research design is thus a complex, evolving, uncertain process. A sufficient level of residual uncertainty in a research design determines its interest and quality (Daft, 1983). This is why, according to Daft, research is based more on expertise than knowledge. This skill is acquired through a learning process, based on experience and frequenting the field. Research quality depends largely on how well prepared the researcher is. Researchers, in order to succeed, must possess certain qualities and dispositions: wisdom and expertise during data collection; perseverance and meticulousness in the analysis phase; along with a solid theoretical training and a taste for uncertainty (Morse, 1994; Daft, 1983; 1995).

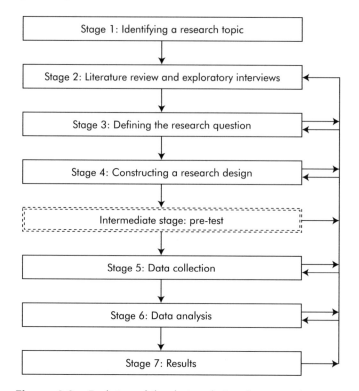

Figure 6.3   *Evolution of the design during the research process*

CONCLUSION

A research design can undergo significant modification according to difficulties encountered or opportunities seized in the course of the research. Nevertheless, though the design may change or even be completely reformulated along the way, the initial design stage is no less necessary. Even though an initial design does not guarantee the final result, the absence of a design increases the risk of encountering problems that may be difficult to solve in subsequent stages of the research.

The process of putting together a research design, even a provisional one, provides other advantages as well. It generally compels researchers to clarify their ideas. It often leads a researcher to refine the research question. By translating the research in terms of definite actions, the initial design makes it easier for researchers to set about the work they are considering. This overall vision of the course of the project can also reduce the anxiety researchers may experience at the beginning of their work (Morse, 1994).

Formalizing the initial design in a tangible document such as a research proposal also provides a communication tool likely to facilitate exchanges with other researchers. It can make it easier for others to evaluate the approach, with the result that peers can provide better-substantiated opinions on the research proposal and give more relevant advice than they might in the absence of a formalized design. In the later stages, this initial design guides the research process. Through it, researchers can avoid trying to do too much at once, which can be costly, particularly in terms of time.

NOTE

1 The term 'research design' is also used by some writers to refer to sequences of stimuli and observations during an experimentation process. In this chapter, however, the term refers to the research design in its entirety.

FURTHER READING

Cook, T.D. and Campbell, D.T., *Quasi-Experimentation: Design and Analysis Issues for Field Settings*, Skokie, IL: Rand Mc Nally, 1979.

Denzin, N. and Lincoln, Y.S. (eds), *Handbook of Qualitative Research*, Thousand Oaks, CA: Sage, 1994.

Glaser, B.G. and Strauss, A.L., *The Discovery of Grounded Theory: Strategy for Qualitative Research*, New York: Adline De Gruyter, 1967.

Jorgensen, D.L., *Participant Observation: A Methodology for Human Studies*, Newbury Park, CA: Sage, 1989.

Miller, D.C., *Handbook of Research Design and Social Measurement*, Newbury Park, CA: Sage, 5th edn, 1991.

Yin, R.K., *Case Study Research: Design and Methods*, Applied Social Research Methods Series, 5, Newbury Park, CA: Sage, 1990.

7

LINKING CONCEPTS AND DATA

Jacques Angot and Patricia Milano

Outline

Establishing a connection between concepts and data is one of the most important and most difficult steps of the research process. This chapter explains this process as a translation procedure incorporating two processes: measurement and abstraction. Measurement consists of deciding upon instruments and indicators to use to translate a concept into data – which some authors refer to as the operationalization or instrumentation of a concept – whereas abstraction involves the translation, through coding and classification, of data into concepts. This chapter aims to help the researcher to develop his or her own translation processes. It demonstrates in what way existing measurements can be used, or improved upon, when researchers want to link existing concepts to the data they have collected, and explains the principles through which data can be assembled or reassembled to establish correspondences with concepts when researchers attempt to realize the translation in reverse.

Two essential modus operandi can be distinguished in management research. Researchers tend to either compare theory to an observed reality, or they try to elicit theoretical elements from reality. In practice this means that, once a research problem has been defined and the researcher has chosen the type of research to undertake, he or she is faced with two possibilities: either to study the literature and extract concepts from it, or to explore reality through fieldwork. The researcher thus assembles either a group of concepts or a body of data. The accumulation of concepts then leads to speculation on the type of data to collect to study these concepts in action, while the accumulation of data leads the researcher to attempt to reveal the concepts underlying this data. Whatever the situation, researchers try to establish links between concepts and data, employing two translation processes to do so: measurement and abstraction.

Measurement involves the 'translation' of concepts into data, and abstraction the 'translation' of data into concepts (it should be noted that, in this chapter, measurement carries the same significance as the traditional concepts of operationalization or instrumentation). Researchers rely on measurement tools and abstraction processes to carry out these translations. Either existing measurements or measurements created by the researcher may be used when translating concepts into data. In translating data into concepts, researchers employ various methods to put together the data they have collected.

SECTION 1　THE TRANSLATION PROCESS

In this section we introduce and outline the principle elements that characterize the translation process.

1. Concepts and Data

1.1 The theoretical realm

The theoretical realm encompasses all the knowledge, concepts, models and theories available, or in the process of being constructed, in the literature on a subject. With respect to translation, however, researchers are primarily concerned with concepts – or to be more precise, with their particular definition of each concept studied. For example, Venkatraman and Grant (1986) found that the concept of strategy is defined in numerous different ways in management research. Rather than being a question of one term referring to multiple concepts, it is more a case of a number of different perspectives being grouped together under one label. Zaltman et al. (1973) also make a valuable distinction between a concept and the terms used to designate it. Consequently, although reading through the literature is the starting point of the research design process, conceptual definitions adopted by the researcher will always condition the translation process he or she employs. For this reason, throughout this chapter the term 'concept' should be understood as synonymous with 'conceptual definition'.

1.2 The empirical realm

The empirical realm encompasses all the data that can be either collected or made use of on the field. This data may include facts (a meeting, the date of an event), opinions, attitudes, observations (of reactions or behaviors) or documents (files, reports). When embarking upon a work of research in management, researchers delimit, by their interest and their attention, an area of study within this empirical realm. This area can relate to a branch of industry, to a population of organizations or a single company, or to particular groups of actors. Moreover, the fieldworker's presence may demarcate this area of study in time; thus it may comprise the lifespan of the studied phenomenon – for example, a project, a structural reform or a change of leadership. Mintzberg (1973), in his study of the role of the manager, defined an area within an empirical realm delimited in space (managers and their activities) and in time (daily life).

When researchers base themselves in the empirical realm, they have a circumscribed body – or a 'closed set' (De Groot, 1969) – of data (facts, opinions, attitudes, observations and documents) at their disposal. Although this data often approximates conceptual items, empirical elements are never able to represent completely, nor to duplicate, the significance of the underlying theoretical concepts (Zeller and Carmines, 1980).

2. Moving from One Realm to the Other

Whichever realm (theoretical or empirical) they are working in, researchers have particular elements at their disposal (concepts or data). To move from one realm to the other, these elements have to be construed in the language of the second realm (Zeller and Carmines, 1980). To go from the theoretical to the empirical involves translating a conceptual definition in order to pinpoint elements of the empirical realm that most closely illustrate it. When, on the other hand, a researcher wants to link empirical elements to the theoretical realm, data collected in the field has to be translated into the concepts that underlie it.

As the following example illustrates, a conceptual definition has no objective correspondence in the empirical realm. That is to say, for any given concept – any given conceptual definition – there is no empirical data that corresponds exclusively to it. Similarly, researchers who wish to move from the empirical to the theoretical work from elements (data) that may be understood to be the manifestation of any of a number of potential concepts.

Example: Non-exclusive correspondence

A researcher may choose to consider the concept of high velocity environments either through the annual rate of innovation within a sector, or through the rate of the renewal of skills within companies operating in this sector. However, the empirical element 'rate of the renewal of skills within companies' could also be used to consider the concept of resources when looking at the correlation between a company's resources and its performance.

As Figure 7.1 illustrates, the translation process consists essentially of connecting a concept to one or more empirical elements (when the researcher has been operating in the theoretical realm) or of connecting one or more empirical elements to a concept (when the researcher has been operating in the empirical realm).

The theoretical and the empirical realms offer the researcher resources of quite different natures (conceptual definitions on the one hand, empirical elements on the other). As we will see, the translation process involves two distinct processes, and the form it takes is closely related to the realm in which the researcher first starts to think about a problem. We call the passage from the theoretical to the empirical 'measurement', and the opposite process, which takes us from the empirical towards the theoretical, 'abstraction'.

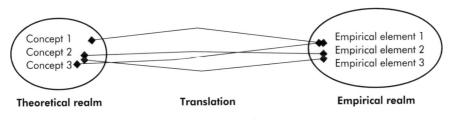

Figure 7.1   *The translation process*

2.1 Measurement

Several definitions of 'measurement' have been proposed by writers in the social sciences. The definition we will use here, is that of DiRenzo (1966), to whom measurement 'refers to the procedures by which empirical observations are made in order … to represent the conceptualizations that are to be explained'. According to Larzarsfeld (1967), however, measurement must be considered in a broader sense in the social sciences than in fields such as physics or biology. A researcher in the social sciences may take measurements that are not necessarily expressed in numbers, in which case the measurement process comprises three, or perhaps four, principal stages. These stages are outlined below.

Stages of the Measurement Process

Lazarsfeld (1967) proposes that there are three stages in the measurement of concepts in the social sciences.

In the first stage the researcher, immersed in the analysis of a theoretical problem, outlines an abstract construction which, little-by-little, takes shape and evolves into an imaged representation that we call a concept.

The second stage consists in ascertaining the components of this concept in order to be able to measure it. These components are called facets or dimensions (or 'definiens' – Zaltman et al., 1973).

In the third stage of the measurement process, the researcher defines the type of data to be collected for each dimension that has been established. To do this, researchers may rely on indicators – empirical elements whose connection to the concept is defined in terms of probability (Lazarsfeld, 1967). A concept studied in a given situation entails the probable manifestation of certain behaviors, the probable appearance of certain facts, and the probable formulation of certain judgements or opinions. Through an indicator, a value or a symbol can be associated to a facet of a concept, either directly or indirectly. An indicator then constitutes a measurement instrument.

We can also add a supplementary stage in the measurement of a concept: the definition of indicators. These are a combination or a synthesis of several indicators, and can, as the following example shows, be used to express a particular dimension of a given concept.

Let us take the example of a study looking at the evolution of organizations (see Figure 7.2). The researcher broaches the study by highlighting the concept of strategic effectiveness (Stage 1). He or she then determines two dimensions of the concept: commercial performance and financial performance (Stage 2). To apprehend the dimension of commercial performance the researcher draws on indicators, such as the turnover and the profits of the organizations he or she is studying (Stage 3). The researcher also builds an index synthesizing the concept of commercial performance, expressed by the ratio of profits to turnover (Stage 4).

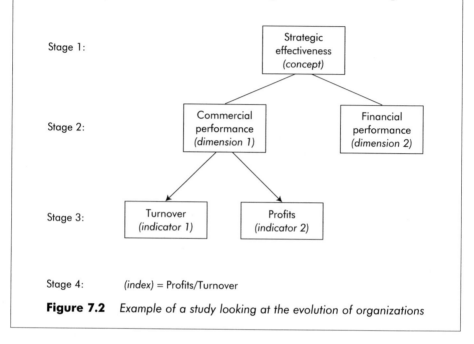

Figure 7.2   *Example of a study looking at the evolution of organizations*

2.2 Abstraction

In the above example we considered a situation in which the researcher moved from the theoretical to the empirical realm. However, research work in management can also begin in the empirical realm, in which case the translation process is no longer a question of taking a measurement, but instead requires the researcher to operate an abstraction. The researcher accumulates a body of data, which he or she then tries to reassemble within a broader framework from which an underlying conceptualization may be established.

For this translation – or abstraction – process, the researcher carries out progressive regroupings of the empirical data collected, so as to draw out more conceptual elements from the facts, observations and documents at hand. The researcher codes the data, formulates indicators (Lazarsfeld, 1967), establishes categories, discovers their properties and, finally, attempts to propose a conceptual definition. As we shall see, abstraction may serve either a descriptive or a theoretical purpose.

Abstraction: Descriptive or Theoretical?

Schatzman and Strauss (1973) identify two distinct methods of abstraction in research projects based on empirical elements: description and theorization. In descriptive work, researchers simply aim at classifying their data into categories. They may draw on the theoretical realm initially, to identify the categories commonly used in the literature, and can establish matrices in which elementary codes, defined with respect to the type of phenomenon being studied, can be cross-collated. The researcher may then opt for a more analytical description, in which case the data collected on the field will itself guide the abstraction process. Through trial and error, the data is analyzed to identify categories and the connections that exist between them. This process can give rise to a number of possible descriptive frameworks.

Abstraction may also be seen from the perspective of theoretical construction, or theorization. In this case the data is initially organized according to the representation of reality on which the researcher has based his or her investigation. The abstraction process then entails grouping similar data together and ascribing conceptual labels to these groups (Strauss and Corbin, 1990). From the initial representation of the studied phenomenon, by identifying concepts and qualifying the relationships that exist between them (cause or effect) a theoretical logic can progressively emerge. This theoretical logic will help the researcher to construct a generalized meaning and, in so doing, to confer an interpretation on the data.

We have seen that the researcher can operate in either the theoretical or the empirical realm. We have also seen that the translation process entails questioning how we can move from one realm into the other. More precisely, it involves translating the elements researchers have at their disposal initially, into the language of the realm to which they wish to go. In the case of measurement, the translation process consists of establishing indicators that correspond to a given concept. In the case of abstraction, the translation process entails deciding how the data that has been gathered is to be categorized.

3. Translation Methods

Several resources are available to the researcher when establishing connections between concepts and data. We will look first at measuring instruments, and then we will consider abstraction processes.

3.1 Measurement instruments

Understanding the nature of indicators   The object of measurement is to establish indicators that correspond to a given concept. These indicators make it possible to associate a value or a symbol with part of the concept, which is why we refer to them as measurement instruments. Either a single indicator alone or a group of indicators can constitute a measurement instrument. Boyd (1990) uses a number of indicators to measure the complexity of an environment, including geographical concentration, the number of firms in the industry and the distribution of market shares. At the same time, however, he uses a single indicator – the rate of sales growth – to measure the environment's dynamism. Indicators can also help the researcher to determine the type of data to collect. In measuring the technological intensity of intercorporate alliances by the ratio of research and development budget to sales, for example, Osborn and Baughn (1990) were led to compile a precise type of information on the firms they studied – putting together a resister of their average research and development budgets and sales figures.

Measurement instruments can be qualitative or quantitative. In their research into the relationship between strategy-making and environment, Miller and Friesen (1983) used a variable broken down into seven items to represent changes that might occur in a company's external environment. A seven-point Likert scale was associated with each of these items. For example, actors were asked to give the following sentence a rating from 1 to 7 (from complete agreement to total disagreement): 'The tastes and preferences of your customers in your principal industry are becoming more stable and more foreseeable'. The measures used were metric and the indicator quantitative – as they were in Osborn and Baughn's research, where the instrument used to measure the technological intensity of intercorporate alliances was a ratio of numerical data.

Controlling the number of indicators   Several indicators can usually be found for a given concept. This means that a researcher working on environmental dynamism will find various types of indicators used in the literature. In Miller and Friesen (1983), for example, this concept is measured by the actors' perceptions of the amount and the predictability of change occurring within an environment (in areas of consumer tastes, production techniques and ways in which companies competed). Boyd (1990), however, measures the concept of environmental dynamism purely on the rate of sales growth.

Pre-existent correspondences between concepts and indicators are available to researchers in the form of proxies. Used often in research in management, a proxy is an indirect measurement of a concept. Performance, for instance, can be measured by the proxy: 'share prices'. Similarly, the turbulence of a branch of industry can be measured by the proxy: 'number of companies entering and leaving the sector'. There are also instruments for which the number of indicators is preset, as illustrated by the work of Miller and Friesen (1983). When researchers use this type of instrument they are typically led to calculate an index: for example, the average of the ratings given to each of the seven items.

In this way, the researcher – as Lazarsfeld (1967) recommends – can define indicators using measuring instruments other than graded scales. Such indicators are particular combinations of indicators that can synthesize a part of a concept. The researcher must take care, however, not to misrepresent or distort the relationship that each of the indicators included have to this concept. For example, a researcher may decide to measure performance by constructing an index expressed by the ratio of turnover to profits. In this case he or she must ensure that variations in the two indicators are reflected by an equally significant variation in the index. The researcher who expects increased performance to be reflected in an increase in turnover and profits, also expects an increase in this index. But where are we then? The increase in the numerator is compensated by that of the denominator: the index remains stable, and the measure becomes inoperative.

3.2 Abstraction methods

If researchers decide to begin their work in the empirical realm, they start out with a body of related empirical data which they then have to interpret. This process entails questioning the level of abstraction to which they wish to subject these empirical elements. They may try to propose a concept or a body of inter-related concepts, or even to establish a model or a theory. The level of abstraction initially envisaged by the researcher has an influence on the level of sophistication of the processes and methods that will be used to carry out this abstraction.

In the abstraction process, researchers are confronted with the problem of coding the empirical elements they have collected. Strauss and Corbin (1990) identify three methods of coding data: open, axial and selective.

Open coding Open coding basically consists of naming and categorizing phenomena by thoroughly examining the data collected in relation to it. By collating this data and classifying it into categories – sets and subsets – the researcher can progressively reduce the number of units that are to be mani-pulated. The researcher then has to try to label these categories. While in some cases existing conceptual definitions can be compared with these new cate-gories and found to be appropriate, it is generally advisable to try to propose original definitions, drawn from fieldwork. Glaser (1978) refers to such defini-tions as 'in vivo'. Once established, these categories should be refined by high-lighting their intrinsic properties and the continuum along which they may fluctuate.

Axial coding A researcher can make the abstraction process more sophisticated by using axial coding. Based on the same principle as open coding, axial cod-ing goes further to specify each category in terms of causality, context, actions and interactions, and their consequences.

Selective coding The principle of selective coding consists in going beyond simple description and towards conceptualization. This involves theoretical integration or construction (Strauss and Corbin, 1990). Selective coding aims at defining a central category, to which the researcher tries to link up all of the properties of the categories that have been established previously. Strongly con-nected to this type of abstraction process is the idea of identifying what Schatzman and Strauss (1973) call a 'key linkage'. This can refer to a metaphor, a model, a general outline or a guiding principle that researchers can use to group their data.

Key linkage serves as a basis for grouping not only data, but also the cate-gories themselves (through similarities in properties and dimensions). After carrying out this abstraction, the researcher obtains central categories that are connected not only on a broad conceptual level, but also to each specific pro-perty of the other categories.

SECTION 2   DESIGNING THE TRANSLATION PROCESS

1. Measurement

Measurement is the process by which we translate from the theoretical realm to the empirical. Once researchers have selected a concept, they have to find a way to measure it – that is, to identify the type of data they need to collect. Drawing on previous works, the researcher begins by looking at how the concept has been interpreted, or translated, in the past. Studying works by other writers can reveal existing translations that may be directly usable, or could be a basis from which certain adjustments need to be made. If these translations appear unsatisfactory, or unsuited to the current study, then the researcher moves to the second stage of the measurement process, that of developing new translations either by improving existing ones or through innovation.

1.1 Drawing on previous works

Once they have located measurements used in previous works, researchers have to choose among them and, if necessary, consider how they can be adapted to the particular context of their own work.

Finding measures   When researchers begin in the theoretical realm, they have access to a body of work with differing levels of relevance to their own field. Published articles, doctorate theses and other works can be used as a basis from which to formulate conceptual definitions or look for available measurements. Table 7.1 illustrates several measurements.

Choosing measurement instruments   To select the measurement instruments most appropriate to their work, researchers need to consider three criteria: 1) reliability, 2) validity and 3) operational feasibility. As reliability and validity are discussed at length in Chapter 10, here we will look only at the third criteria: operational 'feasibility'. Although a number of writers have discussed operational feasibility as a selection criterion (Black and Champion, 1976; De Groot, 1969), it is a quality that is best appreciated by drawing on one's own experience of using a specific measurement.

For example, when considering a scale, operational feasibility is a question of how easy it is to read (the number of items included) and to understand (the vocabulary used). Operational feasibility also relates to the sensitivity of the measurement instruments used, as they need to be able to record subtle variations of the measured concept. The following example illustrates this.

Example: Sensitivity of the measurement instrument

In studying sector-based change in the pharmaceutical industry, a researcher chose to measure the concentration of the sector by calculating the number of companies operating within it. However, she felt that this instrument was not sufficiently

Table 7.1   *Some of the measurements found in management literature*

Sources	Concepts	Dimensions	Indicators
Boyd (1990)	Environment	Dynamism Complexity	Rate of increase in sales over five years Rate of geographic concentration Number of firms in the industry Distribution of market shares
Osborn and Baughn (1990)	Alliance	Intention to form an alliance Technological intensity	Publication of an article announcing the alliance in: – the Asian *Wall Street Journal* – the Japanese *Economic Journal* Average ratio of R and D budget to sales over three years
Miner, Amburgey and Stearns (1990)	Transformation (of daily newspapers)	Area of distribution Contents Format	Number of geographical regions covered Number of changes in the subjects treated Number of pages

sensitive to measure variations in the concept of concentration, as it did not take the size of the companies entering or leaving the sector into account.

Although a company leaving a sector does have an impact on its concentration, the measurement of this variation is identical, whatever the size of the departing company. Yet the size of the companies within the sector can be a significant characteristic of the concept of concentration. The researcher decided to refine the measurement by counting companies according to the following principle: she associated a weighting of almost 1 to large companies, and a weighting closer to 0 for smaller ones.

Even if the measurement instruments used fulfill the requirements of reliability, validity and operational feasibility, researchers may often feel the instruments selected still need to be adapted to suit their particular context.

Making necessary adjustments   The research process entails a targeted approach to the empirical world. Researchers should bear this in mind, whether they are interested in a branch of industry, a type of company, or a given type of actors. By taking this into account, as the following example shows, researchers can contextualize the measuring instruments they use.

Example: Contextualized measurement instruments

In a study that encompassed nearly 100 multinational companies, a researcher looked at the influence of the psycho-sociological characteristics of the members of the board of directors on the success of fusion takeovers. He prepared a questionnaire to measure localization of control, interpersonnel confidence and the social anxiety of board members. Only those companies that had bought out others (and not companies which had been bought out themselves) were included in the study, which concentrated on four branches of industry: pharmaceutical, banking, and the insurance and communication sectors.

> The researcher chose to address his questionnaire to every board member from each of the companies in his sample. This obliged him to re-examine the formulation of certain questions so that they were better adapted to the respondents' areas of expertise (commercial, financial, accounts, legal). In this particular research project, however, an additional adjustment was necessary. As the work concerned multinational corporations, the researcher had to translate his measurement instruments, originally conceived in American English, into German, French and Japanese.

Adapting measurement instruments found in published literature to make them more applicable to a new research project can often entail additional work on the part of the researcher.

Adapting a Scale from one Language to Another

Researchers working in French, for example, might find a scale used in an American study that could be applicable to their current project. But before they could use this measurement instrument, they would have to take a certain number of precautions. A bilingual professional would first have to be called upon to translate the scale in question into French. Once translated, the scale should be retranslated back into English by another bilingual professional. By comparing the final, twice-translated, version with the original scale, the researchers can ensure that the French scale conforms to the original American one. The researchers should then ask the linguistic experts to point out any possible comprehension difficulties that could arise in using the French scale. Finally, the reliability and validity of the scale has to be established anew.

1.2 Ameliorate or innovate?

When the literature does not furnish satisfactory measurement instruments to measure a given concept, researchers are faced with two possibilities. They can either make significant modifications to available measurement instruments, adapting them to their requirements, or, if none are available at all, they can innovate by constructing their own measurements.

For example, in measuring the concept of performance, a researcher might innovate by using the monthly rate of change in share market prices. This could seem more suitable to his or her needs than another, existing, measurement using the ratio of profit to turnover. If a researcher wishes to use a given scale to measure theoretical items, the scale may be improved by removing, adding or substituting certain items.

It is important to stress that improving or creating measurement instruments is a quasi-integral part of the translation process. Of course, whatever the degree of innovation introduced by the researcher, the measurement instruments constructed must always answer to the requirements of reliability, validity and operational 'feasibility'. The degree to which these requirements are satisfied determines the limits of the research, and the scope of its results.

2. Abstraction

Unlike the translation process, which is based on the construction of a measurement, either drawing on existing measurements or adapting them to suit their needs, the abstraction process follows an opposite course. Through abstraction, researchers attempt to establish correspondences, which may be formalized to varying degrees, between the data they have accumulated (behavioral observations, figures, etc.) and underlying concepts – they have to identify the concepts hidden behind their data. In the abstraction process, researchers do not so much aim at processing their data in any definitive way, but at understanding it as accurately as possible.

2.1 Grouping and classifying data

The abstraction process consists of discovering classes of facts, people and events, along with the properties that characterize them. The data a researcher has access to depends essentially on his or her initial field of investigation, which can be used to identify 'key linkages' (Schatzman and Strauss, 1973). Key linkages provide researchers with an order of priorities (or attribution rules) when classifying their data.

A number of different principles of data classification have been proposed (Glaser and Strauss, 1967; Lazarsfeld, 1967; Miles and Huberman, 1984a; Schatzman and Strauss, 1973; Strauss and Corbin, 1990). Classes can be established through comparison, using the principle of similarities between phenomena. Such classes are generally referred to as thematic. For example, in studying the daily activities of an operational unit, a researcher may collect a variety of empirical data – such as notes, memos and exchanges – in which he or she finds words, sentences or parts of text of the type: 'do not forget to write a daily report of your activities', 'we remind you that latecomers will be penalized', and 'please respect the pricing policy'. The researcher can group these elements together by creating a thematic class 'reminders of operational rules'.

Researchers can also establish categories according to a chronological principle – respecting the chronological order of the data. Events that occur simultaneously may, for instance, be differentiated from those that occur sequentially. In the study that looked at the activities of a production plant, the researcher could have ordered his or her data according to the idea of action–reaction chains. This involves classifying events by the order they happen: 1) the decision is made to increase productivity; 2) the rate of absenteeism increases. Similarly, the researcher could classify data according to the idea of simultaneous occurrence (the reaction of the workers and the reaction of the supervisors following the directive to increase production).

Categories may also be determined by structural level of complexity. Data is then collated by distinguishing among the different levels of analysis to which they refer. For example, an actor could be classified according to the department in which he or she works, the company in which he or she is employed or the sector the company is in. Another classification possibility relies on more general conceptual ideas, ordering data according to its degree of abstraction. The idea that 'productivity is closely related to employee satisfaction' can be classified as an individual belief or as a more abstract phenomenon, such as a collective representation.

Data can also be grouped by considering all possible combinations in terms of categories. This can be facilitated by using appropriate indicators, as the following example, taken from Glaser and Strauss (1967: 211), demonstrates.

Example: Using indicators to construct theory from quantitative data

Glaser and Strauss (1967) developed an example of constructing theoretical elements from quantitative data, by studying the role of professional recognition on scientists' motivation. The underlying idea in their study was that recognition is induced by motivation, and that motivation leads to greater recognition.

After collating the information they collected, in order to better understand the relationships between them, Glaser and Straus then sorted the data by creating groups of individuals, based on precise characteristics. They formulated indicators to differentiate the various groups – their initial research outline leading them to construct indicators related to the concepts of recognition and motivation. By combining the modalities they had used to measure the concepts of recognition and motivation, namely high levels and low levels, Glaser and Strauss obtained the following indicators: 'high motivation/low recognition', 'high motivation/ high recognition', 'low motivation/low recognition' and 'low motivation/high recognition'.

These indicators enabled them to differentiate between, and to compare, groups of individuals. More precisely, the authors compared the relative frequency of these various groups to that of a group for which they distinguished only the level of motivation. They found that when motivation was very high there was a difference in the frequency of groups with low recognition and those with high recognition. The comparison allowed them to demonstrate that the effect of recognition is modified by the group's level of motivation.

This example shows how indicators can be used in the abstraction process. By associating level of performance, level of motivation, and level of recognition, effective conceptual tools were developed. The index 'high performance/high motivation' could therefore be referred to as the 'recursive impact of effort' – as suggested by literature in human resource management.

Communicating with other researchers can be useful when applying categorization methods. Talking about their work can help researchers present their research more clearly, and to understand their data in a different light than they might through simply writing about it. This effort clearly tends to objectify the data and any interconnections that naturally appear. As Schatzman and Strauss (1973) put it, an audience serves as a 'conceptual lever'.

The usefulness of these different methods of categorization – as to both the accuracy of the categories and their relevance to the data from which they were created – is appreciated essentially through trial and error (Strauss and Corbin, 1990). To ensure the precision of the abstraction process they employ, or to supplement this process, researchers can draw on formal classification methods (see Chapter 12).

2.2 The researcher as a component of the abstraction

Finally, the researcher too can be considered as an instrument. This concept is closely associated with ethnographic approaches. As Sanday maintains, 'field-workers learn to use themselves as the principal and most reliable instrument of observation, selection, coordination, and interpretation' (1979: 527). The translation process is therefore influenced by qualities inherent to the researcher. However, little is known about the nature of this influence. In his book *Works and Lives*, Geertz (1988), points out that ethnographic work takes on a particular dimension from even the style the researcher uses when transcribing his or her results. The title of his work evokes the ambiguity of the researcher-instrument. There are two realities: that which is studied (there) and that which is reconstructed (here). In studying the style employed by ethnographic researchers, Geertz focuses on transcriptions of research works that do not appear to be objective. This 'deviance' is, however, involuntary – it is inherent in the style of writing. In the effort of conceptualization, ethnographers almost unconsciously try to mask or to promote their own behaviors or attitudes. This can lead to abstractions that have followed somewhat inaccurate guidelines.

Ethnographic work often involves significant immersion of the researcher-instrument in the empirical realm. This immersion is punctuated by periods of intense pleasure and joy, but also by other feelings and more somber emotional states. The natural growth and change that occurs to researchers while carrying out their research modifies the instrument that they themselves represent. This is manifested most particularly in the actors' perception of the researcher. A change in researchers' behavior can modify the answers they are given or the behavior they observe thereafter. As Barley (1990) noted, researchers are often afraid to make a faux pas, and this fear can lead them to becoming self-conscious – preoccupied with the image they project. This can eventually even divert them from their research object. Drawing on his own experience, Barley explained how, while carrying out research on hospitals, he tried to avoid any discussions that might touch on strongly emotional subjects, accentuating or adapting his behavior at times, and controlling himself from expressing his true beliefs and opinions on sensitive subjects: 'even though I could not bring myself to laugh at racist or sexist jokes, I also did not confront their tellers', (1990: 238). Such inhibition cannot be systematic, though, and researchers can help themselves in this respect by taking regular notes on their current emotional states, so that they can 'contextualize' their observations when they read them back at a later date.

CONCLUSION

To link concepts and data researchers have to translate the theoretical or empirical elements they have compiled. We have seen that this involves two processes, and that they each rely on particular principles. For a given concept, measurement enables us to determine indicators or measurement instruments that are needed to apprehend it. On the other hand, abstraction enables us to develop concepts from a body of data, by applying coding and classification methods.

Researchers can employ multiple measurement and/or abstraction processes in the course of their work. They often find they are confronted with a number of concepts, and so with a number of sets of measurement instruments. Similarly, they may acquire diverse sets of data, which can lead them to employ different methods of abstraction.

Having recourse to multiple instruments and abstraction methods poses the problem of the coherence of the translation. In the case of abstraction, researchers should ensure they remain within the one investigative area. In the case of measurement, the use of a number of reliable and valid instruments in conjunction does not necessarily ensure the overall validity of the research. In both cases, the researcher should judge whether the measurements or abstractions employed are coherent with each other, and should make sure that criteria of the reliability and general validity of the research as a whole are satisfied.

FURTHER READING

Black, J. and Champion, D., *Methods and Issues in Social Research*, New York: Wiley, 1976.

Glaser, B. and Strauss, A.L., *The Discovery of Grounded Theory: Strategies for Qualitative Research*, New York: Adline De Gruyter, 1967.

Lazarsfeld, P., *Des concepts aux indices empiriques*, in R. Boudon and P. Lazarsfeld (eds), *Le vocabulaire des sciences sociales*, Paris: Mouton, 1967.

Miles, M. and Huberman, A.M., *Qualitative Data Analysis*, London: Sage, 1984.

Strauss, A.L. and Corbin, J., *Basics of Qualitative Research: Grounded Theory Procedures and Techniques*, Newbury Park, CA: Sage, 1990a.

Zaltman, G., Pinson, C. and Angelmar, R., *Metatheory and Consumer Research*, New York: Holt, Rinehart and Winston, 1973.

Zeller, R. and Carmines, E., *Measurement in the Social Sciences: The Link Between Theory and Data*, Cambridge: Cambridge University Press, 1980.

8

SAMPLING

Isabelle Royer and Philippe Zarlowski

Outline

In this chapter we look at how researchers establish samples – from samples comprised of a large number of elements to those made up of only one element (as in a single-case study). We consider both samples intended for quantitative and qualitative processing.

The chapter presents the range of options open to the researcher when putting together a sample, and guides the researcher's choice by identifying the main criteria to be taken into account. We describe the principal sampling methods, along with aspects that could affect the validity of their results, and explain the factors that should be considered when deciding what sample size is required. The final section of the chapter proposes a number of possible sample selection processes.

Most statistics handbooks define a sample as a subset of elements drawn from a larger unit called a population. In this chapter, however, we use the term 'sample' in a broader sense. A sample is defined as the set of elements from which data is collected. We thus are interested in all types of samples; whatever their size, their nature, the method of selection used and the aims of the study – from the sample comprising only one element, selected by judgement and intended for qualitative processing, to large-scale random sampling aimed at testing hypotheses using advanced statistical techniques. The chapter presents the range of options open to the researcher when drawing a sample, and guides the researcher's choice by indicating the main criteria to be taken into account.

Choices made when drawing a sample will have a determining impact on the external validity as much as the internal validity of the study. External validity refers to the possibility of extrapolating the results obtained from a sample to other elements, under different conditions of time and place. Internal validity consists in ensuring the relevance and internal coherence of the results in line with the researcher's stated objectives. The validity of a study can be linked to three characteristics of the sample: the nature (heterogeneous or homogeneous) of the elements it is composed of; the method used to select these elements; and the number of elements selected.

Various methods can be used to establish a sample. These differ essentially in the way elements are selected and the size of the sample. Choices made concerning these two questions have implications in terms of both possible biases and the potential to generalize from the results. It therefore seems essential to be familiar with the various ways sample elements can be selected, and the criteria to consider when determining sample size, before deciding upon a sampling method.

SECTION 1   SELECTING SAMPLE ELEMENTS

1. Sampling Methods

External validity can be achieved by employing one of two types of inference: statistical or theoretical. Statistical inference uses mathematical properties to generalize from results obtained from a sample to the population from which it was taken. Theoretical inference (or analytical generalization) is another form of generalization, but one that is not based on mathematical statistics. Rather than aiming to generalize from statistical results to a population, theoretical inference aims to generalize across populations on the basis of logical reasoning.

The different sample selection methods can be grouped into four categories (see Figure 8.1). These categories do not employ the same modes of inference. The first category is made up of probability sampling methods, in which each element of a population has a known probability, not equal to zero, of being selected into the sample. These are the only methods that allow the use of statistical inference.

Unlike probability sampling, in which researcher subjectivity is to be eliminated as far as possible, the second category is composed of methods based on personal judgement. Elements are selected according to precise criteria, established by the researcher. The results obtained from a judgement sample lend themselves to an analytical type of generalization.

The third category corresponds to the quota method. Not being a probability sampling method, quota sampling does not, strictly speaking, allow for statistical inference, however, in certain conditions which will be described later, quota sampling can be similar to probability sampling, and statistical inference can then be applied.

Convenience sampling methods make up the fourth group. This term designates samples selected strictly in terms of the opportunities available to the researcher, without applying any particular criteria of choice. This selection method does not allow for statistical inference. Nor does it guarantee the possibility of theoretical inference, although an *ex post* analysis of the composition of the sample may sometimes allow it. For this reason, convenience sampling is generally used in exploratory phases only, the purpose being to prepare for the

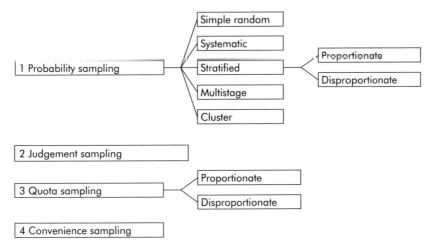

Figure 8.1 *Methods used to select a sample*

next step, rather than to draw conclusions. In this context a convenience sample can be sufficient, and it does present the advantage of facilitating and accelerating the process of data collection.

The choice of methods is often restricted by economic reasons and reasons of feasibility. Nonetheless, the final decision in favor of a particular method must always be based on the objectives of the study.

1.1 Probability sampling

Probability sampling involves selecting elements randomly – following a random procedure. This means that the selection of any one element is independent of the selection of the other elements. When trying to estimate the value of a certain parameter or indicator, probability samples allow researchers to calculate how precise their estimations are. This possibility is one advantage of probability sampling over other selection methods.

Two elements distinguish among different types of probability sampling methods:

- The characteristics of the sampling frame: whether the population is comprehensive or not and whether the frame includes specific information for each population element.
- The degree of precision of the results for a given sample size.

Simple random sampling   Simple random sampling is the most basic selection method. Each element of the population has the same probability of being selected into the sample – this is referred to as equal probability selection. The elements of the sampling frame are numbered serially from 1 to N, and a table of random numbers is used to select them.

The main disadvantage of simple random sampling is that a comprehensive, numbered list of the population is required. This method also tends to select geographically diverse elements, which can make data collection extremely costly.

Systematic sampling   Systematic sampling is closely related to simple random sampling. Its main advantage is that it does not require a numbered list of the population elements. A systematic selection process selects the first element randomly from the sampling frame, then selects the following elements at constant intervals. The selection interval is inversely proportional to the sampling ratio of sample size n divided by population size N. For example, if the sampling ratio is $1/100$, one element will be selected in the list every 100 elements. Nevertheless, it is important to ensure that the selection interval does not correspond to an external reality that could bias the outcome. For example, if the sampling frame supplies monthly data in chronological order and the selection interval is a multiple of 12, all the data collected will refer to the same month of the year.

In practice, this procedure is not always followed strictly. Instead of setting a selection interval in terms of the number of elements, a simple rule is often established to approach this interval. For example, if the sampling frame is a professional directory, and the selection interval corresponds to approximately three pages in the directory, an element will be selected every three pages: the fifth element on the page – for instance – if the first, randomly selected, element was in that position.

Stratified sampling   In stratified sampling, the population is initially segmented on the basis of one or more pre-established criteria. The method is based on the hypothesis that there is a correlation between the phenomenon under observation and the criteria chosen for segmenting the population. The aim is to create strata that are as homogenous as possible in terms of the variable in question. The precision of the estimates is greatest when the elements are homogenous within each stratum and heterogeneous from one stratum to the other. Consequently, in order to choose useful segmentation criteria the researcher must have a reasonably good prior knowledge of both the population and the phenomenon under study. This can be achieved by, for example, examining the results of earlier research.

Sample elements will then be selected randomly within each stratum, according to the sampling ratio, which may or may not be proportional to the relative number of elements in each stratum. When sample size is identical, using a higher sampling ratio for strata with higher variance – to the detriment of the more homogenous strata – will reduce the standard deviation for the whole sample, thereby making the results more precise. A higher sampling ratio might also be used for a subset of the population that requires closer study.

Multistage sampling   Multistage sampling makes repeated selections at different levels. The first stage corresponds to the selection of elements called primary units. At the second stage, subsets, called secondary units, are randomly selected from within each primary unit, and the procedure is repeated until the final stage. Elements selected at the final stage correspond to the units of analysis. One significant advantage of multistage sampling is that it does not require a list of all of the population elements. Also, when stages are defined using geographical criteria, the proximity of the selected elements will, in comparison with simple random sampling, reduce the costs of data collection. The downside of this method is that the estimates are less precise.

In multistage sampling it is entirely possible to choose primary units according to external criteria – in particular, to reduce data collection costs. This practice does not transgress the rules of sampling. In fact, the only thing that matters is the equal probability selection of the elements in the final stage. The sampling ratio for the subsequent stages should however be lower, to compensate for the initial choice of primary unit.

Cluster sampling   Cluster sampling is a particular type of two-stage sampling. The elements are not selected one by one, but by subsets known as clusters, each element of the population belonging to one and only one cluster. At the first stage, clusters are selected randomly. At the second, all elements of the selected clusters are included in the sample.

This method is not very demanding in terms of the sampling frame: a list of clusters is all that is required. Another important advantage is the reduction in data collection costs if the clusters are defined by a geographic criterion. The downside is that estimates are less precise. The efficiency of cluster sampling depends on the qualities of the clusters: the smaller and more evenly sized they are, and the more heterogeneous in terms of the studied phenomenon, the more efficient the sample will be.

We should make it clear that these different sampling methods are not necessarily mutually exclusive. For instance, depending on the purposes of the study, multistage sampling might be combined with stratified sampling, the primary units being selected at random and the elements of the sample being selected into the primary units by the stratification method. One can also, for example, stratify a population, and then select clusters of elements within each stratum. This type of combination can raise the precision level of the estimations, while at the same time taking practical constraints into account (whether or not a comprehensive sampling frame exists, the available budget, etc.). Table 8.1 presents the advantages and disadvantages of each of these probability sampling methods.

1.2 Judgement sampling

The subjectivity of judgement sampling differentiates it from probability sampling, whose very purpose is to eliminate subjectivity. In management research, judgement samples, whether intended for qualitative or quantitative processing, are much more common than probability samples.

Unlike probability sampling, neither a specific procedure nor a sampling frame is needed to put together a judgement sample – as pre-existing sampling frames for organizational phenomena are rare, this is a definite advantage.

Table 8.1   *Comparing probability sampling methods*

	Precision of estimates	Reduced collection costs	Simplicity of the sampling frame	Ease of processing
Simple random sampling	+	–	–	+
Systematic sampling	+	–	+	+
Stratified sampling	+ +	–	– –	–
Multistage sampling	–	+	+	– –
Cluster sampling	– –	+	+ +	–

Even if it were theoretically possible to create one, the difficulty and the cost involved would often rule it out, although in some cases the snowball technique can provide a solution (Henry, 1990). In addition, probability sampling is not always necessary, as research is often aimed more at establishing or testing a proposition than at generalizing results to a given population. For small samples, judgement sampling gives results that are just as good as those obtained from probability sampling, since the variability of the estimates for a small random sample is so high that it creates a bias equally great or greater than that resulting from subjective judgement (Kalton, 1983). Furthermore, a sensitive research subject or an elaborate data collection system can bring about such elevated refusal rates that probability sampling does not make sense. Judgement sampling also allows sample elements to be selected extremely precisely, making it easier to guarantee respect for criteria such as homogeneity, which is required by certain research designs.

Judgement sampling does follow certain theoretical criteria, and to carry it out properly, the researcher must have a good working knowledge of the population being studied. The most common criterion is how 'typical', or conversely, 'atypical', the element is. Typical elements are those the researcher considers to be particularly 'normal' or 'usual' (Henry, 1990) in the population. A second criteria is the relative similarity or dissimilarity of the elements selected.

For both qualitative and quantitative research, selection criteria are guided by the desire to create either a homogenous or a heterogeneous sample. A homogenous sample will make it easier to highlight relationships and build theories. To put together such a sample, similar elements must be selected and atypical ones excluded. When research presenting strong internal validity has enabled a theory to be established, the results may be able to be generalized to a larger or a different population. In order to do this, dissimilar elements must be selected. For example, to increase the scope of a theory, Glaser and Strauss recommend varying the research field in terms of organizations, regions, and/or nations (Glaser and Strauss, 1967).

In experiments aimed at testing a relationship when it is difficult to select random samples large enough to provide significant external validity, one solution is to use samples composed of deliberately dissimilar elements (Cook and Campbell, 1979). The inference principle is as follows: as heterogeneity exercises a negative influence on the significance of the effect, if the relation appears significant despite this drawback, then the results can be generalized further.

1.3 Quota sampling

Quota sampling is a non-random sampling method that allows us to obtain a relatively representative sample of a population. There are a number of reasons for choosing quota sampling, for example, when the sampling frame is not available or is not detailed enough, or because of economical considerations.

As in stratified sampling, the population is segmented in terms of predefined criteria, in such a way that each member of the population belongs to one and only one segment. Each segment has a corresponding quota, which indicates the number of responses to be obtained. The difference between these two methods is found in the means of selecting sample elements, which in the quota method is not random. Two different types of procedures can be used.

The first type of procedure consists of filling the quotas as opportunities present themselves. The risk in this instance is that the sample might contain selection biases, since the first elements encountered may present a particular profile depending, for example, on the interviewer's location, the sampling frame or other reasons.

The second type of procedure is called pseudo-random. For this a list of population elements (for example, a professional directory) is required, although, unlike stratified sampling, segmentation criteria are not needed for this list. The selection procedure consists of selecting the first element of the list at random, then going through the list systematically until the desired number of answers is reached. Even though this method does not scrupulously respect the rules of random sampling (the researcher does not know in advance the probability an element has of belonging to the sample), it does reduce potential selection bias by limiting subjectivity. Empirical studies have shown that the results are not significantly different from those obtained using probability sampling (Sudman, 1976).

2. Matched Samples

Experimental designs often use matched samples. Matched samples present similar characteristics in terms of certain relevant criteria. They are used to ascertain that the measured effect is a result of the variable or variables studied and not from differences in sample composition.

There are two principal methods of matching samples. The most common is randomization, which divides the initial sample into a certain number of groups (equal to the number of different observation conditions) and then randomly allocates the sample elements into these groups. Systematic sampling is often used to do this. For example, if the researcher wants to have two groups of individuals, the first available person will be assigned to the first group, the second to the second, the third to the first, etc. When the elements are heterogeneous, this randomization technique cannot totally guarantee that the groups will be similar, because of the random assignment of the elements.

The second method consists of controlling sample structure beforehand. The population is stratified on the basis of criteria likely to affect the observed variable. Samples are then assembled so as to obtain identical structures. If the samples are large enough, this method has the advantage of allowing data processing to be carried out within each stratum, to show up possible strata differences.

According to Cook and Campbell (1979), matching elements before randomization is the best way of reducing error that can result from differences in sample composition. The researcher performs a pre-test on the initial sample, to measure the observed variable for each sample element. Elements are then classified from highest to lowest, or vice versa, in terms of this variable, and the sample is divided into as many equally sized parts as there are experimental conditions. For example, if there are four experimental conditions, the four elements with the highest score constitute the first part, the next four the second, etc. The elements in each part are then randomly assigned to experimental conditions. The four elements of the first part would be randomly assigned to the four experimental conditions, as would the four elements of the second part, and so on.

3. Sample Biases

Sample biases can affect both the internal and the external validity of a study. There are three categories of biases: sampling variability, sampling bias and non-sampling bias (although sampling variability and estimator's bias affect probability samples only). The sum of these three biases is called the total error of the study (see Figure 8.2).

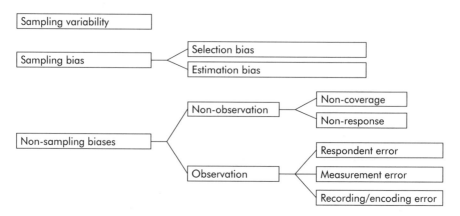

Figure 8.2   *Sample bias*

Sampling variability refers to differences that can be observed by comparing samples. Although one starts with the same population, samples will be composed of different elements. These differences will reappear in the results, which can, therefore, vary from one sample to another. Sampling variability decreases when sample size increases.

Sampling bias is related to the process of selecting sample elements or to the use of a biased estimator. In the case of a random sampling method, selection bias can crop up every time random selection conditions are not respected. Nevertheless, selection bias is much more common in non-random sampling, because it is impossible, by definition, for these methods to control the probability that an element is selected into the sample. For example, quota sampling can lead to significant selection bias insofar as the respondents are, rather subjectively, selected by the investigator. Other sampling biases are related to the estimator selected. An estimator is a statistical tool that enables us to obtain, thanks to the data gathered from a sample, an estimate for an unknown parameter, for example, variance. The mathematical construction of certain estimators presents the 'proper' properties, which establish the 'proper' estimates directly. When this is not the case, we say the estimator is biased.

Biases that are not related to sampling can be of different types, usually divided into two categories: non-observation biases and observation biases. The first can arise either from problems in identifying the study population, which we call coverage bias, or from lack of response. They can affect samples intended for qualitative or quantitative processing. Observation biases, on the other hand, are associated with respondent error, or data-measurement, -recording or -encoding errors. Since observation biases do not stem from the constitution of the sample per se, in the following discussion we will consider non-observation-related biases only.

3.1 Non-coverage bias

A sample presents non-coverage bias when the study population does not correspond to the intended population, which the researcher wishes to generalize the results to. The intended population can encompass individuals, organizations, places or phenomena. It is often defined generically: researchers might say they are studying 'small businesses' or 'crisis management', for example. But researchers must take care to establish criteria that enable the population to be precisely identified. The set defined by the operationalization criteria will then constitute the study population. Two types of error can lead to a less than perfect correspondence between the intended population and the population under study: population-definition errors and listing errors.

Errors in defining the study population are one major source of bias. Inappropriately defined or insufficiently precise operationalization criteria can lead researchers to define the study population too broadly, or conversely, too narrowly. This type of error, for example, can result in different companies being selected for the same intended population. Not all of the sets defined in this way are necessarily pertinent in terms of the question being studied and the purpose of the research. This type of bias can occur in any type of sampling.

Example: Sources of error in defining the population

In a study of strategic choice in small businesses, the set 'small businesses' corresponds to the intended population. Nevertheless, it is important to establish criteria for defining an organization as a 'small business'. Sales figures or the number of employees are two possible operationalization of the qualifier 'small'. Similarly, 'businesses' could be defined in broad terms – as all organizations belonging to the commercial sector – or more restrictively – in terms of their legal status, including only incorporated organizations, and excluding non-profit and economic-interest groups. Choosing an overly strict operationalization of the definition, and including incorporated companies only, for example, will result in a sample that is not truly representative of the small business set. Partnerships, for example, would be excluded, which could create a bias.

Listing errors are a potential cause of bias in the case of probability samples, for which the study population has been materialized as a sampling frame. They often result from recording errors or, even more commonly, from the instability of the population being observed. For example, a professional directory published in 2000, used in the course of the following year will include companies that no longer exist and, conversely, will not include those which have been created since the directory was published. For practical reasons, it is not always possible to be rid of these errors. And yet, the validity of a study depends on the quality of the sampling frame. Researchers should therefore make sure that all the elements in the intended population are on the list, and that all the elements that do not belong to the population are excluded from it. The measures used to increase the reliability of the sampling frame can sometimes be ambivalent. For example, cross-referencing several lists generally helps to reduce the number of missing elements, but it can also lead to including the same element more than once, or to including elements that do not belong to the intended population. In the first case, the conditions of equal probability for each element are no longer maintained. In the second, bias appears which is comparable to the one presented above for definition error. Researchers can reduce these different types of errors before the sample is selected by scrupulously checking the sampling frame.

3.2 Non-response bias

Non-response bias can have two sources: the refusal of elements to participate in the study, or the impossibility of contacting a selected element or elements. If non-responses are not distributed randomly, the results can be biased. This is the case when non-response is connected to characteristics related to the study. For example, for research studying the effect of incentive programs on managerial behavior, non-response may correlate to a certain type of behavior (for example, interventionist) or with certain categories of incentive (for example, stock-option programs).

The higher the non-response rate, the greater the bias may be and the more likely it is to affect the validity of the research. The researcher should therefore try to avoid non-response. Several inducement techniques can be used for this purpose, generally dealing with methods to use when contacting and following up respondents, or with maintaining contact (this subject is dealt with in greater depth in Chapter 9). While these efforts may reduce the non-response rate, they rarely result in the researcher obtaining responses for the entire set of selected elements.

Different techniques can be applied to analyze non-response and, in certain circumstances, correct any possible bias of probability sampling results. These are presented at the end of this chapter, in the section on post sampling.

Because of non-coverage and non-response biases, the observed population hardly ever matches the intended population perfectly. But this does not prevent the researcher from attempting to achieve this goal, as these biases can threaten the validity of the research.

SECTION 2   DETERMINING SAMPLE SIZE

Determining the size of a sample really comes down to estimating the minimum size needed to obtain results with an acceptable degree of confidence. For samples destined for quantitative data processing this means determining the size that enables the study to attain the desired degree of precision or significance level; for qualitative research it is the size that confers an acceptable credibility level.

As a general rule, and all else being equal, the larger the sample, the greater the confidence in the results, whatever type of data processing is used. However, large samples pose problems of practicality, particularly in terms of cost and scheduling. Beyond a certain size, they can also pose problems in terms of reliability, for when a sample is very large, the researcher is often required to farm out data collection. This can increase the number of collection, recording and encoding errors – and may require the instigation of sometimes elaborate verification procedures. Large samples can also turn out to be unnecessarily costly. For example, a small sample is sometimes sufficient to obtain a significant result when the effect of a variable in an experimental design has to be tested.

Determining the appropriate sample size before collecting data is essential in order to avoid the *ex post* realization that a sample is too small. Calculating the sample size required involves evaluating the feasibility of the research's objectives, and, in certain cases, can lead to modifying the research design.

1. Samples Intended for Quantitative Processing

The size required for a sample intended for quantitative data processing depends on the statistical method used. Our intention here is not to provide formulae, but simply to present the factors common to most methods that influence the sample size needed. There are many such factors: the significance level, the desired level of precision, the variance of the studied phenomenon in the population, the sampling technique chosen, the size of the effect being studied, the desired power of the test and the number of parameters to estimate. Which ones need to be taken into consideration depend on the purposes of the study. Nevertheless, two main categories of objectives can be distinguished: describing a population and testing a hypothesis.

1.1 Descriptive research

The principal evaluation criterion for descriptive research is usually precision. Precision depends on several factors: the desired significance level, the population variance and the sampling technique used. To illustrate the incidence of these factors on sample size, we will consider a very familiar statistic: the mean.

Example: Calculating sample size to estimate a mean

In the case of a simple random sample of more than 30 elements selected with or without replacement, but with a sampling ratio smaller than 10 per cent, to reach the desired level of precision, the minimum sample size is

$$ n = \left(\frac{z}{l} s \right)^2 $$

where l is the level of precision, s is the population's standard deviation, n the sample size, and z the value of the normal distribution for the significance level.

Population variance and sample size   The larger the variance s^2, the larger the sample needs to be. Very often, however, the variance of the population is unknown. In that case, it must be estimated in order to calculate the size of the sample. There are several possible ways of doing this. The first is to use results of earlier studies that give suggested variance estimates. Another solution is to perform a pilot study on a small sample. The variance calculated for this sample will provide an estimate for the population variance. A third solution is based on the assumption that the variable being studied follows a normal distribution, which is unlikely for many organizational phenomena. Under this assumption, the standard deviation is approximately one-sixth of the distribution range (maximum value minus minimum value). Finally, when a scale is used to measure the variable, one can refer to the guidelines below.

Guidelines for Estimating Variance for Data using Rating Scales (Churchill, 1991: 588)

Variance depends on the number of scale points and the distribution of responses. The lower the number of scale points, and the more answers tend to concentrate around some middle point (as in normal distribution) the lower the variance. Table 8.2 gives likely values of variance depending on these two factors. The lower values correspond to normal distributions and the higher ones to uniformly distributed responses. It is possible, of course, to encounter still greater variances, particularly with distributions with a mode at each end of the scale.

Table 8.2 *Range of variances, depending on number of scale points*

Number of scale points	Typical range of variances
4	0.7–1.3
5	1.2–2
6	2–3
7	2.5–4
10	3–7

Churchill advises using the highest values to calculate sample size, since data obtained using rating scales are more often uniformly than normally distributed.

Significance level and sample size   Significance level (α) refers to the possibility of rejecting the null hypothesis when it should not have been rejected. By convention, in management research accepted levels are generally from 1 per cent to 5 per cent, or as much as 10 per cent – depending on the type of research. The 1 per cent level is standard for laboratory experiments; for data obtained through fieldwork, 10 per cent could be acceptable. If the significance level is above 10 per cent, results are not considered valid in statistical terms. The desired significance level (α) has a direct influence on sample size: the lower the acceptable percentage of error, the larger the sample needs to be.

Precision level and sample size   The precision level (*l*) of an estimate is given by the range of the confidence interval. The more precise the results need to be, the larger the sample must be. Precision is costly. To increase it twofold, sample size must be increased fourfold.

Sampling method and sample size   The sampling method used affects sampling variability. Every sampling method involves a specific way of calculating the sample mean and standard deviation (for example, see Kalton, 1983). Consequently, sample size cannot always be calculated with the simple formula used in the example on page 158, which is valid for a simple random sample only. However, no matter which sampling method is chosen, it is possible to estimate sample size without having to resort to complex formulae. Approximations can be used. Henry (1990), for example, presents several 'design effect' – or *deff* – adjustment coefficients (see Table 8.3).

By applying these coefficients, sample size can be estimated with a simple calculation derived from the basic formula. The variance is multiplied by the coefficient corresponding to the method used ($s'^2 = s^2 . deff$).

Returning to the formula we used above, with a simple random sample the size is:

$$n = \left(\frac{z}{l} s\right)^2$$

Table 8.3   *Adjustment coefficient of variance depending on sampling methods (Henry, 1990)*

Sampling method	Deff	Notes
Stratified samples	0.5 to 0.95	The ratio decreases with the number of strata and intra-stratum homogeneity.
Multistage sampling	1.25 to 1.5	The effect of this method can be partially reduced through simultaneous use of stratification.
Cluster sampling	1.5 to 3.0	The ratio decreases with the number of clusters, intra-cluster heterogeneity, inter-strata homogeneity and the use of stratification.

With a multistage sample, the maximum deff coefficient is 1.5, so the size is:

$$n = \left(\frac{z}{l}\, s'\right)^2 = \left(\frac{z}{l} s\right)^2 1.5$$

1.2 Hypothesis testing

Other criteria must also be taken into account in the case of samples that will be used to test hypotheses (the most common use of samples in research work). These include effect size, the power of the statistical test and the number of parameters to estimate. These criteria help us to ascertain the significance of the results.

Effect size and sample size   Effect size describes the magnitude or the strength of the association between two variables. Indices measuring effect size depend on the statistics used.

If we take, for example, the test of difference between means, and we assume that the standard deviation is the same for both samples, effect size is given by the ratio *d*:

$$d = \frac{|\bar{y}_1 - \bar{y}_2|}{s}$$

For example, if the average $\bar{y}_1$ of the studied variable in the first sample is 33, the mean $\bar{y}_2$ of the second is 28, and the standard deviation *s* is 10 for each sample, the effect size will be 50 per cent ($d = (33 - 28)/10 = 0.5$).

Effect sizes are generally classified into three categories: small, medium and large. A 20 per cent effect is considered small, a 50 per cent effect medium and an 80 per cent effect large (Cohen, 1988). In terms of proportion of variance, accounted for by an independent variable, these three categories correspond to the values 1 per cent, 6 per cent and 14 per cent.

The smaller the effect the larger the sample size must be if it is to be statistically significant. For example, in a test of difference between means, with two identically sized samples, if the required size of each sample is 20 for a large effect, it will be 50 for a medium one and 310 for a small effect, all else being equal.

Estimating effect size is not easy. As for variance, we can use estimates from earlier research or do a pilot study with a small sample. If no estimate exists, we can also use the minimum effect size that we wish to obtain. For example, if an effect of less than 1 per cent is deemed worthless, then sample size must be calculated with an effect size of 1 per cent.

For management research effect sizes are usually small, as in all the social sciences. When analyzing 102 studies about personality, Sarason et al. (1975) noticed that the median percentage of variance accounted for by an independent variable ranged from 1 per cent to 4.5 per cent depending on the nature of the variable (demographics, personality or situation).

The power of the test and sample size The power of the test could be interpreted as the likelihood of being able to identify the studied effect. When it is low, we cannot determine whether there is no relation between the variables in the population, or whether a relation exists but was not significant because the research was not sufficiently sensitive to it.

The power of the test is expressed with the coefficient $(1 - \beta)$ (see Chapter 11, Comparison Tests).

For example, a power of 25 per cent $(1 - \beta = 0.25)$ means that there is only a 25 per cent chance of correctly rejecting the null hypothesis H_0: that is, there is a 75 per cent chance that no conclusion will be drawn.

The power of the test is rarely mentioned when presenting results, and is not often considered in management sciences (Mazen et al., 1987). Most research presents significant effects only, i.e. for which the null hypothesis H_0 has been able to be rejected. In this case, the decision error is the Type I error α. So it is not surprising to see that Type II error β is not mentioned, since it means accepting H_0 when it is not true.

Cohen (1988) defined standards for β error of 20 per cent and 10 per cent. They are not as strict as those generally accepted for significance level α (5 per cent and 1 per cent). The power of the test depends on the significance level. The relationship between α and β is complex, but, all else being equal, the lower α is, the higher β becomes. Still, it is not advisable to reduce Type II error by increasing Type I error, because of the weight of convention concerning α error. There are other means of improving power. For a given α error, the power of the test increases when sample size increases and variance decreases. If, despite everything, the power of the test is still not acceptable, it may be reasonable to give up on the test in question.

In research comparing two samples, increasing the size of one of them (the control sample) is another way of increasing the power of the test.

When replicating research that did not lead to a rejection of the null hypothesis, Sawyer and Ball (1981) suggest estimating the power of the tests that were carried out – this can be calculated through the results of the research. If the power appears low, it should be increased in order to raise the chance of obtaining significant results. Cook and Campbell (1979) also advise presenting the power of the test in the results when the major research conclusion is that one variable does not lead to another.

Sample size and number of parameters to estimate   Sample size also depends on the number of parameters to be estimated, that is, the number of variables and interaction effects which are to be studied. For any statistical method, the larger the number of parameters that are to be estimated, the larger the sample should be.

When more elaborate statistical methods are used, determining the sample size required in order to achieve the desired significance becomes extremely complex. For means and proportions, simple calculation formulae exist and can be found in any statistics handbook (for example, see Thompson, 1992). On the other hand, for more complicated methods, for example, regression, there are no simple, comprehensive formulae. Researchers often imitate earlier studies for this reason. For most methods, however, calculation formulae or tables exist which enable researchers to estimate sample size for one or more criteria. Rules of thumb often exist as well. These are not, of course, as precise as a formula or a table, but they may be used to avoid major mistakes in estimating sample size.

Advanced Statistical Data Processing

Cohen (1988) supplies tables for several statistics, including multiple regression and variance analysis, which indicate the required sample size depending on the effect size, the significance level, the power of the test and the degrees of freedom.

Milton (1986) proposes a calculation formula and tables for the two most common levels of significance (1 per cent and 5 per cent) for the F-ratio to determine the required sample size when using multiple regression.

MacCallum et al. (1996) offer tables for structural equation models defining the sample size required to obtain a desired global adjustment.

Bentler and Chou (1987) indicate, for structural equation models, that the ratio between sample size and the number of parameters to be estimated can go as low as five to one in the case of normal distribution and ten to one in other cases. These ratios must be increased to obtain significant results for the parameters of the model.

1.3 Usable sample size

The indications presented above for determining sample size concern only the usable sample size – that is, the number of elements retained for statistical analysis. In a random sampling technique, each element selected should be part of the usable sample. If that is not the case, as we mentioned in the first section, then there is bias. It is unusual in management research, though, to obtain all the desired information from each of the randomly selected elements. The reasons for this are many, but they can be classified into four main categories: impossibility of contacting a respondent, refusal to cooperate, ineligibility (that is, the selected element turns out not to belong to the target population) and responses that are unusable (for example, due to incompleteness). The response rate can vary tremendously, depending on a great number of factors related to the data collection methods used (sampling method, questionnaire administration technique, method used to contact respondents, etc.), the nature of the information requested or the amount of time required to supply it. The response rate can often be very low, particularly when data is being gathered through self-administered questionnaires. Certain organizational characteristics can also affect the response rate. The respondent's capacity and motivation can similarly depend on organizational factors (Tomaskovic-Devey et al., 1994). For example, when a questionnaire is addressed to a subsidiary, but decision-making is centralized at the parent company, response probability is lower.

The likely response rate must be taken into account when determining the size of the sample to be contacted. Researchers commonly turn to others who have collected similar data in the same domain when estimating this response rate.

Samples used in longitudinal studies raise an additional problem: subject attrition – that is, the disappearance of certain elements (also referred to as sample mortality). In this type of study, data is gathered several times from the same sample. It is not unusual for elements to disappear before the data collection process is complete. For example, when studying corporations, some may go bankrupt, others may choose to cease cooperating because of a change in management. In researching longitudinal studies published in journals of industrial psychology and organizational behavior, Goodman and Blum (1996) found attrition rates varied from 0 to 88 per cent with a median rate of 27 per cent. In general, the longer the overall data-collection period, the higher the attrition rate. Researchers should always take the attrition rate into account when calculating the number of respondents to include in the initial sample.

1.4 Trading-off sample size and research design

As discussed above, sample size depends on the variance of the variable under study. The more heterogeneous the elements of the sample are, the higher the variance and the larger the sample must be. But it is not always feasible, nor even necessarily desirable, to use a very large sample. One possible answer to this problem is to reduce variance by selecting homogenous elements from a subset of the population. This makes it possible to obtain significant results at lower cost. The drawback to this solution is that it entails a decrease in external validity. This limitation is not, however, necessarily a problem. Indeed, for many studies, external validity is secondary, as researchers are more concerned with establishing the internal validity of results before attempting to generalize from them.

When testing hypotheses, researchers can use several small homogenous samples instead of a single, large heterogeneous sample (Cook and Campbell, 1979). In this case, the approach follows a logic of replication. The researcher tests the hypothesis on one small, homogenous sample, then repeats the same analysis on other small samples, each sample presenting different characteristics. To obtain the desired external validity, at least one dimension, such as population or place, must vary from one sample to another. This process leads to a high external validity – although this is not a result of generalizing to a target population through statistical inference, but rather of applying the principles of analytic generalization across various populations. The smaller samples can be assembled without applying the rigorous sampling methods required for large, representative samples (Cook and Campbell, 1979). This process also offers the advantage of reducing risks for the researcher, in terms of time and cost. By limiting the initial study to a small, homogenous sample, the process is simpler in its application. If the research does not produce significant results, the test can be performed on a new sample with a new design to improve its efficiency. If that is not an option, the research may be abandoned, and will have wasted less labor and expense than a test on a large, heterogeneous sample.

A similar process using several small samples is also an option for researchers studying several relations. In this case the researcher can test one or two variables on smaller samples, instead of testing all of them on a single large sample. The drawback of this solution, however, is that it does not allow for testing the interaction effect among all the variables.

2. Samples Intended for Qualitative Analysis

In qualitative research, single-case studies are generally differentiated from multiple-case studies. In fact, single case studies are one of the particularities of qualitative research. Like quantitative hypothesis testing, sample size for qualitative analysis also depends on the desired objective.

2.1 Single case studies

The status of single-case studies is the object of some controversy. Some writers consider the knowledge acquired from single case studies to be idiosyncratic, and argue that it cannot be generalized to a larger or different population. Others dispute this: for example, Pondy and Mitroff (1979) believe it to be perfectly reasonable to build theory from a single case, and that the single-case study can be a valid source for scientific generalization across organizations. According to Yin (1990), a single-case study can be assimilated to an experiment, and the reasons for studying a single case are the same as those that motivate an experiment. Yin argues that single case studies are primarily justified in three situations. The first is when testing an existing theory, whether the goal is to confirm, challenge or extend it. For example, Ross and Straw (1993) tested an existing prototype of escalation of commitment by studying a single case, the Shoreham nuclear-power plant. Single cases can also be used when they have unique or extreme characteristics. The singularity of the case is then the direct outcome of the rarity of the phenomenon being studied. This was the case, for example, when Vaughan (1990) studied the Challenger shuttle disaster. And finally, the single-case study is also pertinent if it can reveal a phenomenon which is not rare but which had until now been inaccessible to the scientific community. Yin points to Whyte's (1944) research in the Italian community in poor areas of Boston as a famous example of this situation.

2.2 Multiple cases

Like quantitative analysis, the confidence accorded to the results of qualitative research tends to increase with sample size. The drawback is a parallel increase in the time and cost of collecting data. Consequently, the question of sample size is similar to quantitative samples – the goal is to determine the minimum size that will enable a satisfactory level of confidence in the results. There are essentially two different principles for defining the size of a sample: replication and saturation. While these two principles are generally presented for determining the number of cases to study, they can also be applied to respondent samples.

Replication   The replication logic in qualitative research is analogous to that of multiple experiments, with each case study corresponding to one experiment (Yin, 1990). The number of cases required for research depends on two criteria, similar to those existing for quantitative samples intended for hypothesis testing. They are the desired degree of certainty and the magnitude of the observed differences.

There are two criteria for selecting cases. Each case is selected either because similar results are expected (literal replication) or because it will most likely lead to different results for predictable reasons (theoretical replication). The number of cases of literal replication required depends on the scale of the observed differences and the desired degree of certainty. According to Yin (1990), two or three cases are enough when the rival theories are glaringly different or the issue at hand does not demand a high degree of certainty. In other circumstances, when the differences are subtle or the required degree of certainty is higher, at least five or six literal replications would be required.

The number of cases of theoretical replication depends on the number of conditions expected to affect the phenomenon being studied. As the number of conditions increases, so does the potential number of theoretical replications. To compare it to experimentation, these conditions of theoretical replication in multiple case studies fulfill the same purpose as the different conditions of observation in experimental designs. They increase the internal validity of the research.

The saturation principle   Unlike Yin (1990), Glaser and Strauss (1967) do not supply an indication for the number of observation units a sample should contain. According to these authors, the adequate sample size is determined by theoretical saturation. Theoretical saturation is reached when no more information will enable the theory to be enriched. Consequently, it is impossible to know in advance what the required number of observation units will be.

This principle can be difficult to apply, as one never knows with absolute certainty if any more information that could enrich the theory exists. It is up to the researcher therefore, to judge when the saturation stage has been reached. Data collection usually ends when the units of observation analyzed fail to supply any new elements. This principle is based on the law of diminishing returns – the idea that each additional unit of information will supply slightly less new information than the preceding one, until the new information dwindles to nothing.

Above and beyond these two essential principles, whose goal is raising internal validity, it is also possible to increase the number of cases in order to improve external validity. These new cases will then be selected in such a way as to vary the context of observation (for example, geographical location, industrial sector, etc.). Researchers can also take the standard criteria of credibility for the community to which they belong into account when determining the number of elements to include in a sample intended for qualitative processing.

SECTION 3   THE SAMPLE SELECTION PROCESS

Sample selection can follow a number of different procedures, many of which are related to two generic approaches: the traditional approach, typical of probability sampling, and the iterative approach, such as that applied for grounded theory (Glaser and Strauss, 1967). The sample selection process also includes certain procedures that are carried out after data has been collected.

1. Two Standard Approaches

The traditional approach (see Figure 8.3) is typical of probability sampling, but it is also frequently encountered in the quota method. It starts by defining the target population, for which the results will be generalized through statistical inference. The population is operationalized in order to have clear criteria to determine the elements included in or excluded from the study population. The next step is to select a sampling method. It then becomes possible to determine the sample size. If a random sampling method is used, it will be necessary to choose or create a sampling frame in order to carry out random selection. The researcher then selects the sample elements and collects the required data. The elements for which all of the required data could in fact be collected constitute the study's 'usable' sample. The last stage of this procedure is a study of potential biases and, if necessary, adjustment to the sample.

Each stage of this process (sampling method, sample size and element-selection techniques) being related, the outcome of one stage can lead to a reconsideration of earlier choices (Henry, 1990). For example, if the required sample size is too large in terms of the cost of data collection, the population

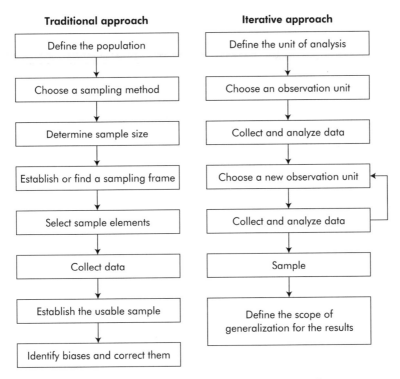

Figure 8.3   *Two ways of constituting a sample*

can sometimes be narrowed to make the sample more homogenous. The significance level required for internal validity is then easier to achieve. If it turns out to be difficult to establish or find a sampling frame, another sampling method might be chosen. Consequently, the choices related to selecting a sample often follow a non-linear process (Henry, 1990).

An iterative approach follows a radically different process. Unlike the classic approach, the scope of generalization for the results is not defined at the outset, but rather at the end of the process. Another important difference between the two procedures lies in the progressive constitution of the sample by successive iterations. Each element of the sample is selected by judgement. The data are then collected and analyzed before the next element is selected. Over the course of successive selections, Glaser and Strauss (1967) suggest first studying similar units in order to enable the emergence of a substantive theory before enlarging the collection to include units with different characteristics. The process is completed when theoretical saturation is reached. Unlike the classic procedure, the size and composition of the sample are not predetermined but, quite the opposite, they arise from the outcome of the iterative process of successive selection of elements. These choices are guided by both the data collected and the theory being elaborated. The scope of generalization of the results is constructed progressively over the course of the procedure and is defined only at the outcome of the process.

Role of the pre-test in the sample selection process   In practice, research often involves a phase of pre-testing. This pre-testing does not specifically concern sampling, but it does supply useful information that can contribute to a better definition of the required size and composition of the final sample. In quantitative studies, the pre-test sample can, in particular, provide an initial estimate for variance and aid in identifying criteria for segmenting a stratified sample. In qualitative research, the pilot case aids in determining the composition and number of cases required. These factors depend on literal and theoretical replication conditions and the magnitude of observed differences (Yin, 1990).

2. Specific Approaches

2.1 Progressive sample selection

The traditional approach is to determine sample size before data collection. However, another possible approach is to collect and process data until the desired degree of precision or level of significance is reached. This involves successive rounds of data collection (Thompson, 1992). According to Adlfinger (1981), this procedure allows us to arrive at a sample half the size it would have been had we determined it in advance. Establishing a minimal size in advance does generally lead to oversized samples as, to be on the safe side, researchers often work from the most pessimistic estimates.

Unfortunately though, researchers are not always in a position to employ this procedure, which can reduce data-collection costs considerably. A study attempting to analyze the impact of a non-reproducible event (such as a merger between two companies) on a variable (for example, executive motivation) illustrates this. Such a study requires data to be collected both before and after the event – it is not possible to increase the number of elements in the sample progressively. The researcher is then obliged to follow the classic procedure – and to determine sample size in advance.

Even if it were possible to constitute the sample progressively, it would still be worthwhile to estimate its size in advance. Without a prior estimate, the researcher runs the risk of not being able to enlarge the sample (for example, for budgetary concerns). The sample might well turn out to be too small to reach the desired significance level.

Determining sample size beforehand enables researchers to evaluate the feasibility of their objectives. This is one way we can avoid wasting time and effort on unsatisfactory research, and it encourages us to consider other research designs that might lead to more significant results.

2.2 Ex post selection

For laboratory experiments, matched samples are constructed by selecting elements, dividing them randomly into the different treatment conditions and collecting data on them. Yet not all phenomena lend themselves to constituting matched samples before data collection. Sample structure can be hard to master, particularly when studying phenomena in real settings, when the phenomena are difficult to access or to identify, or when the population under study is not well known. In these situations, it is sometimes possible to constitute matched samples after data collection – *ex post* – in order to perform a test. To do this, a control group is selected from the target population following the rules of random selection, in such a way that the structure of the control group reproduces that of the observed group.

3. Post-sampling

3.1 Control and adjustment procedures

It is often possible *ex post* to correct non-sampling biases such as non-response and response errors. But researchers should bear in mind that adjusting data is a fall-back solution, and it is always preferable to aim to avoid bias.

Non-response Non-responses can cause representativeness biases in the sample. To detect this type of bias, the researcher can compare the structure of the respondent sample to that of the population, focusing on variables that might affect the phenomenon being studied. If these structures differ noticeably, representativeness bias is probable, and should be corrected.

There are three ways of correcting non-response biases. The first is to survey a subsample of randomly selected non-respondents. The researcher must then make every effort to obtain a response from all of the elements in this subsample (Lessler and Kalsbeek, 1992). The second is to perform an *ex post* stratification, in which responses from sample elements are weighted to reconstruct the structure of the population (Lessler and Kalsbeek, 1992). This method can also be employed in two other situations of non-response bias: when stratification has not been carried out in advance because of technical difficulties (for example, if no sampling frame, or only an insufficiently precise one, was available), or when a new stratification variable is discovered belatedly, during the data analysis phase. In any case, *ex post* stratification can increase the precision of estimations. The third procedure is to replace non-respondents with new respondents presenting identical characteristics, and to compensate by assigning the new respondents a weighted factor (Levy and Lemeshow, 1991). This method can also be applied to adjust for missing responses when replies are incomplete.

If data for certain identifiable subsets of the sample is still missing at the end of this process, the population should be redefined – or, at the very least, this weakness in the study should be indicated.

Response error Response errors can be checked by cross-surveying a sub-set of respondents (Levy and Lemeshow, 1991). This may identify certain types of error, such as errors derived from the interviewer or from respondents misunderstanding the question (although this method is futile if respondents willfully supply erroneous information, which is extremely difficult to detect or correct).

3.2 Small samples

Despite taking all precautions, a sample sometimes turns out to have been too small to obtain the precision or the significance level desired. In this case, the best solution is to carry out a second round of data collection that will enlarge the sample. But this is not always an option (for example, when secondary data is used, when the sampling frame has been entirely exploited, or when the data depend on a particular context which has changed).

When the sample size cannot be increased, the researcher can compensate by generating several samples from the original one. The two main ways of doing this are known as the 'jackknife' and the 'bootstrap' (Mooney and Duval, 1993). These methods enable researchers to establish their results more firmly than they could through standard techniques alone.

The jackknife   The jackknife creates new samples by systematically removing one element from the initial sample. For a sample size of n, the jackknife gives n samples of size $n - 1$. Statistical processing is then carried out on each of these samples, and the results are compared to the initial sample. The more the results converge, the greater the confidence with which we can regard the outcome.

The bootstrap   The bootstrap works on a relatively similar principle, but the samples are constituted differently. They are obtained by random sampling with replacement from the initial sample, and they contain the same number of elements (n). The number of samples drawn from the initial sample can be very high when using the bootstrap, as it does not depend on the size of the initial sample.

Both the jackknife and the bootstrap can be applied to basic statistical measurements, such as variance and mean, and to more complex methods, such as LISREL or PLS.

CONCLUSION

Researchers can draw from a wide range of sampling methods and approaches when putting together their research samples. Although each has its own advantages and disadvantages – particularly in terms of internal and external validity – the choice is often restricted by feasibility criteria. Nevertheless, in choosing a sampling method, one should never lose sight of the desired validity goals; it is vital to ensure the chosen method will allow the study to achieve these. We often have to decide between the two types of validity, as samples that combine both high internal validity and high external validity are generally very costly. In making such methodological choices, researchers must take care to clearly identify the primary objective of their study, and to ensure their samples can allow them to achieve it.

FURTHER READING

Cook, T.D. and Campbell, D.T., *Quasi-Experimentation: Design and Analysis Issues for Field Settings*, Skokie, IL: Rand McNally, 1979.

Glaser, B.G. and Strauss, A.L., *The Discovery of Grounded Theory: Strategy for Qualitative Research*, New York: Adline De Gruyter, 1967.

Henry, G.T., *Practical Sampling*, Newbury Park, CA: Sage, 1990.

Levy, P.S. and Lemeshow, S., *Sampling of Populations: Methods and Applications*, New York: Wiley, 1991.

Yin, R.K., *Case Study Research: Design and Methods*, Applied Social Research Methods Series, 5, Newbury Park, CA: Sage, 1990.

9

DATA COLLECTION AND MANAGING
THE DATA SOURCE

*Jérôme Ibert, Philippe Baumard, Carole
Donada and Jean-Marc Xuereb*

Outline

This chapter begins by looking at ways researchers can collect primary data. We describe techniques used in quantitative research (questionnaire, observation and the experimental method) and in qualitative research (including individual and group interviews and participant and non-participant observation). We then analyze data source management in terms of ease of access and the risks of data contamination or loss of the research site.

Approaches and source management strategies are presented in terms of the formalism of the relationship between the researcher and the individuals used as sources of data, on the secrecy or openness of the investigation and on the degree of intimacy adopted towards the subject-sources. We explore the advantages and the limitations of secondary data – internal or external to the organization – and explain confidentiality conventions and their consequences on the validation of results by subject-sources and on publication.

Data collection is crucial to all research. Through this process researchers accumulate empirical material on which to base their research. But before they begin putting together their empirical base, researchers should ask themselves whether any suitable data is already available. Secondary data (or secondhand data) can offer real advantages, as it relieves researchers from conducting their own fieldwork or reduces the fieldwork required. But it can be difficult to track down suitable secondary data, if it does exist, and once located there is the problem of gaining access to it. Knowing how to identify and access data sources, both external and internal to organizations is central to the collection of secondary data.

In the absence of suitable secondary data, or in addition to such data, researchers can collect their own primary data through fieldwork. This brings us to the question of what methods the fieldworker should use.

Data collection methods vary according to whether the researcher adopts a quantitative or qualitative approach. In this chapter we will make a distinction between techniques that can be used in quantitative research and those more suited to qualitative research.

SECTION 1 COLLECTING PRIMARY DATA FOR QUANTITATIVE RESEARCH

The most developed method of collecting primary data for quantitative research is the questionnaire. We take a particularly close look at mailed questionnaires, as these are used very frequently in management research and necessitate particular techniques. We then present other methods of collecting primary data for quantitative research: observation and experimentation.

1. Surveys

A survey or questionnaire enables researchers directly to question individuals. It is a tool for collecting primary data that adapts well to quantitative research, as it allows the researcher to work with large samples and to establish statistical relationships or numerical comparisons.

Collecting data by survey involves three major steps: initial crafting of the survey and choosing scales, pre-tests to check the validity and reliability of the survey, and then the actual administering of the final version. There are certain procedures that should be followed for each step, to obtain the maximum amount of relevant and usable data. Numerous articles and other published works have gone into lengthy detail about these procedures (Albreck and Settle, 1989; Fink and Kosecoff, 1998; Rossi et al., 1985; Schuman, 1996), but we have chosen here to focus on a number of fundamental points.

1.1 Choosing scales

To craft a survey for quantitative research is, in fact, to construct a measuring instrument. Before tackling the problems of wording the questions and organizing the structure of the questionnaire, the researcher must first choose which scales to use (the different types of scales – nominal, ordinal, interval or proportional – are presented in Chapter 4). Not only do researchers need to determine the type of scale to use, they also have to choose between using pre-existent scales or creating their own.

Using pre-existent scales   Most questionnaires used in management research combine a number of scales. A researcher may choose to use scales already constructed and validated by other researchers. These are generally published in the annex of the article or the work in which they are first employed, or they can be obtained by requesting them directly from the researcher who created them. A number of publications (Bearden et al., 1993; Robinson et al., 1991) present a large range of scales. Researcher should be aware, though, that the validity of these pre-existent scales is strongly linked to the context in which they are used. A scale designed to measure the degree of radicalness of an innovation in the biotechnology industry may not be able to be transposed to a study of the literary editing sector. Scales developed in a particular country (most often the USA) or socio-cultural context may need to be adapted for use in other contexts. When using scales in other contexts than that for which they were created, researchers must always verify that they are indeed valid in the new context.

Constructing new scales   If appropriate scales cannot be found, researchers have to construct their own measuring instruments. Detailed interviews are a good way to obtain a better picture of the phenomenon under study, and they enable the researcher to define coherent items that will be understood by the population being studied. This should then be followed by an initial pre-test phase, to refine the list of questions and to validate the scale.

For a complete description of all the steps to be followed to create new scales, the researcher can refer to detailed works such as Aaker and Day (1990), Devellis (1991) or Tull and Hawkins (1987).

1.2 Designing and pre-testing a questionnaire

Designing the questionnaire   Preparing the questions is complex work. The researcher needs to avoid errors in the formulation and organization of the questions as well as in the choice of possible responses. Specialized works on the design of questionnaires make quite precise recommendations (Converse and Presser, 1986; Fink, 1995; Rossi et al., 1985; Schuman, 1996). Here we will simply summarize several fundamental points.

A questionnaire (or survey) generally begins with relatively simple and closed questions. It is preferable to group together questions that are more involved, complex or open at the end of the document. The questions should, as far as possible, follow a logical order that uses thematic groupings and facilitates the passage from one theme to another. There are two common sources of error that should be avoided when formulating and deciding the order of the questions. The halo effect results from associating a series of successive questions that are too similar to each other. This can occur, for example, when a long series of questions uses the same scale for all modes of response. To avoid the halo effect, the researcher can introduce a change in the form of the questions, or propose an open question. The contamination effect occurs when one question influences the subsequent question or questions. To guard against this bias, one needs to be scrupulously careful about the order of the questions. The unit of analysis (the industrial sector, the organization, a product line, a particular department …) that a question or a series of questions relates to must always be made clear, and any change of unit should be systematically acknowledged. When the survey includes questions relating to different subjects, it is useful to draw the respondent's attention to this by introducing the new subject with a short phrase separating the groups of questions.

The pre-test Once the researcher has prepared a first draft of the question-naire, he or she will need to carry out a pre-test – to test the form of the questions and their order, to ensure that respondents understand the questions and to assess whether the proposed modes of reply are relevant (Hunt et al., 1982). Ideally, the draft should be given to several respondents in face-to-face interviews, so that their non-verbal reactions can be noted. Following this, it is recommended that researchers carry out a pre-test using the same method they propose to use for the definitive questionnaire, and under the same conditions of interaction (or non-interaction) with the respondents. Data collected during the pre-test(s) also allows researchers to measure the internal validity of their scales. Through this phase the list of items can be refined so that only those which really measure the phenomenon being studied are retained. By the end of the pre-test phase, the questionnaire should be pertinent, efficient and clear for the researcher as well as for the respondents.

1.3 Administering a questionnaire

There are several ways of administering the questionnaire. It can be administered electronically – via e-mail, Internet or intranet – interviews can be conducted face to face or by video and telephone, or it can be sent out by mail. While each of these methods has a number of specific considerations, it must be remembered that administering the questionnaire harbors its own particular difficulties in each individual case, and always calls for prudence. A danger faced by all researchers is the risk of a weak response rate, which can call the whole research project into question. The issue here is the problem of managing data sources in the context of a survey conducted by questionnaire. Different researchers specializing in crafting questionnaires have proposed administration methods that enable researchers to obtain high response rates (Childers and Skinner, 1979; Dillman, 1978; Linsky, 1975; Yammarino et al., 1991) and we present the most elementary points here. Researchers need to be prepared to adapt these techniques to suit the socio-cultural context of their research and the means at their disposal. Finally, different techniques are used depending on whether the survey is administered by mail, in face to face interviews, by telephone or using information technology.

Administering a mailed questionnaire Mailed questionnaires are somewhat particular in that they are auto-administered by the respondents. Given the importance of motivating correspondents to complete a mailed questionnaire, great care must be taken over the document's general presentation. The questionnaire should be printed on white paper,[1] and should be in booklet form. There should be no questions on the first page – this page is often reserved for the title of the study and recommendations for the respondent. An illustration may also be used; sufficiently neutral to avoid the questionnaire being turned into an advertising brochure. It is also preferable to leave the final page free of questions. This page is reserved for the respondent's comments. To date, researchers have been unable to agree on the ideal length of a mailed questionnaire. Logically, subjects are more reticent about replying to a lengthy questionnaire, which requires more of their time. Certain specialists say questionnaires should not exceed ten pages, while others say they should be limited to four pages.

It is generally recommended to send an accompanying letter with a mailed questionnaire.

The Accompanying Letter

Under whose auspices is the questionnaire being sent out?

The organizations and people carrying out the research should be acknowledged, as well as those sponsoring it. If foreign organizations are involved or if the questionnaire is to be sent abroad then the names and descriptions of such organizations should be translated, or local equivalents cited as examples. The prestige and image of a sponsoring institution can play an important role.

Why carry out such a study?

This involves highlighting the objectives of the questionnaire and the themes it addresses.

Why take the trouble to reply to the questionnaire?

You should state clearly how the study will help increase understanding about the subject area concerned. You should also explain to respondents why their participation in the study is important – why they have been included in the sample. The respondents' specific qualities should be brought to the forefront. Direct financial rewards are rarely used in Europe and are not really feasible in the framework of university research. One can, nevertheless, offer to provide the respondent with a managerial summary of the research results. In the case of questionnaires that would only take up to 10–15 minutes to fill out, pointing out the time it should take permits the respondent to evaluate the cost of his or her participation.

Should anonymity be guaranteed?

Tests on the effect of subject anonymity on questionnaire return rates give contradictory results. On the basis of our own experience we concur with Dillman (1978), that one should state clearly that responses are anonymous, and that if respondents wish to contact the researcher, they can send their professional card in a separate envelope to that in which they return the completed questionnaire. It should be noted that respecting anonymity goes against the recommendations of several specialists who stress the need to personalize the relationship with the subjects of the study. However, studies show that such personalization yields divergent results (Linsky, 1975; Kanuk and Berenson, 1975).

Should the questionnaire be signed and dated?

It is important that the researcher signs each questionnaire so as to personalize it. Specialists frequently recommend setting a deadline to increase the return rate of a questionnaire that is auto-administered. However, this technique can rule out the possibility of a relaunch. Moreover, certain subjects will not return the questionnaire once the deadline has passed. This technique is, therefore, double-edged.

Once the questionnaire and accompanying letter have been drawn up, there is the auto-administration of the mailed questionnaire to think about. The fact that the subjects solicited are not in direct contact with the researcher leads to certain difficulties (Bourque and Fielder, 1995). It is impossible to be insistent, to rely on one's physical presence to help lessen a subject's reticence. One needs to alleviate these difficulties by developing other forms of contact or conduct. In the following we present some techniques for optimizing auto-administration of a mailed questionnaire.

Optimizing Auto-Administration of a Mailed Questionnaire

How does one establish contact with prospective subjects?

The researcher can contact respondents in advance to explain the objectives of the study and seek their cooperation. There are different forms of contact to choose from: contact by mail or e-mail, in person or by telephone. Contacting respondents by telephone seems the most efficient, as it enables the relationship between the subjects and the researcher to be personalized at reasonable cost.

How can you facilitate return of the questionnaire?

Certain authors propose including a reply envelope or, better still, a postage-paid envelope, although this can become costly. Failing this, providing a fax number or e-mail address can increase the likelihood of questionnaires being returned.

How should you deal with the phenomenon of non-response?

Dillman (1978) suggested a three-stage plan for reviving the subjects' interest. One week after sending out the questionnaire, the researcher telephones respondents to check they have received it, and to encourage them to reply. Three weeks after mailing it, a first letter of reminder can be sent to those who have not yet replied. Seven weeks after the initial mailing, a second reminder should be sent out along with a new copy of the questionnaire. The Dillman method seems effective (the author guarantees a return rate of more than 60 per cent). Sosdian and Sharp (1980) confirmed the need for a reminder: 10 per cent of the subjects who had received a questionnaire had filled it in, but simply forgotten to mail it. We have established through our own research that a reminder increases return rates by between 20 and 30 per cent. We therefore advise researchers to send respondents at least one reminder, including a new copy of the questionnaire in case they have not kept it. The only drawback of this procedure is its cost, which can be high if the study involves a large sample in several countries.

Administering a questionnaire face to face   This procedure allows the researcher to reply directly to any queries respondents may have about the actual nature of the questions. It also makes it easier to check that the sample is representative. The main limitation is that the researcher must always guard against expressing any opinion or sign of approval, or disapproval, at the risk of influencing the respondent. Moreover, this method blocks the responses of certain people who consider them too personal to be expressed face to face. When using this technique to administer a questionnaire, researchers still need to present the study clearly to the respondents, and involve them in its aims. The researcher should have a suitable text prepared to present the questionnaire, confronting the same issues as those discussed above for a letter accompanying a mailed questionnaire.

Administering a questionnaire by telephone   It is pointless to pretend that a respondent is anonymous during a telephone conversation. Yet when telephone interviews are used to complete a questionnaire, the researcher is confronted with the dilemma of choosing between personalizing the relationship and maintaining the subject's anonymity as much as is possible. One compromise solution can be to personalize the conversation while guaranteeing to respect the subject's anonymity. As with the preceding techniques, the researcher must begin the interaction by explaining the aims of the research and the contribution it will make. Preliminary contact by mail enables the researcher to prepare potential respondents and to explain their particular importance to the study. This technique avoids the element of surprise and lessens the negative reaction that the disturbance of a telephone call can so often provoke.

Administering a questionnaire using information technology   There are two possible ways information technology can be used to administer a questionnaire. The researcher may send out a file, a diskette, or a CD-ROM containing a program the respondents can load into their computers so as to reply directly to the questionnaire. The respondent then sends back a completed file. It is equally possible to ask respondents to connect to a web site – a link can be included in an e-mail – where they will find the questionnaire and can reply to it directly. These two methods have the advantage of freeing the researcher from the unappetizing tasks of envelope-stuffing and mailing, and inputting replies. It can provide data that can be directly used for statistical analyses. Dillman (1999) has gone into lengthy detail on the procedures to follow in his book.

1.4 Advantages and limitations of questionnaires

The questionnaire seems to be one of the most efficient ways of collecting primary data. It also offers the possibility of standardizing and comparing scales, and enables the anonymity of the data sources to be preserved. Nevertheless, data collection by questionnaire has certain limitations. It is not flexible. Once the administration phase is under way, it is no longer possible to backtrack. The researcher can no longer offset a lack of sufficient data or an error in the scale used. Furthermore, standardization of the measurement instrument has a downside: the data gathered using standardized methods is necessarily very perfunctory. Collecting data by questionnaire also exposes the researcher to the bias of the person making the statements. There is a commonly cited difference between declaratory measurements and behavioral measurements.

Some of the advantages and disadvantages inherent to the different methods of administering questionnaires are presented in Table 9.1.

2. Other Ways to Collect Data

There are other ways of collecting primary data for quantitative use. These are principally observation procedures and experimental methods.

Table 9.1   *Different ways to administer a questionnaire*

	Modes of administration			
	Post	Face to face	By telephone	By computer
Cost	Average: postage cost and cost of reproduction	High, if not carried out by the researcher.	High, if not carried out by the researcher.	Average if sent by mail, or low via the Internet
Sample monitoring	Weak. No means of knowing who has replied	High	High	Weak. No means of knowing who has replied
Time required	About two months	Depends heavily on the sample and number of researchers	Depends heavily on the sample and number of researchers	Quite short, except in the case of a relaunch

2.1 Observation

As noted by Silverman (1993), observation is not a collection method that is used very often in quantitative research. It is difficult to observe large samples, and to obtain a sample that is statistically large enough can require mobilizing several observers. This can entail another problem, that of the reliability of the measurement – as there is a risk that the observations will not be homogeneous. When using this collection method the researcher needs to develop and validate a standard (or systematic) observation framework from which to uniformly describe the types of behavior observed (Bouchard, 1976).

Taking account of the rigidity of such a system, the researcher will need to guard against possible errors of content (resulting from simplification of the observation) or context (inherent to the link between data and situations) and against instrumental bias (due to the researcher's judgements and assumptions) (Weick, 1968).

2.2 Experimental methods

Certain experimental methods enable us to draw out quantitative results and to make statistical use of the data collected. The quality of such experimentation rests above all on creating optimum conditions for the participants (behavior, willingness to participate, environment, etc.). Participants should never feel obliged to adopt special behavior to suit the experimentation situation. The researcher's job, therefore, is to create conditions that encourage participants to behave as naturally as possible. There are a number of different methods that can be employed to conduct the experimentation. The researcher can use the protocol method, where subjects are invited to reconstruct and describe 'out loud' their internal method of processing information when they need to make a decision. Another experimental method involves the subjects taking part in role-playing.

These experimental methods offer a wealth of information for the researcher. The variables are measurable and can be controlled, and the researcher can establish comparisons and test causal relationships between events. However, experimental methods are sometimes too simplistic and can be limited in terms of external validity. The results should always be analyzed with care, as they often give only limited scope for generalization.

SECTION 2   COLLECTING PRIMARY DATA FOR QUALITATIVE RESEARCH

Primary data collection cannot be a discreet step in the research process, particularly in qualitative research, which requires prolonged investigation in the field. This being the case, managing the interaction between the researcher and the data sources is a vital issue. We will conclude this section by presenting several approaches and source management strategies that can be used for collecting primary data.

1. Principal Methods

1.1 Interviewing

Interviewing is a technique aimed at collecting, for later analysis, discursive data that reflects the conscious or unconscious mind-set of individual interviewees. It involves helping subjects to overcome or forget the defense mechanisms they generally use to conceal their behavior or their thoughts from the outside world.

Individual interviews   In qualitative research, the interview involves questioning the subject while maintaining an empathetic demeanor: that is, accepting the subject's frame of reference, whether in terms of feelings or relevance. Subjects can say anything they wish, and all elements of their conversation have a certain value because they refer directly or indirectly to analytical elements of the research question. This is the opposite of following a set series of predetermined questions, designed to aggregate the thoughts or knowledge of a large number of subjects, as is characteristic of interviewing for quantitative research (Stake, 1995).

If such a principle is followed, the degree to which the researcher directs the dynamics of the interview can vary (Rubin and Rubin, 1995). Traditionally, a distinction is drawn between two types of interview: unstructured and semi-structured. In an unstructured interview, the interviewer defines a general subject area or theme without intervening to direct the subject's remarks. He or she limits interventions to those that facilitate the discussion, express understanding, provide reminders based on elements already expressed by the subject, or go more deeply into discursive elements already expressed. In a semi-structured interview, also called a 'focused' interview (Merton et al., 1990), the researcher applies the same principles, except that a structured guide allows the researcher to broach a series of subject areas defined in advance. This guide is completed during the course of the interview, with the aid of other questions

'Main questions' can be modified if, in the course of the interview, the subject broaches the planned subject areas without being pressed by the interviewer. In some cases certain questions may be abandoned, for example if the subject shows reticence about particular subjects and the researcher wishes to avoid blocking the flow of the face to face encounter. An interview rarely follows a predicted course. Anything may arise during the interview – interviewing demands astuteness and lively interest on the part of the researcher! In practice, a researcher who is absorbed in taking notes risks not paying enough attention to be able to take full advantage of opportunities that emerge in the dynamics of the interview. For this reason it is strongly advised to tape-record the interview, even though this can make the interviewee more reticent or circumspect in his or her remarks. An added advantage is that the taped data will be more exhaustive and more reliable. More detailed analyses can then be carried out on this data, notably content analyses.

Two different interviewing procedures are possible. Researchers can either conduct a systematic and planned series of interviews with different subjects, with an eye to comparing their findings, or they can work heuristically, using information as it emerges to build up their understanding in a particular field. Using the first method, the researcher is rigorous about following the same guide for all of the interviews, which are semi-directed. Using the second method, the researcher aims for a gradual progression in relation to the research question. Researchers might start with interviews that are only slightly structured, with the research question permanently open to debate, which allows subject participation in establishing the direction the research will take. They would then conduct semi-structured interviews on more specific subject areas. The transition from a 'creative' interview to an 'active' interview can provide an illustration of this procedure (see below).

Moving from a 'Creative' Interview to an 'Active' Interview

In the first encounters, conversation is a useful means of delving more deeply into a situation. This interviewing method falls within the category of 'creative' interviewing, as there is 'mutual revelation' on the part of the researcher and the subject, combined with a 'generation of emotion' (Douglas, 1985). A researcher's ability to expose himself or herself is, for the subjects, a measure of authenticity, and subjects are more likely to open up themselves if this happens. Clearly, 'emotion' cannot be generated in a single interview with a subject. For this to be possible, there needs to be a repeat interview. Subjects get to know the researcher better, and this in turn encourages them to be more open themselves. The researcher can then move in the direction of an 'active' interview, introducing rationality to counterbalance emotion (Holstein and Gubrium, 1995).

When research involves several actors within an organization or a sector, they might not have the same attitude to the researcher or the same view of the research question. The researcher may have to adapt to the attitude of each actor. According to Stake (1995), each individual questioned must be seen as having particular personal experiences and specific stories to tell. The way they are interviewed can therefore be adapted in relation to the information they are best able to provide (Rubin, 1994). Researcher flexibility is, therefore, a key factor in the successful collection of data by interview. It may be useful to organize the interviews so they are partly non-directive, which leaves room for suggestions from the subjects, and partly semi-directive, with the researcher specifying what kind of data is required. As Stake (1995: 65) points out; 'formulating the questions and anticipating probes that evoke good responses is a special art'.

Group interviews   A group interview involves bringing different subjects together with one or more animators. Such an interview places the subjects in a situation of interaction. The role of the animator(s) is delicate, as it involves helping the different individuals to express themselves, while directing the group dynamic. Group interviewing demands precise preparation, as the aims of the session and the rules governing the discourse must be clearly defined at the beginning of the interview: who is to speak and when, how subjects can interject and what themes are to be discussed.

Specialists in qualitative research differ on the effectiveness of group interview. Some argue that a group interview enables researchers to explore a research question or identify key information sources (Fontana and Frey, 1994). The interaction between group members stimulates their reflection on the problem put before them (Bouchard, 1976). Others point out that, in group interviews, subjects can become reticent about opening up in front of other participants (Rubin and Rubin, 1995). In management research, the biases and impediments inherent to group interviews are all the more obvious. Care is required when judging the authenticity of the discussion, as power games and the subjects' ambitions within the organization can influence the flow of the interview. If the inquiry is actually exploring these power games, a group interview will tend to reveal elements that the researcher can then evaluate using other collection methods. A group interview can also be used to obtain confirmation of latent conflicts and tensions within an organization that have already been suggested by other collection methods.

As in individual interviews, the animator of a group interview must be flexible, empathetic and astute. However, running a group interview successfully requires certain specific talents as well, to avoid altering the interview dynamic, which would distort the data collected (see below). For example, according to Merton et al. (1990), the researcher who is running a group interview must:

- prevent any individual or small coalition from dominating the group
- encourage recalcitrant subjects to participate
- obtain from the group as complete an analysis as possible of the subject of the inquiry.

Fontana and Frey (1994) point to another useful talent: knowing how to strike a balance between playing a directive role and acting as a moderator, so as to pay attention both to guiding the interview and to maintaining the group dynamic.

Finally, the group must contain as few superfluous members as possible and should fully represent all actors the research question relates to (Thompson and Demerath, 1952).

Taking into account the points we have just covered, group interviewing, with rare exceptions, cannot be considered a collection technique to be used on its own, and should always be supplemented by another method.

1.2 Observation

Observation is a method of data collection by which the researcher directly observes processes or behaviors in an organization over a specific period of time. With observation, the researcher can analyze factual data about events that have definitely occurred – unlike verbal data, the accuracy of which should be treated with some caution.

Two forms of observation can be distinguished, in relation to the viewpoint the researcher takes towards the subjects being observed (Jorgensen, 1989; Patton, 1980). The researcher may adopt either an internal viewpoint, using an approach based on participant observation, or an external viewpoint, by conducting non-participant observation. Between these two extremes, the researcher can also opt for intermediate solutions. Junker (1960) and Gold (1970) define four possible positions the researcher in the field may adopt: the complete participant, the participant as observer, the observer as participant and the complete observer.

Participant observation   When carrying out fieldwork, researchers must choose the degree to which they wish to 'participate'. We distinguish three degrees of researcher participation.

The researcher can, first, be a 'complete participant'. In this case, he or she does not reveal his or her role as a researcher to the subjects observed. The observation is thus covert. Complete participation presents both advantages and disadvantages. The data collected is not biased by the reactivity of the subjects (Lee, 1993). According to Douglas (1976), one of the few supporters of 'covert' observation via complete participation, this data collection technique is justified by the conflictual nature of social existence, and the resistance that exists *vis-à-vis* any type of investigation, even scientific. However, in opting for 'covert' observation, researchers may find it difficult to dig deeper, or confirm their observations through other techniques, such as interviewing. They also run the crippling risk of being discovered. The 'complete participant' is often led to use sophisticated methods of recording data so as to avoid detection (Bouchard, 1976). They have very little control over selection of their data sources, and their position in the field remains fixed: it cannot be modified, which means important opportunities may be missed (Jorgensen, 1989). Finally, 'covert' observation poses serious ethical problems (Punch, 1986). It can only be justified in exceptional circumstances, and cannot be defended by simply arguing that one is observing subjects so as to collect 'real data' (Lincoln and Guba, 1985).

The researcher can opt for a lesser degree of participation, taking the role of 'participant as observer'. This position represents a compromise. The researcher has a greater degree of freedom to conduct the investigations, and he or she can supplement his or her observations with interviews. Nevertheless, the researcher exposes himself or herself to subject reactivity, as he or she is appointed from within the organization. The researcher's very presence will have an impact on subject-sources of primary data, who may become defensive in face of the investigation. Take the case of a salaried employee in an organization who decides to do research work. His status as a member of the organization predominates over his role as researcher. The conflict of roles which arises can make it difficult for the researcher to maintain his or her position as a fieldworker.

Finally, the researcher can be an 'observer as participant'. His or her participation in the life of the organization being studied remains marginal, and his or her role as a researcher is clearly defined for the subject-sources. At the beginning of the study, the researcher risks encountering resistance from those being observed. However, such resistance can lessen with time, enabling the researcher to improve his or her capacity to conduct the observation. The researcher's behavior is the determining factor here. If he or she succeeds in gaining the confidence of the subject-sources, he or she then has more latitude to supplement the observation with interviews and to control the selection of data sources. The key is to remain neutral in relation to the subjects.

Non-participant observation   There are two types of non-participant observation: casual and formal. Casual observation can be an elementary step in an investigation, with the aim of collecting preliminary data in the field. It can also be considered as a complementary data source. Yin (1989) notes that, during a field visit to conduct an interview, researchers may observe indicators, such as the social climate or the financial decline of the organization, which they could then include in their database. If they decide to supplement verbal data obtained in interviews by systematically collecting observed data (such as details on the interviewee's attitude and any non-verbal communication that may take place), the observation can then be described as formal. Another way of carrying out formal observation as part of qualitative research can be systematically to observe certain behaviors over specific periods of time.

1.3 'Unobstrusive' methods

There is another way of collecting primary data that bisects the classification of collection methods that we have adopted so far. This involves using 'unobstrusive' methods. The primary data collected in this way is not affected by the reactivity of the subjects, as it is gathered without their knowledge (Webb et al., 1966). As demonstrated in Chapter 4, data obtained in this fashion can be used to supplement or confirm data collected 'obtrusively'.

Webb et al. (1966) proposed a system of classifying the different elements the researcher can use to collect data 'unobtrusively' into five categories:

- Physical traces: such as the type of floor covering used (generally more hard-wearing when the premises are very busy), or the degree to which shared or individual equipment is used.
- Primary archives used (running records): includes actuarial records, political and judicial records, other bureaucratic records, mass media.
- Secondary archives, such as episodic and private records: these can include sales records, industrial and institutional records, written documents.
- Simple observations about exterior physical signs: such as expressive movements, physical location, use of language, time duration.
- Behavior recorded through various media: includes photography, audio-tape, video-tape.

2. Coordinating Data Sources

One of the major difficulties facing a researcher who wants to conduct qualitative management research lies in gaining access to organizations and, in particular, to people to observe or interview. Researchers need to show flexibility when interacting with the subject-sources of primary data. As the sources are reactive, researchers can run the risk of contaminating them.

2.1 Accessing sources of primary data

Authorized access   It is crucial for researchers to establish beforehand whether they need to obtain authorized access to the site they wish to study. Such authorization is not given systematically. Many organizations, either to foster a reciprocal relationship with the research community, or simply by giving in to the mutual curiosity that exists between researchers and potential subjects, do allow access to their employees and sites (offices, production plants, etc.). Other organizations cultivate a culture of secrecy and are more inclined to oppose investigation by researchers. That said, should one refrain from working on a particular site because the company does not allow access? If this were the case, many research projects would never have seen the light of day. A great deal of information can be accessed today without the permission of those it concerns. It is also possible, if need be, to conduct interviews without the express agreement of the company involved. It is, however, more prudent to make the most of opportunities to access organizations that welcome researchers. By adopting this standpoint you can avoid having to confront conflict situations which, even if they do not call the actual research project into question, are nevertheless costly, as they demand extra effort on the part of the researcher. It is therefore useful to gain access to primary data-sources.

Building up trust   Negotiating access to a site requires time, patience, and sensitivity to the rhythms and norms of a group (Marshall and Rossman, 1989). Taking things gradually can minimize the potential threat the researcher may represent, and avoid access to the site being blocked (Lee, 1993). Researchers can use collection methods such as participant observation and in-depth interviewing to familiarize themselves with the context in which they are working and avoid, or at least delay, making any potentially damaging faux pas. These methods provide an opportunity to build the kind of trust that is the key to accessing data. While a subject's trust in a researcher does not guarantee the quality of the data collected, an absence of trust can prejudice the data significantly (Lincoln and Guba, 1985). To win the trust of the data sources, the researcher may need to obtain the sponsorship of an actor in the field. The sponsorship technique saves considerable time. Lee (1993) discusses the most well-known and best example of this technique: Doc, the leader of the Norton gang studied by Whyte (1944) in *Street Corner Society*. It is, in fact, thanks to Doc that Whyte, whose first attempts to enter the Street Corner Society were a failure, was finally able to gain access. This example illustrates the fundamental nature of a sponsor: he or she must have the authority to secure the other subjects' acceptance of the researcher.

  While having the backing of someone in the field is sometimes very useful, it can nevertheless lead to serious disadvantages in data collection. There are three different roles that sponsors may adopt (Lee, 1993). They can serve as a 'bridge' to an unfamiliar environment. They can also serve as a 'guide', suggesting directions and, above all, alerting the researcher to any possible faux pas in relation to the subjects. Finally, they can be a sort of 'patron' who helps the researcher to win the trust of the other subjects by exerting a degree of control over the research process. Access to the field is obtained indirectly via the 'bridge' and the 'guide' and, directly, via the 'patron'. Lee (1993) highlights the other side of the coin in relation to access with the help of a sponsor. In bringing the researcher onto the site, or sites, being studied, patrons exert an influence inherent to their reputation, with all the bias this entails. Moreover, according to our own observations, the sponsor as 'patron' can limit the study through the control he or she exercises over the research process. Sponsors can become adversaries if the process takes what they consider to be a threatening turn. Researchers must therefore take care not to turn systematically to the same sponsor, or they run the risk of introducing a 'heavy' instrumental bias. Subjects will unavoidably be selected through the prism of the sponsor's perception, rather than according to theoretical principles. To avoid this type of phenomenon, researchers should take advantage of their familiarity with the terrain and seek the patronage of other actors.

Flexibility   Always indispensable when using secondary data (for example, in relation to data availability), researcher flexibility (or opportunism) becomes even more necessary when managing primary data sources. It is pointless to envisage a research project without taking into account the interaction between the researcher and the sources of primary data. The researcher is confronted by the element of the unknown as 'what will be learned at a site is always dependent on the interaction between investigator and context' and 'the nature of mutual shapings cannot be known until they are witnessed' (Lincoln and Guba, 1985: 208).

2.2 Source contamination

One of the critical problems in managing primary data lies in the various contamination phenomena researchers have to confront. While they need not operate in a completely neutral fashion, they must both be conscious of and carefully manage the contamination risks engendered by their relationships with their sources.

Three types of contamination can occur: intra-group contamination, contamination between the researcher and the population interviewed, and contamination between primary and secondary data sources. We can define contamination as any influence exerted by one actor upon another, whether this influence is direct (persuasion, seduction, the impression one makes, humor, attitude, behavior, etc.) or indirect (sending a message via a third party, sending unmonitored signals to other actors, circulation of a document influencing the study sample, the choice of terms used in an interview guide, etc.).

Intra-group contamination is born of the interaction between the actors interviewed. When a researcher is conducting a long-term investigation on a site, those involved talk among themselves, discussing the researcher's intentions and assessing what motivates his or her investigations. If a sponsor introduced the researcher, the actors will tend to consider the sponsor's motivation and that of the researcher as one and the same. The researcher can appear to be a 'pioneering researcher' guided by the sponsor. The subject-sources of primary data will tend to contaminate each other when exchanging mistaken ideas about the researcher's role. The effect is that a collective attitude is generated towards the researcher, which can heavily influence the responses of the interviewees. When a researcher is working on a sensitive site, the collective interests associated to the site's sensitivity tends to increase intra-group contamination (Mitchell, 1993). The sponsor's role as a mediator and conciliator becomes essential in ensuring that the researcher continues to be accepted. However, while well intentioned, sponsors – if not sufficiently briefed by the researcher – can do more harm than good by giving the group a biased picture of the research objectives so as to make their 'protégé' better accepted.

The sponsor can also contaminate the researcher. This happens quite often, as the sponsor, in providing access to the actors will, at the same time, 'mold' the interviewee population and the sequence of the interviews. This first type of influence can be benign as long as the sponsor does not take it upon himself or herself to give the researcher his or her personal opinion about – or evaluation of – 'the actor's real role in the organization'. It is very important that researchers plan exactly how they are going to manage their relationship with the sponsor, as much in the sense of limiting this key actor's influence on the research process, as in relation to ensuring that those being studied do not lose their confidence in the research and the researcher.

Finally, secondary sources can be both contaminated and contaminating at the same time. Where internal documents are concerned, researchers must take care they have clearly identified the suppliers and authors of the secondary sources used. Actors may influence, or may have influenced, these sources. For example, actors have a tendency to create firewalls and other barriers when archiving or recording internal data so as to hide their errors by accentuating the areas of uncertainty in the archives. In large industrial groups, these fire-walls are constructed using double archiving systems that separate Head Office archives from those labeled 'General Records' or 'Historical Records'. This works as a filtering mechanism to shield the motivations behind, or the real conditions surrounding, the organization's decisions. This is all the more true in a period of crisis, when urgent measures are taken to deal with archives (the destruction of key documents, versions purged before being archived). In such a case the data available to researchers will hamper their work, as it portrays a situation as has been 'designed' by the actors involved.

While one cannot circumvent this problem of contamination, one solution lies in the researcher systematically confronting actors with any possibilities of contamination discovered during the course of the research. Researchers can resort to double-sourcing, that is, confirming information supplied by one source with a second source. They can make the actors aware of the possibility of contamination, asking for their help to 'interpret' the available secondary sources. Another solution lies in replenishing one's sources, and removing those sources that are too contaminated. This demands a heavy sacrifice on the part of the researcher, who must discard as unusable any data that is likely to be contaminated. Such an approach nevertheless enables researchers to guarantee the validity of their results.

3. Strategies for Approaching and Managing Data Sources

We present several strategies for approaching and managing data sources. We describe the options open to researchers depending on their research question, the context of their data collection and their personal affinities.

3.1 Contractual and oblative approaches

To avoid misunderstanding, and as protection if any disputes arise, one can consider bringing the research work within the terms of a contract. This can reassure the organization that the researcher's presence on their premises will be for a limited time period. Indeed, access to all of an organization's data sources, both primary and secondary, can be conditional to the existence of such a contract. The contract generally relates to the researcher's obligation to provide the organization in question with a report of the research. To protect their own interests, researchers should be as honest and precise as possible about the purpose of their research.

A contractual framework can influence the research work. The contract should clearly specify which data collection methods are to be employed, as such precision can be very useful if any disputes arise. Although researchers may at times seek funding from an organization to finance their work, if they wish to have a significant degree of freedom, they should avoid placing themselves in a subordinate position. It could be in the researcher's interest to place reasonable limits on any contractual responsibility. The most crucial part of a research contract with an organization concerns the confidentiality of the results and publication rights. It is legitimate for an organization to protect the confidentiality of its skills, designs, methods, codes, procedures and documents. While it is useful to submit one's work to the organization before final publication, the researcher must not become a 'hostage' to the organization's wishes. In fact, a researcher can set a deadline for the organization to state any disagreement, after which authorization to publish is considered to have been given. Finally, it is worthwhile remembering that researchers retain intellectual property rights over their work, without any geographic or time limit. Negotiations over intellectual property rights can very quickly become difficult, particularly if the research concerns the development of management instruments.

In contrast to this contractual arrangement, the researcher can take a much more informal approach, which we will describe as *oblative*, as it is based on a spirit of giving. While it may well seem anachronistic to refer to a gift in management research, this kind of approach can turn out to be highly productive in terms of obtaining rare and relevant data. If the researcher is keen for the subjects to participate in crafting the research question, and establishes an interpersonal relationship that is specific to each case and is based on mutual trust, patiently built up, subjects can become the source of invaluable data. An oblative approach is founded on trust and keeping one's word. The choice of an oblative approach can be justified if the researcher wishes to maintain a large degree of flexibility in his or her relationship with the primary data sources.

3.2 Covert or overt approaches

In approaching data sources, researchers face the following dilemma: should they employ a 'covert' approach – retaining absolute control over the management of the primary data sources and conducting an investigation in which they hide their research aims – or should they opt for an 'overt' approach – in which they do not hide their objectives from the subject-sources, but offer them greater control over the investigation process. Each of these options presents advantages and disadvantages.

The choice of a 'covert' investigation greatly limits a researcher's movements in the field, as actors may harbor suspicions about the researcher's intentions (Lee, 1993). Also, because it leaves the subject no latitude, this type of data-source management raises difficulties regarding the morality of the underlying method (Whyte, 1944). The researcher cannot assume 'the right to deceive, exploit, or manipulate people' (Warwick, 1982: 55).

The choice of an 'overt' approach, whereby researchers do not hide their research aims, means they have to confront the phenomenon of subject reactivity. 'If the researcher must expose all his intentions in order to gain access, the study will be hampered' (Marshall and Rossman, 1989: 56). The researcher also runs the risk of being refused access to the site. An 'overt' approach must be parsimonious, and take account of the specificity of the interaction with each subject, the maturity of the researcher–subject relationship, and its limits. Choosing such an approach involves going beyond the strictly technical and calling upon qualities such as 'empathy, sensitivity, humor and sincerity', which 'are important tools for the research' (Rubin and Rubin, 1995: 12).

All told, we consider that, if data is to be collected 'overtly', that is with the subjects' knowledge, managing primary data-sources involves a certain transparency. The 'covert' approach, though, seems to us only to be compatible with more discreet collection techniques: collection without the subjects' knowledge. Such an approach needs to be justified from an ethical point of view: by the fact that the reactivity of the subjects would constitute an instrumental bias, and by the innocuous nature of the research results as far as the subjects are concerned.

3.3 Distance or intimacy in relation to the data source

Should one develop an intimate relationship, or should a certain distance be maintained in relation to the subjects? It is necessary, in this respect, to take account of the 'paradox of intimacy' (Mitchell, 1993). The more the researcher develops 'intimacy' with those being questioned, the more the interviewees will tend to reveal themselves and disclose information. However, such an attitude on the part of the researcher can have an extremely negative impact on the research in terms of internal validity. The more a researcher becomes involved in 'dis-inhibiting' a research subject-source, the more he or she will tend to enter into agreement with the actor, offering a reciprocal degree of intimacy. As Mitchell has pointed out, the researcher also exposes himself or herself to the possibility that the subjects will 'turn against him or her' when his or her work is published. After publishing a study of mountain-climbers, Mitchell (1983) was accused of having 'spied' on them to obtain his information, when the data had, in fact, become available because the author developed strong intimacy with certain subject-sources. Intimacy with sources can pose very serious problems of loyalty in the relationship after the research work has been completed.

Managing the dilemma of distance versus intimacy also poses problems relating to the amount of information the researcher acquires in the field and

Affect

Low ——————————————————————→ High

Unsympathetic   Sympathetic

	'Spy': informed and unsympathetic	'Ally': informed and sympathetic

High
 	
↑
 	
Informed
 	
Cognition
	+ Faster access to data
	+ Researcher not involved
	   in situation (expert)
	+ Independance *vis-à-vis* actors
	− Threatens intragroup
	   solidarity
	− Belief in 'transparent
	   disguise'
	− Risk of dispassionate
	   observation
		+ Facilitates intergroup solidarity
		+ Protects access to the
		   field (sponsor)
		+ Permits long interviews
		− Problem of 'paradox of
		   intimacy'
		− Risk of contamination
		   the sources
		− Political games
		   (something wanted in return)

	'Outsider': naïve and unsympathetic	**'Novice': naïve and sympathetic**

Naïve
 	
Low
	+ Facilitates intragroup solidarity
	+ Less implicating for the source
	+ The researcher is not a menace
	− Difficult to catch
	   theatrical behavior
	− Sources use formal
	   language
	− Actors remain onlookers,
	   not involved
		+ Researcher is 'socialized'
		+ Source gains confidence
		+ Spirit of giving freely
		− The researcher becomes
		   a 'prey'
		− Feeling of 'treason' after
		   the fact
		− Researcher exploited
		   (for political ends)

Figure 9.1   *Perception of the researcher's role based
on knowledge and emotional involvement*

the emotional involvement developed with the actors concerned. Mitchell suggests two key aspects that should be considered when looking at the researcher's role: the knowledge researchers acquire about the site, and their emotional involvement with the subjects (see Figure 9.1.).

SECTION 3   COLLECTING SECONDARY DATA

Secondary data is data that already exists. It is advisable to systematically begin a research project by asking whether any appropriate secondary data is available. Use of such data presents numerous advantages. It is generally inexpensive, it has already been assembled, and it does not necessarily require access to the people who supplied it. It has historical value and is useful for establishing comparisons and evaluating primary data. However, secondary data can be difficult to obtain, or obsolete, and can vary in the degree to which it is approximate or exhaustive. Moreover, it is possible that the data format does not fully correspond with that used by the researcher, in which case it has to be changed from its original form into a format better suited to present needs. Researchers, therefore, have to understand exactly why the data was originally put together before they can decide to use it or not.

1. Internal Secondary Data

Internal secondary data is information that has already been produced by organizations or private individuals. The data was not collected to respond to the specific needs of the researcher, but constitutes a veritable data-source for those consulting it. Archives, notes, reports, documents, rules and written procedures, instructions and press cuttings are just some of the types of internal data the researcher can use.

There are several advantages with such data. First, analyzing it enables one to reconstitute past actions that have had an influence on events and decisions and involved individuals. The use of internal data, indispensable within the framework of an historical and longitudinal procedure (monography, process analysis over a lengthy period), generates information that actors do not discuss spontaneously during face to face interviews. It is, therefore, normal for researchers to begin by gathering documentation and informing themselves about their subject by collecting such data. Finally, it is often necessary to analyze internal data in order to triangulate the data and validate its reliability.

However, analyzing archives and internal documents can pose problems. First, documentary sources can be difficult to use on their own. In terms of content, such data cannot always be easily validated, and one must, therefore, identify any possible bias on the part of those who compiled it or authorized its compilation. We saw in Section 2 of this chapter that contamination of primary data can spread to secondary data. We also underlined the bias that exists when one is not aware of a system of double archives. As researchers do not always have sufficient information to discover the context in which particular documents were drawn up, they must interpret them subjectively, and give thought to any possible validation problems that might arise when using this kind of source.

To collect such data, the researcher needs to be in contact with people on the site being studied. With semi-private data, access can be relatively easy. This is the case, for example, with reports of the activities of firms quoted on the stock exchange, and with university research or public studies. It is also possible to consult certain archives belonging to chambers of commerce, trade unions and political organizations and, more generally, all the administrative bodies that are responsible for keeping public or semi-public statistics. However, such documents are not always very accessible for reasons of confidentiality or poor distribution. Access to internal secondary data is, therefore, neither automatic nor easy to obtain.

How to process the information depends on the type of data collected. When data is presented purely in the form of documents, researchers generally analyze their content. When it is in numerical form, they would be more likely to conduct statistical or accounting analyses.

In summary, the main advantage of collecting internal data is the low cost of accessing the information, but one should take great care when processing it.

2. External Secondary Data

To collect external secondary data, it is worthwhile going to libraries and other documentation centers with a large stock of periodicals and other works dealing with the research field one has in mind. Access to theses and studies that have already been published or are in progress is indispensable to the spread of knowledge and evolution of research. Two important steps are to identify and to read works by researchers working on the same question. When one is starting a research project, these steps enable better targeting and justification of the subject. During the course of the research, they enable the researcher to remain permanently in touch with the evolution of the subject and any changes in the views of other researchers. Governmental publications (such as official documents or ministerial studies), publications produced by public and/or international organizations and private publications are all important sources of external data. Finally, press cuttings and private directories (*Kompass*, *Who Owns Who* ...) are easy to access in order to build up files on the organizations being studied. To sum up, many findings are the fruit of chance discoveries on library shelves, chatroom discussions over the Internet, or the consultation of web sites related to the subject.

SECTION 4 DATA-SOURCE CONFIDENTIALITY

Management research is carried out in a context that can be 'sensitive', and the degree of sensitivity can vary. The researcher's investigation may constitute a threat to the organizations being studied and their members. This potential threat can be internal, relating to the risk of actors' attitudes or behavior being revealed, which can have consequences on the life of the organization. 'The presence of a researcher is sometimes feared because it produces a possibility that deviant activities will be revealed' (Lee, 1993: 6). The researcher may represent a threat *vis-à-vis* the world outside the organization, as that which relates to the management of an organization can have an impact on the organization's relationship with its environment. It is, therefore, imperative to underline that all management research is characterized by varying degrees of confidentiality. The degree of confidentiality will also vary depending on the personality of the actors the researcher is brought into contact with.

Confidentiality imposes three kinds of constraint on the researcher. First there is the question of protecting confidentiality during the course of the research. Confidentiality can also have implications on the validation of results by subject-sources. The final problem relates to publication of the research results.

1. Protecting Data Confidentiality

Researchers working on 'sensitive' topics must understand the risks their data sources may run. In this situation researchers are confronted with the need to protect the results of the inquiry – their notes and the transcriptions of their interviews. They need to ensure that the anonymity of the subjects being questioned or observed, and the organizations being studied, is protected.

Researchers who truly wish to protect the anonymity of their interviewees and the confidentiality of their data are forced to become involved in a complex process. The destruction of any material that connects pseudonyms with real actors, along with the wiping of tape or video recordings, protects data confidentiality and guarantees complete anonymity. Such measures, notably the wiping of tapes, can increase the confidence of actors and considerably improve the quality of the data collected. It may be worthwhile using cryptographic software to protect transcriptions from any accidental disclosure (loss or theft of a computer, for example). Before each analysis and editing session, one needs to decode the material saved and re-encode it at the end. It is, however, advisable to keep a non-coded version of the data in a totally safe place as encoding and decoding operations can be subject to failures which will alter the files.

2. Using Data-sources to Validate Results

In the April 1992 edition of the *Journal of Culture and Ethnography*, Whyte was criticized for failing to follow the deontological principle of submitting the results of his analysis of Cornerville society to all those he met and observed. Whyte replied that, at the time he carried out his work, he had never heard of such a principle and that, most importantly, his analysis could have unfortunate consequences on relationships between the actors concerned and on the image they had cultivated of themselves (Whyte, 1993). This latter point seems to us to be essential. Although the principle of having subjects validate research results is justly recommended by numerous authors (Miles and Huberman, 1984b; Lincoln and Guba, 1985) in accordance with the research principle of refutation (Glaser and Strauss, 1967), if actors are to be 'required' to read the researcher's findings so as to provide an alternative formulation or interpretation (Stake, 1995), it is no less necessary to take account of the possible 'sensitive' character of the elements brought forward. One solution is to conceal certain results according to the specific position of the actors consulted. We agree with Whyte in considering it pointless to require all subjects questioned or observed to participate in validating the results of a research project. Both the results that are presented and the subjects they are presented to must be selected judiciously. It is clear that the familiarity the researcher will have acquired with the field (Miles and Huberman, 1984b), will be of great help in this procedure.

3. Publishing the Research

Publication of research results is the final issue to consider as far as the issue of managing data sources is concerned, whether the terrain is considered to be 'sensitive' or not. Maintaining the anonymity of data sources means other researchers are less able to verify the research results. However, cooperation of those in the field may be conditional on the use of pseudonyms. In this case, the researcher must take care that the link between the pseudonyms and the real actors is not too easy to establish. It may be useful to submit all publication plans to these sources to obtain their agreement. Nevertheless, this method has the disadvantage of being heavy to manage; it also imposes restrictions on the researcher, as the sources may abuse their discretionary power. The researcher may be faced with the dilemma between respecting the moral contract established with the subject-sources and the need to publish the final work (Punch, 1986).

CONCLUSION

In our efforts to present strategies for data collection and source management, we have drawn inspiration from our respective experiences and made extensive use of the available literature on these subjects. We have considered the different predicaments researchers may face. Novice researchers may find certain of our notions and suggestions complex. They are, nevertheless, very useful, and we have turned to them ourselves in many situations. There are those who fear that digging too deeply into published works will delay their investigation in the field, and we can only emphasize to them that solutions to the many problems posed by data collection and source management will not necessarily be found in a formal guide. Certain modalities and solutions still have to be developed by researchers individually, as each research situation has its own particularities as much in relation to the personality of the researcher as to the management situation he or she wishes to analyze. Researchers are, above all, invited to ask themselves those questions most useful to them, given the particular situation in which they find themselves. They will find the answers either by delving into relevant literature, or through their own inspiration.

NOTE

1 LaGarce and Kuhn (1995) showed that questionnaires printed on colored paper had a lower return rate than those printed on white paper (all else being equal). The positive impact on return rates of the use of color in logos and titles has, however, been amply demonstrated.

FURTHER READING

Bearden, W.O., Netmeyer, R.G. and Mobley, M.F., *Handbook of Marketing Scales*, Thousand Oaks, CA: Sage, 1993.
Fink, A., *The Survey Kit*, Thousand Oaks, CA: Sage, 1995.
Lincoln, Y.S. and Guba, E.G., *Naturalistic Inquiry*, Beverly Hills, CA: Sage, 1985.
Miles, A.M. and Huberman, A.M., *Analysing Qualitative Data: A Sourcebook for New Methods*, Beverly Hills, CA: Sage, 1984a.

10

VALIDITY AND RELIABILITY

Carole Drucker-Godard, Sylvie Ehlinger and Corinne Grenier

Outline

Both during their research work and once it is completed, researchers must always consider the validity and the reliability of their research. This chapter discusses issues of the reliability and validity of our measuring instruments, and the reliability as well as the internal and external validity of our research as a whole. The chapter then provides researchers with some methods that can be used to improve the validity and reliability of their work.

One of the questions researchers often ask is how their research can be both precise and of practical use to other researchers. To what extent can their results contribute to the area of science in which they work? To answer these questions researchers need to evaluate their work in relation to two criteria, that of validity and of reliability.

To assess the overall validity of our research (and its reliability, as we will see later on), it is necessary to be sure of various more specific types of validity. These include construct validity, the validity of the measuring instrument, the internal validity of the research results and the external validity of those same results. These different kinds of validity concern both the research in its entirety (internal and external validity), and individual research components (the concepts or the measuring instruments used).

Although this chapter analyzes each of these different types of validity individually, it is not always possible to determine tests specific to each one.

More generally, there are two main concerns in relation to validity: assessing the relevance and the precision of research results, and assessing the extent to which we can generalize from these results. The first is a question of testing the validity of the construct and the measuring instrument, and the internal validity of the results – these three tests can in some cases involve very similar techniques. The extent to which we can generalize from research results is essentially a question of assessing the external validity of these results.

In assessing reliability we try to establish whether the study could be repeated by another researcher or at another time with the same results. This concept, like validity, involves two different levels: the reliability of the measuring instrument and the more overall reliability of the research. Even though these criteria have long been considered as applying only to quantitative research, the question of the validity and reliability of research applies as much to qualitative as to quantitative work. There is an essential difference, however, in that we test quantitative research to *assess* its validity and reliability, whereas with qualitative research, rather than testing, we take precautions to *improve* validity and reliability.

There is no single method for testing the validity and reliability of a research project. Some techniques used for quantitative research can be inappropriate for qualitative research, which has led recent studies (Miles and Huberman, 1984a; Silverman, 1993) to propose validation techniques appropriate to a qualitative methodology.

SECTION 1   CONSTRUCT VALIDITY

1. Definition and Overview

The concept of construct validity is peculiar to the social sciences, where research often draws on one or several abstract concepts that are not always directly observable (Zaltman et al., 1973). These can include change, performance, or power. Concepts are the building blocks of propositions and theories used to describe, explain or predict organizational phenomena. As they are abstract forms that generally have several different meanings, it is often difficult to find rules to delimit them. Because of this it is important that the researcher's principal concern is the need to establish a common understanding of the concepts used. This poses the question of the validity of these concepts, and in the following discussion and in Table 10.1 we present several different approaches to concept validity (Zaltman et al., 1973).

Among the different types of validity, those most often used are *criterion-related* validity content validity and construct validity. However, as Carmines and Zeller (1990) emphasize, *criterion* validation procedures cannot be applied to all of the abstract concepts used in the social sciences. Often no relevant criterion exists with which to assess a measure of a concept. (For example while the meter-standard forms a reference criterion for assessing distance, there is no universal criterion for assessing a measure of organizational change). In the same way, content validity assumes we can delimit the domain covered by a concept. For example, the concept 'arithmetical calculation' incorporates addition, subtraction, multiplication and division. But what is covered by concepts such as organizational change or strategic groups? Content validity is therefore quite difficult to apply in the social sciences (Carmines and Zeller, 1990). As pointed out by Cronbach and Meehl (1955: 282),[1] it seems that only construct validity is really relevant in social sciences: 'construct validity must be investigated whenever no criterion on the universe of content is accepted as entirely adequate to define the quality to be measured'.

Table 10.1   *Types of concept validity*
(Zaltman et al., 1973: 44)

1. Observational validity	The degree to which a concept is reducible to observations
2. Content validity	The degree to which an operationalization represents the concept about which generalizations are to be made
3. Criterion-related validity	The degree to which the concept under consideration enables one to predict the value of some other concept that constitutes the criterion
3a. Predictive validity	A subtype of criterion-related validity in which the criterion measured is separated in time from the predictor concept
3b. Concurrent validity	A subtype criterion-related validity in which criterion and the predictor concepts are measured at the same time
4. Construct validity	The extent to which an operationalization measures the concept which it purports to measure
4a. Convergent validity	The degree to which two attempts to measure the same concept through maximally different methods are convergent. It is generally represented by the correlation between the two attempts
4b. Discriminant validity	The extent to which a concept differs from other concepts
4c. Nomological validity	The extent to which predictions based on the concept which an instrument purports to measure are confirmed
5. Systemic validity	The degree to which a concept enables the integration of previously unconnected concepts and/or the generation of a new conceptual system
6. Semantic validity	The degree to which a concept has a uniform semantic usage
7. Control validity	The degree to which a concept is manipulatable and capable of influencing other variables of influence

One of the main difficulties in assessing construct validity in management research lies in the process of operationalization. Concepts are reduced to a series of operationalization or measurement variables. For example, the concept 'organizational size' can be operationalized through the variables turnover, number of employees or total assets. Such variables are observable or measurable indicators of a concept that is often not directly observable. We call this operationalized concept the 'construct' of the research. When we address construct validity, we do not attempt to examine the process of constructing the research question, but the process of operationalizing it. Research results are not measures of the theoretical concept itself, but measures of the *construct* – the concept as it is put into operation. In questioning the validity of the construct we must ensure that the operationalized concept expresses the theoretical concept.

2. Assessing Construct Validity

2.1 Quantitative research

Testing construct validity in a quantitative research project consists most often in determining whether the variables used to measure the phenomenon being studied are a good representation of it.

To achieve this, researchers need to ensure that different variables used to measure the same phenomenon correlate strongly with each other ('convergent validity') and that variables used to measure different phenomena are not perfectly correlated ('discriminant validity'). In other words, testing construct validity comes down to confirming that variables measuring the same concept converge, and differ from variables that measure different concepts. To measure the correlation between items, researchers can use Campbell and Fiske's (1959) multitrait-multimethod matrix.

The researcher can equally well turn to other statistical data-processing tools. In particular, factor analysis can be used to measure the degree of construct validity (Carmines and Zeller, 1990).

2.2 Qualitative research

For qualitative research we need to establish that the variables used to operationalize the studied concepts are appropriate. We also need to evaluate the degree to which our research methodology (both the research design and the instruments used for collecting and analysing data) enables us to answer the research question. It is therefore essential, before collecting data, to ensure that the unit of analysis and the type of measure chosen will enable us to obtain the necessary information: we must define what is to be observed, how and why.

We must then clearly establish the initial research question, which will guide our observations in the field. Once this has been done, it is then essential to define the central concepts, which more often than not are the dimensions to be measured. For example, in order to study organizational memory, Girod-Séville (1996) first set out to define its content and its mediums. She defined it as the changeable body of organizational knowledge (which is eroded and enhanced over time) an organization has at its disposal, and also clearly defined each term of her definition.

The next step consists of setting out, on the basis of both the research question and existing literature, a conceptual framework through which the various elements involved can be identified. This framework provides the basis on which to construct a methodology, and enables the researcher to determine the characteristics of the observational field and the units of the analysis. The conceptual framework describes, most often in a graphic form, the main dimensions to be studied, the key variables and the relationships which are assumed to exist between these variables. It specifies what is to be studied, and through this determines the data that is to be collected and analyzed.

The researcher should show that the methodology used to study the research question really does measure the dimensions specified in the conceptual framework. To this end, writers such as Yin (1989) or Miles and Huberman (1984a) propose the following methods to improve the construct validity of qualitative research:

- Use a number of different sources of data.
- Establish a 'chain of evidence' linking clues and evidence that confirm an observed result. This should enable any person outside the project to follow

exactly how the data has directed the process, leading from the formulation of the research question to the statement of the conclusions.
- Have the case study verified by key actors.

> **Example: Strategies used in qualitative research to improve construct validity (Miles and Huberman, 1984a; Yin, 1989)**
>
> **Multiple data-sources:** interviews (open, semi-directive, to correlate or to validate), documentation (internal documents, union data, internal publications, press articles, administrative records, etc.), the researcher's presence in the field (obtaining additional information about the environment, the mood in the workplace, seeing working conditions firsthand, observing rituals such as the coffee-break, informal meetings, etc.).
>
> **Having key informants read over the case study:** this includes those in charge of the organizational unit being studied, managers of other organizational units, managers of consultant services that operate within the organization.

SECTION 2 RELIABILITY AND VALIDITY OF THE MEASURING INSTRUMENT

1. Definition and Overview

In the social sciences, measurement can be defined as the process that enables us to establish a relationship between abstract concepts and empirical indicators (Carmines and Zeller, 1990). Through measurement, we try to establish a link between one or several observable indicators (a cross in a questionnaire, a sentence in a meeting or a document, an observed behavior, etc.) and an abstract concept, which is not directly observable, nor directly measurable, and which we aim to study. We try to determine the degree to which a group of indicators represents a given theoretical concept. One of the main preoccupations of researchers is to verify that the data they plan to collect in the field relates as closely as possible to the reality they hope to study. However, numerous occasions for error are likely to arise, making every method of measuring phenomena or the subject being observed more difficult. These errors can include: actors giving false information; tired observers transcribing their observations badly; changes in the attitudes of respondents between two surveys; or errors in the process of transforming qualitative data into quantitative data. It is therefore essential to ensure that empirical indicators (or field data) are comparable to the measurements employed. This will provide the best possible representation of the phenomenon being investigated. The researcher must, then, consider – for each measurement used – the question of its reliability and its validity. This in turn makes it necessary to address the process by which this measurement has been obtained or arrived at: researchers must demonstrate that the instrument or the instruments used enable them to obtain reliable and valid measurements.

Reliability and Validity of a Measuring Instrument

Let us suppose that a pediatrician measures two of her patients, each one separately every year, with a tape-measure. The children's mother measures them similarly, with the same tape-measure. If she measures each child to be the same height as the pediatrician measures them, we would say that the measurement is reliable.

  Imagine though, if an old tape-measure were used, one missing the first two inches. In this case, although the tape-measure accurately measures inches, the results obtained in measuring the children, for example, will not be correct – the children will measure two inches less than the true measurement. The tool, the tape-measure, is therefore not valid. Let us suppose that, in addition, someone confuses the measuring instruments and uses scales to measure the children's height. The tool in this case, the scales, is not suited for the information (height) which it is expected to collect. This tool is therefore also invalid.

To be reliable, a measuring instrument must allow different observers to measure the same subject with the same instrument and arrive at the same results, or permit an observer to use the same instrument to arrive at similar measures of the same subject at different times. To be valid, the instrument must on the one hand measure what it is expected to measure, and on the other hand give exact measures of the studied object.

The validity, just as much as the reliability, of a measuring instrument is expressed in degrees (more or less valid, more or less reliable) and not in absolute terms (valid or not valid, reliable or not reliable). Researchers can assess the validity or reliability of an instrument in comparison with other instruments.

2. Assessing the Reliability of a Measuring Instrument

In assessing reliability, the researcher is assessing whether measuring the same object or the same phenomenon with the same measuring instrument will give results that are as similar as possible. Correlations between duplicated or reproduced measurements of the same object or phenomenon, using the same instrument, need to be calculated. This duplication can be carried out either by the same observer at different times, or by different observers simultaneously.

2.1 Measuring instruments used in quantitative research

To assess the reliability and validity of quantitative measuring instruments, researchers are most often drawn to refer to the true value model. This consists of breaking the result of a measurement into different elements: the true value (theoretically the perfect value) and error terms (random error and non-random error).

The measure obtained = true value + random error + non-random error

- 'Random error' occurs when the phenomenon measured by an instrument is subject to vagaries, such as circumstances, the mood of the people being questioned, or fatigue on the part of the interviewer. It is important, however, to note that the very process of measuring introduces random error. The distinction between different indicators used should not be made according to whether or not they induce random error, but rather according to the degree of random error. Generally, random error is inversely related to the degree of reliability of the measuring instrument: the greater the reliability, the smaller the random error.
- 'Non-random error' (also called 'bias'), refers to a measuring instrument producing a systematic biasing effect on the measured phenomenon. A thermometer that measures 5 degrees more than the real temperature is producing a non-random error. The central problem of the validity of the measuring instrument is bound to this non-random error. In general terms, the more valid the instrument, the smaller the non-random error.

Later in this chapter (section 3.1) we will discuss techniques used to improve measurement validity.

In the following discussion we will focus essentially on measuring scales (used in questionnaires), as these constitute the main group of tools used with quantitative approaches. As the reliability of a measurement is linked to the risk that it will introduce random error, we present below four methods used to estimate this reliability.

'Test-retest'   This method consists in carrying out the same test (for example posing the same question) on the same individuals at different times. We can then calculate a correlation coefficient between the results obtained in two successive tests. However, these measurements can be unstable for reasons independent of the instrument itself. The individuals questioned might themselves have changed; to limit this possibility, there should not be too much delay between the two tests. The fact of having been given the test previously may also sensitize a subject to the question, and predispose him to respond differently in the second test – subjects may have given the problem some thought, and perhaps modified their earlier opinions. It has also been observed, conversely, that if the time lapse between two measurements is too short, actors often remember their first response and repeat it despite apparent changes.

Alternative forms   This method also involves administering two tests to the same individuals, the difference being that in this case the second test is not identical to the first; an alternative questionnaire is used to measure the same object or phenomenon, with the questions formulated differently. Although this method limits the effect that memory can have on test results (a source of error with the test-retest method), it is sometimes difficult in practice to design two alternative tests.

'Split-halves'   This method consists of giving the same questionnaire at the same time to different actors, but in this case the items are divided into two

halves. Each half must present the phenomenon the researcher seeks to measure, and contain a sufficient number of items to be significant. A coefficient correlation of the responses obtained in each half is then calculated (one of the most commonly used of such coefficients is that of Spearman-Brown (Brown, 1910; Spearman, 1910). The difficulty of this method lies in the division of questionnaire items – the number of ways of dividing these items increases greatly as the number of items contained in a scale increases. This problem of dividing the items is a limitation of this method, as the coefficients obtained will vary in line with the division method used. One solution to this problem consists in numbering the items and dividing the odd from the even.

Internal consistency   Methods have been developed to estimate reliability coefficients that measure the internal cohesion of a scale without necessitating any dividing or duplicating of items. Of these coefficients the best known and most often used is Cronbach's Alpha (Cronbach, 1951).

   Cronbach's Alpha is a coefficient that measures the internal coherence of a scale that has been constructed from a group of items. The number of items initially contained in the scale is reduced according to the value of the coefficient alpha, so as to increase the reliability of the construct's measurement. The value of α varies between 0 and 1. The closer it is to 1, the stronger the internal cohesion of the scale (that is, its reliability). Values equal to 0.7 or above it are generally accepted. However, studies (Cortina, 1993; Kopalle and Lehman, 1997; Peterson, 1994) have shown that interpretation of the alpha coefficient is more delicate than it may seem. The number of items, the degree of correlation between the items and the number of dimensions of the concept being studied (a concept may be unidimensional or multidimensional) all have an impact on the value of α. If the number of items contained in the scale is high, it is possible to have an α of an acceptable level in spite of a weak correlation between the items or the presence of a multidimensional concept (Cortina, 1993). It is therefore necessary to make sure before interpreting an alpha value that the concept under study is indeed unidimensional. To do this a preliminary factor analysis should be carried out. The α coefficient can be interpreted as a true indicator of the reliability of a scale only when the concept is unidimensional, or when relatively few items are used (six items, for example).

   Of the methods introduced above, the alternative forms method and the Cronbach Alpha method are most often used to determine the degree of reliability of a measuring scale, owing to the limitations of the test-retest and the split halves methods (Carmines and Zeller, 1990).

2.2 Measuring instruments used in qualitative research

While we face the problem of reliability just as much for qualitative instruments as for quantitative instruments, it is posed in different terms. As Miles and Huberman (1984a: 46) point out:

   continuously revising instruments puts qualitative research at odds with survey research, where instrument stability (for example test-retest reliability) is required to assure reliable measurement. This means that in qualitative research issues of instrument validity and reliability ride largely on the skills of the researcher. Essentially a person – more or less fallibly – is observing, interviewing and recording while modifying the observation, interviewing and recording devices from one field trip to the next.

The continual revision of instruments makes qualitative research the exact opposite of quantitative research, in which the stability of the instrument is essential for a reliable measure. In qualitative research, instrument validity and reliability depend largely on the skills of the researcher – a person, fallible to differing degree, who observes, questions and records, while at the same time modifying his or her observation, interview and recording tools 'from one field trip to the next' (Miles and Huberman, 1984a: 46). Thus, reliability is assessed partly by comparing the results of different researchers, when there are several of them, and partly through the work of coding raw data obtained through interviews, documents or observation (see Chapter 16). Different coders are asked to analyze data using a collection of predetermined categories and in accordance with a coding protocol. Inter-coder reliability is then assessed through the rate of agreement between the different coders on the definition of the units to code and their categorization. This reliability can also be calculated from the results obtained by a single coder who has coded the same data at two different periods, or by two coders working on the same data simultaneously.

Assessing Inter-Coder Reliability

Having set up an initial coding scheme, the researcher may decide to employ different coders (most often two). A first stage consists of having the same data sample (an extract from an interview or a document) coded independently by different coders, in order to test the coding system. From the coded samples, the level of consistency among the coders can be established, both in the definition of the units to code (so as to make sure that each coder interprets the definitions in the same way) and in categorizing the units. The coding rules are then defined according to the differences encountered and the coding process can be repeated with the entire body of data.

One difficulty in this method lies in choosing the inter-coder reliability rate. There are a number of different ways of calculating inter-coder reliability, according to the practical details of the coding and the data that is to be coded. Among the common rates accepted in management research (Cohen, 1960; Guetzkow, 1950; Robinson, 1957), Cohen's kappa coefficient of consistency (derived from the k of Kruskal) is the most often used. This coefficient allows us to evaluate consistency between coders, accounting for the probability of a similar coding being solely dependent on chance. Its formula is as follows:

$K = (Po - Pc) / (1 - Pc)$, where Po = true agreement and Pc = agreement due to chance ($Pc = \sum Pi1 * Pi2$, where $Pi1$ = proportion of units classed by Coder 1 in Category i and $Pi2$, = proportion of units classed by Coder 2 in Category i)

Kappa can have a value of between -1 and $+1$: -1 expresses complete disagreement between coders, 0 means agreement due solely to chance, and $+1$ refers to perfect agreement.

There are, however, three essential conditions to be met when using this coefficient:

- The units are to be coded must be independent of each other.
- The coding categories must be independent, mutually exclusive, and exhaustive.
- Coders must work independently.

Reliability of observations   Studies based on observation are often criticized for not providing enough elements to enable their reliability to be assessed. To respond to this criticism researchers are advised to accurately describe the note-taking procedures and the observation contexts that coders should follow (Kirk and Miller, 1986), so as to ensure that different observers are assessing the same phenomenon in the same way, noting the phenomena observed according to the same norms. We can then assess the reliability of the observations by comparing how the different observers qualified and classified the observed phenomena.

To obtain the greatest similarity in results between the different observers, it is recommended that researchers use trained and experienced observers and set out a coding protocol that is as clear as possible. In particular, the protocol will have to establish exactly which elements of the analysis are to be recorded, and clearly define the selected categories.

Reliability of documentary sources   Researchers have no control over the way in which documents have been established. Researchers select the documents that interest them, then interpret and compare their material. Reliability depends essentially on the work of categorizing written data in order to analyze the text (see Chapter 16), and different coders interpreting the same document should obtain the same results. An assessment of reliability is then essentially a question of determining the degree of inter-coder reliability (see the discussion on assessing inter-coder reliability above).

Reliability of interviews   Unstructured interviews are generally transcribed and analyzed in the same way as documents; the question of reliability comes back then to determining inter-coder reliability.

In the case of more directive interviews, interview reliability can be enhanced by ensuring that all the interviewees understand the questions in the same way, and that the replies can be coded unambiguously. For this reason it is necessary to pre-test questionnaires, to train interviewers and to verify inter-coder reliability for any open questions.

3. Assessing the Validity of a Measuring Instrument

3.1 Measuring instruments used in quantitative research

We recall that validity is expressed by the degree to which a particular tool measures what it is supposed to measure rather than a different phenomenon. An instrument must also be valid in relation to the objective for which it has been used. Thus, while reliability depends on empirical data, the notion of validity is in essence much more theoretical, and gives rise to the question: 'Valid for what purpose?'

We have seen in Section 2.1 above that the validity of a measuring instrument is tied to the degree of non-random error that it contains (or any bias introduced by using the tool or by the act of measuring). Improving the validity of a measuring instrument then consists of reducing as far as possible the level of non-random error connected to the application of that instrument.

One type of validity by which we can assess a measuring instrument is content validity: this means validating the application of a tool on the basis of a consensus within the research community as to its application. It is also useful to assess whether the tool used permits different dimensions of the phenomenon under study to be measured. In the case of quantitative instruments (particularly measuring scales), the notion of instrument validity is very close to the notion of construct validity; both assess whether the indicators used (by way of the measurement scale) are a good representation of the phenomenon (see Section 1, 2.1 above).

3.2 Measuring instruments used in qualitative research

In discussing qualitative research, Miles and Huberman (1984a: 230) assert that 'the problem is that there are no canons, decision rules, algorithms, or even any agreed upon heuristics in qualitative research, to indicate whether findings are valid'. However, the accumulation of experimental material in qualitative research has led more and more researchers to put forward methodologies which can improve the validity of qualitative tools such as observation, interviews or documentary sources.

Improving the validity of interviews   The question of the validity of interviews used in a qualitative process poses a problem, as it is difficult to assess whether this instrument measures exactly what it is supposed to measure. The fact that the questions posed concern the problem being studied is not enough to assess the validity of the interview. While it is possible to assess whether an interview is a good instrument for comprehending facts, such an assessment becomes more tenuous when we are dealing with opinions for which there is no external criterion of validity. Certain precautions exist that are designed to reduce errors or possible biases, but the subject of the validity of interviews remains debatable, raising the question of whether researchers should give priority to the accuracy of their measurements or to the richness of the knowledge obtained (Dyer and Wilkins, 1991).

Improving the validity of document analyses   When an analysis can describe the contents of a document and remain true to the reality of the facts being studied, we can consider that this analysis is valid. Its validity will be that much stronger if the researcher has taken care to clearly define how categories and quantification indices are to be constructed, and to describe the categorization process in detail. We must note, however, that it is easier to show the validity of a quantitative content analysis, which aims for a more limited goal of describing obvious content, than to show the validity of a qualitative content analysis, which can have the more ambitious goals of prediction, explanation and analysis of the latent content (see Chapter 16). Validity can also be verified by comparing the results obtained through content analysis with those obtained through different techniques (interviews, measurements of attitudes, observation of behavior).

Improving the validity of observation techniques External criteria do not always exist with which to verify whether the observations really measure what they are supposed to measure. Different observation techniques are possible (see Silverman, 1993), and validity depends more on the methodological system employed than on the instrument itself (Miles and Huberman, 1984a).

SECTION 3 INTERNAL VALIDITY

1. Definition and Overview

Internal validity consists in being sure of the pertinence and internal coherence of the results produced by a study; researchers must ask to what degree their inferences are correct, and whether or not rival explanations are possible. They must assess, for example, whether variations of the variable that is to be explained are caused solely by the explanatory variables. Suppose that a researcher has established the causal relationship: 'Variable A brings about the appearance of Variable B.' Before asserting this conclusion, the researcher must ask himself or herself whether there are other factors causing the appearance of A and/or B, and whether the relationship established might not be rather of the type: 'Variable X brings about the appearance of variables A and B.'

While internal validity is an essential test for research into causality, the concept can be extended to all research that uses inference to establish its results (Yin, 1989).

Testing internal validity is designed to evaluate the veracity of the connections established by researchers in their analyses.

There is no particular method of ensuring the 'favourable' level of internal validity of a research project. However, a number of techniques (which are more tests of validity in quantitative research and precautions to take in qualitative research) can be used to assess this internal validity.

2. Techniques for Assessing Internal Validity

We will not make any distinctions between techniques used for quantitative or qualitative research. Testing for internal validity applies to the research process, which poses similar problems regardless of the nature of the study.

The question of internal validity must be addressed from the stage of designing the research project, and must be pursued throughout the course of the study.

To achieve a good standard of internal validity in their research, researchers must work to remove the biases identified by Campbell and Stanley (1966). These biases (see Table 10.2) are relative: to the context of the research (the history effect, the development effect, the effect of testing); to the collection of data (the instrumentation effect); or to sampling (the statistical regression effect, the selection effect, the effect of experimental mortality, the contamination effect).

It is essential to anticipate, from the outset, effects that might be damaging to internal validity, and to design the research so as to limit the most serious of them.

Using a specific case study as an example, Yin (1989) presents a number of tactics to strengthen internal validity. These tactics can be extended to all qualitative research. He suggests that researchers should test rival hypotheses and compare the empirical patterns that are revealed with those of existing theoretical propositions. In this way, researchers can assess whether the relationship they establish between events is correct, and that no other explanation exists.

It is then necessary to describe and explain, in detail, the analysis strategy and the tools used in the analysis. Such careful explanation increases the transparency of the process through which results are developed, or at least makes this process available for criticism.

Finally, it is always recommended to try to saturate the observational field (to continue data collection until the data brings no new information and the marginal information collected does not cast any doubt on the construct design). A sufficiently large amount of data helps to ensure the soundness of the data collection process.

Miles and Huberman (1984a) reaffirm many of Yin's suggestions, and propose a number of other tactics to strengthen internal validity. Researchers can, for example, examine the differences between obtained results and establish contrasts and comparisons between them: this is the method of 'differences'. They can also verify the significance of any atypical cases – exceptions can generally be observed for every result. Such exceptions may either be ignored or the researcher may try to explain them, but taking them into account allows researchers to test and strengthen their results. Researchers can also test the explanations they propose. To do so, they will have to discard false relationships – that is, researchers should try to eliminate the possible appearance of any new factor which might modify the relationship established between two variables. Researcher can also test rival explanations that may account for the phenomenon being studied. Researchers rarely take the time to test any explanation other than the one they have arrived at. A final precaution is to seek out contradictory evidence. This technique involves actively seeking out factors that may invalidate the theory the researcher maintains as true. Once a researcher has established a preliminary conclusion, he or she must ask whether there is any evidence that contradicts this conclusion or is incompatible with it.

Table 10.2 *Biases limiting internal validity (Campbell and Stanley, 1966)*

Biases limiting internal validity	Meaning	How to avoid the bias
History effect	Events which are external to the study and take place during the study period have falsified the results	Reduce the time span of the study Look critically at the period set
Maturation effect	The subjects of the analysis have changed during the course of the study	Reduce the study period
Test effect	Individuals have undergone the same test several times in quick succession during a longitudinal study, and their responses the second time around have been biased through the fact of having previously responded to this test	Work with several samples with the same characteristics
Instrumentation effect	The questions used to collect data have been badly formulated	The researcher should be an expert The number of interviewers should be reduced The collection of data should be very formulized
Effect of statistical regression	The individuals selected have been chosen on the basis of extreme scores	Correct the way that the sample is constituted
Selection effect	The sample studied is not representative of the population which is pertinent to the study	Accord great importance to the sampling procedure
Effect of experimental mortality	Subjects have disappeared during the study	Replace the subjects if necessary without changing the characteristics of the sample
Contamination effect	An individual being questioned has learnt from others about the purpose of the study, which has falsified the results	Conclude the study as quickly as possible or make very sure of the confidentiality of the procedures

SECTION 4   RELIABILITY

Doing research takes time and involves a community of researchers. However, it would be very prejudicial if the soundness or precision of results produced in this way were dependent on the individual method of each researcher in conducting a project, or again, on conditions peculiar to that study. The reliability of research results, over time and across a community of researchers, is an important consideration.

1. Definitions and Overview

Evaluating the reliability of research (that is, the reliability of its results) consists in establishing and verifying that the various processes involved will be able to be repeated with the same results being obtained by different researchers and/or at different periods. Researchers who are integrated into a scientific team must be able to convey as faithfully as possible their method of carrying out a project. This is the concept of diachronic reliability (Kirk and Miller, 1986), which examines the stability of an observation over time. Researchers must be also able to duplicate exactly a study they have previously conducted, for example, when they are conducting multi-site research over several months (synchronic reliability, Kirk and Miller, 1986, which examines the similarity of observations over the same period of time).

Kirk and Miller (1986) and Silverman (1993) both mention the quixotic reliability dimension of a research project's reliability, which evaluates the circumstances in which the same method of observation will lead to the same results. This dimension of reliability is strongly linked to the reliability of the measuring instrument (refer to Section 2 of this chapter).

The question of reliability concerns all operational stages of quantitative or qualitative research. These include data collection, coding, and all other processes of preparing and analyzing data, including the presentation of the results when the vocabulary or the tables used are specific to the research. It is important for researchers to precisely describe their research design, so as to aim for a higher degree of reliability. Research is a complex process (whose evolution is never linear) and often takes place over a long period of time. Researchers may forget what they have done, and why and how they did it, by the time they attempt to repeat their research or initiate a research team within a different observational field.

A social science that is situated in time, research is also a personal exercise that relies on the intuition of the researcher. It is an imaginative practice: 'the process of theory construction in organizational studies is portrayed as imagination disciplined by evolutionary processes analogous to artificial selection' (Weick, 1989: 516). An aptitude for imagination, for perception when doing fieldwork, is not transmissible, but the process of questioning is. The degree to which a researcher will be able to duplicate a study will depend also on the accuracy of his or her description of the research process employed.

The principle techniques for attaining sound reliability in research are presented below. In general these relate to the organization and the quality of the research protocol.

2. Assessing Research Reliability

2.1 Methods common to both quantitative and qualitative research

Most importantly, researchers should always pay great attention to the communication of methodological information (the research process) from one researcher to another, or from one observational field to another. The different stages in the research should be clearly described, including discussion of the choice of observational field, the methods used in the collection and analysis of data, and the steps taken to control the effect the researcher may have on the observational field.

There must be a concern at all times to control the effect of the researcher on the observational field, and not only in the case of the solitary qualitative researcher. In fact, in quantitative research, the administration of a questionnaire can be disrupted by the attitude of a researcher who appears, for example, to be hurried, or who might be judgemental about the responses of the people being questioned. This kind of attitude cannot fail to disturb and to influence respondents.

At the same time, particular attention should also be given to certain other aspects of the research, according to its type. In the case of quantitative research, research reliability seems to depend more on the reliability of the measuring instrument. In the case of qualitative research, it seems to depend more on the ability of the researcher to understand and reconstruct the observational field.

2.2 Qualitative research

The reliability of qualitative research depends partly on the reliability of the measuring instrument. However, the interaction between the researcher and the observational field and the role of the researcher in administering the measuring instrument have a greater impact on research reliability in the case of qualitative research than quantitative, by reason of the very nature of the measuring instruments used (the qualitative instrument). Researchers must pay particular attention to writing concise instructions if qualitative measuring instruments are to be used by several people or at different times. They should explain how to use the instrument, how to understand questions that may be posed if respondents want further explanation before replying, how to select people to be questioned and, finally, how to take notes (extensive or pre-coded, for example) on the interviewee's replies. These instructions can take different forms; such as a manual for the observer in the studied observational field, or as notes accompanying a guide to the interviewing technique, explaining the contents of the questionnaire and how it is to be administered. Carrying out a pre-test can be an appropriate occasion for developing these guidelines, which can also be used in the post-test. Finally, particular importance must be given to training those who will administer this measuring instrument.

The reliability of qualitative research depends mainly on the ability and honesty of the researcher in describing the entire research process employed, particularly in the phases which relate to condensing and analyzing the collected data (Miles and Huberman, 1984a). The operation of condensing data consists of a group of processes of selection, grouping, simplifying and transforming the raw data collected (Miles and Huberman, 1984a). The researcher arrives at a set of data that has been simplified, transformed and reduced in number (condensed), and the task of data analysis is made easier.

The dependence of reliability on the ability and honesty of the researcher concerns both the qualitative and the quantitative researcher. However, quantitative research makes use of numerous techniques, statistical tools and tests which can be explained very precisely. This emphasis on the analysis process appeared for a long time to be less important to the qualitative researcher, particularly as no specific analysis techniques exist for such research.

The following discussion is based on an article by Gioia and Thomas (1996), who give their readers a precise description of their research procedure in such a way that it can be reproduced. This description is interesting in that it gives a direct account of the methodical progression of the research, from the phase of data collection to data analysis. If research relies on a logical progression of analysis phases (Glaser and Strauss, 1967), an explanation of the process must account for this.

A Precisely Described Methodology

(Gioia and Thomas, 1996: 370–403)
Gioia and Thomas sought to explain the phenomenon of the persistence or non-persistence of the identity and image of an organization when confronted with radical strategic change. They looked at the problem of change that faces presidents of American universities: how to make changes in order to be among the 'top 10' universities in the USA?

The observational field was comprised of American universities. A large part of the research methodology used was qualitative and inductive. (A second part of the project tested, from a quantitative perspective, a model based on data drawn from the qualitative analysis).

The purpose of the study was to extract, through analysis of qualitative data, different categories of concepts explaining the content of and the relationships between actors' representations of the radical change taking place in American universities. To do this, the authors outlined with precision the principal steps in their process:

- Interviews with three members of the universities' administrative council, discussing the process of change that was occurring, were conducted on several occasions over a six-month period, using a long, open, questionnaire.

- One of the two authors asked the questions while the other took notes and occasionally posed supplementary questions: this division of tasks resulted in a high quality of notes taken during interviews.
- Each interview was written up and discussed 24 hours after its completion, in order to avoid errors resulting from forgetting or memory distortion.
- Each person was questioned several times to assure the meaning of his or her comments, or to add to them as the research progressed.
- The data sources were triangulated, to supplement and to validate the information collected.
- Two processes were used to draw conceptual categories from the qualitative data. The authors describe these two data analysis techniques, and provide clear references so that an interested researcher can refer to these sources for further information.

Similarly, Miles and Huberman (1984a), as well as Silverman (1993), recommend drawing up and using identical note-taking formats so as to compare different sites and to quickly develop a methodology for gathering raw data that is easy to repeat. Miles and Huberman (1984a) propose different techniques (in the form of a matrix presenting and analyzing data) to improve research reliability.

The use of matrices to present, reduce, and analyze qualitative data collected in the field allows the researcher to increase the level of reliability of the research. But particular care should be taken to describe the reasons behind (the why) and the methods used (the how) in the construction of these matrices. The process of compiling and analyzing data then seems more precise, or 'objective', as it is no longer based on only a few personal and inaccessible methods used by a particular researcher, but instead is based on clearly explained methods.

All the same, it would not be extreme to recommend the inclusion in research projects of a certain amount of data relating to the researcher himself or herself (professional background, academic training, etc.).

SECTION 5   EXTERNAL VALIDITY

1. Definition and Overview

To assess the external validity of a research project we examine the possibilities and conditions for generalizing and appropriating the model to other sites. There are two facets to external validity, which we present in the following discussion; these correspond to a logical progression in two stages in assessing research validity.

The researcher must first examine the degree to which results found from a sample can be generalized to the whole parent population (supposedly represented by the sample, which has been established for the research at hand). It is only in a second stage that we can evaluate to what extent these results can be transferred or appropriated to the study and understanding of other observational fields.

The potential to generalize from research results is a concern that is more familiar to researchers who apply a quantitative methodology than to those who use qualitative methods. Quantitative researchers are generally used to working with samples, as accessing the whole population is either too difficult or too costly, or may not even be necessary (a statistically representative number of individuals of a population may be sufficient). Quantitative researchers are familiar with having to define the characteristics of the population under study. These characteristics provide them with criteria to use when selecting the units that will make up their study samples. Research results may then be extrapolated, taking certain statistical precautions, to the entire target population – and the status of these results can be established. However, this concern with the need to be able to generalize from their results should not be neglected by researchers who carry out qualitative work.

The status of the case studies conducted during a qualitative study can sometimes be poorly defined. Say, for example, that an in-depth case study has been carried out on company 'X' to study a process of industrial restructuring. Are we than to consider 'X' as a representative sample of a population of companies possessing similar characteristics, or confronted with identical strategic issues or, on the contrary, does it constitute a specific population? The status of the results of qualitative research is dependent on the answer to this question.

In both quantitative and qualitative research, the sample studied and the population targeted must be defined before we can determine the generalization perimeter of the results. To do this, qualitative research draws on a process of statistical generalization, whereas qualitative research draws on a process of analytical generalization (Yin, 1989).

The second facet of external validity – that of the transferability of results – concerns both work that assesses the potential to extrapolate research into other observational fields, and researchers who incorporate into their own research approach results imported from a different domain to that in which they are studying. In both of these situations researchers should always consider the possible contextual dependence of the research results they are working with. Contextual dependence is a measure of whether a result demonstrated in one observational field is dependent solely on one or more of the research variables, or whether it depends also on other characteristics particular to the studied field – in which case the research is culturally, historically or socially anchored to some extent to the field (contextualization). Although this problem is no impediment to research in itself, it should be taken into account when determining the possibilities or conditions for extrapolating results to other observational fields which do not necessarily present the same contextual characteristics.

This problem is very often raised in assessing the external validity of qualitative research, when the results have been drawn from analysis of a single case or a small number of cases. Whereas qualitative research is often criticized for being too contextualized, Guba and Lincoln (1994) consider that work based on quantitative data too often favors precision to the detriment of contextualization. Transferability can be limited if the aggregate data has no particular application to practical cases in management. Quantitative researchers working with large amounts of data should not be under the illusion that they understand the studied observational field in all its principal contextual characteristics (Silverman, 1993). Qualitative research can give invaluable information about the context from which the results are derived, and consequently about the contexts in which these results can be used again. In more general terms, a detailed, rich and intimate knowledge of the context of their research enables researchers to estimate the possibilities of, and the conditions for, generalizing or transferring their results to other settings.

Although they are often linked, the two facets of external validity discussed above (that is, generalization and transferability of results) should be distinct in each research project. Researchers may not necessarily aim to produce results that can be generalized to the entire population, nor to assess the possibilities for transferring their results to other observational fields. Or researchers may consider the question of generalization without having to consider that of the transferability of the results (and vice versa). It is important, though, for researchers to define their research objectives and, consequently, to marshal appropriate techniques and methods to ensure their results meet one or the other of these conditions of external validity.

2. Assessing External Validity

We set out, below, a number of techniques, tests or procedures (the list is not exhaustive) that can be used to improve the external validity of research results, according to whether the research is quantitative or qualitative. For both types of research we outline, where necessary, any problem areas with regard to the generalization and transferability of research results.

The external validity of a study depends essentially on the external validity of the measuring instrument used in the case of quantitative research, and of the research procedure itself in the case of qualitative research. For this reason, external validity techniques or tests differ greatly according to the nature of the research.

Before examining these techniques of improving external validity, let us point out that researchers will be far better able to ensure the external validity of their research if they take a hard look at the particularities of their observational field from the outset.

In particular, researchers can include certain control variables in their measuring instrument, from its conception, to delimit and accurately characterize the population they are studying. By doing so they will improve the level of external validity of the results they obtained on completion of the study.

Researchers should also examine very carefully the variables they use in their study. Generalizing from research, or moving from one context to another, often implies modifying how these variables are operationalized. For example, the relationship between capacity to change and organizational size presupposes that the variable 'size of the organization' is to be measured. In the industrial sector, size may be measured by the turnover of the businesses under study. In the non-profit sector, a different measure will have to be devised (for example, the number of volunteers working for these organizations).

2.1 Quantitative research

The researcher must first determine the degree to which the results drawn from a sample can be taken as applying to the whole population, and to what degree these results can be compared to the norms or standards generally accepted about this population (as a result of previous studies for example). These two questions relate to the practice of statistical inference in quantitative research, and a number of statistical tests are available to researchers to answer them. These tests are discussed in Chapter 14.

When research has been carried out on a sample, researchers often hope to generalize their results to the population from which the sample has been drawn. The results of quantitative research are often presented in statistical form, to reduce the large amount of numerical data involved (percentages, means, standard deviations, etc.). To generalize from these results researchers must apply statistical generalization. Correspondingly, statistical formulae are used to evaluate results that have been generalized from a sample to a population. These formulae differ according to whether the results are in the form of a mean or a proportion. In both cases, we speak of the error margin within which the result generalized to the whole population lies. To determine this error margin, the researcher has to know the size of the sample and its confidence level (generally 95 per cent).

As we have shown in this chapter, the question of the transferability of results from one study to other related observational fields depends essentially on the following two factors:

- the external validity of the measuring instrument used (this is discussed further in Section 2 of this chapter)
- the validity of inferring from results from one population to another (this is discussed further in Chapter 14).

We emphasize that researchers should make use of appropriate statistical tests, which are called non-parametric tests, when working on small samples. Chapter 14 explains how these tests can be used during the research process to assure its external validity.

2.2 Qualitative research

When qualitative research produces figures in the form of proportions or means, the techniques we have presented above for quantitative research can equally be applied to generalize a result within a set margin of error, or to transfer results using statistical tests. The sample should in this case, however, comprise at least 30 units (companies observed, managers questioned, etc.), a number which is not abnormal in qualitative research.

However, the results of a qualitative study are generally presented in the form of a proposition or a written statement derived from qualitative data, in which case the use of statistical tests is not possible.

The passage from qualitative data, collected in a large quantity and often diverse in nature, to a conclusion in the form of a proposition of results, depends above all on a certain number of techniques of data collection, reduction (condensing) and analysis (Altheide and Johnson, 1994; Miles and Huberman, 1984a; Silverman, 1993). It depends, too, on the expertise and the experience of the researcher in collating this mass of information. For this reason, techniques aimed at assuring the external validity of qualitative research apply principally to the research process (Silverman, 1993). Only the researcher is really in a position to say how much the observational field has been taken into account and how he or she intends to allow for specific local factors in each case, in order to be able to generalize the results to a much greater arena. Researchers should always question their methods of working. They should examine the relationship between their research question and the broader historical and social context of their work, and give consideration to the relationship between the observer, the observed and the place of observation, and to the observer's point of view and his or her interpretation of the observational field.

Two aspects of the qualitative research procedure need to be examined in more detail, however, as they have a direct bearing on the external validity of the research: the method used to select the observational field, and the method used to analyze the collected data.

A number of different techniques may be used when a researcher wishes to generalize from case study results that might be considered as idiosyncratic situations. Numerous authors recommend using several case studies (Eisenhardt, 1989; Guba and Lincoln, 1994) to vary the contextual characteristics of qualitative research and to limit or control as much as possible particularities of individual cases. A poorly thought-out choice of several cases does not always provide any real improvement to the external validity of the results. The following methods can be used to avoid this trap.

First, repeating a case study (Yin, 1989) will normally help to reach a theoretical and literal generalization. In repeating a study, the researcher may either select a case for which the same results are predicted (literal replication) or select a case for which different results are produced, but for anticipated reasons (theoretical replication). The results of the qualitative study may then be compared or contrasted according to the characteristics – identical or different – of the cases available to the researcher.

For such case comparison to be effective, certain criteria (carefully chosen in line with the research question) must be included in each case, and the cases should vary in relation to these criteria. A good knowledge of the observational field is then vital when formulating these criteria – a knowledge based at the least on a detailed description of the field's general framework and the activities or actors being studied. These criteria may be determined at the outset of the study or they may be formulated as the research progresses, in relation to early results obtained.

The process of choosing different sites for case studies has to be carried out with care, as researchers can be influenced by a 'representativeness bias' (Miles and Huberman, 1994). Researchers sometimes have a tendency to select 'similar' cases, so that their results converge and they avoid being temporarily thrown off the track by contradictory or unforeseen results. Researchers should always set down clearly the criteria they have used for selecting cases to study, and consider them with a critical eye; it can be useful to seek an external opinion on this selection.

There are no fixed rules setting a maximum number of repeated case studies below which a research study can maintain its qualitative nature, or above which the researcher must use statistical tools to deal with too great an amount of information. Although it is generally accepted that an understanding of local causality becomes crucial when there are more than 15 sites, this depends to a great extent on the researcher's expertise in carrying out such qualitative studies.

The external validity of qualitative research depends also on the way in which the collected data is condensed and analyzed. Different techniques have been proposed (see Miles and Huberman, 1984a) with which researchers can move from a local explanation (causality) to an inter-site explanation, and reach a higher level of external validity. These techniques are based essentially on the use of data analysis matrices.

Although researchers do not always have the opportunity or the time to carry out a multi-site study, they can try to assure the external validity of their results by using paradox, or apparent contradiction (Quinn and Cameron, 1988) – by comparing their results with the work of other researchers (Eisenhardt, 1989) so as to interpret their single case study in a different way.

CONCLUSION

Research results are most often evaluated and criticized in relation to the criteria of validity and reliability that we have described in this chapter. For this reason, we encourage researchers to assess the research they are undertaking in these terms from the beginning stages and throughout the research project, as the structure of the research evolves.

Knowing that the precision of the theoretical analysis and methodology employed strengthens the validity and reliability of research, initial choices must be evaluated in relation to their impact on the validity and reliability of the research. These choices include for example, the definition of the concepts to be studied, the measuring instruments to be used and methods of accessing the observational field(s).

It is, however, important to note that, while it is possible to test the reliability of a measuring instrument and to approach a maximum threshold (for example 100 per cent agreement between two analysts), the other evaluation criteria we have described in this chapter involve a more quali- tative estimation. Although it is possible to ascertain that a study is invalid, there is no such thing as perfect validity in research. Researchers must adopt a critical attitude to their work, and incorporate into it some of the techniques that we have explained in this chapter (selecting techniques applicable to each objective and to the type of research). In this way the results of the research can be judged as reproducible, cumulative and able to be generalized.

NOTE

1 Cited in Carmines and Zeller (1990: 22).

FURTHER READING

Carmines, E. and Zeller, R., *Reliability and Validity Assessment*, London: Sage, 1990.

Kirk, J. and Miller, M., *Reliability and Validity in Qualitative Research*, London: Sage, 1986.

Silverman, D., *Interpretative Qualitative Data: Methods for Analysing Talk, Text and Interaction*, London: Sage, 1993.

Yin, R., *Case Study Research: Design and Methods*, Applied Social Research Methods Series, 5, Newbury Park, CA: Sage, 1990.

PART III

ANALYSIS

In this third part we enter more technical areas of research. Here we find the toolbox. The techniques developed in this book have not been chosen arbitrarily. They correspond to the questions researchers in management generally have to confront. The order in which they are presented does not correspond, however, to any 'ideal' sequence. The analysis phase poses a multitude of questions. Researchers may want to compare variables with one another, or to appraise whether their results are random, or if they do reveal meaning. Since analysis involves statistical inference, it is important to recognize the hypotheses underlying the use of such tests if we are to obtain results that are significant on more than just the statistical level. Another frequently encountered problem is determining whether relationships of cause and effect do exist between variables. To construct and test causal relationships, researchers have to specify the phenomenon, identify its concepts and variables, and describe the relationships between these concepts and variables – and then test these relationships. Researchers often have to manipulate large amounts of data. Two classes of techniques for doing so are presented here. Classification methods enable us to break up a large body of data into a smaller number of categories, while structuring methods allow us to discover the internal structure of a data set. The study of networks, whether of individuals or organizations, is central to more and more research designs. We categorize the particular techniques needed for such studies as social network analyses. These techniques allow us to identify connections between individual analysis units, and to elucidate situations which, at first encounter, might seem complex. Sometimes, too, research can involve understanding a dynamic – an evolution over the course of time. Again, specific techniques are required. These include sequential methods, event analyses, cohort analyses and the use of chronological matrices. Finally, for some studies it is necessary to dissect, classify and analyze information contained in a document, a communication or a discourse. Once again, this is a question of making sense of a considerable mass of data – in this case, verbal and written. For this, two major types of methods are generally used: content analysis and cognitive mapping.

11

COMPARISON TESTS

Ababacar Mbengue

Outline

Used extensively in management research, comparison tests allow the researcher to test hypotheses formulated in terms of the equality of certain elements or the existence of a relationship between variables. This chapter describes the basic logic of such tests, and presents the rules and modes of their use. As well as establishing a general distinction between parametric and non-parametric tests, different comparison tests are presented in relation to the different questions posed by management researchers: whether they want to compare means, proportions or percentages, variances, correlation coefficients or linear regressions, variables or populations.

Researchers in management often find they want to test hypotheses. For example, a researcher may want to test the hypothesis that the introduction of formalized strategic planning improves the financial performance of banks (Robinson and Pearce, 1983). Comparison tests are powerful tools for testing such a research hypothesis.

Statistical tests generally fall into one of two categories: parametric tests and non-parametric tests. Aside from a number of differences, which we will look at later in this chapter, parametric and non-parametric tests essentially share the same basic logic. This common logic is presented in the first section of this chapter. The second and third sections then describe how these two types of statistical tests can be applied as part of the research process. Both of these sections are organized according to questions that commonly arise during the research process, along with appropriate statistical tests. So that readers can use this chapter to go directly to the test corresponding to their research question, I have systematically repeated information about the conditions under which each test should be applied, together with the rules to follow when deciding upon a test. The conclusion to the chapter presents an effective strategy with which to approach statistical testing.

SECTION 1   STATISTICAL TESTS

In this section we explore the general context in which researchers carry out statistical tests. We define the essential concepts involved and outline the general steps followed when using this type of test.

1. Inference and Statistics

Inference has a very important place in management research. Conclusions or generalizations often have to be established on the basis of observations or results, and in some cases statistics can add to their precision. As inference is often at the heart of the reasoning by which the statistician generalizes from a sample to a population, the branch of statistics devoted to this type of approach is called *inferential statistics*. The goal of inferential statistics is to evaluate hypotheses through information collected from a selected sample. Statistical tests are thus at the very core of inferential statistics.

2. Research Hypotheses

Research hypotheses are unproven statements about a research field. They may be based on existing theoretical material, previous empirical results, or even personal impressions or simple conjecture. For instance, one of Robinson and Pearce's (1983: 201) research hypotheses was 'Banks engaging in formal planning will have a significantly higher mean performance ranking than non-formal planning banks from 1977 and 1979'. If researchers want to use statistical tests to prove a research hypothesis, they must first translate the hypothesis into a statistical hypothesis.

3. Statistical Hypotheses

A statistical hypothesis is a quantified statement about the characteristics of a population. More precisely, it describes the distribution of one or more random variables. It might describe the parameters of a given distribution, or a probability distribution of an observed population.

Parameters

A parameter is a quantifiable aspect such as mean, variance, a percentage, or any quantity specific to the population in question. A population's parameters are usually unknown. It is possible, however, to estimate them using statistical methods applied to a sample. Conventionally, population parameters are represented by Greek letters (μ, σ, π, etc.). *Probability distribution* describes the general shape of the frequency distribution for this population. It can be said to be a model representing the frequency distribution of a random variable.

A statistical hypothesis is generally presented in two parts: the *null hypothesis* and the *alternative* or *contrary hypothesis*. These two hypotheses are incompatible. They describe two complementary states. The null hypothesis describes a situation in which there is no major shift from the status quo, or there is an absence of difference between parameters. The alternative hypothesis – that there *is* a major shift from the status quo, or that there *is* a difference between parameters – is generally the hypothesis the researcher wishes to establish. In this case the alternative hypothesis corresponds to the research hypothesis – the researcher believes it to be true (Sincich, 1996). The researcher's goal is then to disprove the null hypothesis in favor of the alternative hypothesis (Sincich, 1996; Zikmund, 1994).

The null hypothesis is generally marked H_0 and the alternative (or contrary) hypothesis H_1 or H_a. It is important to bear in mind that statistical tests are designed to *refute* and not to *confirm* hypotheses. In other words, these tests do not aim to prove hypotheses, and do not have the capacity to do so. They can only show that the level of probability is too low for a given statement to be accepted (Kanji, 1993). For this reason, statistical hypotheses are normally formulated so that the alternative hypothesis H_1 corresponds to the research hypothesis one is trying to establish. In this way, rather than attempting to prove that this hypothesis is correct, the goal becomes to reject the null hypothesis.

4. Statistical Tests

Statistical tests are used to assess the validity of statistical hypotheses. They are carried out on data collected from a representative sample of the studied population. A statistical test should lead to rejecting or accepting an initial hypothesis: in most cases the null hypothesis.

Statistical tests generally fall into one of two categories: *parametric tests* and *non-parametric* tests.

Parametric and Non-Parametric Tests

A parametric test is a statistical test that presumes a particular distribution of one of the parameters of a population. For example, a parametric test might be used if a researcher believes that a population is distributed normally. The Student test is a parametric test that aims to compare the means of two normally distributed populations.

A non-parametric test is a statistical test in which it is not necessary to specify the parametric distribution within the population. Examples of non-parametric tests are the sign test, the Wilcoxon test, the Mann-Whitney U test, the Kruskal-Wallis test or the Kolmogorov-Smirnov test.

Statistical tests were first used in the experimental sciences and in management research. For instance, the Student test was designed by William Sealy Gosset (who was known as 'Student'), when working with Guinness breweries. But the mathematical theory of statistical tests was developed by Jerzy Neyman and Egon Shape Pearson. These two authors also stressed the importance of considering not only the null hypothesis, but also the alternative hypothesis (Lehmann, 1991).

In a statistical test focusing on *one parameter of a population*, for instance its mean or variance, if the null hypothesis H_0 states one value for the parameter, the alternative hypothesis H_1 would state that the parameter is different from this specific value.

In a statistical test focusing on the *probability distribution of a population*, if the null hypothesis H_0 states that the population follows a specific distribution, for example a normal distribution, the alternative hypothesis H_1 would state that the population does not follow this specific distribution.

4.1 A single population

The number of populations being considered will influence the form of the statistical test. If a single population is observed, the test may compare a parameter θ of the population to a given value θ_0.

For example, Robinson and Pearce (1983: 201) hypothesized that companies with a formal planning policy will perform better than companies without such a policy. In this case the statistical test used would be a one-tail test to the right (a right-tail test). If the hypothesis had suggested that inferior performance resulted from formal planning, a one-tail test to the left (a left-tail test) would be used. If, however, the two authors had simply hypothesized that formal planning would lead to a difference in performance, without specifying in which direction, a two-tail test would have been appropriate. These three alternative hypotheses would be formulated as follows:

- $H_1: \theta > \theta_0$ (unidirectional to the right)
- $H_1: \theta < \theta_0$ (unidirectional to the left)
- $H_1: \theta \neq \theta_0$ (bi-directional)

where θ corresponds to the performance of companies with a formal planning policy, and θ_0 to the performance of companies without such a policy.

Example: Statistical testing of a population percentage

A researcher studying cooperation agreements between companies may wish to test the hypothesis that the percentage of companies that sign such agreements within his chosen population is 50 per cent. After sending out a survey and analyzing the responses, he finds that 45 per cent of the companies in his sample had signed cooperation agreements. He then wonders if this observed percentage differs significantly from his predicted 50 per cent for the entire population. The null hypothesis, in this case, could be formulated as

$$H_0: \pi = 0.5$$

π being the percentage of the population being estimated.

He then carries out a two-tail test in order to establish whether the percentage for the entire population is different from 50 per cent. Here's the alternative hypothesis:

$$H_1: \pi \neq 0.5$$

On the other hand, if the researcher's hypothesis had been that the percentage of cooperation agreements was less than 50 per cent, he would have carried out a left-tail test. The hypotheses system would then be.

$$H_0: \pi - 0.5 \text{ and } H_1. \pi < 0.5$$

Sometimes, the null hypothesis can also be expressed as an inequation. This gives the following hypotheses systems:

$$H_0: \theta \leq \theta_0 \text{ and } H_1: \theta > \theta_0$$

or

$$H_0: \theta \geq \theta_0 \text{ and } H_1: \theta < \theta_0$$

In these cases, the symbols '$\leq$' (less than or equal to) and '$\geq$' (greater than or equal to) are used in formulating the null hypothesis H_0 in order to cover all cases in which the alternative hypothesis H_1 is not valid.

However, the general convention is to express H_0 as an equation. The reasoning behind this convention is the following: if the alternative hypothesis is stated as an inequation, for instance $H_1: \theta > \theta_0$, then every test leading to a rejection of the null hypothesis $H_0: \theta = \theta_0$ and therefore to the acceptance of the alternative hypothesis $H_1: \theta > \theta_0$, would also lead to the rejection of every hypothesis $H_0: \theta = \theta_i$, for every θ_i inferior to θ_0. In other words, $H_0: \theta = \theta_0$ represents the most unfavorable situation possible (from the researcher's point of view) if the alternative hypothesis $H_1: \theta > \theta_0$ turned out to be incorrect. For this reason, expressing the null hypothesis as an equation covers all possible situations.

4.2 Two populations

When a statistical test focuses on the parameters of two populations, the goal is to find out whether the two populations described by a specific parameter are different. If θ_1 and θ_2 represent the parameters of the two populations, the null hypothesis predicts the equality of these two parameters:

$$H_0: \theta_1 = \theta_2, \text{ or } H_0: \theta_1 - \theta_2 = 0$$

The alternative hypothesis may be expressed in three different ways:

- $H_1: \theta_1 > \theta_2$, or $H_1: \theta_1 - \theta_2 > 0$
- $H_1: \theta_1 < \theta_2$, or $H_1: \theta_1 - \theta_2 < 0$
- $H_1: \theta_1 \neq \theta_2$, or $H_1: \theta_1 - \theta_2 \neq 0$

Example: Comparing two proportions

The same researcher may then want to test a second hypothesis, according to which cooperation agreements between companies would be more frequent in the automobile industry than in the computer sector. Here, a right-tail test is appropriate. The hypotheses system could be written as follows:

$$H_0: \pi_1 = \pi_2$$
$$H_1: \pi_1 > \pi_2$$

π_1 and π_2 being the percentages of cooperation agreements within the respective populations: the automobile and the computer sectors.

4.3 More than two populations

A statistical test on k populations aims to determine if these populations differ on a specific parameter. $\theta_1, \theta_2, \ldots, \theta_k$ are the k parameters describing the k populations being compared. The null hypothesis would be that the k parameters are identical:

$$H_0: \theta_1 = \theta_2 = \ldots = \theta_k$$

The alternative hypothesis would then be formulated as follows:

H_1: *the values of* θ_i $(i = 1, 2, \ldots, k)$ are not all identical.

This means that the null hypothesis will be rejected in favor of the alternative hypothesis if the value for any single parameter is found to be different from that of another.

Example: Comparing k proportions ($k > 2$)

Say the researcher now wanted to test the hypothesis that the percentage of inter-company cooperation agreements differs from one sector to another for the five different sectors represented in his sample (automobile, computers, aeronautics, textile and metallurgy). The null hypothesis could be formulated as:

$$H_0: \pi_1 = \pi_2 = \pi_3 = \pi_4 = \pi_5,$$

$\pi_1, \pi_2, \pi_3, \pi_4$ and π_5 being the percentages of agreements, at the level of the population, for the five sectors.

A two-tail test would then be used to find out whether the percentage of agreements within the population as a whole differed according to sectors. The alternative hypothesis could read:

H_1: *at least two* π_i differ from each other $(i = 1 - 5)$.

5. Risk of Error

Statistical tests are used to give an indication as to what decision to make – for instance, whether to reject or not to reject the null hypothesis H_0. As this decision is, in most research situations, based on partial information only, derived from observations made of a sample of the population, a margin of error is involved (Sincich, 1996; Zikmund, 1994). A distinction is made between two types of error in statistical tests: error of the first type, or Type I error (α), and error of the second type, or Type II error (β).

5.1 Type I and Type II error

By observing the sample group, a researcher may be lead mistakenly to reject the null hypothesis – when in fact the population actually *fulfills* the conditions

Table 11.1   *Type I and Type II error in statistical tests*

		Real situation in the population	
		H_0 is true	H_0 is false
Decision	Not reject H_0	Right decision	Type II error (β)
	Reject H_0	Type I error (α)	Right decision

of this hypothesis. Type I error (α) measures the probability of rejecting the null hypothesis when it is in fact true. Conversely, a researcher's observations of a sample may not allow the null hypothesis to be rejected, when in fact the population actually satisfies the conditions of the alternative hypothesis. Type II error (β) measures the probability of not rejecting the null hypothesis when it is in fact false.

As the null hypothesis may be true or false and the researcher may reject it or not reject it, there are only four possible and mutually exclusive outcomes of a statistical test. These are presented in Table 11.1.

Only two of the four cases in Table 11.1 involve an error. Type I error can only appear if the null hypothesis is rejected. In the same way, Type II error is only possible if the null hypothesis is not rejected. The two types of error can never be present at the same time.

It is tempting to choose a minimal value for Type I error α. Unfortunately, decreasing this value increases Type II error, and vice versa. The only way to minimize both α and β is to use a larger sample (Sincich, 1996). Otherwise, a compromise must be sought between α and β, for example by measuring the power of the test.

**The Power of a Statistical Test, Effectiveness
Curves and Confidence Level**

The power of a statistical test is the probability $(1 - \beta)$ of accurately rejecting the null hypothesis when it is indeed false. The smaller the Type II error is, the greater the power of the test.

An effectiveness curve is the curve representing Type II error (the probability of not rejecting the null hypothesis when it is false) as a function of the statistically calculated values for which the alternative hypothesis H_1 should be accepted. The probability $(1 - \alpha)$ of accepting the null hypothesis when it is true is called the confidence level of a statistical test.

When using statistical tests, it is preferable not to speak of *accepting* the null hypothesis, but rather of not rejecting it. This semantic nuance is important: if the aim of the test was to accept H_0, the validity of its conclusion would be measured by Type II error β – the probability of not rejecting the null hypothesis when it is false. However, the value of β is not constant. It varies depending on the specific values of the parameter, and is very difficult to calculate in most statistical tests (Sincich, 1996). Because of the difficulty of calculating β, making a decision based upon the power of the test or the effectiveness curve can be tricky.

There is actually another, more practical solution; to choose a null hypothesis in which a possible Type I error α would be much more serious than a Type II error β. For example, to prove a suspect guilty or innocent, it may be preferable to choose as the null hypothesis 'the suspect is innocent' and as the alternative hypothesis 'the suspect is guilty'. Most people would probably agree that in this case, a Type I error (convicting someone who is innocent) is more serious than a Type II error (releasing someone who is guilty). In such a context, the researcher may be content to minimize the Type I error α.

5.2 Significance level

Before carrying out a test, a researcher can determine what level of Type I error will be acceptable. This is called the *significance level* of a statistical test.

A significance level is a probability threshold. A significance level of 5 per cent or 1 per cent is common in management research. In determining a significance level, a researcher is saying that if Type I error – the probability of wrongly rejecting a null hypothesis – is found to be greater than this level, it will be considered significant enough to prevent the null hypothesis H_0 from being rejected.

In management research, significance level is commonly marked with asterisks. An example is the notation system employed by Horwitch and Thiétart (1987): $p < 0.10^*$; $p < 0.05^{**}$; $p < 0.01^{***}$; $p < 0.001^{****}$, where one asterisk corresponds to results with a 10 per cent significance level, two asterisks 5 per cent, three asterisks 1 per cent and four asterisks 0.1 per cent (that is, one in one thousand). If no asterisk is present, it means the results are not significant.

6. To Reject or not to Reject?

6.1 Statistic X

The decision to reject or not to reject the null hypothesis H_0 is based on the value of a relevant statistic – which we refer to as a statistic X. A statistic X is a random variable, appropriate to the null hypothesis H_0. It is calculated from data collected from one or more representative samples from one or more populations (Kanji, 1993). A statistic X may be quite simple, such as the mean or the variance, or it may be a complex function of these and other parameters. We will look at different examples later in this chapter.

A good statistic should present three characteristics (Kanji, 1993):

1 It must behave differently according to whether H_0 is true (and H_1 false) or vice versa.
2 Its probability distribution when H_0 is true must be known and calculable.
3 Tables defining this probability distribution must be available.

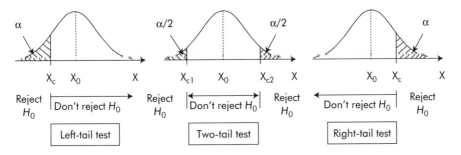

Figure 11.1 Type I error, acceptance region and rejection region

6.2 Rejection region, acceptance region, and critical value

The set of values of the statistic X that lead to rejecting the null hypothesis is called the *rejection region* (or the *critical region*). The complementary region is called the *acceptance region* (or, more accurately, the *non-rejection region*). The value representing the limit of the rejection region is called the *critical value*. In a one-tail test, there is only one critical value X_c, while in a two-tail test, there are two; X_{c1} and X_{c2}. The acceptance region and the rejection region are both dependant on Type I error α, since α is the probability of rejecting H_0 when it is actually true, and $1-\alpha$ is the probability of not rejecting H_0 when it is true. This relationship is illustrated by Figure 11.1.

Rules for rejecting or not rejecting the null hypothesis

- For a left-tail test, the null hypothesis is rejected for any value of the statistic X lower than the critical value X_c. The rejection region therefore comprises the values of X that are 'too low'.
- For a two-tail test, the null hypothesis H_0 is rejected for values of the statistic X that are either less than the critical value X_{c1} or greater than the critical value X_{c2}. The rejection region here comprises the values of X that are either 'too low' or 'too high'.
- Finally, for a right-tail test, the null hypothesis is rejected for any value of the statistic X greater than the critical value X_c. The rejection region in this case comprises the values of X that are 'too high'.

6.3 P-value

Most statistical analysis software programs provide one very useful piece of information, the p value (also called the observed significance level). The p value is the probability, if the null hypothesis were true, of obtaining a value of X as extreme as the one found for a sample. The null hypothesis H_0 will be rejected if the p value is lower than the pre-determined significance level α (Sincich, 1996).

It is becoming increasingly common to state the p value of a statistical test in published research articles (for instance Horwitch and Thiétart, 1987). Readers can then compare the p value with different significance levels and see for themselves if the null hypothesis should be rejected or not. The p value also locates the statistic X in relation to the critical region (Kanji, 1993). For instance, if some data indicates that the null hypothesis H_0 should not be rejected, the p value may be just below the chosen significance level; while if the data provides solid reasons to reject the null hypothesis, the p value would be noticeably lower than the significance level.

7. Defining a Statistical Test – Step-by-Step

Statistical tests on samples generally follow the following method.

Statistical Tests on Samples

1.   Formulate hypotheses (the null hypothesis H_0 and the alternative hypothesis H_1).
2.   Choose a significance level α for the test – that is, determine the level of risk of wrongly rejecting a true null hypothesis that would be considered significant enough to prohibit its rejection (normally between 1 per cent and 10 per cent).
3.   Obtain a sample of random observations from the population.
4.   For parametric tests, determine the probability distribution of the sample population (normal distribution, Poisson distribution, etc.).
5.   Determine a statistic X (that is, a criterion that is dependant on the data) of which the probability distribution is known when the null hypothesis is true.
6.   From the significance level, calculate the critical value(s) (X_c or X_{c1} and X_{c2}), and so the rejection region and the acceptance region for the null hypothesis H_0.
7.   Establish the rules for decision-making:
     (a) if the statistic observed for the sample is within the acceptance region, the null hypothesis will not be rejected;
     (b) if the statistic observed for the sample is within the rejection region, the null hypothesis will be rejected in favor of the alternative hypothesis.
8.   Calculate the statistic and determine whether it is in the rejection region or the non-rejection region of the null hypothesis H_0.
9.   Make the decision to reject or not to reject the null hypothesis H_0, on the basis of the test carried out on the sample.

In practice, the task is much easier than this. Most statistical analysis software (SAS, SPSS, etc.) determine the statistic X appropriate to the chosen test, calculate its value, and indicate the p value of the test. Some programs, such as Statgraphics, will even go one step further and suggest whether the null hypothesis should be rejected or not according to the significance level fixed by the researcher.

The major difficulty researchers face, though, is to choose the right test. The two following sections provide guidelines for making this choice, first looking at parametric and then at non-parametric tests. The tests are presented in terms of research aims and the research question, and the conditions attached to the application of each test are enumerated.

SECTION 2   PARAMETRIC TESTS

1. Tests on Means

1.1 Comparing the mean m of a sample to a reference value μ_0 when the variance σ_2 of the population is known

Research question   Does the mean m, calculated from a sample taken from a population with a known variance of σ_2, differ significantly from a hypothetical mean μ_0?

Application conditions

- The variance σ_2 of the population is known (this is a very rare case!) but the mean μ is not known (the hypothesis suggests it equals μ_0).
- A random sample is used, containing n independent observations
- The size n of the sample should be greater than 5, unless the population follows a normal distribution, in which case the size has no importance. Actually, this size condition is to guarantee the mean of the sample follows a normal distribution (Sincich, 1996).

Hypotheses

The null hypothesis to be tested is H_0: $\mu = \mu_0$,
the alternative hypothesis is H_1: $\mu \neq \mu_0$ (for a two-tail test)
or H_1: $\mu < \mu_0$ (for a left-tail test)
or H_1: $\mu > \mu_0$ (for a right-tail test)

Statistic   The statistic calculated is

$$Z = \frac{(m - \mu_0)}{\sigma / \sqrt{n}}.$$

It follows a standard normal distribution (mean = 0 and standard deviation = 1). This is called a z test or a z statistic.

Interpreting the test

- In a two-tail test, H_0 will be rejected if $Z < -Z_{\alpha/2}$ or $Z > Z_{\alpha/2}$
- in a left-tail test, H_0 will be rejected if $Z < -Z_\alpha$
- in a right-tail test, H_0 will be rejected if $Z > Z_\alpha$

where α is the defined significance level (or Type I error), and Z_α and $Z_{\alpha/2}$ are the normal distribution values that can be found in the appropriate tables.

Example: Comparing a mean to a given value (the variance of the population is known)

A sample of 16 observations is drawn from a population with a known standard deviation $\sigma = 40$ but an unknown mean μ. It is proposed by hypothesis that the mean $\mu_0 = 500$. The mean observed on the sample is $m = 493$. Could the mean $\mu_0 = 500$ be accepted for the population, if a Type I error α of 5 per cent is assumed?

The size of the sample ($n = 16$, that is, it is greater than 5) dispenses with the hypothesis of normality.

$$Z = \frac{(493 - 500)}{40 / \sqrt{16}} = -0.70.$$

The normal distribution table gives us the values $Z_{\alpha/2} = Z_{0.025} = 1.96$ and $Z_\alpha = Z_{0.05} = 1.64$.

Two-tail test: As $-Z_{\alpha/2} \le Z \le Z_{\alpha/2}$ ($-1.96 \le -0.70 \le 1.96$), the results are within the acceptance region for H_0, and the hypothesis that the mean of the population equals 500 ($\mu = 500$) cannot be rejected.

Left-tail test: As $Z > -Z_\alpha$ ($-0.70 > -1.64$), the results are within the acceptance region for H_0, and the hypothesis that the mean of the population equals 500 ($\mu = 500$) cannot be rejected.

Right-tail test: As $Z < Z_\alpha$ ($-0.70 < 1.64$), the results are within the acceptance region for H_0, and the hypothesis that the mean of the population equals 500 ($\mu = 500$) cannot be rejected.

1.2 Comparing the mean m of a sample to a reference value μ_0 when the variance σ_2 of the population is unknown

Research question   Does the mean m, calculated from a sample taken from a population with an unknown variance σ^2, differ significantly from a hypothetical mean μ_0?

Application conditions

- The variance σ^2 of the population is not known and has to be estimated from the sample. The mean μ is also unknown (the hypothesis suggests it equals μ_0).
- A random sample is used, containing n independent observations.
- The size n of the sample is greater than 30, unless the population follows a normal distribution, in which case the size has no importance.

Hypotheses

Null hypothesis, H_0: $\mu = \mu_0$,
alternative hypothesis, H_1: $\mu \ne \mu_0$ (for a two-tail test)
or H_1: $\mu < \mu_0$ (for a left-tail test)
or H_1: $\mu > \mu_0$ (for a right-tail test).

Statistic   The unknown variance (σ_2) of the population is estimated from the sample, with $n - 1$ degrees of freedom, using the formula

$$s^2 = \frac{1}{n-1}\sum_{i=1}^{n}(x_i - m)^2.$$

The statistic calculated is

$$T = \frac{(m-\mu_0)}{s/\sqrt{n}}.$$

It follows Student's distribution with $n - 1$ degrees of freedom, and is called a *t test* or a *t statistic*.

Interpreting the test   When n is large, that is, greater than 30, this statistic approximates a normal distribution. In other words:

$$T = \frac{(m-\mu_0)}{s/\sqrt{n}} \approx Z = \frac{(m-\mu_0)}{\sigma/\sqrt{n}}.$$

The decision to reject or not to reject the null hypothesis can therefore be made by comparing the calculated statistic T to the normal distribution values. We recall that the decision-making rules for a standard normal distribution are:

- in a two-tail test, H_0 will be rejected if $Z < -Z_{\alpha/2}$ or $Z > Z_{\alpha/2}$
- in a left-tail test, H_0 will be rejected if $Z < -Z_\alpha$
- in a right-tail test, H_0 will be rejected if $Z > Z_\alpha$.

where α is the significance level (or Type I error) and Z_α and $Z_{\alpha/2}$ are normal distribution values, which can be found in the appropriate tables.

But for smaller values of n, that is, lower than 30, the Student distribution (at $n - 1$ degrees of freedom) cannot be replaced by a normal distribution. The decision rules then become the following:

- In a two-tail test, H_0 will be rejected if $T < -T_{\alpha/2;\,n-1}$ or $T > T_{\alpha/2;\,n-1}$
- in a left-tail test, H_0 will be rejected if $T < -T_{\alpha;\,n-1}$
- in a right-tail test, H_0 will be rejected if $T > T_{\alpha;\,n-1}$.

Example: Comparing a mean to a given value (variance is unknown)

This time, the sample is much larger, containing 144 observations. The mean found in this sample is again $m = 493$. The estimated standard deviation is s = 46.891. Is it still possible to accept a mean in the population $\mu_0 = 500$, if we adopt a significance level α of 5 per cent?

The relatively large size of the sample ($n = 144$, and so is greater than 30) justifies the approximation of the statistic T to a normal distribution. Thus

$$T = \frac{(493 - 500)}{46.891/\sqrt{144}},$$

which gives –1.79. The tables provide values of $Z_{0.025} = 1.96$ and $Z_{0.05} = 1.64$.
Two-tail test: As $-Z_{\alpha/2} \le T \le Z_{\alpha/2}$ ($-1.96 \le -1.79 \le 1.96$), the null hypothesis, stating that the mean of the population equals 500 ($\mu = 500$), cannot be rejected.

Left-tail test: as $T < -Z_\alpha$ (−1.79 < −1.64), the null hypothesis is rejected, to the benefit of the alternative hypothesis, according to which the mean in the population is less than 500 ($\mu < 500$).

Right-tail test: as $T \leq Z_\alpha$ (−1.79 ≤ 1.64), the null hypothesis cannot be rejected.

As mentioned above, the major difficulty researchers face when carrying out comparison tests is to choose the appropriate test to prove their research hypothesis. To illustrate this, in the following example we present the results obtained by using proprietary computer software to analyze the above situation. For this example we will use the statistical analysis program, Statgraphics, although other software programs provide similar information.

Example: Using statistical software to generate statistical tests

When using proprietary statistics software, the researcher begins by indicating the variable that is to be examined. In this example, this is the mean of the 144 observations. The software then presents an input screen, for which a number of fields have to be filled out manually: 1) the hypothetical mean μ_0 (500 in our example) corresponding to the null hypothesis H_0; 2) the alternative form of the hypothesis, which is defined by choosing from three different operators: 'different', 'less than' and 'greater than'. In this example, the alternative hypothesis reads $H_1: \mu \neq \mu_0$ for a two-tail test, $H_1: \mu < \mu_0$ for a left-tail test, or yet $H_1: \mu > \mu_0$ for a right-tail test. 3) the significance level α chosen by the researcher.

After processing this data, the program provides the following results:

Sample statistics:
Number of observations: 144
Mean: 493
Variance: 2198.77
Standard deviation: 46.891

Test:
H_0: Mean = 500   Calculated Statistic $T = -1.79139$
H_1: Different   Observed significance level = 0.0753462
For a significance level Alpha = 0.05:→   do not reject H_0

Test:
H_0: Mean = 500   Calculated Statistic $T = -1.79139$
H_1: Less than   Observed significance level = 0.0376731
For a significance level Alpha = 0.05:→   reject H_0

Test:
H_0: Mean = 500   Calculated Statistic $T = -1.79139$
H_1: Greater than   Observed significance level = 0.962327
For a significance level Alpha = 0.05: →   do not reject H_0

The software carries out all the calculations, and even indicates the decision to make (to reject the null hypothesis or not) on the basis of the statistic T and the significance level α set by the researcher. In addition, it provides the *p* value, or the observed significance level. We have already mentioned the importance of the *p* value, which can provide more detailed information, and so refine the decision. In the first test (two-tail test), the null hypothesis is not rejected for a significance level of 5 per cent, but it would have been rejected if the Type I error risk had been 10 per cent. The *p* value (0.0753462) is greater than 5 per cent but less than 10 per cent. In the second test (left-tail test), the null hypothesis is rejected for a significance level of 5 per cent, while it would not have been rejected for a significance level of 1 per cent. The *p* value (0.0376731) is less than 5 per cent but greater than 1 per cent. Finally, in the last test (right-tail test), examining the *p* value (0.962327) suggests that there are good reasons for not rejecting the null hypothesis, as it is well above any acceptable significance level.

1.3 Comparing the difference of two means to a given value, when the variance of the two populations is known

Research question   Is the difference between the two means μ_1 and μ_2 of two populations of known variances σ_1^2 and σ_2^2 significantly different from a given value D_0 (for instance zero)?

Application conditions

- The variances σ_1^2 and σ_2^2 of the two populations are known. The means μ_1 and μ_2 are unknown.
- Both samples are random and contain n_1 and n_2 independent observations respectively.
- Either the mean for each population follows a normal distribution, or the size of each sample is greater than 5.

Hypotheses

Null hypothesis, H_0: $\mu_1 - \mu_2 = D_0$,
alternative hypothesis, H_1: $\mu_1 - \mu_2 \neq D_0$ (for a two-tail test)
or H_1: $\mu_1 - \mu_2 < D_0$ (for a left-tail test)
or H_1: $\mu_1 - \mu_2 > D_0$ (for a right-tail test).

Statistic

The statistic calculated is

$$Z = \frac{m_1 - m_2 - D_0}{\sigma_d},$$

x_{1i} = the value of variable X for observation i in population 1,
x_{2i} = the value of variable X for observation i in population 2,

$$m_1 = \frac{\sum_{i=1}^{n_1} x_{1i}}{n_1}, \; m_2 = \frac{\sum_{i=1}^{n_2} x_{2i}}{n_2}$$

and

$$\sigma_d = \sqrt{\frac{\sigma_1^2}{n_1} + \frac{\sigma_2^2}{n_2}}$$

is the standard deviation of the difference $(m_1 - m_2)$.
   Z follows a standard normal distribution.

Interpreting the test   The decision rules are the following:

- In a two-tail test, H_0 will be rejected if $Z < -Z_{\alpha/2}$ or $Z > Z_{\alpha/2}$
- in a left-tail test, H_0 will be rejected if $Z < -Z_\alpha$
- in a right-tail test, H_0 will be rejected if $Z > Z_\alpha$.

1.4 Comparing the difference of two means to a given value, when the two populations have the same variance, but its exact value is unknown

Research question   Is the difference between the two means μ_1 and μ_2 of two populations that have the same unknown variance σ^2 significantly different from a given value D_0 (for instance zero)?

Application conditions

- The two populations have the same unknown variance (σ^2). The two means μ_1 and μ_2 are not known.
- Both samples are random and contain n_1 and n_2 independent observations respectively.
- Either the mean for each population follows a normal distribution, or the size of each sample is greater than 30.
- The hypothesis of equality of the variances is verified (see Section 3.2 of this chapter).

Hypotheses

Null hypothesis, H_0: $\mu_1 - \mu_2 = D_0$,
alternative hypothesis, H_1: $\mu_1 - \mu_2 \neq D_0$ (for a two-tail test)
or H_1: $\mu_1 - \mu_2 < D_0$ (for a left-tail test)
or H_1: $\mu_1 - \mu_2 > D_0$ (for a right-tail test).

Statistic
The statistic calculated is:

$$T = \frac{m_1 - m_2 - D_0}{s_d},$$

x_{1i} = the value of the observed variable X for observation i in population 1,

x_{2i} = the value of the observed variable X for observation i in population 2,

$$m_1 = \frac{\sum_{i=1}^{n_1} x_{1i}}{n_1}, \quad m_2 = \frac{\sum_{i=1}^{n_2} x_{2i}}{n_2}, \quad s_d = \sqrt{\frac{(n_1-1)s_1^2 + (n_2-1)s_2^2}{n_1+n_2-2}} \times \sqrt{\left(\frac{1}{n_1} + \frac{1}{n_2}\right)}$$

$$s_1^2 = \frac{\sum_{i=1}^{n_1}(x_{1i} - m_1)^2}{n_1 - 1} \quad and \quad s_2^2 = \frac{\sum_{i=1}^{n_2}(x_{2i} - m_2)^2}{n_2 - 1}.$$

This statistic follows Student's t distribution with $n_1 + n_2 - 2$ degrees of freedom.

Interpreting the test   The decision rules are the following:

- in a two-tail test, H_0 will be rejected if $T < -T_{\alpha/2;\, n1+n2-2}$ or $T > T_{\alpha/2;\, n1+n2-2}$
- in a left-tail test, H_0 will be rejected if $T < -T_{\alpha;\, n1+n2-2}$
- in a right-tail test, H_0 will be rejected if $T > T_{\alpha;\, n1+n2-2}$.

When the sample size is sufficiently large (that is, $n_1 \geq 30$ and $n_2 \geq 30$), the distribution of the statistic T approximates a normal distribution, in which case

$$T = \frac{(m - \mu_0)}{s/\sqrt{n}} \approx Z = \frac{(m - \mu_0)}{\sigma/\sqrt{n}}.$$

The decision to reject or not to reject the null hypothesis can then be made by comparing the calculated statistic T to the normal distribution. In this case, the following decision rules should apply:

- In a two-tail test, H_0 will be rejected if $T < -Z_{\alpha/2}$ or $Z > Z_{\alpha/2}$
- in a left-tail test, H_0 will be rejected if $T < -Z_{\alpha}$
- in a right-tail test, H_0 will be rejected if $T > Z_{\alpha}$.

1.5 Comparing two means, when the variances of the populations are unknown and differ

Research question Do the two means μ_1 and μ_2 of two populations of unknown variances σ_1^2 and σ_2^2 differ significantly from each other?

Application conditions

- The variances σ_1^2 and σ_2^2 of the two populations are unknown and different. The means μ_1 and μ_2 are unknown.
- Both samples are random and contain n_1 and n_2 independent observations respectively.

- For both populations, the mean follows a normal distribution.
- The two samples are of practically the same size.
- At least one of the samples contains fewer than 20 elements.
- The hypothesis of the inequality of variances is fulfilled (see Section 3.2 of this chapter).

Hypotheses

Null hypothesis, H_0: $\mu_1 = \mu_2$,
alternative hypothesis, H_1: $\mu_1 \neq \mu_2$ (for a two-tail test)
or H_1: $\mu_1 < \mu_2$ (for a left-tail test)
or H_1: $\mu_1 > \mu_2$ (for a right-tail test).

Statistic Using the same notations as in Section 1.4 of this chapter, the statistic calculated is:

$$T' = \frac{m_1 - m_2}{\sqrt{\dfrac{s_1^2}{n_1} + \dfrac{s_2^2}{n_2}}}$$

This statistic T' is called an Aspin-Welch test. It approximates a Student T distribution in which the number of degrees of freedom v is the closest integer value to the result of the following formula:

$$\frac{1}{v} = \frac{1}{n_1 - 1}\left(\frac{\dfrac{s_1^2}{n_1}}{s_d^2}\right)^2 + \frac{1}{n_2 - 1}\left(\frac{\dfrac{s_2^2}{n_2}}{s_d^2}\right)^2$$

Interpreting the test The decision rules then become the following:

- in a two-tail test, H_0 will be rejected if $T' < -T_{\alpha/2;\,v}$ or $T' > T_{\alpha/2;\,v}$
- in a left-tail test, H_0 will be rejected if $T' < -T_{\alpha;\,v}$
- in a right-tail test, H_0 will be rejected if $T' > T_{\alpha;\,v}$.

1.6 Comparing *k* means (μ_k): analysis of variance

Research question Do k means, $m_1, m_2 \ldots, m_k$ observed on k samples differ significantly from each other?
This question is answered through an analysis of variance (Anova).

Application conditions

- All k samples are random and contain $n_1, n_2 \ldots n_k$ independent observations.
- For all k populations, the mean approximates a normal distribution with the same, unknown, variance (σ^2).

Hypotheses

Null hypothesis, H_0: $\pi_1 = \pi_2 = \ldots = \pi_k$,
alternative hypothesis, H_1: the values of π_i ($i - 1, 2, \ldots , k$) are not all identical. This means that one single different value would be enough to reject the null hypothesis, thus validating the alternative hypothesis.

Statistic   The statistic calculated is

$$F = \frac{\text{Variance between groups}}{\text{Variance within groups}}$$

The statistic F follows a Fisher distribution with $k - 1$ and $n - k$ degrees of freedom, where n is the total number of observations.

Interpreting the test   The decision rule is the following:
H_0 will be rejected if $F > F_{k - 1; n - k}$.
   The analysis of variance (Anova) can be generalized to the comparison of the mean profiles of k groups according to j variables X_j. This analysis is called a Manova, which stands for 'multivariate analysis of variance'. Like the Anova, the test used is Fisher's F test, and the decision rules are the same.

1.7 Comparing k means (μ_k): multiple comparisons

Research question   Of k means m_1, $m_2 \ldots , m_k$ observed on k samples, which if any differ significantly?
   The least significant difference test, or LSD, is used in the context of an Anova when examination of the ratio F leads to the rejection of the null hypothesis H_0 of the equality of means, and when more than two groups are present. In this situation, a classic analysis of variance will only furnish global information, without indicating which means differ. LSD tests, such as the Scheffé, Tukey, or Duncan tests, compare the groups two by two. These tests are all included in the major statistical analysis computer programs.

Application conditions

* All k samples are random and contain n_1, $n_2 \ldots n_k$ independent observations.
* For all k populations, the mean approximates a normal distribution with the same, unknown, variance (σ^2).

Hypotheses

Null hypothesis, H_0: $\pi_1 = \pi_2 = \cdots = \pi_k$,
alternative hypothesis, H_1: the values of π_i ($i = 1, 2, \ldots , k$) are not all identical. This means that one single different value would be enough to reject the null hypothesis, thus validating the alternative hypothesis.

Statistic

The statistic calculated is

$$T_{ij} = \frac{Y_i - Y_j}{\sqrt{S_1^2 \left(\dfrac{1}{n_i} + \dfrac{1}{n_j} \right)}}$$

where Y_i is the mean of Group i, Y_j the mean of group j, n_i the number of observations of group i, n_j the number of observations of group j, and S_1^2 the estimation of the variance within each group. This statistic T_{ij} follows a Student distribution with $n - k$ degrees of freedom, where n is the total number of observations. This signifies that the mean of all the two-by-two combinations of the k groups will be compared.

Interpreting the test   The decision rule is the following:
H_0 will be rejected if one T_{ij} is greater than $T_{\alpha/2; n-k}$. When $T_{ij} > T_{\alpha/2; n-k}$, the difference between the means Y_i and Y_j of the two groups i and j in question is judged to be significant.

1.8 Comparing k means (μk): analysis of covariance

Research question   Do k means $m_1, m_2 \dots , m_k$ observed on k samples differ significantly from each other?
    Analysis of covariance permits the differences between the means of different groups to be tested, taking the influence of one or more metric variables, X_j called concomitants, into account. This essentially involves carrying out a linear regression to explain the means in terms of the X_j concomitant variables, and then using an analysis of variance to examine any differences between groups that are not explained by the linear regression. Analysis of covariance is therefore a method of comparing two or more means. Naturally, if the regression coefficients associated with the explicative concomitant metric variables are not significant, an analysis of variance will have to be used instead.

Application conditions

- All k samples are random and contain $n_1, n_2 \dots n_k$ independent observations.
- For all k populations, the mean approximates a normal distribution with the same, unknown, variance (σ^2).
- The choice of structure of the k groups should not determine the values of the concomitant metric variables.

Hypotheses

Null hypothesis, H_0: $\pi_1 = \pi_2 = \cdots = \pi_k$,
alternative hypothesis, H_1: the values of π_i ($i = 1, 2, \dots , k$) are not all identical. This means that one single different value would be enough to reject the null hypothesis, thus validating the alternative hypothesis.

Statistic

The statistic calculated is

$$F = \frac{\text{Explained variance}}{\text{Residual variance}}$$

where the *explained variance* is the estimation made from the sample of the variance between the groups, and the *residual variance* is the estimation of the variance of the residues. This statistic F follows a Fisher distribution, with $k - 1$ and $n - k - 1$ degrees of freedom, n being the total number of observations.

Interpreting the test   The decision rule is the following:
H_0 will be rejected if $F > F_{k-1;\, n-k-1}$. The statistic F and the observed significance level are automatically calculated by statistical analysis software.

The analysis of covariance (Ancova) can be generalized to the comparison of the mean profiles of k groups according to j variables X_j. This is called a Mancova, for 'multivariate analysis of covariance'. The test used (that is, Fisher's F test) and the decision rules remain the same.

1.9 Comparing two series of measurements: the hotelling T^2 test

Research question   Do the mean profiles of two series of k measurements (m_1, m_2 ... , m_k) and (m'_1, m'_2, ... , m'_k), observed for two samples, differ significantly from each other?

The Hotelling T^2 test is used to compare any two matrices or vectors, particularly correlation matrices, variance or covariance matrices, or mean-value vectors.

Application conditions

- The two samples are random and contain n_1 and n_2 independent observations respectively.
- The different measurements are independent and present a normal, multivariate distribution.

Hypotheses

Null hypothesis, H_0: the two series of measurements present the same profile, alternative hypothesis, H_1: the two series of measurements present different profiles.

Statistic

The statistic calculated is

$$F = \frac{n_1 + n_2 - k - 1}{k(n_1 + n_2 - 2)} T^2$$

where T^2 is Hotelling's T^2, k the number of variables, and n_1 and n_2 are the number of observations in the first and second sample.

The statistic F follows a Fisher distribution with k and $n_1 + n_2 - k - 1$ degrees of freedom.

Interpreting the test   The decision rule is the following:
H_0 will be rejected if $F > F_{k-1; n1 + n2 - k - 1}$.

2. Proportion Tests

2.1 Comparing a proportion or a percentage to a reference value π_0: binomial test

Research question   Does the proportion p, calculated on a sample, differ significantly from a hypothetical proportion π_0?

Application conditions

- The sample is random and contains n independent observations.
- The distribution of the proportion in the population is binomial.
- The size of the sample is relatively large (greater than 30).

Hypotheses

Null hypothesis, H_0: $\pi = \pi_0$,
alternative hypothesis, H_1: $\pi \neq \pi_0$ (for a two-tail test)
or H_1: $\pi < \pi_0$ (for a left-tail test)
or H_1: $\pi > \pi_0$ (for a right-tail test).

Statistic

The statistic calculated is

$$Z = \frac{p - \pi_0}{\sigma_p}$$

where

$$\sigma_p = \sqrt{\frac{\pi_0 (1 - \pi_0)}{n}}.$$

It follows a standard normal distribution.

Interpreting the test   The decision rules are the following:

- in a two-tail test, H_0 will be rejected if $Z < -Z_{\alpha/2}$ or $Z > Z_{\alpha/2}$
- in a left-tail test, H_0 will be rejected if $Z < -Z_{\alpha}$
- in a right-tail test, H_0 will be rejected if $Z > Z_{\alpha}$.

2.2 Comparing two proportions or percentages p_1 and p_2 (with large samples)

Research question   Do the two proportions or percentages p_1 and p_2, observed in two samples, differ significantly?

Application conditions

- The two samples are random and contain n_1 and n_2 independent observations respectively.
- The distribution of the proportion in each population is binomial.
- Both samples are large ($n_1 \geq 30$ and $n_2 \geq 30$).

Hypotheses

Null hypothesis, H_0: $\pi_1 = \pi_2$,
alternative hypothesis, H_1: $\pi_1 \neq \pi_2$ (for a two-tail test)
or H_1: $\pi_1 < \pi_2$ (for a left-tail test)
or H_1: $\pi_1 > \pi_2$ (for a right-tail test).

Statistic

The statistic calculated is

$$Z = \frac{p_1 - p_2}{\sqrt{p_0 (1 - p_0)\left(\dfrac{1}{n_1} + \dfrac{1}{n_2}\right)}}$$

where

$$p_0 = \frac{n_1 p_1 + n_2 p_2}{n_1 + n_2}.$$

It follows a standard normal distribution.

Interpreting the test   The decision rules are the following:

- in a two-tail test, H_0 will be rejected if $Z < -Z_{\alpha/2}$ or $Z > Z_{\alpha/2}$
- in a left-tail test, H_0 will be rejected if $Z < -Z_{\alpha}$
- in a right-tail test, H_0 will be rejected if $Z > Z_{\alpha}$.

2.3 Comparing k proportions or percentages p_k (large samples)

Research question   Do the k proportions or percentages $p_1, p_2 \ldots, p_k$, observed in k samples, differ significantly from each other?

Application conditions

- The k samples are random and contain $n_1, n_2 \ldots n_k$ independent observations.
- The distribution of the proportion or percentage is binomial in each of the k populations.

- All the samples are large (n_1, n_2 ... and $n_k \geq 50$).
- The k proportions p_k as well as their complements $1 - p_k$ represent at least five observations, that is: $p_k \times n_k \geq 5$ and $(1 - p_k) \times n_k \geq 5$.

Hypotheses

Null hypothesis, H_0: $\pi_1 = \pi_2 = \ldots = \pi_k$,
alternative hypothesis, H_1: the values of π_i ($i = 1, 2, \ldots , k$) are not all identical. This means that one single different value would be enough to reject the null hypothesis, thus validating the alternative hypothesis.

Statistic

The statistic calculated is

$$\chi = \sum_{j=1}^{k} \frac{(x_j - n_j p)^2}{n_j p \, (1 - p)}$$

where x_j = the number of observations in the sample j corresponding to the proportion p_j, and

$$p = \frac{\displaystyle\sum_{j=1}^{k} x_j}{\displaystyle\sum_{j=1}^{k} n_j}$$

The statistic χ follows a chi-square distribution, with $k - 1$ degrees of freedom.

Interpreting the test   The decision rule is the following:
H_0 will be rejected if

$$\chi > \chi^2_{\alpha; \, k-1}$$

3. Variance Test

3.1 Comparing the variance σ^2 to a reference value σ_0^2

Research question   Does the variance s^2 calculated from a sample differ significantly from a hypothetical variance σ_0^2?

Application conditions

- The sample is random and contains n independent observations.
- The distribution of the variance in the population is normal, the mean and standard deviation are not known.

Hypotheses

Null hypothesis, H_0: $\sigma^2 = \sigma_0^2$,
alternative hypothesis, H_1: $\sigma^2 \neq \sigma_0^2$ (for a two-tail test)

or H_1: $\sigma^2 < \sigma_0^2$ (for a left-tail test)
or H_1: $\sigma^2 > \sigma_0^2$ (for a right-tail test).

Statistic

The statistic calculated is

$$\chi = (n-1)\frac{s^2}{\sigma_0^2} = \frac{\displaystyle\sum_{i=1}^{n}(x_i - m)^2}{\sigma_0^2}$$

where σ_0^2 is the given variance, s^2 the variance estimated from the sample, and m the mean estimated from the sample. The statistic χ follows a chi-square distribution with $n - 1$ degrees of freedom, which is written $\chi^2(n - 1)$.

Interpreting the test   The decision rules are the following:

- In a two-tail test, H_0 will be rejected if

$$\chi > \chi^2_{\alpha/2;\, n-1} \ \text{ or } \ \chi < \chi^2_{1-\alpha/2;\, n-1}$$

- in a left-tail test, H_0 will be rejected if

$$\chi < \chi^2_{1-\alpha;\, n-1}$$

- in a right-tail test, H_0 will be rejected if

$$\chi > \chi^2_{\alpha;\, n-1}$$

3.2 Comparing two variances

Research question   Do the variances σ_1^2 and σ_2^2 of two populations differ significantly from each other?

Application conditions

- Both samples are random and contain n_1 and n_2 independent observations respectively.
- The distribution of the variance of each population is normal, or the samples are large ($n_1 \geq 30$ and $n_2 \geq 30$).

Hypotheses

Null hypothesis, H_0: $\sigma_1^2 = \sigma_2^2$,
alternative hypothesis, H_1: $\sigma_1^2 \neq \sigma_2^2$ (for a two-tail test)
or H_1: $\sigma_1^2 < \sigma_2^2$ (for a left-tail test)
or H_1: $\sigma_1^2 > \sigma_2^2$ (for a right-tail test).

Statistic

The statistic calculated is

$$F = \frac{s_1^2}{s_2^2}$$

where

$$s_1^2 = \frac{\sum_{i=1}^{n_1}(x_{1i} - x_1)^2}{n_1 - 1}$$

and

$$s_2^2 = \frac{\sum_{i=1}^{n_2}(x_{2i} - x_2)^2}{n_2 - 1}$$

x_{1i} = the value of variable X for observation i in population 1,
x_{2i} = the value of variable X for observation i in population 2,
x_1 = the mean estimated from the sample of variable X in population 1,
x_2 = the mean estimated from the sample of variable X in population 2. If required, the numbering of the samples may be inverted to give the numerator the greater of the two estimated variances,

$$\frac{\sum_{i=1}^{n}(x_1 - x_2)^2}{n_1 - 1} \text{ and } s_2^2$$

The statistic F follows a Fisher-Snedecor distribution, $F(n_1 - 1, n_2 - 1)$.

Interpreting the test   The decision rules are the following:

- In a two-tail test, H_0 will be rejected if $F > F_{\alpha/2; n1 - 1, n2 - 1}$ or $F < F_{1 - \alpha/2; n1 - 1, n2 - 1}$
- in a left-tail test, H_0 will be rejected if $F > F_{\alpha; n2 - 1, n1 - 1}$
- in a right-tail test, H_0 will be rejected if $F > F_{\alpha; n1 - 1, n2 - 1}$.

3.3 Comparing k variances: Bartlett test

Research question   Do k variances $\sigma_1^2, \sigma_2^2, \dots, \sigma_k^2$ observed in k samples, differ significantly from each other?

Application conditions

- All k samples are random and contain $n_1, n_2 \dots n_k$ independent observations.
- The distribution of the variance of all k populations is normal.
- None of the observed variances equals zero.

Hypotheses

Null hypothesis, H_0:

$$\sigma_1^2 = \sigma_2^2 = \dots = \sigma_k^2$$

alternative hypothesis, H_1: the values of σ_i^2 ($i = 1, 2, \dots, k$) are not identical

Statistic

The statistic calculated is

$$\chi = v \ln s^2 - \sum_{i=1}^{k} v_i \ln s_i^2$$

where $v_i = n_i - 1$,

$$s_i^2 = \frac{\sum_{j=1}^{n} (x_{ij} - x_i)^2}{v_i}, \quad v = \sum_{i=1}^{k} v_i, \quad s^2 = \frac{1}{v} \sum_{i=1}^{k} v_i s_i^2,$$

x_{ij} = the value of variable X for observation j in population i,
x_i = the mean of variable X in population i, estimated from a sample of size n_i,
s_i^2 = the variance of variable X in population i, estimated from a sample of size n_i.
   The statistic χ follows a chi-square distribution with v degrees of freedom.

Interpreting the test   The decision rule is the following:
H_0 will be rejected if

$$\chi > \chi^2_{\alpha; k-1}$$

3.4 Comparing k variances: Cochran test

Research question   Do k variances $\sigma_1^2, \sigma_2^2, \ldots, \sigma_k^2$, observed in k samples, differ significantly from each other?
   More precisely, the Cochran test examines if the greatest of the k variances is significantly different to the $k - 1$ other variances

Application conditions

- The k samples are random and contain a same number n of independent observations.
- The variance in each of the k populations follows a normal distribution, or at least a uni-modal distribution.

Hypotheses

Null hypothesis, H_0: $\sigma_1^2 = \sigma_2^2 = \ldots \sigma_k^2$,
alternative hypothesis, H_1: the values of σ_i^2 ($i = 1, 2, \ldots, k$) are not identical.

Statistic

The statistic calculated is

$$C = \frac{S^2_{max}}{\sum_{i=1}^{k} S_i^2}$$

where the values of s_i^2 are the estimated variances calculated with $v = n - 1$ degrees of freedom, and S^2_{max} is the greatest estimated variance within the k samples.
   The statistic C is compared to the critical value C_α, as read from a table.

Interpreting the test   The decision rule is the following:
H_0 will be rejected if $C > C_\alpha$.

4. Correlation Tests

4.1 Comparing a linear correlation coefficient r to zero

Research question   Is the linear correlation coefficient r of two variables X and Y significant – that is, not equal to zero?

Application conditions

- The observed variables X and Y are, at least, continuous variables.

Hypotheses

Null hypothesis, H_0: $\rho = 0$,
alternative hypothesis, H_1: $\rho \neq 0$ (for a two-tail test)
or H_1: $\rho < 0$ (for a left-tail test)
or H_1: $\rho > 0$ (for a right-tail test)

Statistic

The statistic calculated is

$$T = \frac{r\sqrt{n-2}}{\sqrt{1-r^2}}.$$

It follows a Student distribution with $n - 2$ degrees of freedom.

Interpreting the test   The decision rules are the following:

- in a two-tail test, H_0 will be rejected if $T < -T_{\alpha/2;\, n-2}$ or $T > T_{\alpha/2;\, n-2}$
- in a left-tail test, H_0 will be rejected if $T < -T_{\alpha;\, n-2}$
- in a right-tail test, H_0 will be rejected if $T > T_{\alpha;\, n-2}$.

For large values of n ($n - 2 > 30$), this statistic approximates a standard normal distribution. The decision to reject or not to reject the null hypothesis can then be made by comparing the calculated statistic T to values of the standard normal distribution, using the decision rules that have already been presented earlier in this chapter.

4.2 Comparing a linear correlation coefficient r to a reference value ρ_0

Research question   Is the linear correlation coefficient r of two variables X and Y, calculated from a sample, significantly different from a hypothetical reference value ρ_0?

Application conditions

- The observed variables X and Y are, at least, continuous variables.

Hypotheses

Null hypothesis, H_0: $\rho = \rho_0$,
alternative hypothesis, H_1: $\rho \neq \rho_0$ (for a two-tail test)
or H_1: $\rho < \rho_0$ (for a left-tail test)
or H_1: $\rho > \rho_0$ (for a right-tail test)

Statistic

The statistic calculated is

$$Z = \frac{1}{2} \frac{\ln\left(\dfrac{1+r}{1-r} \times \dfrac{1-\rho_0}{1+\rho_0}\right)}{\sqrt{\dfrac{1}{n-3}}}.$$

It follows a standard normal distribution.

Interpreting the test   The decision rules are the following:

- in a two-tail test, H_0 will be rejected if $Z < -Z_{\alpha/2}$ or $Z > Z_{\alpha/2}$
- in a left-tail test, H_0 will be rejected if $Z < -Z_\alpha$
- in a right-tail test, H_0 will be rejected if $Z > Z_\alpha$.

4.3 Comparing two linear correlation coefficients, ρ_1 and ρ_2

Research question   Do the two linear correlation coefficients ρ_1 and ρ_2 differ significantly from each other?

Application conditions

- The two linear correlation coefficients r_1 and r_2 are obtained from two samples of size n_1 and n_2 respectively.

Hypotheses

Null hypothesis, H_0: $\rho_1 = \rho_2$,
alternative hypothesis, H_1: $\rho_1 \neq \rho_2$ (for a two-tail test)
or H_1: $\rho_1 < \rho_2$ (for a left-tail test)
or H_1: $\rho_1 > \rho_2$ (for a right-tail test).

Statistic

The statistic calculated is
It follows a standard normal distribution.

$$Z = \frac{1}{2} \frac{\ln\left(\dfrac{1+r_1}{1-r_1} \times \dfrac{1-r_2}{1+r_2}\right)}{\sqrt{\dfrac{1}{n_1-3} + \dfrac{1}{n_2-3}}}.$$

Interpreting the test   The decision rules are thus the following:

- in a two-tail test, H_0 will be rejected if $Z < -Z_{\alpha/2}$ or $Z > Z_{\alpha/2}$
- in a left-tail test, H_0 will be rejected if $Z < -Z_{\alpha}$
- in a right-tail test, H_0 will be rejected if $Z > Z_{\alpha}$.

5. Regression Coefficient Tests

5.1 Comparing a linear regression coefficient β to zero

Research question   Is the linear regression coefficient β of two variables X and Y significant, that is, not equal to zero?

Application conditions

- The observed variables X and Y are, at least, continuous variables.
- β follows a normal distribution or the size n of the sample is greater than 30.

Hypotheses

Null hypothesis, H_0: $\beta = 0$,
alternative hypothesis, H_1: $\beta \neq 0$ (for a two-tail test)
or H_1: $\beta < 0$ (for a left-tail test)
or H_1: $\beta > 0$ (for a right-tail test).

Statistic

The statistic calculated is

$$T = \frac{b}{s_b},$$

where b represents the regression coefficient β and s_b its standard deviation, both estimated from the sample. The statistic T follows a Student distribution with $n - 2$ degrees of freedom.

Interpreting the test   The decision rules are the following:

- in a two-tail test, H_0 will be rejected if $T < -T_{\alpha/2;\, n-2}$ or $T > T_{\alpha/2;\, n-2}$
- in a left-tail test, H_0 will be rejected if $T < -T_{\alpha;\, n-2}$
- in a right-tail test, H_0 will be rejected if $T > T_{\alpha;\, n-2}$.

5.2 Comparing a linear regression coefficient β to a reference value β_0

Research question   Is the linear regression coefficient β of two variables X and Y significantly different from a reference value β_0?

Application conditions

- The observed variables X and Y are, at least, continuous variables.
- β follows a normal distribution or the size n of the sample is greater than 30.

Hypotheses

Null hypothesis, H_0: $\beta = \beta_0$,
alternative hypothesis, H_1: $\beta \neq \beta_0$ (for a two-tail test)
or H_1: $\beta < \beta_0$ (for a left-tail test)
or H_1: $\beta > \beta_0$ (for a right-tail test).

Statistic

The statistic calculated is

$$T = \frac{b - \beta_0}{s_b},$$

where b represents the regression coefficient β and s_b its standard deviation, both estimated from the sample. The statistic T follows a Student distribution with $n - 2$ degrees of freedom.

Interpreting the test   The decision rules are the following:

- in a two-tail test, H_0 will be rejected if $T < -T_{\alpha/2; n-2}$ or $T > T_{\alpha/2; n-2}$
- in a left-tail test, H_0 will be rejected if $T < -T_{\alpha; n-2}$
- in a right-tail test, H_0 will be rejected if $T > T_{\alpha; n-2}$.

5.3 Comparing two linear regression coefficients β and β in two populations

Research question   Do the two linear regression coefficients β and β', observed in two populations, differ significantly from each other?

This is again a situation in which the difference between two means b and b' with estimated variances s_b^2, and $s_{b'}^2$, is tested. Naturally we must distinguish between cases in which the two variances are equal and cases in which they are not equal. If these variances differ, an Aspin-Welch test will be used.

Application conditions

- β and β' represent the values of the regression coefficient in two populations, from which two independent, random samples have been selected.
- The observed variables X and Y are, at least, continuous variables.

Hypotheses

Null hypothesis, H_0: $\beta = \beta'$,
alternative hypothesis, H_1: $\beta \neq \beta'$ (for a two-tail test)
or H_1: $\beta < \beta'$ (for a left-tail test)
or H_1: $\beta > \beta'$ (for a right-tail test).

Statistic

The statistics calculated and the interpretations of the tests are the same as for the tests on differences of means, described in parts 1.1 through 1.5 in this chapter.

In addition, it is possible to use the same kind of tests on a constant (β_0) of the linear regression equation. However, this practice is rarely used due to the great difficulties in interpreting the results. Similarly, more than two regression coefficients may be compared. For instance, the Chow test (Chow, 1960; Toyoda, 1974), which uses the Fisher-Snedecor distribution, is used to determine whether the coefficients of a regression equation are the same in two or more groups. This is called an *omnibus test*, which means that it tests whether the full set of equation coefficients are identical.

When comparing two groups, a neat and quite simple alternative to the Chow test is the introduction of a 'dummy variable' to the regression, indicating the group it belongs to. The original variables are multiplied by the dummy variable thus obtaining a set of new variables. The coefficients of the dummy variable represent the differences between the constants (β_0) for the two groups, and the coefficients of the new variables represent the differences between the coefficients of the explicative variables for the two groups. These coefficients can then be tested globally (as the Chow test does) or individually (see Sections 5.1 through 5.3 in this chapter) to identify which coefficient behaves differently according to the group.

SECTION 3 PRACTICING NON-PARAMETRIC TESTS

Non-parametric tests use statistics (that is, calculations) that have been established from observations, and do not depend on the distribution of the corresponding population. The validity of non-parametric tests depends on very general conditions that are much less restrictive than those that apply to parametric tests.

Non-parametric tests present a number of advantages, in that they are applicable to:

- small samples
- various types of data (nominal, ordinal, intervals, ratios)
- incomplete or imprecise data.

1. Testing One Variable in Several Samples

1.1 Comparing a distribution to a theoretical distribution: goodness-of-fit test

Research question Does the empirical distribution D_e, observed in a sample, differ significantly from a reference distribution D_r?

Application conditions

- The sample is random and contains n independent observations arranged into k classes.
- A reference distribution, D_r, has been chosen (normal distribution, Chi-square, etc.).

Hypotheses

Null hypothesis, H_0: $D_e = D_r$,
alternative hypothesis, H_1: $D_e \neq D_r$,

Statistic

The statistic calculated is

$$\chi = \sum_{i=1}^{k} \frac{(O_i - T_i)^2}{T_i}$$

where, for each of the k classes, O_i is the number of observations made on the sample and T_i is the theoretical number of observations calculated according to the reference distribution D_r.

The statistic χ follows a chi-square distribution with $k - 1 - r$ degrees of freedom, where r is the number of parameters of the reference distribution that have been estimated with the aid of observations.

Interpreting the test   The decision rule is the following: H_0 will be rejected if

$$\chi > \chi^2_{\alpha; k-1-r}$$

1.2 Comparing the distribution of a variable X in two populations (Kolmogorov-Smirnov test)

Research question   Is the variable X distributed identically in two populations, A and B?

The Kolmogorov-Smirnov test may also be used to compare an observed distribution to a theoretical one.

Application conditions

- The two samples are random and contain n_A and n_B independent observations, taken from populations A and B respectively.
- The variable X is an interval or a ratio variable of any distribution.
- The classes are defined in the same way in both samples.

Hypotheses

Null hypothesis, H_0: The distribution of variable X is identical in A and B,
alternative hypothesis, H_1: The distribution of variable X is different in A and B.

Statistic

The statistic calculated is:

$$d = Maximum \left| F_A(X) - F_B(X) \right|$$

where $FA(x)$ and $FB(x)$ represent the cumulated frequencies of the classes in A and in B. These values are compared to the critical values d_0 of the Kolmogorov-Smirnov table.

Interpreting the test   The decision rule is the following:
H_0 will be rejected if $d > d_0$.

1.3 Comparing the distribution of a variable X in two populations: Mann-Whitney U test

Research question   Is the distribution of the variable X identical in the two populations A and B?

Application conditions

- The two samples are random and contain n_A and n_B independent observations from populations A and B respectively (where $n_A > n_B$). If required, the notation of the samples may be inverted.
- The variable X is ordinal.

Hypotheses

Null hypothesis, H_0: The distribution of the variable X is identical in A and B, alternative hypothesis, H_1: The distribution of the variable X is different in A and B.

Statistic

$(A_1, A_2, ..., A_{nA})$ is a sample, of size n_A, selected from population A, and $(B_1, B_2, ..., B_{nB})$ is a sample of size n_B selected from population B. $N = n_A + n_B$ observations are obtained, which are classed in ascending order regardless of the samples they are taken from. Each observation is then given a rank: 1 for the smallest value, up to N for the greatest.
   The statistic calculated is:

$$U = Minimum\left(n_A\, n_B + \frac{n_A\,(n_A + 1)}{2} - R_A;\ n_A\, n_B + \frac{n_B\,(n_B + 1)}{2} - R_B \right)$$

where R_A is the sum of the ranks of the elements in A, and R_B the sum of the ranks of the elements in B. The statistic U is compared to the critical values U_α of the Mann-Whitney table.

Interpreting the test   The decision rule is the following:
H_0 will be rejected if $U < U_\alpha$.
   For large values of n_A and n_B (that is, > 12),

$$U' = \frac{U - \dfrac{n_A\, n_B}{2}}{\sqrt{\dfrac{n_A\, n_B\,(n_A + n_B + 1)}{12}}}$$

tends rapidly toward a standard normal distribution. U' may then be used, in association with the decision rules of the standard normal distribution for rejecting or not rejecting the null hypothesis.

1.4 Comparing the distribution of a variable X in two populations: Wilcoxon test

Research question   Is the distribution of the variable X identical in the two populations A and B?

Application conditions

- The two samples are random and contain n_A and n_B independent observations from populations A and B respectively.
- The variable X is at least ordinal.

Hypotheses

Null hypothesis, H_0: The distribution of variable X is identical in A and B, alternative hypothesis, H_1: The distribution of variable X is different in A and B.

Statistic

$(A_1, A_2, ..., A_{nA})$ is a sample, of size n_A, selected from population A, and $(B_1, B_2, ..., B_{nB})$ is a sample of size n_B selected from population B. $N = n_A + n_B$ observations are obtained, which are classed in ascending order regardless of the samples they are taken from. Each observation is then given a rank: 1 for the smallest value, up to N for the greatest.

The statistic calculated is:

$$T = \frac{R - n_A(N+1)/2}{\sqrt{n_A\, n_B\,(N+1)/12}}$$

where $R(A_i)$ is the rank of observation A_i, $i = 1, 2, ..., n_A$ and

$$R = \sum_{i=1}^{n_A} R(A_i)$$

the sum of all the ranks of the observations from sample A.

The statistic T is compared to critical values R_α available in a table.

Interpreting the test   The decision rule is the following:
H_0 will be rejected if $R < R_\alpha$.

If N is sufficiently large (that is, $n \geq 12$), the distribution of T approximates a standard normal distribution, and the corresponding decision rules apply, as described above. When a normal distribution is approximated, a mean rank can be associated with any equally placed observations, and the formula becomes:

$$T = \frac{R - n_A(N+1)/2}{\sqrt{\dfrac{n_A\, n_B}{12}\left(N + 1 - \dfrac{\sum_{i=1}^{g} t_i\,(t_i^2 - 1)}{N(N-1)}\right)}}$$

where g is the number of groups of equally-placed ranks and t_i is the size of group i.

1.5 Comparing variable distribution in two populations: testing homogenous series

Research question   Is the distribution of the variable X identical in the two populations A and B?

Application conditions

- The two samples are random and contain n_A and n_B independent observations from the populations A and B respectively.
- The variable X is at least ordinal.

Hypotheses

Null hypothesis, H_0: The distribution of the variable X is identical in A and B, alternative hypothesis, H_1: The distribution of the variable X is different in A and B.

Statistic

$(A_1, A_2, \ldots, A_{nA})$ is a sample, of size n_A, selected from population A, and $(B_1, B_2, \ldots, B_{nB})$ is a sample of size n_B selected from population B. $N = n_A + n_B$ observations are obtained, which are classed in ascending order regardless of the samples they are taken from. Each observation is then given a rank: 1 for the smallest value, up to N for the greatest.
   The statistic calculated is:
$R =$ the longest 'homogenous series' (that is, series of consecutive values belonging to one sample) found in the general series ranking the $n_A + n_B$ observations.
   The statistic R is compared to critical values C_α available in a table.

Interpreting the test   The decision rule is the following:
H_0 will be rejected if $R < C_\alpha$.
   For large values of n_A and n_B (that is, > 20),

$$R' = \frac{\dfrac{2n_A\, n_B}{n_A + n_B} - 0.5}{\sqrt{\dfrac{2n_A\, n_B\, (2n_A\, n_B - n_A - n_B)}{(n_A + n_B)^2\, (n_A + n_B - 1)}}}$$

tends towards the standard normal distribution. R' may then be used instead, in association with the decision rules of the standard normal distribution for rejecting or not rejecting the null hypothesis.

1.6 Comparing the distribution of a variable X in k populations: Kruskal-Wallis test or analysis of variance by ranking

Research question   Is the distribution of the variable X identical in the k populations $A_1, A_2, \ldots, A_k$?

Application conditions

- The two samples are random and contain $n_1, n_2, \ldots n_k$ independent observations from the populations $A_1, A_2, \ldots A_k$.
- The variable X is at least ordinal.

Hypotheses

Null hypothesis, H_0: The distribution of the variable X is identical in all k populations,
alternative hypothesis, H_1: The distribution of the variable X is different in at least one of the k populations.

Statistic

$(A_{11}, A_{12}, \ldots, A_{1n1})$ is a sample of size n_1 selected from population A_1 and $(A_{21}, A_{22}, \ldots, A_{2n2})$ is a sample of size n_2 selected from population A_2.

$$N = \sum_{i=1}^{k} n_i$$

observations are obtained, which are classed in ascending order regardless of the samples they are taken from. Each observation is then given a rank: 1 for the smallest value, up to N for the greatest. For equal observations, a mean rank is attributed. R_i is the sum of the ranks attributed to observations of sample A_i.

The statistic calculated is:

$$H = \left(\frac{12}{N(N+1)} \sum_{i=1}^{k} \frac{R_i^2}{n_i} \right) - 3(N+1).$$

If a number of equal values are found, a corrected value is used:

$$H' = \frac{H}{\dfrac{\sum_{i=1}^{g}(t_i^3 - t_i)}{N^3 - N}}$$

where g is the number of groups of equal values, and t_i the size of group i.

Interpreting the test   The decision rule is the following:
H_0 will be rejected if H (or, the case being, H') $> \chi^2_{1-\alpha;\, k-1}$ or a corresponding value in the Kruskal-Wallis table.

If the Kruskal-Wallis test leads to the rejection of the null hypothesis, it is possible to identify which pairs of populations tend to be different. This requires the application of either the Wilcoxon signed test or the sign test if the samples are matched (that is, logically linked, such that the pairs or n-uplets of observations in the different samples contain identical or similar individuals), or a Mann-Whitney U or Wilcoxon test if the samples are not matched. This is basically the same logic as used when associating the analysis of variance and the LSD test. The Mann-Whitney U is sometimes called analysis of variance by rank.

1.7 Comparing two proportions or percentages (small samples)

Research question   Do the two proportions or percentages p_1 and p_2, observed in two samples, differ significantly from each other?

Application conditions

- The two samples are random and contain n_1 and n_2 independent observations respectively.
- The size of the samples is small ($n_1 < 30$ and $n_2 < 30$).
- The two proportions p_1 and p_2 as well as their complements $1-p_1$ and $1-p_2$ represent at least 5 observations.

Hypotheses

Null hypothesis, H_0: $\pi_1 = \pi_2$,
alternative hypothesis, H_1: $\pi_1 \neq \pi_2$.

Statistic

The statistic calculated is

$$\chi = \frac{(x_1 - n_1 p)^2}{n_1 p \, (1-p)} + \frac{(x_2 - n_2 p)^2}{n_2 p \, (1-p)}$$

where x_1 is the number of observations in sample 1 (size n_1) corresponding to the proportion p_1, x_2 is the number of observations in sample 2 (size n_2) corresponding to the proportion p_2, and

$$p = \frac{x_1 + x_2}{n_1 + n_2}.$$

This statistic χ follows a chi-square distribution with 1 degree of freedom.

Interpreting the test   The decision rule is the following:
H_0 will be rejected if $\chi > \chi^2_{\alpha;\, 1}$

2. Tests on More than One Variable in One or Several Matched Samples

Two or more samples are called matched when they are linked in a logical manner, and the pairs or n-uplets of observations of different samples contain identical or very similar individuals. For instance, samples comprised of the same people observed at different moments in time may comprise as many matched samples as observation points in time. Similarly, a sample of n individuals and another containing their n twins (or sisters, brothers, children, etc.) may be made up of matched samples in the context of a genetic study.

2.1 Comparing any two variables: independence or homogeneity test

Research question Are the two variables X and Y independent?

Application conditions

- The sample is random and contains n independent observations.
- The observed variables X and Y may be of any type (nominal, ordinal, interval, ratio) and are illustrated by k_X and k_Y classes.

Hypotheses

Null hypothesis, H_0: X and Y are independent,
alternative hypothesis, H_1: X and Y are dependent

Statistic

The statistic calculated is

$$\chi = \sum_{ij} n\frac{\left(n_{ij} - \frac{n_i \cdot n_j \cdot}{n}\right)^2}{n_i \cdot n_j \cdot}$$

where n_{ij} designates the number of observations presenting both characteristics X_i and Y_j (i varying from 1 to k_X; j from 1 to k_Y),

$$n_i \cdot = \sum_{j=1}^{k_x} n_{ij}$$

is the number of observations presenting the characteristics X_i and

$$n \cdot_j = \sum_{i=1}^{k_x} n_{ij}$$

is the number of observations presenting the characteristics X_j.
This statistic χ follows a chi-square distribution with $(k_X - 1)(k_Y - 1)$ degrees of freedom.

Interpreting the test The decision rule is the following:
H_0 will be rejected if $\chi > \chi^2_{\alpha;(kx-1)(ky-1)}$

2.2 Comparing two variables X and Y measured from two matched samples A and B: sign test

Research question Are the two variables X and Y, measurable for two matched samples A and B, identically distributed?

Application conditions

- The two samples are random and matched.
- The n pairs of observations are independent.
- The variables X and Y are at least ordinal.

Hypotheses

Null hypothesis, H_0: The distribution of the two variables is identical in the two matched samples,
alternative hypothesis, H_1: The distribution of the two variables is different in the two matched samples.

Statistic

The pairs (a_1, b_1), (a_2, b_2), ... , (a_n, b_n) are n pairs of observations, of which the first element is taken from population A and the second from population B. The difference $a_i - b_i$ is calculated for each of these n pairs of observations (a_i, b_i). The number of positive differences is represented by $k+$, and the number of negative differences by $k-$. The statistic calculated is:

$K = $ Minimum $(k+, k-)$.

The statistic K is compared to critical values C_α available in a table.

Interpreting the Test   The decision rule is the following:
H_0 will be rejected if $K < C_\alpha$.
    For sufficiently large values of n (that is, $n > 40$),

$$K' = \frac{2K - n + 1}{\sqrt{n}}$$

tends towards the standard normal distribution. K' may then be used instead, in association with the decision rules of the standard normal distribution for rejecting or not rejecting the null hypothesis.

2.3 Comparing variables from matched samples: Wilcoxon sign test

Research question   Are the two variables X and Y, measured from two matched samples A and B, identically distributed?

Application conditions

- The two samples are random and matched.
- The n pairs of observations are independent.
- The variables X and Y are at least ordinal.

Hypotheses

Null hypothesis, H_0: The distribution of the two variables is identical in the two matched samples, alternative hypothesis, H_1: The distribution of the two variables is different in the two matched samples.

Statistic

(a_1, b_1), (a_2, b_2), ... , (a_n, b_n) are n pairs of observations, of which the first element is taken from the population A and the second from the population B. For each pair of observations, the difference $d_i = a_i - b_i$ is calculated. In this way n differences d_i are obtained, and these are sorted in ascending order. They are ranked from 1, for the smallest value, to n, for the greatest. For equal-value rankings, a mean rank is attributed. Let $R+$ be the sum of the positive differences and $R-$ the sum of the negative ones.

The statistic calculated is:

$R = \text{Minimum } (R+, R-)$

The statistic R is compared to critical values R_α available in a table.

Interpreting the test   The decision rule is the following:
H_0 will be rejected if $R < R_\alpha$.
For large values of n (that is, $n > 20$),

$$R' = \frac{R - \dfrac{n(n+1)}{4}}{\sqrt{\dfrac{1}{24} n (n+1)(2n+1)}}$$

tends towards a standard normal distribution. R' may then be used in association with the decision rules of the standard normal distribution for rejecting or not rejecting the null hypothesis.

2.4 Comparing variables from matched samples: Kendall rank correlation test

Research question   Are the two variables, X and Y, measured for two matched samples A and B, independent?

Application conditions

- The two samples are random and matched.
- The n pairs of observations are independent.
- The variables X and Y are at least ordinal.

Hypotheses

Null hypothesis, H_0: X and Y are independent,
alternative hypothesis, H_1: X and Y are dependent.

Statistic

The two variables (X, Y) observed in a sample of size n give n pairs of observations (X_1, Y_1), (X_2, Y_2), ... , (X_n, Y_n). An indication of the correlation between variables X and Y can be obtained by sorting the values of X_i in ascending order and counting the number of corresponding Y_i values that do not respect this order. Sorting the values in ascending order guarantees that $X_i < Xj$ for any value of $i < j$.

Let R be the number of pairs (X_i, Y_j) such that, if $i < j$, $X_i < X_j$ and $Y_i < Y_j$. The statistic calculated is:

$$S = 2R - \frac{n(n-1)}{2}.$$

The statistic S is then compared to critical values S_α available in a table.

Interpreting the test   The decision rule is the following:
H_0 will be rejected if $S > S_\alpha$. In case of rejection of H_0, the sign of S indicates the direction of the dependency.

For large values of n (that is, $n > 15$),

$$S' = \frac{S+1}{\sqrt{n(n+1)(2n+5)/18}}$$

tends towards a standard normal distribution. S' may then be used instead, in association with the decision rules of the standard normal distribution for rejecting or not rejecting the null hypothesis.

2.5 Comparing two variables X and Y measured from two matched samples A and B: Spearman rank correlation test

Research question   Are the two variables X and Y, measured for two matched samples A and B, independent?

Application conditions

- The two samples are random and of the same size, n.
- The observations in each of the samples are independent.
- The variables X and Y are at least ordinal.

Hypotheses

Null hypothesis, H_0: X and Y are independent,
alternative hypothesis, H_1: X and Y are dependent.

Statistic

The two variables (X, Y) observed in a sample of size n give n pairs of observations $(X_1, Y_1), (X_2, Y_2) \dots (X_n, Y_n)$. The values of X_i and Y_j can be classed separately in ascending order. Each of the values X_i and Y_j is then attributed a rank between 1 and n. Let $R(X_i)$ be the rank of the value X_i, $R(Y_i)$ the rank of the value Y_i and $d_i = R(X_i) - R(Y_i)$.

The Spearman rank correlation coefficient is:

$$R = 1 - \frac{6\sum\limits_{i=1}^{n} d_i^2}{(n^3 - n)}$$

Interpreting the test   The Spearman rank correlation coefficient R can be evaluated in the same way as a classical correlation coefficient (see Sections 4.1 through 4.3 in main Section 2).

2.6 Comparing classifications

Research question   Are k classifications of n elements identical?

This type of test can be useful, for instance, when comparing classifications made by k different experts, or according to k different criteria or procedures.

Application conditions

- A set of n elements $E_1, E_2, ..., E_n$ has been classified by k different procedures

Hypotheses

Null hypothesis, H_0: the k classifications are identical,
alternative hypothesis, H_1: At least one of the k classifications is different from the others

Statistic   The statistic calculated is:

$$S = \sum_{i=1}^{n} \left(\sum_{i=1}^{k} r_{ij} - \frac{k(n+1)}{2} \right)^2$$

where r_{ij} is the rank attributed to the element E_i by the procedure j (expert opinion, criteria, method ...).

The statistic X is compared to critical values X_α available in a table.

Interpreting the test   The decision rule is the following:
H_0 will be rejected if $S > X_\alpha$.

CONCLUSION

Statistical tests are very useful to researchers who hope to prove a certain number of research hypotheses, or who wish to generalize from results observed from a sample of a population. This chapter has tried to clarify the logical context of this type of test, and to provide a practical guide to their application.

Fortunately, statistical analysis software can do a lot of the heavy calculus work for researchers; the remaining key difficulty is to define which test is appropriate to the research question. For this reason, two sections of this chapter have been dedicated to the operationalization of statistical tests (parametric and non-parametric), organized according to typical research questions.

For each test, the conditions of its use, the statistical form of the hypotheses and the decision rules for rejecting or not rejecting the null hypothesis have been described in detail. Statistical calculations relevant to these tests are also outlined. However, the reader may choose not to pay close attention to these calculations, as what is most important is to know how to define which test is appropriate and how to interpret the results.

A practical way for researchers to use this chapter would therefore be to:

1 Identify their research question in the Table of Contents.
2 Choose the corresponding test.
3 Use one of the principal statistical analysis computer programs.
4 Read the p value provided by the software.

If this p value is lower than the chosen significance level, the null hypothesis should be rejected. If not, it cannot be rejected.

The list of comparison tests described in this chapter is not exhaustive but, at the least, I hope it has provided a useful presentation of the general logic of this type of tests and a practical guide to the tests that are most relevant to management research.

FURTHER READING

Kanji, G.K., *100 Structural Tests*, Thousand Oaks, CA: Sage, 1993.
Sincich, T., *Business Statistics by Example*, 5th Edn, Upper Saddle River, NJ: Prentice-Hall, 1996.

12

CAUSAL ANALYSIS AND MODELING

Ababacar Mbengue and Isabelle Vandangeon-Derumez

Outline

This chapter explains how to construct and test a causal model – a model representing a network of causal relationships between variables. Causal modeling is presented in four stages:

1 Identifying the phenomenon to be modeled.
2 Identifying the model's concepts and variables.
3 Identifying the relationships among the model's concepts and variables.
4 Testing the model's validity.

Although we present these stages in a linear and sequential fashion, the modeling procedure is in reality complex, and researchers often find they have to regularly loop back through the four phases. The chapter shows how, at each of these four stages, the researcher can adopt either an inductive or a deductive approach, and apply either qualitative or quantitative methods.

Management research generally aims to describe, understand, explain or predict phenomena related to organizations. But whatever the ultimate aim may be, researchers often need to examine the cause, or causes, of the phenomena they study. At the same time, the world of organizations is a complex one, and in most cases it is impossible for researchers to paint a fully detailed picture of these phenomena. They must, therefore, find a simplified way of representing them. Modeling is one solution.

Modeling has other uses than its capacity for enabling simplified representation. In everyday management practice it is widely used as a decision-making tool. In management research, modeling is just as useful in describing or understanding phenomena or systems as it is for explaining or predicting them.

An analysis is considered to be causal when it studies cause and what constitutes it or what it implies. Such analyses aim to establish causal relationships between variables (at the empirical level) or concepts (at the theoretical level), with causality being defined as the relationship between a cause and the effect it produces. As a rule, a variable is considered to be a cause when it brings about or has an impact on a result: causes refer to the factors that induce phenomena to occur or to change (Zaltman et al., 1973).

It is important to draw a clear distinction between causality and association. Showing that two variables are linked is not enough to establish the existence of a causal relationship: we must also clearly determine the mechanism by which a variable (the cause) affects another variable (that on which the effect is measured). The theories and hypotheses a researcher puts forward can be very useful in identifying this mechanism. But while association does not establish causality, it is a necessary condition for causality. In other words, it is impossible to conclude that a causal relationship exists between two variables if one cannot first demonstrate an association, or a correlation, between them.

A proposition linking two variables, X and Y through a causal relationship theoretically assumes that an environment exists within which any variation in the single variable X will produce a change in Y (Zaltman et al., 1973). To demonstrate causality between two variables, we must first control the effects of each variable in the environment in question. But it is extremely difficult, if not impossible, to control all of the variables in a given environment – and so testing and demonstrating causality empirically does not enable a researcher to conclude with absolute certainty that the initial causal proposition is true.

Modeling can be defined as the activity of constructing a model. As a model is a simplified, or abstract, representation of a given phenomenon or system, modeling is then a process of constructing an abstraction – an entity comprised solely of its definition – in order to study a real phenomenon. There are as many models of a phenomenon as there are objectives underlying its simplification or abstract representation.

Various types of models are possible, including descriptive, explanatory, predictive or prescriptive, simulation or dynamic. A general distinction can be made between explanatory and non-explanatory models. Explanatory models are used to investigate causal relationships between the model's elements, and therefore incorporate causal analysis. When a model is non-explanatory, the model-maker views the system as a black hole and does not even glance inside. Explanatory models are then the only type of models to which causal analysis is really appropriate. This is why, in this chapter, we have decided to deal exclusively with this type of model.

SECTION 1   SPECIFYING THE PHENOMENON OR SYSTEM TO BE MODELED

Models can be defined as abstract representations of real phenomena. They represent the components of the phenomena studied as much as they do the interrelationships among these components. Identifying the phenomenon or system to be modeled is a three-step process. The first step is to determine its components. The interrelationships between these components must then be specified. Finally, because these models are representations, the researcher will want to formalize them through a graphic or mathematical description of the components and their presumed interrelations. Most often, a model will be represented by circles, rectangles or squares linked by arrows, curves, lines, etc.

1. Components of a Model

A model, in its most simple form (a relationship of cause and effect between two variables), essentially comprises two types of variables with different functions: independent variables (also called explanatory or exogenous variables) and dependent variables (also called variables to be explained, or endogenous variables). In this causal relationship, the independent variable represents the cause and its effect is measured on the dependent variable.

Quite often, the phenomenon being studied includes more elements than simply an independent variable and a dependent variable. A single dependent variable is liable to have multiple causes. Several independent variables may explain one dependent variable. These variables are considered as causes in the same way as the initial causal variable, and produce an additive effect. They are an addition to the model and explain the dependent variable.

The introduction of new variables within a simple causal relationship between two independent and dependent variables may also produce an interactive effect. In this case, the dependent variable is influenced by two causal variables whose effect can only be seen if these two associated variables intervene at the same time.

Figure 12.1 schematizes the additive and interactive effects linked to the introduction of a third variable, Z, into a simple causal relationship between two variables, X and Y.

Finally, variables can intervene in the direct causal relationship between the dependent variable or variables and the independent variable. These variables, described as intervenors, take two forms: mediator or moderator.

When the effect of the independent variable X on the dependent variable Y is measured by the intermediary of a third variable Z, we call this third variable a mediator. The association or causality observed between X and Y results from the fact that X influences Z, which in turn influences Y (Baron and Kenny, 1986).

A moderator variable modifies the intensity (increasing or decreasing) and/or the sign of the relationship between independent and dependent variables (Sharma et al., 1981). The moderator variable enables researchers to identify when certain effects are produced and then to break down a population into subpopulations, according to whether the measured effect is present or not. Figure 12.2 schematizes the mediator and moderator effects relative to the introduction of a third variable in the relationship between independent and dependent variables.

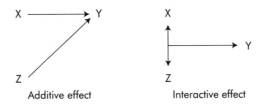

Figure 12.1 *Additive and interactive effects linked to the introduction of a third variable in a causal relationship between two variables*

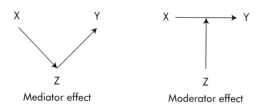

Figure 12.2   *Mediator and moderator effects linked to the introduction of a third variable in a causal relationship between two variables*

To move from a phenomenon to a model, it is not enough just to identify the different variables involved. One must also determine the status of these variables: dependent, independent (with an additive or interactive effect), moderator or mediator.

2. Relationships

Three types of relationship are possible between two of a phenomenon's variables (Davis, 1985). The first two are causal, while the third involves simple association:

- The first possibility is a simple causal relationship between the two variables: $X => Y$ (X influences Y, but Y does not influence X).

Example: A simple causal relationship

Introducing the theory of the ecology of populations to explain organizational inertia and organizational change, Hannan and Freeman (1984) postulate that selection mechanisms favor companies whose structures are inert. They present organizational inertia as the result of natural selection mechanisms. The variable 'natural selection' therefore acts on the variable 'organizational inertia'.

- The second relationship involves a reciprocal influence between two variables: $X => Y => X$ (X influences Y, which in turn influences X).

Example: A reciprocal causal relationship

Many authors refer to the level of an organization's performance as a factor that provokes change. They consider that weak performance tends to push organizations into engaging in strategic change. However, others point out that it is important to take the reciprocal effect into account. According to Romanelli and Tushman (1986), organizations improve their performance because they know how to make timely changes in their action plan. There is, therefore, a reciprocal influence between performance and change, which can be translated as follows: weak performance pushes companies to change and such change enables performance to be improved.

- The third relationship demonstrates that an association exists between the two variables. However, it is not possible to determine which causes the other: $X <=> Y$ (X relates to Y and Y to X).

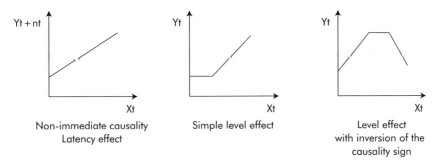

Figure 12.3 *Representation of latency and level effects in a relationship between two variables*

Once the nature of the relationship has been determined, it is important to establish its sign. This is either:

- positive, with X and Y varying in the same direction
- or negative, with X and Y varying in opposite directions.

In a causal relationship, the sign translates as follows. It is positive when an increase (or reduction) in X leads to an increase (or decrease) in Y and it is negative when an increase (or decrease) in X leads to a decrease (or increase) in Y. In the case of an association between two variables, X and Y, the sign of the relationship is positive when X and Y are high or low at the same time and negative when X is high and Y is low and vice versa.

In a relationship between two variables, causality is not always immediate. Indeed, there can be a latent effect – a period during which the effect of a variable is awaited. This effect is particularly significant when researchers use correlation to test relationships between two temporal sets. They need to determine what period of time elapses between the cause and effect, and to separate the two series accordingly to conduct this test. It is possible that the relationship or causality will only be effective below a certain level. As long as the value of X remains below this level, X has no influence on Y (or there is no relationship between X and Y). When the value of X goes beyond this level, then X has an influence on Y (or there is a relationship between the two variables X and Y). An effect related to level may also influence the relationship's sign. For example, below a certain level, the relationship is positive. Once this level has been attained, the sign is inverted and becomes negative. Figure 12.3 schematizes these different effects.

Whatever the nature or sign of the relationship, causality can only be specified in two ways: deductively, starting from theory, or inductively, by observation. Researchers must begin with the hypothesis of a causal relationship between two variables, either based on theory or because observation is tending to reveal it. Only then should they evaluate and test the relationship, either quantitatively or qualitatively.

3. Formal Representation

Models are usually represented in the form of diagrams. This formalization responds, above all, to the need to communicate information. A drawing can be much clearer and easier to understand than a lengthy verbal or written description, not least when the model is complex (that is, contains several variables and interrelations).

Over the years, a diagrammatic convention has developed from 'path analysis' or 'path modeling', (see Section 3). According to this convention, concepts or variables that cannot be directly observed (also called latent variables, concepts or constructs) are represented by circles or ellipses. Variables that can be directly observed (manifest and observed variables, and measurement variables or indicators) are represented by squares or rectangles. Causal relationships are indicated by tipped arrows, with the arrowhead indicating the direction of causality. Reciprocal causality between two variables or concepts is indicated by two arrows going in opposite directions. Simple associations (correlations or covariance) between variables or concepts are indicated by curves without arrowheads, or two arrowheads going in opposite directions at the two ends of the same curve. A curve that turns back on one variable or concept indicates variance (covariance of an element with itself). Arrows without origin indicate errors or residues.

Figure 12.4 is an example of a formal representation of a model examining the relationship between strategy and performance. In this example, 'product lines' or 'profit margin' are directly observable variables, and 'scale' or 'profitability' are concepts (that is, variables that are not directly observable). The hypothesis is that three causal relationships exist between the concepts of 'segments', 'resources' and 'scale', on the one hand, and that of 'profitability' on the other. There is also assumed to be an association relationship between the three concepts 'segments', 'resources' and 'scale'. Finally, all the directly observable variables contain terms of error as well as the concept of 'profitability'.

There is scope for the notion of a model to be very widely accepted in quantitative research. Many statistical methods aim to measure causal relationships between variables by using a model to indicate the relationship system. This is often expressed by equations predicting the dependent or explained variables that are to be explained by other variables (known as independent or explanatory variables). An example is linear regression or analysis of variance.

These explanatory methods are particular examples of more general techniques through which causal relationship networks can be examined (Hoyle, 1995). These techniques are known by various names; such as 'path analysis' or 'path modeling', which we have already mentioned, 'causal model analysis' or 'causal modeling', 'structural equations analysis' or 'structural equation modeling' and 'latent variable analysis of structural equations'. Some of them even just carry the name of a computer program, such as LISREL, PLS or AMOS. In this chapter, we have decided to use the term 'causal model' to indicate these techniques for examining causal relationship networks.

Causal models do not necessarily have to be represented graphically. They can also be represented mathematically. As a rule, causal models are expressed

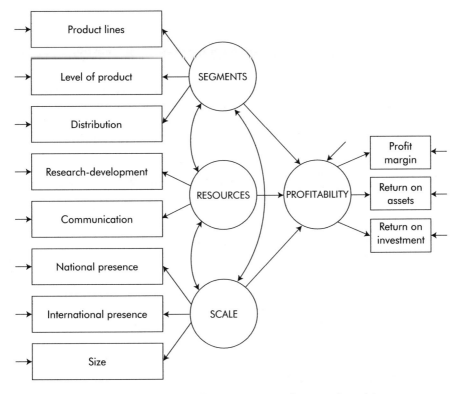

Figure 12.4   *Formal representation of a causal model*

in the form of equations. These are often matrix equations, in which case the general notation takes the following form:

$$Y = \Lambda_Y \eta + \varepsilon,$$
$$X = \Lambda_X \xi + \delta,$$
$$\eta = \Gamma \xi + \beta \eta + \zeta,$$

Y = vector of the observed endogenous (that is, dependent) variables

X = vector of the observed exogenous (that is, independent) variables

η = vector of the latent endogenous variables

ξ = vector of the latent exogenous variables

Λ_Y = matrix of coefficients linking the latent endogenous variables to the observed endogenous variables

Λ_X = matrix of coefficients linking the latent exogenous variables to the observed exogenous variables

ε = vector of residues for the observed endogenous variables

δ = vector of residues for the observed exogenous variables

ζ = vector of residues for the latent endogenous variables

Γ = the matrix of causal relationships between the latent
    exogenous and the endogenous variables
β = the matrix of causal relationships between the latent
    endogenous variables.

Causal models are interesting not only because they produced the convention for formally representing phenomena or modeling systems. They are also the most successful technique for modeling causal relationships quantitatively, illustrating the quantitative process that takes place at each stage.

SECTION 2   SPECIFYING VARIABLES AND CONCEPTS

Specifying a model's different concepts and variables is, above all, dependent on the researcher's chosen approach, which can be inductive or deductive, qualitative or quantitative. There are two levels of specification. One is conceptual, and enables researchers to determine the nature of concepts. The other is operational, and enables researchers to move from concepts to the variables that result from field observation. An inductive approach specifies conceptual and operational levels simultaneously, whereas a deductive approach moves from the conceptual level to the operational level. But even with a deductive approach, the researcher may need to return to both of these two levels at a later stage.

1. Qualitative Method

A particular characteristic of qualitative methods is that they do not necessitate numerical evaluation of the model's variables. Specification therefore involves describing the model's concepts without quantifying them. We can, however, evaluate concepts according to a number of dimensions, representing the various 'forms' they can take. There is no reason why researchers should not use quantitative data to specify certain of their model's concepts.

1.1 Qualitative inductive method

When researchers decide to employ a qualitative/inductive method, field data is used to draw out the concepts that represent the phenomenon being studied. Glaser and Strauss (1967) propose an inductive method of coding, which they call 'open coding'. This method enables 'the process of breaking down, examining, comparing, conceptualizing, and categorizing data' (Strauss and Corbin, 1990: 61) to occur. It has four interactive phases:

Phase 1: Labeling phenomena   This phase involves taking an observation – spoken or written – and giving a name to each incident, idea, or event it contains. To facilitate this first 'conceptualization' (passage from data to concept) researchers can ask themselves the following questions: what is it? and what does that represent?

Phase 2: Discovering categories   This phase involves grouping together the concepts resulting from the first phase, to reduce their number. For this categorization, researchers can group together those concepts that are most closely related to each other. Alternatively, they can group together their observations, while keeping the concepts in mind.

Phase 3: Naming a category   Researchers can invent this name themselves or borrow it from the literature. It can also be based on words or phrases used by interviewees.

Phase 4: Developing categories in terms of their properties and dimensions   Now the researcher defines the 'properties' and 'dimensions' of each of the categories created during the previous phases. Properties are a category's characteristics or attributes, while dimensions represent the localization of each property on a continuum. Dimensions translate the different forms the property can take (a phenomenon's intensity, for example). They enable researchers to construct different profiles of a phenomenon, and to represent its specific properties under different conditions.

Miles and Huberman (1984a) propose a process which, while remaining inductive, is based on a conceptual framework and gives researchers a focus for collecting data in the field. They suggest a number of tactics for drawing out these concepts, which we will explain briefly. The aim of the first tactic is to calculate, or isolate items that recur during interviews or observations. This tactic aims at isolating the model's concepts (which the authors also call themes). The second tactic involves grouping the elements in one or several dimensions together to create categories. This can be done by association (grouping together similar elements) or dissociation (separating dissimilar elements). The third tactic is to subdivide the categories created earlier; to explore whether a designated category might actually correspond to two or more categories. Researchers need to be cautious about wanting to subdivide each category, and so guard against excessive atomization. The fourth tactic is to relate the particular to the general – to ask: of what is this element an example? and does it belong to a larger class?

The fifth and final tactic involves factorizing. The term 'factor' stems from factor analysis, a statistical tool used to reduce a large number of observed variables to a small number of concepts that are not directly observed. Factorization occurs in several stages. First, researchers take an inventory of items arising during their interviews or observations. They then group the items according to a logical rule they have defined in advance. The rule could be that items arising concomitantly during the interviews should be grouped together. Alternatively, one could group together items translating a particular event. At the end of this phase, researchers have several lists of items at their disposal. They then describe the various items so as to produce a smaller list of code names. They group these code names together under a common factor, which they then describe.

The two methods explained above enable researchers to draw out the model's variables, and then its concepts, from observations in the field: to specify the model's components. These methods are inductive, but can still be used in a theoretical framework. In both cases, researchers are advised to loop back continually between fieldwork data and relevant literature during the coding process. In this way, they should be able to specify and formalize the variables (or concepts) they have defined.

1.2 The qualitative deductive method

With this method researchers draw up a list of the concepts that make up the phenomenon being studied, using information gleaned from the results of earlier research. They then operationalize these concepts using data from the empirical study so as to obtain variables. However, researchers adopting this method are advised to enrich and remodel the concepts obtained from the literature using data gathered in the field (Miles and Huberman, 1984a). To do this, they can turn to techniques for specifying variables that are appropriate for use in inductive research.

> **Example: Specifying a model's variables using a qualitative deductive method**
>
> The principle of this method is to start with a list of codes or concepts stemming from a conceptual framework, research questions or initial hypotheses (or research propositions). These concepts are then operationalized into directly observed variables. In their study on teaching reforms, Miles and Huberman (1984a) initially conceptualized the process of innovation 'as a reciprocal transformation of the innovation itself, of those making use of it, and the host classroom or school' (Miles and Huberman, 1984a: 98). They drew up a list of seven general codes (or concepts): property of innovation (PI), external context (EC), internal context (IC), adoption process (AP), site dynamic and transformation (SDT), and new configurations and final results (NCR). This list breaks down into subcodes (or variables), which can be directly observed in the field (operationalization of concepts). For example the code internal context breaks down into: characteristics of the internal context (CI-CAR), norms and authority (CI-NORM) and history of the innovation (CI-HIST), etc.

2. The Quantitative Method

Quantitative causal modeling techniques place the identifying variables and concepts center-stage. They have systematized the theoretical distinction between variables and concepts.

Usually, causal models contain variables that are not directly observable (known as latent variables, concepts or constructs) and directly observable variables (known as manifest or observed variables, indicators, or variables of measurement). The notion of a latent variable is central in human and social sciences. Concepts such as intelligence, attitude or personality are latent variables. Manifest variables are approximate measurements of latent variables. A score in an IQ test can be considered as a manifest variable that is an approximation of the latent variable 'intelligence'. In causal modeling, it is recommended that each latent variable should be measured by several manifest variables. The latent variable is defined by what happens within the community of diverse manifest variables that are supposed to measure it (Hoyle, 1995). From this point of view, latent variables correspond to the common factors we recognize in factor analysis. They can, as a result, be considered as devoid of measurement errors.

2.1 The quantitative deductive method

In specifying concepts, there are several possibilities. The model's concepts may already be precisely defined. In strategy, for example, the concept of a strategic group univocally indicates a group of firms in a given sector that have the same strategy. Researchers using such a concept in their model will not be spending time redefining it. Johansson and Yip (1994) provide other examples of identifying the concepts of industry structure, global strategy, organization structure, etc. Already defined methods of operationalizing concepts may even be available. This is true in the case of the aforementioned strategic groups. Strategic groups can be operationalized through a cluster analysis of companies, characterized by variables that measure strategic positioning choices and resource allocation. If a method of operationalizing concepts is already available, the researcher's main preoccupation will be to verify its validity.

That said, even when the concepts are defined and the operationalization method has been determined, researchers are still advised systematically to try and enrich and remodel the variables/concepts stemming from earlier works by means of observation or theory.

Researchers need to clearly define their concepts and clearly formulate their method of operationalization. They can opt for either an inductive, qualitative or quantitative method to specify the concepts.

2.2 Quantitative inductive method

While quantitative methods are more readily associated with deductive research, they can very well be called into use for inductive research. It is altogether possible, when specifying a model's variables and concepts, to use statistical methods to draw out these concepts from the available data. This practice is very common in what is known as 'French' data analysis, which was popularized by Jean-Paul Benzécri's team (see Benzécri, 1980; Lebart et al., 1984). In general, it involves using a table of empirical data to extract structures, classes and regularities.

Data analysis methods such as correspondence analysis, factor analysis or cluster analysis (classification analysis) are fruitful and very simple methods for drawing out concepts from empirical data. For example, several strategic management researchers have been able to use factor analysis to identify 'generic strategies' that can be classed as factors stemming from data. The work of Dess and Davis (1984) illustrates this process. Equally, many other researchers have turned to cluster analysis to identify 'strategic groups' – classes stemming from classification analyses. Thomas and Venkatraman (1988) present many such research works.

SECTION 3   IDENTIFYING RELATIONSHIPS AMONG A MODEL'S VARIABLES AND CONCEPTS

As with identifying the model's concepts and variables, identifying relationships depends above all on the method the researcher adopts: qualitative or quantitative, inductive or deductive. Its aim is to determine whether there is a relationship between the model's concepts (and variables), the nature of this relationship (causal or simple association) and the relationship's sign (positive or negative).

1. Qualitative Method

Specifying qualitative relationships involves determining the elements that characterize the relationship. It is not a case of evaluating the relationship mathematically or statistically. However, nothing prevents the researcher from using a coding procedure to quantify the data before evaluating the relationship quantitatively.

1.1 Qualitative inductive method

In the case of inductive methods, Glaser and Strauss (1967) propose an 'axial coding' technique comprising a set of procedures by which the data is grouped together to create links between categories (Strauss and Corbin, 1990). The aim of axial coding is to specify a category (which the authors also call a phenomenon) according to the following categories:

- Causal conditions. These conditions, which the authors call 'causal conditions' or antecedent conditions, are identified with the help of the following questions: Why? When? How? Until when? There may be several causal conditions for one phenomenon.
- The context of all the phenomenon's properties: its geographical and temporal position, etc. The researcher identifies the context by posing the following questions: When? For how long? With what intensity? According to which localization?, etc.
- Action/interaction strategies engaged to drive the phenomenon.
- Intervening conditions, represented by the structural context, which facilitate or restrict actions and interactions. These include time, space, culture, economic status, technical status, careers, history, etc.
- Consequences linked to these strategies. These take the form of events, and active responses to initial strategies. They are current or potential and can become causal conditions of other phenomena.

The phenomenon (or category) corresponds to the model's central idea. It is revealed by the following questions: To what does the data refer? What is the aim of the actions and interactions?

1.2 Qualitative deductive method

As when specifying variables or concepts, researchers can use a qualitative/ deductive method to establish relationships between variables using the results of earlier research (available literature). Relationships established in this way can also be supplemented by other relationships stemming from initial observations in the field. So, before testing a model that was constructed *a priori*, researchers are advised to conduct several interviews, or collect information that will enable them to demonstrate other relationships than those stemming from the literature. The next stage involves operationalizing these relationships.

Example: Identifying relationships using a qualitative deductive method

In researching the relationship between sensemaking at a strategic level and organizational performance, Thomas et al. (1993) studied public hospitals in one US state and sought to relate the search for information to how this information is interpreted, the action then taken, and the results. Through an analysis of the literature, Thomas et al. were able to describe the relationships between their model's different elements (see Figure 12.5).

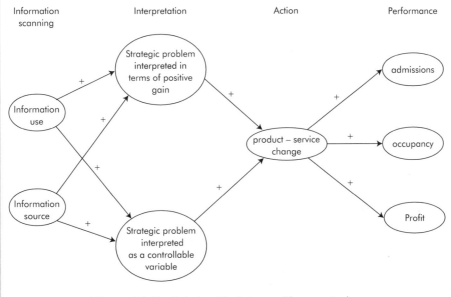

Figure 12.5 *Relationship between Thomas et al. (1993) model's different elements*

Information scanning was operationalized according to two variables: 'information use' and 'information source' (which could be internal or external). The concept of interpretation incorporated the two variables 'positive gain' and 'controllability'. Strategic change was measured at the level of 'product – service change' over the period 1987 to 1989. Performance was measured using three variables: 'occupancy', 'profit per discharge' and 'admissions'.

2. Quantitative Methods

Causal models provide a good example of the quantitative method of specifying causal relationships within a model. While quantitative methods are generally associated with a deductive approach, we will see that they can also be used in inductive research.

2.1 Quantitative deductive method

We can distinguish between two situations researchers may encounter in specifying the relationships between a model's variables/concepts. When consulting the available literature, they may find specific hypotheses that clearly detail the nature and sign of the relationships between the variables/concepts. In this case, their main preoccupation will be to verify the validity of these hypotheses. The problem then essentially becomes one of testing the hypotheses or causal model. This question of testing causal models is dealt with in the fourth and final section of this chapter.

However, very often, researchers do not have a set of hypotheses or propositions prepared in advance about the relationships between the model's concepts and variables. They then have to proceed to a full causal analysis. Although any of the qualitative techniques presented in the first part of this might be used, quantitative methods (that is, causal models) are more profitable.

Causal models can be defined as the union of two conceptually different models:

- A measurement model relating the latent variables to their measurement indicators (that is, manifest or observed variables).
- A model of structural equations translating a group of cause-and-effect relationships between latent variables or observed variables that do not represent latent variables.

Relationships between latent variables and their measurement indicators are called epistemic. There are three types: non-directional, reflective and formative. Non-directional relationships are simple associations. They do not represent a causal relationship but a covariance (or a correlation when variables are standardized). In reflective relationships, measurement indicators (manifest variables) reflect the underlying latent variable (that is, the latent variable is the cause of the manifest variables). In formative relationships, measurement indicators 'form' the latent variable (that is, they are the cause). The latent variable is entirely determined by the linear combination of its indicators. It can be difficult to determine whether a relationship is reflective or formative. For example, intelligence is a latent variable linked by reflective relationships to its measurement indicators, such as IQ. (Intelligence is the cause of the observed IQ.) However, the relationships between the latent variable, socio-economic status and measurement indicators such as the income or level of education are, by nature, formative (income and level of education effect economic status).

In the example in Figure 12.4, the 'measurement model' relates to measurement of the four latent variables 'scope', 'resources', 'scale' and 'profitability'. The epistemic relationships are all reflective. Measurement models are analogous to factor analysis (on the manifest variables). Structural models look at causal relationships between latent variables, and are analogous to a series of linear regressions between latent variables (here, the relationships are between 'scope', 'resources' and 'scale', on the one hand, and 'profitability', on the other). Causal models can be presented as a combination of factor analysis (on the manifest variables) and linear regressions on the factors (latent variables). We can see how causal models are a generalization of factor and regression analyses.

Researchers who choose a quantitative process to specify relationships must systematically distinguish between the different kinds of relationship between their model's variables (association, simple causality and reciprocal causality). In the language of causal models, association relationships are also called non-directional relationships, and represent covariance (or correlations when the variables are standardized). Simple causal relationships are known as uni-directional, while reciprocal causal relationships are known as bi-directional. On a very general level, all relationships can be broken down into two effects: causal and non-causal (association). Causal effects, comprise two different effects: direct and indirect. A direct effect represents a direct causal relationship between an independent variable and a dependent variable. However, in causal models, one particular variable can, at the same time, be dependent on one direct effect and independent of another. This possibility for a variable to be both independent and dependent in one model goes to the heart of the notion of indirect effect.

Indirect effect is the effect of an independent variable on a dependent variable via one or several mediator variables. The sum of the direct and indirect effects constitutes the total effect. On-causal effects (association) also break down into two. First, there are association effects due to a common identified cause (that is, one or several variables within the model constitute the common cause of the two associated variables). Then, there are the non-analyzed association effects (that is, for various reasons, the researcher considers that the variables are associated). Researchers may do this when, for two related variables, they are unable to differentiate between cause and effect, or when they know that the two variables have one or several causes in common outside of the model. In causal models, non-analyzed associations translate as covariance (or correlations) and are represented by curves that may have arrow heads at each end.

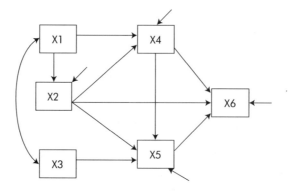

Figure 12.6   *Example of a path analysis model*

A model is said to be recursive if it has no bi-directional causal effect (that is, no causal relationship that is directly or indirectly reciprocal). While the terms can seem misleading, it should be noted that recursive models are unidirectional, and non-recursive models bi-directional. Recursive models occupy an important position in the history of causal models. One of the most well-known members of this family of methods, path analysis, uses only with recursive models. The other major characteristic of path analysis is that it only considers manifest variables. Path analysis is a case in point among causal models (Maruyama, 1998). Figure 12.6 presents an example of a path analysis model.

Identifying causal relationships in the framework of a quantitative approach can be more precise than just specifying the nature of these relationships (association, unidirectional or bi-directional). It is also possible to fix the sign of the relationships and even their intensity. Equality or inequality constraints may be taken into account. For example, the researcher may decide that one particular relationship is equal to a given fixed value (0.50, for instance), that another should be negative, that a third will be equal to a fourth, which will be equal to double a fifth, which will be less than a sixth, etc. Intentionally extreme, this example illustrates the great flexibility researchers have when they quantitatively specify the relationships between variables and concepts in a causal model.

2.2 Quantitative inductive methods

Quantitative methods can be used inductively to expose causal relationships between variables or concepts. By analyzing a simple matrix of correlations between variables, researchers can draw out possible causal relationships (between pairs of variables that are strongly correlated). It is also possible to make exploratory use of 'explanatory' statistical methods (for example, linear regression or analysis of variance) to identify statistically significant 'causal' relationships between different variables. However, explanatory methods are a case in point in terms of causal methods, and we prefer here to discuss the subject more generally.

Joreskog (1993) distinguishes between three causal modeling situations: confirmation, comparison and model generation. In the strictly confirmatory situation, researchers build a model which they then *test* on empirical data. When the test results lead to the model being rejected or retained, no other action is taken. It is very rare for researchers to follow such a procedure. The two other situations are much more common. In the alternative models situation, researchers start off with several alternative models. They evaluate each one using the same set of data and then compare them so as to retain the best ones. This is common when concurrent theories exist and when the area of interest has not yet reached a mature phase or there is uncertainty about the relationships between variables and concepts. In model generation, researchers begin with an already determined model, test it on a set of relevant data and then refine it (in particular, by eliminating the non-significant relationships and adding significant relationships omitted earlier). Aaker and Bagozzi (1979) make the following observation: while, ideally, a single model of structural equations corresponds to a given theory and researchers then calculate that model's parameters, the situation is often different in practice. Most often, researchers begin with an initial version of the model of structural equations which they then test and improve iteratively before gradually obtaining a satisfactory version. According to Aaker and Bagozzi, this phenomenon arises because of the immaturity of the theories involved, the complexity of the management problems and the presence, at every stage of the research process, of uncertainties which translate as measurement errors.

While the strictly confirmatory situation is more in keeping with a deductive process, model generation and alternative models are totally compatible with an inductive approach. But as the existence of a (statistically significant) relationship does not mean there is necessarily a causal effect, researchers must always supplement their exploratory quantitative analyses with theoretical causal analysis.

SECTION 4   EVALUATING AND TESTING THE MODEL

Evaluating and testing a model does not simply mean testing the hypotheses or relationships between the model's concepts or variables one after the other, but also judging its internal global coherence.

1. Qualitative Methods

In some studies, researchers want to test the existence of a causal relationship between two variables without having recourse to sophisticated quantitative methods (such as those presented in the second part of this section). In fact, situations exist in which the qualitative data (resulting from interviews or documents) cannot be transformed into quantitative data or is insufficient for the use of statistical tools. In this case, researchers identify within their data the arguments that either invalidate or corroborate their initial hypothesis about the existence of a relationship between two variables. They then establish a decision-making rule for determining when they should reject or confirm their initial hypothesis. To establish such a rule, one needs to refer back to the exact nature of the researcher's hypotheses (or propositions). Zaltman et al. (1973) identify three types of hypotheses that can be tested empirically: those that are *purely confirmable*, those that are *purely refutable* and those that are *both refutable and confirmable*.

1   Hypotheses are considered to be purely confirmable when contrary arguments, discovered empirically, do not allow the researcher to refute them. For example, the hypothesis that 'there are opinion leaders in companies that change', is purely confirmable. In fact, if researchers discover contrary arguments, such as companies changing without opinion leaders, this does not mean they should refute the possibility of finding such leaders in certain cases.

2   Hypotheses are considered to be purely refutable when they cannot be confirmed. A single negative instance suffices to refute them. Asymmetry therefore exists between verifiability and falsifiability). For example, the hypothesis 'all companies which change call upon opinion leaders' is purely refutable. In fact, finding just one case of a company changing without an opinion leader is sufficient to cast doubt on the initial hypothesis. Universal propositions form part of this group of hypotheses. Indeed, there are an infinite number of possibilities for testing such propositions empirically. It is, therefore, difficult to demonstrate that all possible situations have been thought of and empirically tested.

The testing of such hypotheses is not undertaken directly. One needs to derive sub-hypotheses from the initial hypothesis and then confirm or refute them. These sub-hypotheses specify the conditions under which the initial proposition will be tested. For example, from the hypothesis 'all companies which change call upon opinion leaders' one derives the hypothesis that 'type A companies call upon opinion leaders' and the auxiliary hypothesis that 'type A companies have changed'. It is therefore possible, to identify clearly all the companies belonging to group A and test the derived hypothesis among them. If one company in the group has not called on an opinion leader in order to implement change then the derived hypothesis is refuted and, as a result, so is the initial hypothesis. If all type A companies have called upon opinion leaders when instituting change, the derived hypothesis is then confirmed. But the researcher's cannot conclude that the initial hypothesis is also confirmed.

3   The final group consists of hypotheses that are both confirmable and refutable. As an example, let us consider the hypothesis 'small companies change more often than large ones'. To test such a hypothesis, it suffices to calculate the frequency with which small and large companies change, then compare these frequencies. The presence of a single contrary argument does not systematically invalidate the initial hypothesis. Conversely, as Miles and Huberman (1984a) point out, one cannot use the absence of contrary evidence as a tactic of decisive confirmation.

To move from testing a relationship to testing a model, it is not enough to juxtapose the relationships between the model's variables. In fact, as we saw in the introduction to this section, we must ascertain the model's global coherence. Within the framework of a qualitative method, and particularly when it is inductive, researchers face three sources of bias that can weaken their conclusions (Miles and Huberman, 1984a):

- The holistic illusion: according events more convergence and coherence than they really have by eliminating the anecdotal facts that make up our social life.
- Elitist bias: overestimating the importance of data from sources who are clear, well informed and generally have a high status while underestimating the value of data from sources that are difficult to handle, more confused, or of lower status.
- Over-assimilation: losing one's own vision or ability to pull back, and being influenced by the perceptions and explanations of local sources (Miles and Huberman, 1984a).

The authors propose a group of tactics for evaluating conclusions, ranging from simple monitoring to testing the model. These tactics permit the researcher to limit the effects of earlier bias.

2. Quantitative Methods

Causal models illustrate a quantitative method of evaluating and testing a causal model. However, evaluating a model is more than simply evaluating it statistically. It also involves examining its reliability and validity. These two notions are developed in detail in Chapter 10. We have, therefore, chosen to emphasize a system that is the most rigorous method for examining causal relationships, and permits the researcher to increase the global validity of causal models. This is experimentation.

2.1 Experimental methods

The experimental system remains the favored method of proving that any variable is the cause of another variable. Under normal conditions, researchers testing a causal relationship have no control over the bias that comes from having multiple causes explaining a single phenomenon or the bias that occurs in data collection. Experimentation gives researchers a data collection tool that reduces the incidence of such bias to the maximum.

Experimentation describes the system in which researchers manipulate variables and observe the effects of this manipulation on other variables (Campbell and Stanley, 1966). The notions of factor, experimental variables, independent variables and cause are synonymous, as are the notions of effect, result and dependent variables. Treatments refer to different levels or modalities (or combinations of modalities) of factors or experimental variables. An experimental unit describes the individuals or objects that are the subject of the experimentation (agricultural plots, individuals, groups, organizations, etc.). In experimentation, it is important that each treatment is tested on more than one experimental unit. This basic principle is that of repetition.

The crucial aim of experimentation is to neutralize those sources of variation one does not wish to measure (that is, the causal relationship tested). When researchers measure any causal relationship, they risk allocating the observed result to the cause being tested when the result is, in fact, explained by other causes (that is, the 'confounding effect'). Two tactics are available for neutralizing this confounding effect (Spector, 1981). The first involves keeping constant those variables that are not being manipulated in the experiment. External effects are then directly monitored. The limitations of this approach are immediately obvious. It is impossible to monitor all the non-manipulated variables. As a rule, researchers will be content to monitor only the variables they consider important. The factors being monitored are known as secondary factors and the free factors are principal factors. The second tactic is random allocation, or randomization. This involves randomly dividing the experimental units among different treatments, in such a way that there are equivalent groups for each process. Paradoxically, on average, the groups of experimental units become equivalent not because the researcher sought to make them equal according to certain criteria (that is, variables), but because they were divided up randomly. The monitoring of external effects is, therefore, indirect. Randomization enables researchers to compare the effects of different treatments in such a way that they can discard most alternative explanations (Cook and Campbell, 1979). For example, if agricultural plots are divided up between different types of soil treatment (an old and a new type of fertilizer), then the differences in yields cannot result from differences in the amount of sunshine they receive or the soil composition because, on the basis of these two criteria, the experimental units (agricultural plots) treated with the old type of fertilizer are, on average, comparable with those treated with the new type. Randomization can be done by drawing lots, using tables of random numbers or by any other similar method.

All experimentation involves experimental units, processing, an effect and a basis for comparison (or control group) from which variations can be inferred and attributed to the process (Cook and Campbell, 1979). These different elements are grouped together in the experimental design, which permits researchers to:

- select and determine the method for allocating experimental units to the different processes
- select the external variables to be monitored
- choose the processes and comparisons made as well as the timing of their observations (that is, the measurement grades).

There are two criteria researchers can use to classify their experimental program, with a possible crossover between them. They are the number of principal factors and the number of secondary (or directly monitored) factors being studied in the experimentation. According to the first criterion, the researcher studies two or more principal factors and possibly their interactions. A factor analysis can either be complete (that is, all the processes are tested) or it can be fractional (that is, certain factors or treatments are monitored). According to the second criterion, total randomization occurs when there is no secondary factor (that is, no factor is monitored with a control). The experimental units are allocated randomly to different treatments in relation to the principal factors studied (for example, if there is one single principal factor which comprises three modalities, it constitutes three treatments, whereas if there are three principal factors with two, three and four modalities, that makes 2 × 3 × 4, or 24 treatments). When there is a secondary factor, we refer to a random bloc plan. The random bloc plan can even be complete (that is, all the treatments are tested within each bloc) or it can be incomplete. The experimental system is the same for total randomization, except that experimental units are divided into subgroups according to the modalities of the variable being monitored, before being allocated randomly to different treatments within each subgroup. When there are two secondary factors, we refer to Latin squares. When there are three secondary factors, they are Greco-Latin squares, and when there are four or more secondary factors they are hyper-Greco-Latin squares. The different systems of squares require that the number of treatments and the number of modalities, or levels of each of the secondary factors, are identical.

In the experimental systems presented earlier, experimental units were randomly allocated to treatments. Agricultural plots are easier to randomize than individuals, social groups or organizations. It is also easier to conduct randomization in a laboratory than in the field. In the field, researchers are often guests whereas, in the laboratory, they can feel more at home and often have virtually complete control over their research system. As a result, randomization is more common in the case of objects than people, groups or organizations and is more often used in the laboratory than during fieldwork.

Management researchers, who essentially study people, groups or organizations and are the most often involved in fieldwork, rarely involve themselves in experimentation. In fact, in most cases, they only have partial control over their research system. In other words, they can choose the 'when' and the 'to whom' in their calculations but cannot control the spacing of the stimuli, that is, neither the 'when' or the 'to whom' in the treatments, nor their randomization, which is what makes true experimentation possible (Campbell and Stanley, 1966). This is 'quasi-experimentation'.

Quasi-experimentation describes experimentation that involves treatments, measurable effects and experimental units, but does not use randomization. Unlike experimentation, a comparison is drawn between groups of non-equivalent experimental units that differ in several ways, other than in the presence or absence of a given treatment whose effect is being tested. The main difficulty for researchers wishing to analyze the results of quasi-experimentation is trying to separate the effects resulting from the treatments from those due to the initial dissimilarity between of groups of experimental units.

Cook and Campbell (1979) identified two important arguments in favor of using the experimental process in field research. The first is the growing reticence among researchers to content themselves with experimental studies in a controlled context (that is, the laboratory), which often have limited theoretical and practical relevance. The second is researcher dissatisfaction with non-experimental methods when making causal inferences. Quasi-experimentation responds to these two frustrations. Or, more positively, it constitutes a middle way, a kind of convergence point for these two aspirations. From this point of view, there is bound to be large-scale development in the use of quasi-experimentation in management.

So far in this section we have been talking essentially about drawing causal inferences using variables manipulated within the framework of an almost completely controlled system. In the following paragraphs, we focus on another family of methods that enable causal inferences to be made using data that is not necessarily experimental. These are causal models.

2.2 Statistical methods

There are three phases in the evaluation and testing of causal models: identification, estimation and measurement of the model's appropriateness.

Every causal model is a system of equations in which the unknowns are the parameters to be estimated and the values are the elements of the variance/covariance matrix. Identifying the causal model involves verifying whether the system of equations which it is made of has zero, one or several solutions. In the first instance (no solution), the model is said to be under-identified and cannot be estimated. In the second case (a single solution), the model is said to be just identified and possesses zero degree of freedom. In the third case (several solutions), the model is said to be over-identified. It possesses several degrees of freedom, equal to the difference between the number of elements in the matrix of the variances/covariance (or correlations) and the number of parameters to be calculated. If there are p variables in the model, the matrix of the variances/covariance is counted as $p(p + 1)/2$ elements and the matrix of correlations $p(p - 1)/2$ elements. These two numbers have to be compared with those of the parameters to be calculated. However, in the case of complex models, it can be difficult to determine the exact number of parameters to be calculated. Fortunately, the computer software currently available automatically identifies the models to be tested and displays error messages when the model is under-identified.

Statistically testing a causal model only has interest and meaning when there is over-identification. Starting from the idea that the S matrix of the observed variances/covariance, which is calculated on a scale, reflects the true Σ matrix of the variances/covariance at the level of all of the population, one can see that, if the model's system of equations is perfectly identified (that is, the number of degrees of freedom is null), then the C matrix reconstituted by the model will equal the S matrix. However, if the system is over-identified (that is, the number of degrees of freedom is strictly positive) then the correspondence will probably be imperfect because of the presence of errors related to the sample. In the latter case, estimation methods permit researchers to calculate parameters which will approximately reproduce the S matrix of the variances/covariance observed.

After the identification phase, the model's parameters are estimated, most often using the criterion of least squares. A distinction can be drawn between simple methods (unweighted least squares) and iterative methods (maximum likelihood or generalized least squares, etc.). With each of these methods, the researcher has to find estimated values for the model's parameters that permit them to minimize an F function. This function measures the difference between the observed values of the matrix of the variances/covariance and those of the matrix of variances/covariance predicted by the model. The parameters are assessed iteratively by a non-linear optimization algorithm. The F function can be written as follows:

$$F = 0.5 \times Tr[(W(S - C))2]$$

S being the matrix of the observed
  variances/covariance
C is the matrix of the variances/covariance
  predicted by the model
W is the weighting matrix
Tr signifies the trace of the matrix.

In the method of unweighted least squares, W equals I, the matrix identity. In the method of generalized least squares, W equals S – 1, the inverse of the matrix of the observed variances/covariance. In the method of maximum likelihood, W equals C – 1, the inverse recalculated at each iteration of the matrix of variances/covariance predicted.

After the estimation phase, the researcher has to verify the model's appropriateness in relation to the empirical data. The appropriateness of a model in relation to the empirical data used to test it is greater when the gap between the matrixes of predicted and observed variances and covariance (S) is weak. However, the more parameters the model has to be estimated, the greater the chance that the gap will be reduced. For this reason, evaluation of the model must focus as much on the predictive quality of the variance/covariance matrix as on the statistical significance of each of the model's elements.

Causal models offer a large number of criteria to evaluate the degree to which a theoretical model is appropriate in relation to empirical data. At a very general level, we can distinguish between two ways of measuring this appropriateness:

- the appropriateness of the model can be measured as a whole (the Khi2 test, for example)
- the significance of the model's different parameters can be measured (for example, the t test or z test).

Software proposing iterative estimation methods, such as generalized least squares or maximum likelihood, usually provide a Khi2 test. This test compares the null hypothesis with the alternative. The model is considered to be acceptable if the null hypothesis is not rejected (in general, $p > 0.05$). This runs contrary to the classic situation in which models are considered as acceptable when the null hypothesis is rejected. As a result, Type II errors (that is, the probability of not rejecting the null hypothesis while knowing it is false) are critical in the evaluation of causal models. Unfortunately, the probability of Type II errors is unknown.

In order to offset this disadvantage, one can adopt a comparative rather than an absolute approach, and sequentially test a number of models whose differences are established by the addition or elimination of constraints (that is, 'nested models'). In fact, if researchers have two models, one of which has added constraints, they can test the restricted model versus the more general model by assessing them separately. If the restricted model is correct, then the difference between the Khi2 of the two models approximately follows a Khi2 distribution and the number of degrees of freedom is the difference in degrees of freedom between the two models.

It is, however, worth noting two major limitations of the Khi2 test:

- When the sample is very big, even very slight differences between the model and the data can lead to a rejection of the null hypothesis.
- This test is very sensitive to possible discrepancies from a normal distribution.

As a result, other indices have been proposed to supplement the Khi2 test. The main software packages, such as LISREL, EQS, AMOS or SAS, each offer more than a dozen. Certain of these indices integrate explained variance percentage allowances. Usually, the models considered to be good models are those whose indices are above 0.90. However, the distribution of these indices is unknown and one should therefore exclude any idea of testing appropriateness statistically. A second category groups together a set of indices which take real values and which are very useful for comparing models that have different numbers of parameters. It is usual, with these indices, to retain as the best those models whose indices have the lowest values.

In addition to these multiple indices for globally evaluating models, numerous criteria exist to measure the significance of models' different parameters. The most widely used criterion is that of 't' (that is, the relation between the parameter's value and its standard deviation). This determines whether the parameter is significantly non-null. Likewise, the presence of acknowledged statistical anomalies such as negative variances and/or determination coefficients that are negative or higher than the unit are naturally clear proof of a model's deficiency.

All in all, to meet strict requirements, a good model must present a satisfactory global explanatory value, contain only significant parameters and present no statistical anomalies.

In general, the use of causal models has come to be identified with the computer program LISREL, launched by Joreskog and Sorbom (1982). As renowned as this software might be, we shouldn't forget that there are other methods of estimating causality which may be better suited to certain cases. For example, the PLS method, launched by Wold (1982), does not require most of the restrictive hypotheses associated with use of maximum likelihood technique generally employed by LISREL (that is, a large number of observations and multi-normality in the distribution of variables). Variants of the LISREL program, such as CALIS (SAS Institute, 1989) or AMOS (Arbuckle, 1997), and other programs such as EQS (Bentler, 1989) are now available in the SAS or SPSS software packages. In fact, the world of software for estimating causal models is evolving constantly, with new arrivals, disappearance and, above all, numerous changes.

CONCLUSION

This chapter has tried to reply to the question of how to construct and test a causal model; that is, a model reproducing a network of causal relationships between concepts and variables. After emphasizing the diversity of possible methods (qualitative or quantitative and inductive or deductive), we highlighted the four essential stages in the process of modeling causal relationships:

1 Specifying the phenomenon or system to be modeled.
2 Specifying the model's variables and concepts.
3 Specifying the relationships between the model's variables and concepts.
4 Testing the model.

However, these four stages do not always follow directly on from each other, nor do they always occur in this order. To the contrary, the modeling process is often iterative and non-linear.

An important message of this chapter is that causal modeling is a difficult task, and causal analysis must be given a priority position in the process. While either quantitative or qualitative research may suggest a causal relationship, it is theory that forms the basis for this relationship and, in the end, justifies it, whether the researcher adopts an inductive or deductive approach. With an inductive approach, theory is the outcome of the process of constructing and testing the causal model, while, with a deductive approach, it forms the basis for the process.

Some recent developments in modeling are worth mentioning. According to certain authors, current procedures are lacking because they do not enable researchers to discern the complexity of phenomena. From this deficiency, new approaches develop; taking their inspiration, for example, from biological processes such as genetic algorithms and neuron networks. The researcher is no longer trying to explain phenomena with the help of analysis, in the aim of reducing the number of parameters, but is instead emphasizing research results while conserving a wealth of parameters. These new practices, which constitute a kind of bridge between traditional explanatory causal models and simulation models, are being used increasingly in the study of phenomena associated with organizations (Cheng and Van De Ven, 1996).

FURTHER READING

Campbell, D.T. and Stanley, J.C., *Experimental and Quasi-Experimental Designs for Research*, Chicago: Rand McNally College Publishing Company, 1966.

Cook, T.D. and Campbell, D.T., *Quasi-Experimentation: Design and Analysis Issues for Field Settings*, Boston, MA: Houghton Mifflin Company, 1979.

Davis, J.A., *The Logic of Causal Order*, Sage University paper, Series: Quantitative Applications in the Social Sciences, 1985.

Glaser, B. and Strauss, A.L., *The Discovery of Grounded Theory: Strategy for Qualitative Research*, New York, Aldine de Gruter, 1967.

Hayduk, L.A., *LISREL Issues, Debates, and Strategies*, Baltimore, MD: Johns Hopkins University Press, 1996.

Hoyle, R.H. (ed.), *Structural Equation Modeling: Concepts, Issues, and Applications*, Thousand Oaks, CA: Sage Publications, 1995.

Maruyama, G.M., *Basics of Structural Equation Modeling*, Thousand Oaks, CA: Sage, 1998.

Miles, B. and Huberman, M., *Analyzing Qualitative Data Analysis: A Source Book of New Methods*, Beverley Hills, CA: Sage, 1984.

Strauss, A. and Corbin, J., *Basics of Qualitative Research*, Newbury Park, CA: Sage, 1990.

Zaltman, C., Pinson, C. and Angelmar, R., *Metatheory and Consumer Research*, New York: Holt, Reinhart and Winston, 1973.

13

CLASSIFYING AND STRUCTURING

Carole Donada and Ababacar Mbengue

Outline

Strategic management researchers frequently find they have to synthesize large sets of data, often working with tables containing several tens or even hundreds of lines and columns. They may need to transform a body of data comprising a great number of different objects into a small number of organized classes of identical or similar objects; or they may want to highlight, through a small number of key factors, the internal structure of a data set. Classification and structuring methods are the most practical techniques for such analysis. In this chapter we distinguish between two classes of methods available to the researcher: cluster analysis and factor analysis.

Classification and structuring methods combine different techniques to break down large data sets into a smaller number of classes or general factors. These methods have many basic features in common, notably in their objectives but also in the preliminary treatment given to the data and in data analysis methods.

SECTION 1 METHODS

Data analysis manuals (Aldenderfer and Blashfield, 1984; Everitt, 1993; Hair et al., 1992; Kim and Mueller, 1978; Lebart et al., 1984) provide a detailed presentation of the mathematical logic on which classification and structuring methods are based. We have chosen here to define these methods and their objectives, and consider the preliminary questions that would confront a researcher wishing to use them.

1. Definitions and Objectives

Classifying, condensing, categorizing, regrouping, organizing, structuring, summarizing, synthesizing and simplifying are just some of the procedures that can be done with a data set using classification and structuring methods. Taking this list as a starting point, we can formulate three propositions. First, the different methods of classification and structuring are aimed at condensing a relatively large set of data to make it more intelligible. Second, classifying data is a way of structuring it (that is, if not actually highlighting an inherent structure within the data, at least presenting it in a new form). Finally, structuring data (that is, highlighting key or general factors) is a way of classifying it – essentially by associating objects (observations, individuals, cases, variables, characteristics, criteria) with these key or general factors. Associating objects with particular dimensions or factors boils down to classifying into categories represented by these dimensions or factors.

The direct consequence of the above propositions is that, conceptually, the difference between methods of classification and methods of structuring is relatively slim. Although traditionally observations (individuals, cases, firms) are classified, and variables (criteria, characteristics) are structured, there is no reason, either conceptually or technically, why variables cannot be classified or observations structured.

While there are many different ways to classify and structure data, these methods are generally grouped into two types: *cluster analysis* and *factor analysis*. The main aim of cluster analysis is to group objects into homogeneous classes, with those objects in the same class being very similar and those in different classes being very dissimilar. For this reason, cluster analysis falls into the domain of 'taxonomy' – the science of classification. However, while it is possible to classify in a subjective and intuitive way, cluster analyses are automatic methods of classification using statistics. 'Typology', 'cluster analysis', 'automatic classification' and 'numeric taxonomy' are actually synonymous terms. Part of the reason for the diversity of terms is that cluster analyses have been used in many different disciplines such as biology, psychology, economics and management – where they are used, for example, to segment a firm's markets, sectors or strategies. In management, cluster analyses are often used in exploratory research or as an intermediary step during confirmatory research.

Strategic management researchers have often needed to gather organizations together into large groupings to make them easier to understand. Even early works on strategic groups (Hatten and Schendel, 1977), organizational clusters (Miles and Snow, 1978; Mintzberg, 1989), taxonomies (Galbraith and Schendel, 1983) or archetypes (Miller and Friesen, 1978) were already following this line of thinking. Barney and Hoskisson (1990) followed by Ketchen and Shook (1996) have provided an in-depth discussion and critique of the use of these analyses.

The main objective of factor analysis is to simplify data by highlighting a small number of general or key factors. Factor analysis combines different statistical techniques to enable the internal structure of a large number of variables and/or observations to be examined, with the aim of replacing them with a small number of characteristic factors or dimensions.

Factor analysis can be used in the context of confirmatory or exploratory research (Stewart, 1981). Researchers who are examining the statistical validity of observable measurements of theoretical concepts (Hoskisson et al., 1993;

Venkatraman, 1989; Venkatraman and Grant, 1986) use factor analysis for confirmation. This procedure is also followed by authors who have prior knowledge of the structure of the interrelationships among their data, knowledge they wish to test. In an exploratory context, researchers do not specify the structure of the relationship between their data sets beforehand. This structure emerges entirely from the statistical analysis, with the authors commenting upon and justifying the results they have obtained. This approach was adopted by Garrette and Dussauge (1995) when they studied the strategic configuration of interorganizational alliances.

It is possible to combine cluster and factor analysis in one study. For example, Dess and Davis (1984) had recourse to both these methods for identifying generic strategies. Lewis and Thomas (1990) did the same to identify strategic groups in the British grocery sector. More recently, Dess et al. (1997) applied the same methodology to analyze the performance of different entrepreneurial strategies.

2. Preliminary Questions

Researchers wishing to use classification and structuring methods need to consider three issues: the content of the data to be analyzed, the need to prepare the data before analyzing it and the need to define the notion of proximity between sets of data.

2.1 Data content

Researchers cannot simply take the available data just as they find it and immediately apply classification and structuring methods. They have to think about data content and particularly about its significance and relevance. In assessing the relevance of our data, we can focus on various issues, such as identifying the *objects to be analyzed*, fixing spatial, temporal or other *boundaries*, or *counting* observations and variables.

The researcher must determine from the outset whether he wishes to study observations (firms, individuals, products, decisions, etc.) or their characteristics (variables). Indeed, the significance of a given data set can vary greatly depending on which objects (observations or variables) researchers prioritize in their analysis. A second point to clarify relates to the spatial, temporal or other boundaries of the data. Defining these boundaries is a good way of judging the relevance of a data set. It is therefore extremely useful to question whether the boundaries are natural or logical in nature, whether the objects of a data set are truly located within the chosen boundaries, and whether all the significant objects within the chosen boundaries are represented in the data set. These last two questions link the issue of data-set boundaries with that of counting objects (observations or variables). Studies focusing on strategic groups can provide a good illustration of these questions. In such work, the objects to be analyzed are observations rather than variables. The time frames covered by the data can range from one year to several. Most frequently, the empirical context of the studies consists of *sectors*, and the definition criteria are those of official statistical organizations (for example, Standard Industrial Classification – SIC).

Another criterion used in defining the empirical context is that of *geographic* or *national borders*. A number of research projects have focused on American, British or Japanese industries. Clearly, the researcher must consider whether it is relevant to choose national borders to determine an empirical context. When the sectors studied are global or multinational, such a choice is hardly appropriate. It is also valid to ask whether a sector or industry defined by an official nomenclature (for example SIC) is the relevant framework within which to study competitive strategies. One can check the relevance of such frameworks by questioning either experts or those actually involved in the system. Finally, one needs to ask whether data covering a very short *time span* is relevant, and to consider, more generally, the significance of cross-sectional data. When studying the dynamics of strategic groups or the relationship between strategic groups and performance, for example, it is important to study a longer time span.

As for the *number* and *nature* of observations and variables, these depend greatly on the way the data is collected. Many studies now make use of commercially established databases (Pims, Compustat, Value Line, Kompass, etc.), which give researchers access to a great amount of information. Determining the number of variables to include leads us to the problem of choosing which ones are relevant. Two constraints need to be respected: *sufficiency* and *non-redundancy*. The sufficiency constraint demands that no relevant variable should be omitted, and the non-redundancy constraint insists that no relevant variable should appear more than once, either directly or indirectly. These two constraints represent extreme requirements – in reality it is difficult to entirely fulfill them both, but clearly the closer one gets to fulfilling them, the better the results will be. To resolve these selection difficulties, the researcher can turn to theory, existing literature, or to expertise. Generally, it is preferable to have too many variables rather than too few, particularly in an exploratory context (Ketchen and Shook, 1996).

The problem of the number of observations to include poses the same constraints: *sufficiency* and *non-redundancy*. For example, in the study of strategic groups, the sufficiency constraint demands that all firms operating within the empirical context are included in the study. The non-redundancy constraint insists that no firm should appear among the observations more than once. The difficulty is greater here than when determining which variables to include. In fact, the increase in diversification policies, mergers, acquisitions and alliances makes it very difficult to detect *relevant strategic entities* (or *strategic actors*). One solution lies in basing the study on *legal entities*. As legal entities are subject to certain obligations in their economic and social activities, this choice at least has the merit of enabling access to a minimum of economic and social information relating to the study at hand. Here, even more than in the case of variables, sector-based expertise must be used. Identifying relevant observations (such as strategic actors in a study of strategic groups) is an essentially qualitative process.

As a rule, researchers need to consider whether they have enough observations at their disposal. For factor analyses, some specialists recommend more than 30 observations per variable, and even as many as 50 or 100. Others say there must be 30 or 50 more observations than there are variables. There are also those who recommend four or five times more observations than variables. Hair et al. (1992) have argued that these criteria are very strict – they point out that quite often, researchers have to handle data in which the number of observations is hardly double the number of variables. Generally, when the number of observations or variables seems insufficient, the researcher must be doubly careful in interpreting the results.

2.2 Preparing data

Preparing data ahead of applying classification and structuring methods is essentially a question of tackling the problems of missing values and outliers, and of standardizing variables.

Missing values   The problem of missing values can be dealt with in a number of ways, depending both on the analysis envisaged and the number of observations or variables involved.

Cluster analysis programs automatically exclude observations in which any values are missing. The researcher can either accept this imposed situation, or attempt to estimate the missing values (for example, by replacing the missing value with an average or very common value). If the researcher replaces the missing values with a fixed value – using, for instance, the mean or the mode of the variable in question – there is a risk of creating artificial classes or dimensions. This is because having an identical value recurring often in the data set will increase the proximity of the objects affected.

The question of missing data is, therefore, all the more important if a large number of values are missing, or if these missing values relate to observations or variables that are essential to the quality of the analysis.

Outliers   The question of how to treat outliers is also an important issue, as most of the proximity measurements from which classification and structuring algorithms are developed are very sensitive to the existence of such points. An outlier is an anomalous object, in that it is very different from the other objects in the database. The presence of outliers can greatly distort analysis results, transforming the scatter of points into a compact mass that is difficult to examine. For this reason it is recommended that the researcher eliminates them from the database during cluster analysis and reintegrates them after obtaining classes from less atypical data. Outliers can then supplement results obtained using less atypical data, and can enrich the interpretation of these results. For example, an outlier may have the same profile as the members of a class that has been derived through analysis of more typical data. In such a case, the difference is, at most, one of degree – and the outlier can be assigned to the class whose profile it matches. Equally, an outlier may have a profile markedly different from any of the classes that have resulted from the analysis of more typical data. Here, the difference is one of nature, and the researcher must explain the particular positioning of the outlier in relation to the other objects. Researchers can use their intuition, seek expert opinions on the subject, or refer to theoretical propositions which justify the existence or presence of an outlier.

Standardizing variables   After attending to the questions of missing values and outliers, the researcher may need to carry out a third manipulation to prepare the data: he or she must now standardize, or normalize, his or her variables. This operation allows the same weight to be attributed to all of the variables that have been included in the analysis. It is a simple statistical operation that in most cases consists of centering and reducing variables around a zero mean, with a standard deviation equal to one. This operation is strongly recommended by certain authors – such as Ketchen and Shook (1996) – when database variables have been measured using different scales (for example, turnover, surface area of different factories in square meters, number of engineers, etc.). Although standardization is not essential if database variables have been measured using comparable scales, this has not prevented some researchers from conducting statistical analyses on untreated variables and then on standardized variables so as to compare the results. Here, the solution is to select the analysis with the greater validity.

Some specialists remain skeptical about how useful the last two preparatory steps really are (for example, Aldenderfer and Blashfield, 1984). Nevertheless, it is worthwhile for researchers to compare the results of analyses obtained with and without standardizing variables and integrating extreme data (outliers). If the results are found to be stable, the validity of the classes or dimensions identified is strengthened.

2.3 Data proximity

The notion of proximity is central to classification and structuring algorithms, all of which are aimed at grouping more similar objects together and separating those that are farthest removed from each other. Two types of measurements are generally employed to specify which measure of proximity to use: distance measurements and similarity measurements. In general, distance measurements are used for classification analyses and similarity measurements for factor analyses.

Researchers' choices are greatly limited by the kind of analyses they intend carrying out and, above all, by the nature of their data (category or metric). With category data, the appropriate measurement to use is the distance of the chi-square. With metric data, the researcher can use the correlation coefficient for factor analyses and Euclidean distance for cluster analyses. Mahalanobis distance is recommended in place of Euclidean distance in the specific case of strong co-linearity among variables. It must be noted that factor analyses function exclusively with similarity measurements, whereas cluster analyses can be used with both distance measurements and, although it is very rare, similarity measurements (for example, the correlation coefficient).

In classifying observations, distance measurements will associate observations that are close across all of the variables while similarity measurements will associate observations that have the same profile – that is, that take their extreme values from the same variables. It can be said that similarity measurements refer to *profile* while distance measurements refer to *position*.

A researcher may then quite possibly obtain different results depending on the proximity measurement (similarity or distance) used. If the results of classification or structuring are stable whichever proximity measurements are used, a cluster or factor structure probably exists. If the results do not correspond, however, it could be either because the researcher measured different things, or because there is no real cluster or factor structure present.

SECTION 2   APPLICATION

This section puts the principal methods into practice. We recommend researchers seeking a more detailed discussion of the practical application of these structuring and classifying methods refer to a specialized data analysis manual, such as Hair et al. (1992).

1. Cluster Analysis

After clearly defining the environment from which the objects to be classified have been drawn, and then preparing the data appropriately, a researcher who undertakes to conduct a cluster analysis must choose a classification algorithm, determine the number of classes necessary and then validate them.

1.1 Choosing a classification algorithm

Choosing a classification algorithm involves deciding which procedure, hierarchical or non-hierarchical, to use in order to correctly group discrete objects into classes.

Several classification algorithms exist. Two different types of procedure are commonly distinguished: hierarchical procedures and non-hierarchical procedures.

Hierarchical procedures break down a database into classes that fit one inside the other in a hierarchical structure. These procedures can be carried out in an agglomerative or a divisive manner. The agglomerative method is the most widely used. From the start, each object constitutes a class in itself. The first classes are obtained by grouping together those objects that are the most alike. The classes that are the most alike are then grouped together – and the method is continued until only one single class remains. The divisive method proceeds by successive divisions, going from classes of objects to individual objects. At the start, all of the objects constitute a single class – this is then divided to form two classes, which are as heterogeneous as possible. The procedure is repeated until there are as many classes as there are different objects.

Several hierarchical classification algorithms exist. The Ward algorithm is the most often used in management research, as it favors the composition of classes of the same size. For a more in-depth discussion of the advantages and limits of each algorithm, the researcher can consult specialist statistical works, different software manuals (SAS, SPSS, SPAD, etc.), or articles that present meta-analyses of algorithms used in management research (Ketchen and Shook, 1996).

Non-hierarchical procedures – often referred to as *K-means methods* or *iterative methods* – involve groupings or divisions which do not fit one inside the other hierarchically. After having fixed the number (K) of classes he or she wishes to obtain, the researcher can, for each of the K classes, select one or several typical members – 'core members' – to input into the program.

Each of these two approaches has its strengths and its weaknesses. Hierarchical methods are criticized for being very sensitive to the environment from which the objects that are to be classified have been drawn, to the preparatory processing applied to the data (to allow for outliers and missing values, and to standardize variables) and to the method chosen to measure proximity. They are also criticized for being particularly prone to producing classes which do not correspond to reality. Non-hierarchical methods are criticized for relying completely on the subjectivity of the researcher who selects the core members of the classes. Such methods demand, meanwhile, good prior knowledge of the environment from which the objects being classified have been drawn; which is not necessarily the case in exploratory research. However, non-hierarchical methods are praised for not being over-sensitive to problems linked to the environment of the objects being analyzed – in particular, to the existence of outliers.

In the past, hierarchical methods were used very frequently, certainly in part for reasons of opportunity: for a long time these methods were the most well documented and the most readily available. Non-hierarchical methods have since become more accepted and more widespread. The choice of algorithm depends, in the end, on the researcher's explicit or implicit hypotheses, on his or her degree of familiarity with the empirical context and on the prior existence of a relevant theory or published work.

Several specialists advise a systematic combination of the two types of methods (Punj and Steward, 1983). A hierarchical analysis can be conducted initially, to obtain an idea of the number of classes necessary, and to identify the profile of the classes and any outliers. A non-hierarchical analysis using the information resulting from hierarchical analysis (that is, number and composition of the classes) then allows the classification to be refined with adjustments, iterations and reassignments within and across the classes. This double procedure increases the validity of the classification (see Section 2, subsection 1.3 in this chapter).

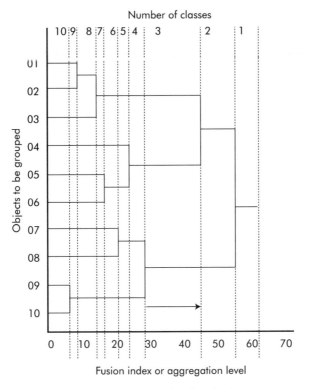

Figure 13.1 *An example of a dendogram*

1.2 Number of classes

Determining the number of classes is a delicate step that is fundamental to the classification process. For non-hierarchical procedures, the number of classes must be established by the researcher in advance – whereas for hierarchical procedures it is deduced from the results. While no strict rule exists to help researchers determine the 'true' or 'right' number of classes, several useful criteria and techniques are available to them (Hardy, 1994; Molière, 1986; Ohsumi, 1988).

Virtually all hierarchical classification software programs generate graphic representations of the succession of groupings produced. These graphs – called *dendograms* – consist of two elements: the *hierarchical tree* and the *fusion index* or *agglomeration coefficient*. The hierarchical tree is a diagrammatic reproduction of the classified objects. The fusion index or agglomeration coefficient is a scale indicating the level to which the agglomerations are effected. The higher the fusion index or agglomeration coefficient, the more heterogeneous the classes formed.

Figure 13.1 shows an example of a dendogram. We can see that the objects that are the closest, and are the first to be grouped together, are objects 09 and 10. Aggregations then occur reasonable regularly, without any sudden rises, until

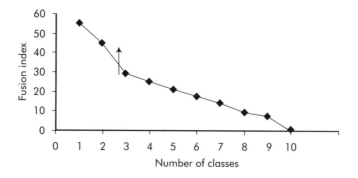

Figure 13.2   *Evolution of the fusion index in relation to number of classes*

the number of classes has been reduced to three. However, when we pass from three classes to two (see arrow on Figure 13.2), there is a big 'leap' in the fusion index (see the arrow on the graph). The conclusion is that three classes should be kept.

The researcher may be faced with situations where there is no visible leap in the fusion index, or where there are several. The first situation may signify that there are not really any classes in the data. The second signifies that several class structures are possible.

Finally, another often used criterion is the CCC (Cubic Clustering Criterion). This is a means of relating intra-class homogeneity to inter-class heterogeneity. Its value for each agglomeration coefficient (that is, each number of classes) is produced automatically by most automatic classification software programs. The number of classes to use is the number for which the CCC reaches a maximum value – a 'peak'. Several researchers have used this criterion (Ketchen and Shook, 1996).

1.3 Validating the classes

The final step in using cluster analyses is to verify the validity of the classes obtained. The aim is to ensure the classification has sufficient internal and external validity (the concept of validity is presented in detail in Chapter 10). In the case of cluster analyses, there are three important aspects to consider: reliability, predictive validity and external validity.

The reliability of the instruments used can be evaluated in several ways. The researcher can apply different algorithms and proximity measurements then compare the results obtained. If the classes highlighted remain the same, the classification is reliable (Hair et al., 1992; Ketchen and Shook, 1996; Lebart et al., 1984). Equally, one can divide a sufficiently large database into two parts and carry out the procedures on each of the separate parts. Concordance of the results is an indication of their reliability. Hambrick's (1983) research on mature industrial environments is a good example of this method.

Predictive validity should always be examined in relation to an existing conceptual base. Thus, the many authors who have used cluster analyses to identify strategic groups would be able to measure the predictive validity of their classifications by studying the relationship between the classes they obtained (that is, the strategic groups) and performance. In fact, the strategic groups theory stipulates that membership of a strategic group has a determining influence on performance (Porter, 1980). If a classification enables us to predict performance, it has a good predictive validity.

There are no tests specifically designed to test the external validity of cluster analyses. One can still, however, appreciate the quality of the classification by carrying out traditional statistical tests (Fisher's F, for example) or analyses of the variance between the classes and external measurements. For example, a researcher may set about classifying industrial supply firms and find two classes; that of the equipment suppliers and that of the subcontractors. To test the validity of his or her typology, the researcher may carry out a statistical test on the classes obtained and on a variable not taken into account in the typology. If the test is significant, he or she will have strengthened the validity of the classification. If the reverse occurs, he or she will need to examine the reasons for this non-validation. The researcher could question, for instance, whether the external measurement he or she has chosen is suitable, whether there are errors in his or her interpretation of the classes and whether the algorithms he or she has chosen are consistent with the nature of the variables and his or her research method.

The external validity of a classification can also be tested by carrying out the same analysis on another database and comparing the results obtained (Hair et al., 1992). This method is difficult to use in most research designs in management, however, as primary databases are often small and it is not easy to access complementary data. It is rarely possible to divide the data into different sample groups. Nevertheless, this remains possible when the researcher is working with large secondary databases.

1.4 Conditions and limitations

There are numerous possible ways cluster analyses can be useful research tools. Not only are they fundamental to studies aimed at classifying data, but they are also regularly used to investigate data, because they can be applied to all kinds of data.

In theory, we can classify everything. But while this may be so, researchers should give serious thought to the logic of their classification strategies. They must always consider the environmental homogeneity of the objects to be classified, and the reasons for the existence of natural classes within this environment – and what these may signify.

The subjectivity of the researcher greatly influences cluster analysis, and represents one of its major limitations. Even though there are a number of criteria and techniques available to assist researchers in determining the number of classes to employ, the decision remains essentially up to the researcher alone.

Justification is easier when these classes are well defined, but in many cases, class boundaries are less than clear-cut, and less than natural.

In fact, cluster analysis carries a double risk. A researcher may attempt to divide a logical continuum into classes. This is a criticism that has been leveled at empirical studies that attempt to use cluster analysis to validate the existence of the two modes of governance (hierarchical and market) proposed by Williamson. Conversely, the researcher may be attempting to force together objects that are very isolated and different from each other. This criticism is sometimes leveled at works on strategic groups which systematically group firms together (Barney and Hoskisson, 1990).

The limitations of classification methods vary according to the researcher's objectives. These limitations are less pronounced when researchers seek only to explore their data than when their aim is to find true object classes.

2. Factor Analysis

Factor analysis essentially involves three steps: choosing an analysis algorithm, determining the number of factors and validating the factors obtained.

2.1 Choosing a factor analysis technique

Component analysis and common and specific factors analysis   There are two basic factor analysis techniques (Hair et al., 1992): 'classic' factor analysis, also called *common and specific factor analysis*, or CSFA, and *component analysis*, or CA. In choosing between the two approaches, the researcher should remember that, in the framework of factor analysis, the total variance of a variable is expressed in three parts: (1) *common*, (2) *specific* and (3) *error*. Common variance describes what the variable shares with the other analysis variables. Specific variance relates to the one variable in question. The element of error comes from the imperfect reliability of the measurements or to random component in the variable measured.

In a CSFA, only common variance is taken into account. The variables observed, therefore, are the linear combinations of non-observed factors, also called *latent variables*. Component analysis, on the other hand, takes total variance into account (that is, all three types of variance). In this case it is the 'factors' obtained that are linear combinations of the observed variables. The choice between CSFA and CA methods depends essentially on the researcher's objectives. If the aim is simply to summarize the data, then CA is the best choice. However, if the aim is to highlight a structure underlying the data (that is, to identify latent variables or constructs) then CSFA is the obvious choice. Both methods are very easy to use and are available in all major software packages.

Correspondence factor analysis   A third, albeit less common, type of factor analysis is also possible: correspondence factor analysis (Greenacre, 1993;

Greenacre and Blasius, 1994; Lebart and Mirkin, 1993). This method is used only when a data set contains *categorical variables* (that is, nominal or ordinal). Correspondence factor analysis was invented in France and popularized by Jean-Paul Benzécri's team (Benzécri, 1992). Technically, correspondence factor analysis is similar to conducting a CA on a table derived from a categorical database. This table is derived directly from the initial database using correspondence factor analysis software. However, before beginning a correspondence factor analysis, the researcher has to categorize any metric variables present in the initial database. An example of such categorization is the transformation of a metric variable such as 'size of a firm's workforce' into a categorical variable, with the modalities 'small', 'medium' and 'large'. All metric variables can be transformed into a categorical variable.

Otherwise, aside from the restriction of it being solely applicable to the analysis of categorical variables, correspondence factor analysis is subject to the same constraints and same operating principles as other types of factor analysis.

2.2 Number of factors

Determining the number of factors is a delicate step in the structuring process. While again there is no general rule for determining the 'right' number of factors, a number of criteria are available to assist the researcher in approaching this problem (Stewart, 1981). We can cite the following criteria:

'A priori specification' This refers to situations when the researcher already knows how many factors need to be included. This approach is relevant when the research is aimed at testing a theory or hypothesis relative to the number of factors involved, or when the researcher is replicating earlier research and wishes to extract exactly the same number of factors.

'Minimum restitution' The researcher fixes in advance a level corresponding to the minimum percentage of information (that is, of variance) that is to be conveyed by all of the factors retained (for example, 60 per cent). While in the exact sciences, percentages of 95 per cent are frequently required, in management percentages of 50 per cent and even much lower are often considered satisfactory (Hair et al., 1992).

The Kaiser rule According to the Kaiser rule, the researcher includes only those factors whose eigenvalues (calculated automatically by computer software) are greater than one. The Kaiser rule is frequently applied in management science research – although it is only valid without restrictions in the case of a CA carried out on a correlation matrix. In the case of a CSFA, the Kaiser rule is too strict. According to this rule, the researcher can retain a factor whose eigenvalue is less than one, as long as this value is greater than the mean of the variables' *communalites* (common variances). This rule gives the most reliable results for cases including from 20 to 50 variables. Below 20 variables, it tends to reduce the number of factors, and above 50 variables, to increase it.

Example: Factors and associated eigenvalues

Table 13.1 presents the results of a factor analysis. Eleven variables characterizing 40 firms were used in the analysis. For each variable, communality represents the share of common variance. The first six factors are examined in the example. According to the Kaiser rule, only the first four factors must be retained (they have an eigenvalue of more than 1). In total, these first four factors reproduce 77.1 per cent of the total variance.

Table 13.1   *Eigenvalues and variance*

Variable	Communality	Factor	Eigen value	Percentage of variance	Percentage accumulated
Assets	0.95045	1	4.09733	37.2	37.2
Turnover	0.89745	2	1.89810	17.3	54.5
Communication	0.67191	3	1.42931	13.0	67.5
Workforce	0.92064	4	1.05872	9.6	77.1
Export	0.82043	5	0.76011	6.9	84.0
France	0.61076	6	0.61232	5.6	89.6
International	0.76590				
Margin	0.68889				
R&D	0.66600				
Economic return	0.82788				
Financial return	0.66315				

The eigenvalues are classified in decreasing order and any definite leveling-out of the curve is noted. The number of factors to include is then the number corresponding to the point where this leveling-out begins. Factor analysis software packages can generate a graphic visualization – called a 'scree plot' or a 'scree test' – of eigenvalues, which facilitates detection of such leveling. Figure 13.3 shows an example of a 'scree plot'. It represents the eigenvalues of the first 14 factors resulting from a CA. We note that, after the fourth factor, the eigenvalues stabilize (see arrow on Figure 13.3). The number of factors to retain is, therefore, four.

Factor interpretation is at the heart of factor analysis; notably CSFA, where it is often important to understand and sometimes to *name* the latent variables (that is, the factors). One frequently used technique is *rotation*. Rotation is an operation that simplifies the structure of the factors. Ideally, each factor would load with only a small number of variables and each variable would load with only a small number of factors, preferably just one. This would enable easy differentiation of the factors. A distinction needs to be made between *orthogonal* rotations and *oblique* rotations. In an orthogonal rotation, the factors remain orthogonal in relation to each other while, in an oblique rotation, this constraint is removed and the factors can load with each other. The rotation operation consists of two steps. First, a CA or a CSFA is carried out. On the basis of the previously mentioned criteria, the researcher chooses the number of factors to retain; for example, two. Rotation is then applied to these factors. We can cite three principal types of orthogonal rotation: *Varimax*, *Quartimax* and *Equamax*.

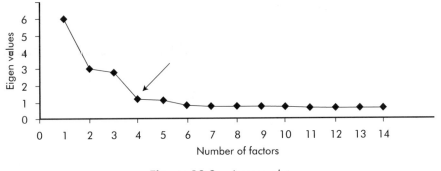

Figure 13.3 *A scree plot*

The most widespread method is Varimax, which seeks to minimize the number of variables strongly loaded with a given factor. For each factor, variable correlations (factor loading) approach either one or zero. Such a structure generally facilitates interpretation of the factors, and Varimax seems to be the method that gives the best results. The Quartimax method aims to facilitate the interpretation of the variables by making each one strongly load with one factor, and load as little as possible with all the other factors. This means that several variables can be strongly loaded with the same factor. In this case, we obtain a kind of general factor linked to all the variables. This is one of the main defects of the Quartimax method. The Equamax method is a compromise between Varimax and Quartimax. It attempts to somewhat simplify both factors and variables, but does not give very incisive results and remains little used. Oblique rotations are also possible, although these are given different names depending on the software used (for example, Oblimin on SPSS or Promax on SAS). Oblique rotations generally give better results than orthogonal rotations.

To interpret the factors, the researcher must decide on which variables are significantly loaded with each factor. As a rule, a loading greater than 0.30 in absolute value is judged to be significant and one greater than 0.50 very significant. However, these values must be adjusted in relation to the size of the sample, the number of variables and factors retained. Fortunately, many software packages automatically indicate which variables are significant.

Example: Matrix, rotations and interpretation of the factors

Tables 13.2 and 13.3 follow from the factor analysis results presented above in Table 13.1. These tables reproduce the standard output of factor analysis software. We should remember that the first four factors were retained according to the Kaiser rule (eigenvalue greater than one). Table 13.2 presents the matrix of the factors before rotation. One can conclude that the variables 'assets', 'workforce' and 'turnover' are strongly and essentially loaded to Factor 1 and that the variable 'financial profitability' is strongly and essentially loaded to Factor 2. However, the other variables are strongly loaded to several factors at once. Such a situation makes interpretation relatively difficult. It can, therefore, be useful to proceed to a factor rotation.

Table 13.3 presents the matrix of factors after a Varimax rotation. One can conclude that the variables 'assets', 'workforce' and 'turnover' are always strongly and essentially loaded to Factor 1. The variables 'economic profitability', 'financial profitability'

Table 13.2   *Matrix of factors before rotation*

Variable	Factor 1	Factor 2	Factor 3	Factor 4
Assets	**0.90797**	−0.04198	−0.30036	0.18454
Turnover	**0.88159**	−0.02617	−0.31969	0.13178
Communication	0.53730	−0.54823	−0.05749	−0.28171
Workforce	**0.90659**	0.00130	−0.30151	0.08849
Export	0.23270	−0.41953	**0.76737**	−0.03787
USA	0.48212	0.36762	−0.11265	−0.48009
International	0.60010	−0.46029	0.43955	−0.02691
Margin	0.58919	0.41630	0.33545	−0.23646
R&D	0.24258	−0.10944	0.16083	**0.75453**
Economic profitability	0.57657	0.57524	0.40565	−0.00026
Financial profitability	0.00105	**0.74559**	0.21213	0.24949

Table 13.3   *Matrix of factors after a Varimax rotation*

Variable	Factor 1	Factor 2	Factor 3	Factor 4
Assets	**0.95422**	0.14157	0.10597	0.09298
Workforce	**0.93855**	0.17384	0.09755	−0.00573
Turnover	**0.93322**	0.13494	0.08345	0.03720
Economic profitability	0.25123	**0.85905**	0.16320	−0.01262
Financial profitability	−0.13806	**0.70547**	−0.32694	0.19879
Margin	0.28244	**0.69832**	0.25400	−0.23865
Export	−0.13711	0.11330	**0.87650**	0.14331
International	0.34327	0.05113	**0.79908**	0.08322
Communication	0.50704	−0.28482	**0.52309**	−0.24510
R&D	0.22953	0.08582	0.12415	**0.76846**
USA	0.38221	0.40220	−0.02817	**−0.54965**

and 'margin' seem to be strongly and essentially loaded to Factor 2. The variables 'export' and 'international' as well as, to a lesser degree, the variable 'communication', are strongly and essentially loaded to Factor 3. Finally, the variable 'R&D' and, to a lesser degree, the variable 'USA' are strongly and essentially loaded to Factor 4. In conclusion, the interpretation of the factors is simplified: Factor 1 represents 'size', Factor 2 'profitability', Factor 3 'internationalization policy' and Factor 4 'research and development policy'.

2.3 Validation

The final step in a factor analysis involves examining the validity of the factors obtained. The same methods that may be applied to increase the reliability of cluster analyses (that is, cross-correlating algorithms, dividing a database) can also be used for factor analyses.

Factor analyses are often aimed at identifying latent dimensions (that is, variables that are not directly observable) that are said to influence other variables. In strategic management, for example, numerous 'factors' have been found to influence the performance of companies. These include strategy, organizational structure, planning, information and decision-making systems. Researchers wanting to operationalize such factors (that is, latent variables) could study the predictive validity of the operationalizations obtained. For example, researchers who undertake to operationalize the three 'generic strategies' popularized by Porter (1980) – overall low cost, differentiation and focus – would then be able to examine the predictive validity of these three factors by evaluating their relationship to the firms' performances.

Researchers can test the external validity of their factor solutions by replicating their study in another context or with another data set. That said, in most cases it would not be possible for the researcher to access a second empirical context. The study of external validity can never simply be a mechanical operation. A thorough preliminary consideration on the content of the data to be analyzed, as developed in the first section of this chapter, can provide a good basis for studying the external validity of a factor analysis.

2.4 Conditions and limitations

Factor analysis is a very flexible tool, with several possible uses. It can be applied to all kinds of objects (observations or variables) in various forms (tables of metric or categorical data, distance matrices, similarity matrices, contingency and Burt tables, etc.).

As with cluster analyses, the use of factor analysis entails a certain number of implicit hypotheses relating to the environment of the objects to be structured. Naturally, there is no reason why the factors identified should necessarily exist in a given environment. Researchers wishing to proceed to a factor analysis must, therefore, question the bases – theoretical or otherwise – for the existence of a factor structure in the particular environment of the objects to be structured. Most factor analysis software automatically furnishes indicators through which the probability of a factor structure existing can be determined and the quality of the factor analysis assessed. Low quality is an indication of the absence of a factor structure or the non-relevance of the factorial solution used by the researcher.

Finally, it must be noted that the limitations of factor analysis vary depending on the researcher's objectives. Researchers wishing simply to explore or synthesize data have much greater freedom than those who propose to find or to construct underlying factors.

CONCLUSION

In this chapter we have presented classification and structuring methods. We have distinguished between two classes of statistical methods available to the researcher: cluster analyses and factor analyses. The two types of methods have many basic features in common, which are presented in the first section of the chapter. These features relate, in particular, to the aims of these methods, the consideration that must be given to data content, and the task of data preparation. A second section was devoted to the practical application of the different techniques. While each technique involves distinct processes, the same three essential steps apply in each case:

1   Choosing an analysis procedure.
2   Determining the number of classes or factors.
3   Validating the results obtained.

In the literature on this subject, we can find several meta-analyses of management research projects that have applied cluster or factor analysis. For example, Ketchen and Shook (1996) examined articles in 16 academic strategic management revues and listed 45 research papers published between 1977 and 1993. One thing we learn from their work is that relatively little research based exclusively on cluster analysis manages to make it into publication. As no normative and objective rule exists to judge the work (that is, cluster analyses), reading committees remain cautious and reject a large number of these articles. Those that do make it through are primarily articles on exploratory research, whose authors have constructed their analysis using multiple procedures (standardizing and not standardizing variables, conserving and not conserving outliers, etc.), diversifying their algorithms (using the hierarchical agglomerative method, then the divisive method, the non-hierarchical method, etc.) and testing the validity of the classification in several ways (statistical tests, external measurements, sampling procedures, etc.).

We believe another promising publishing opportunity exists in the area of associating cluster or factor analyses with other techniques within a framework of confirmatory research. For example, as Thomas and Venkatraman (1988) have already discussed, a researcher can combine cluster analysis and causality models to test certain hypotheses of strategic group theory.

Researchers wishing to carry out a classification or a structuring analysis will considerably improve the quality of their work if they take the following precautions:

- Use relevant data, and assess its significance.
- Use a sufficient amount of data in order to meet the demands of these statistical methods.
- Use 'true' data, taking care to consider the issues of missing values, outliers and variables whose scales and variances differ greatly.
- Choose the similarity or distance measurement in relation to the aims being pursued (paying particular attention to profile or position) and to the nature of the data (metric or categorical).
- Use a number of different algorithms to more precisely identify classes and factors.
- Use a number of different criteria to decide the number of classes or factors to be included.
- Examine the validity of the cluster or factor solutions found.

FURTHER READING

Aldenderfer, M.-S. and Blashfield, R.-K., *Cluster Analysis*, Newbury Park, CA: Sage, 1984.

Everitt, B., *Cluster Analysis*, 3rd edn, New York: Halsted, 1993.

Hair, J.-F., Anderson, R.-E., Tatham, R.-L. and Black, W.-C., *Multivariate Data Analysis*, 3rd edn, New York: Macmillan, 1992.

Kim, J.-O. and Mueller, C.W., *Factor Analysis: Statistical Methods and Practical Issues*, Newbury Park, CA: Sage, 1978.

14

ANALYZING SOCIAL NETWORKS

Jacques Angot and Emmanuel Josserand

Outline

By studying the structure of social and organizational networks – networks of individuals, of groups, and of organizations – we can develop a clearer perception of the links both between and across them. This chapter is primarily concerned with helping the researcher to understand the particularities of the different network analysis methods available to them, and to identify the data needed to make use of these methods. We also look at the principal tools available to the researcher, and the precautions to take when applying these methods and tools.

Network analysis groups together methods used in the human sciences to study the relations or links that exist between units (individuals, groups or organizations). In management, these methods enable researchers to understand a diverse range of phenomena. These could include the structure of relations between individual actors within an organization, the links between the departments making up the organization, or the relations that exist between it and other organizations. Network analysis can also be used to identify homogenous subgroups or individuals who play a particular role in an organization, or, more broadly, simply as an aid in considering the formal and the informal structure of the organization as a whole. Finally, network analysis helps us to understand inter- or intra-organizational power and communication relations.

The common point between the different analyses we present in this chapter is their interest in relations – the links between the individuals or the units studied. Network analysis then provides researchers with methods enabling them to think of reality in terms of relations.

SECTION 1   GENERAL PRESENTATION AND DATA COLLECTION

Network analysis essentially involves revealing the links that exist between units. These units can be individuals, actors, groups, organizations or projects.

When researchers decide to use network analysis methods, and to look at links between units of analysis, they should be aware that they are implicitly entering into the paradigm of structural analysis. Structural sociology proposes going beyond the opposition that exists in sociology between holistic and individualistic traditions, and for this reason gives priority to relational data.

Analysis methods can be used by researchers taking a variety of different approaches, whether inductive, hypothetico-deductive, static or dynamic. Different ways of using the methods are presented in the first part of this section. Researchers may find they face difficulties that are linked as much to data collection as to the sampling such collection requires. These problems are dealt with in the second part.

1. Using Social Network Analysis Methods

A researcher may often be led to approach a particular management problem by using social network analysis in many different ways. The flexibility of these methods means they can be used inductively or to test a conceptual framework or a set of hypotheses. Moreover, recent developments in network analysis have made it easier to take the dynamics of the phenomena into account.

1.1 Inductive or hypothetico-deductive approaches

The descriptive power of network analysis can make it a particularly apt tool with which to seek a better understanding of a structure. Faced with a reality that can be difficult to grasp, researchers need tools that enable them to interpret this reality, and the data processing methods of network analysis are able to meet this need. General indicators or a sociogram (the graphic representation of a network) can, for example, help researchers to better understand a network as a whole. Calculation of the centrality score or detailed analysis of the sociogram can then enable the central individuals of the structure to be identified. Finally, and still using a sociogram or the grouping methods (which are presented in the second section of this chapter), researchers may reveal the existence of strongly cohesive subgroups within the network (individuals strongly linked to each other), or of groups of individuals who have the same relationships with the other members of the network. Network analysis can thus be used as 'an inductive method for describing and modeling relational structure [of a network]' (Lazega, 1994: 293). Lazega's case study of a firm of business lawyers (see the example below) illustrates the inductive use of network analysis. Studying cliques within this company (groups of individuals in which each is linked to every other member of the clique) enabled him to show how organizational barriers are crossed by small groups of individuals.

With an inductive approach, it is often advisable to use network analysis as a research method that is closely linked to the collection of qualitative data. In fact, as Lazega (1994) underlines, network analysis often only makes sense when qualitative analysis is also used – to provide the researcher with a real understanding of the context, so that the results obtained can be properly understood and interpreted.

Inductive use of network analysis

In his study of a firm of business lawyers, Lazega (1992) sought to understand how a collegial organization functions. To do this, he studied three internal networks: networks of collaborators, of advisers and of friends. Lazega's analysis revealed numerous small cliques (strongly cohesive subgroups) which crossed the formal organizational boundaries. The boundaries that existed within the organization were boundaries of status (between associates and non-associates), geographical boundaries (the firm had three offices) and boundaries between specialties. Collaborative cliques crossed the status boundaries, advice-giving cliques crossed geographical boundaries, and friendship cliques crossed specialty boundaries. So, the differentiation effect linked to the existence of formal groups was compensated for in this type of structure by the existence of small informal groups.

Network analysis is by no means restricted to inductive use. It can, in fact, enable a large number of concepts to be operationalized. There is a great deal of research in which structural data has been used to test hypotheses. For example, centrality scores are often used as explanatory variables in studies of power within organizations. In general, all the methods used in network analysis can be used hypothetico-deductively. Not only are there methods aimed at drawing out individual particularities, but researchers can also use the fact that someone belongs to a subgroup in an organization or network as an explanatory or explained variable. This is what Roberts and O'Reilly are doing when they use a structural equivalence measurement to evaluate whether individuals are 'active participants' or not within the United States' Navy (see example below).

Example: Hypothetico-deductive use of network analysis

In their study conducted within the US Navy, Roberts and O'Reilly (1979) focused on the individual characteristics of 'participants' – people who play a communicative role in the organization. Three networks were analyzed, each relating to communication of different kinds of information. One network related to authority, another was a 'social' network (unrelated to work) and the third related to expertise. The individual characteristics used were: rank, level of education, length of time they had been in the navy, need to accomplish, need for power, work satisfaction, performance, involvement and perceived role in communications. The hypotheses took the following form: 'participants have a higher rank than non-participants' or 'participants have greater work satisfaction than non-participants'. A questionnaire was used to collect both structural data and data on individual characteristics. Network analysis then enabled participant and non-participant individuals to be identified. Actors were grouped into two classes of structural equivalence – participants and non-participants – according to the type of relationship they had with the other people questioned. The hypotheses were then tested by means of discriminant analyses.

1.2 Static or dynamic use of network analysis methods

Network analysis methods have often been criticized for being like a photograph taken at one precise moment. It is, in fact, very rare for researchers to be in a position to conduct a dynamic study of a network's evolution. This can only be achieved by reconstituting temporal data using an artefact (video-surveillance tapes, for example) or by having access to direct observations on which to base the research. More often, the network observed is a photograph, a static observation. Static approaches can nevertheless lead to very interesting results, as the two examples presented below clearly show. However, references to the role time plays within networks can be found in the literature. Following on from Suitor et al. (1997), many works examine the dynamics of networks, principally asking how this can be taken into account so as to improve the quality of the data collected.

For example, in certain studies, data is collected at successive moments in time. Researchers then present the evolution of the network as a succession of moments in the same way that the construction of discrete variables approximates a continuous phenomenon. This type of research could be aimed at improving our understanding of the stability of networks, and their evolution over time. Here, the researcher seeks to describe or explain the way in which the number of links, their nature or even their distribution evolves. As an illustration, we can cite Welman et al. (1997). Taking a longitudinal approach, they show that neither an individual's centrality nor a network's social density are linked to the preservation of the links between actors. Similarly, the fact that a link is strong does not mean it will be long-lasting.

Collecting dynamic data about networks also enables researchers to carry out work for which the implications are more managerial than methodological. For example, Abrahamson and Rosenkopf (1997) propose an approach that enables researchers to track the diffusion of an innovation. Here, the approach is truly dynamic and the research no longer simply involves successive measurements.

2. Data Collection

Data collection is a delicate phase of network analysis. The analyses carried out are, in fact, sensitive to the slightest variations in the network analyzed. Leik and Chalkley (1997) outline some potential reasons for change: the instability inherent in the system (for example, the mood of the people questioned), change resulting from the systems' natural dynamics (such as maternity leave) and external factors (linked, for example, to the dynamics of the sector of activity). It is, therefore, essential to be extremely careful about the way in which data is collected, the tools that are used, the measurements taken to assess the strength of the links, and how the sample is constructed (how to define the network's boundaries).

2.1 Collection tools

Network analysis is about relationships between individual or collective units. The data researchers obtain is relational data. In certain situations the collection of such data poses no particular problem – it may be possible to collect data using secondary sources, which often prove to be entirely reliable. This is the case, for example, with research that makes use of the composition of boards of directors or inter-company cooperative ventures. The fact that this type of data is often used indicates that it is reliable relational information that is often relevant and easily accessible. For example, Mizruchi and Stearns (1994) use data on the boards of directors of large American companies taken from Standard and Poor's and Moody's annual directories. These directories enabled them to find out who was on the boards of directors and trace the boards' evolution. The authors were particularly interested in the presence of bank representatives on these boards.

Direct observation is sometimes feasible. One might, for example, study interactions in a particular place such as an office or a tea-room. However, in practice such possibilities for direct observation are quite rare. It is also possible to use certain relational artefacts, such as the minutes of meetings.

Most research based on network analysis uses surveys or interviews to collect data. It is, in fact, difficult to obtain precise data about the nature of the relationships between individuals in the network being analyzed by any other means. The obvious advantage of surveys is that they can reach a large number of people. However, the data collected is often more 'flimsy' than that obtained in interviews. The researcher's presence during the interview means he or she can reply directly to questions raised by the respondent during the research. In an interview situation researchers can also make sure that respondents fully understand what is asked of them and that, from start to finish, they are serious in their replies.

Name generators   Whether researchers use surveys or conduct interviews, relational data can be collected by means of 'name generators'. A name generator is a question either about the links the person being questioned has with the other members of the network or about his or her perception of the links that exist between members of the network. Table 14.1 gives some examples of name generators used in management research. Several collection techniques are possible.

One technique involves asking the respondent to cite the people concerned, possibly in order of importance (or frequency). Researchers can facilitate responses by supplying a list of names (all the members of the organization, for example). Another technique involves asking who they would choose as recipients if a message had to be sent to people with a certain profile.

The use of name generators is a delicate matter. They rely on the respondents' capacity to recall the actors with whom they are linked in a given type of relationship (for example, the people they have worked with over the past month).

Table 14.1   *Examples of name generators used in research in management*

Authors	Nature of the connection studied and the corresponding name generator
Roberts and O'Reilly (1979)	*Authority connection*: If you are upset about something related to the Navy or to your job, to whom in the squadron are you most likely to express your dissatisfaction (gripe) formally? *Expertise connection*: When you need technical advice in doing your job, who are the people you are most likely to ask? *Social connection*: With which people in this squadron are you most likely to have social conversations (not work-related) in the course of a work day?
Tichy et al. (1979)	*Work collaboration connection*: Think back over the past month. Consider all the people in your department; i.e., your superiors, your subordinates and people at the same level as yourself. Please write down the names of those with whom you have spent the most time on work matters. List the names, in order, so that the first person is the one with whom you have spent the most time.
Bovasso (1992)	*Contact connection*: – Cite the other members of the top management with whom you have had telephone and written contact? – Cite the other members of the top management with whom you have had face to face contacts? – Cite the other members of the top management with whom you have had visits outside the workplace? *Influence connection*: – Cite the other members of the top management who influence your ideas? – Cite the other members of the top management whose ideas you influence?

Valued data   Not solely the existence, but also the strength of a link can be evaluated. These evaluations produce a valued network. If a flow of information or products circulates among the actors, we also talk about flow measurements. There are a number of ways of collecting this type of data.

The time an interaction takes, for example, can be included in a direct observation of the interaction. Certain secondary data can enable us to assess the strength of a link. If we return to the example of links between boards of directors, the number of directors or the length of time they are on the board can both be good indicators. The following example illustrates another way that secondary data can be used to evaluate the strength of links.

Using Valued Structural Data

Seungwha (1996) looks at the effect that cooperative relationships between investment banks have on their performance. His structural data was taken mainly from the 'Investment Dealers' Digest' which, whenever new shares are issued, provides the name of the overseeing bank, the names of the banks forming the syndicate, and the sales figures. This information enabled a matrix of the exchanges between the 98 banks included in the study to be established. The performance of the relationships was assessed through the strength of the link between two banks and the relational strategy used by each bank. The strength of the link between two banks was measured by the number of exchanges that occurred between these two banks over the period of the study. The authors used the structural data to identify the type of relational strategy adopted by each of the banks to increase the number of operations they handled. Certain banks adopted an expansive strategy, that is, they sought to increase the number of partners with whom they had a relationship. There were numerous links in their network, but they were weak. Other banks did the opposite: adopting a popularity strategy, they sought to increase the number of contracts they had with the same partners. They had fewer, but stronger links. The study concludes that an expansive strategy improves long-term profitability and a popularity strategy lessens it.

In the many cases in which surveys or interviews are used, researchers must include a specific measurement in their planning to evaluate the strength of relational links. They can do this in two ways. They can either introduce a scale for each relationship, or they can classify individuals in order of the strength of the relationship. The use of scales makes the survey or interview much more cumbersome, but does enable exact evaluation of the links. Likert scales are most commonly used, with five or seven levels ranging, for example, from 'very frequent' to 'very infrequent' (for more information on scales, see Chapter 9). It is easier to ask respondents to cite actors in an order based on the strength of the relationship, although the information obtained is less precise. In this case, the researcher could use several name generators, and take as the relationship's value the number of times an individual cites another individual among their n first choices.

Biases   To conclude this part of the chapter, we will now examine the different types of biases researchers may face during data collection.

First, there is associative bias. Associative bias occurs in the responses if the individuals who are cited successively are more likely to belong to the same social context than individuals who have not been cited successively. Such a bias can alter the list of units cited and, therefore, the final network. Research has been carried out recently which compares collection techniques to show that this type of bias exists (see, for example, Brewer, 1997). Burt (1997) recommends the parallel use of several redundant generators (that is, relating to relationships of a similar nature). This redundancy can enable respondents to mention a different name, which can in turn prompt them to recall other names.

Another problem researchers face is the non-reciprocity of responses among members of the network. If A cites B for a given relationship, B should, in principle, cite A. For example, if A indicates that he or she has worked with B, B should say that he or she has worked with A. Non-reciprocity of responses can be related to a difference in cognitive perception between the respondents (Carley and Krackhardt, 1996). Researchers must determine in advance a fixed decision-making rule for dealing with such non-reciprocity of data. They might, for example, decide to eliminate any non-reciprocal links.

The question also arises of the symmetry of the relationships between individuals. One might expect, for example, that links relating to esteem should be symmetrical. If A esteems B, one might assume that B esteems A. Other relationships, like links relating to giving advice or lending money, are not necessarily reciprocal. It is, however, risky to assume, without verification, that a relationship is symmetrical. Carley and Krackhardt (1996) show that friendship is not a symmetrical relationship.

2.2 Sampling: determining the boundaries and openness of a network

Choosing which individuals to include and setting network boundaries is a delicate area in network analysis. It is very rare for a network to present clearly demarcated natural boundaries. Networks make light of the formal boundaries we try to impose on organizations (structures, flow charts, job definitions, localization, etc.). Consequently, there is bound to be a certain degree of subjectivity involved when researchers delimit the network they are analyzing. Demarcation of the area being studied is all the more important because of the very strong influence this has on the results of the quantitative analyses being conducted (Doreian and Woodard, 1994). Moreover, research into the 'small world' phenomenon shows that it is possible, on average, to connect two people chosen at random anywhere in the world by a chain of six links – or six degrees. It is clear, therefore, that if a network is not controlled, it very quickly leads us outside any organizational logic.

For their data to be of any real use, researchers must restrict themselves to a relatively limited field of investigation and obtain the agreement of all (or almost all) of the individuals who enter within this field. While researchers can begin their investigations without having their field of study written in stone, they do have to determine its boundaries sufficiently early on.

According to Laumann et al. (1983), it is possible to specify the boundaries of a network while using either a realist or a nominalist approach. In a realist approach, the researcher adopts the actors' point of view, and when taking a nominalist approach the researcher adopts certain formal criteria in advance (for example, taking only the first three people cited into account). In both cases, the boundary can be defined in terms of the actors themselves, the relationships between them, or their participation in an activity (a meeting, for example). As a general rule, the research question should serve as a guide in defining the boundaries.

Researchers sometimes need to go beyond this way of thinking about boundaries to take into account the openness of networks. Networks are often analyzed as if they are closed – the actors are considered to be a closed group. However, in many situations this presupposition poses problems.

Doreian and Woodard (1994) propose a systematic process that enables researchers to control sample snowballing. Their method enables researchers to build a sample during the course of their research and to avoid closing off the boundaries of the networks too early, while keeping a check on the individuals included in the network. The first stage consists of obtaining a list of actors included in the network, using strict realist criteria. Those on the list are then asked about the other actors who are essential to their network. Of these new actors, the researcher includes only those who meet a nominalist criterion (for example, taking into account the first three actors cited) – the strictness of the criterion used is determined by the researcher. This criterion is used until no new actors can be included in the network. It is the control the researcher has on the strictness of the nominalist criterion used that enables researchers to halt any snowballing of the sample, and which sets the limits of the network while taking its openness into account from the start.

SECTION 2   ANALYSIS METHODS

Once researchers have collected sociometric data (data that measures links between individuals), and so know which actors have links with which other actors, they then need to reconstitute the network, or networks, of actors before they can conduct a global network analysis (or analyses). The methods of analysis fall into two main categories. In the first, the researcher's aim is to identify homogenous groups within the network. In the second, the focus is on individual particularities and the researcher concentrates on each actor's position within the network.

1. Formalizing Data, and Initial Analyses

1.1 From adjacency matrix to sociogram

In most cases, computer software is used to process data. The first step is to put the data into the form of a matrix. A matrix is produced for each type of relationship (supervision, work, friendship, influences, financial flow, flow of materials, etc.). The matrix can then be used to obtain a graphic representation.

To construct an adjacency matrix, all of the actors involved are listed along both the columns and the rows of the matrix. If individual A has a relationship with individual B, a number 1 is placed in the corresponding space at the intersection of line *a* and column *b*. If the relationship is directed, its direction must be taken into account. For example, the researcher might study simply the fact that individual A worked with B during the previous three months, or they may study whether A supervised the activity of individual B during this period. In the first case, the working relationship is not directed. A and B worked together and the adjacency matrix is, therefore, symmetrical. The number 1 is placed at the intersection of line *a* and column *b* and at the intersection of line *b* and column *a*. In the case of the network of supervision, however, the relationship is directed. While A supervises B, B does not necessarily supervise A. The number 1 is simply placed at the intersection of line *a* and column *b* and one obtains a non-symmetrical adjacency matrix.

Once the adjacency matrix has been constructed, it can be represented in the form of a graph. The graph obtained in this way is a sociogram. Figure 14.1

Adjacency matrix

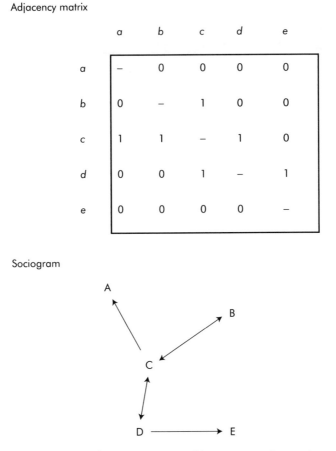

Sociogram

Figure 14.1 *An adjacency matrix and its corresponding sociogram*

gives an example of an adjacency matrix for a directed network, and its corresponding sociogram.

Sociograms enable us to make a certain number of summary interpretations, and can be sufficient for analyzing simple networks. In the example of Figure 14.1, we can immediately identify C as an important actor. If the relationship being studied is one of advice, C is probably an expert. If it is a supervision relationship, C is probably a departmental head. However, once the size of the networks involved increases, visual interpretation of the graph becomes particularly difficult. It also becomes hazardous in the sense that the choices made in arranging the elements of the graph have a strong influence on the way it can be interpreted. Researchers need standardized tools that enable systematic analysis.

1.2 General analyses

In analyzing the general structure of a network, indicators can help researchers to assess the overall reality of the structure of the relationships between individuals.

As an example of how indicators can be used, we present below the two most frequently used indicators: density and multiplexity. We will then show how a number of networks can be compared.

Density of a network   In any given network, density corresponds to the relationship between the number of existing links and the number of possible links. By existing links we mean those that the researcher has been able to reveal. Possible links refer to all the links that could have existed, taking into account the number of individuals involved. Thus, for n individuals, there are $n(n-1)/2$ possible links.

The density measurement does not say very much in itself. The researcher can simply make a subjective judgement on the value obtained. However, density becomes particularly interesting if we wish to compare different groups of individuals or different organizations.

To give an example, the communication network in Production Unit A of an organization may be more dense than that in Production Unit B. If we hypothesize that the density of the communication network is a factor of performance, we can conclude, from a descriptive viewpoint, that Unit A performs better than Unit B. We could also test this hypothesis by seeing if there is a link between the density of a department's communications network and the evaluation that members of upper management make of that department's performance.

Network multiplexity   Multiplexity relates to the existence of different kinds of links between individuals. Let us take the example of the relationships within a group of company directors. Between the directors of two companies there can exist relationships of trust, friendship or even guidance. The more dimensions the relationship involves, the more it is said to be multiplex. If n is the number of different links existing between the units being studied (individuals, companies, etc.) and p is the number of units cited as being linked, the degree of multiplexity is the relationship n/p. This general indicator requires delicate handling. It does not take into account the distribution of multiplexity within the network – two networks can have the same degree of multiplexity but very different structures. For example, similar multiplexity is obtained in the two following cases. In the first case, a minority of individuals have very multiplex links (that is, involving direction, influence, assistance and advice) while the others have simple links. In the second case, most of the individuals have just two kinds of link (for example, assistance and advice).

Other indices   It is possible to compare networks using other means than general indices that measure either density or multiplexity. Researchers can assess how much overlap there is between the networks. Software packages can calculate the number of common links between adjacency matrices. Random networks can be generated and compared to the empirical data. This comparison enables researchers to assess the specific nature of the data they collect: does the network obtained have a direction (an underlying order) or does it present the same characteristics as a network constructed 'by chance'? Software packages can also carry out statistical internetwork analyses. Ucinet IV, for example, can analyze the correlation between two different networks. This tool can be used to test whether it is relevant to use relationships about which there is available information to approximate relationships that are difficult to evaluate. For example, is it relevant, in a given context, to evaluate the trust between a network's units (information that is difficult to collect on a wide scale) from the flow of information between them? If, when using a test sample, we notice that the network of trust is strongly correlated with the telephone communications network (taken as a proxy for information flow), then the answer is yes.

2. Grouping Methods

Analyzing the general structure of a network provides useful initial information, but researchers quite often need to go beyond this type of analysis. There are a series of methods available that enable researchers to group together individuals within a network. Using these methods, they can identify collective actors, according to an essential grouping principle: cohesion. A second principle, that of equivalence, is used to group together individuals who occupy similar positions within the network.

2.1 Strongly cohesive groups

The principle of cohesion involves grouping together individuals within a network on the basis of them being 'close' to each other – of distinguishing subgroups by their strong density. Research into subgroups within a network corresponds in general terms to a desire to reveal the existence of 'collective' actors (for example, a dominant coalition) within an organization, and to study how the relationships between these actors are structured.

A 'collective' actor is often represented in the world of networks by a clique – a set of individuals who are all interconnected. In the example below we present a sociogram of cliques. Within a clique, links are direct (all the individuals are linked to each other, without an intermediary). Generally, for a clique to exist at all, all the individuals must be connected by strong links. This means that if the relationship is directed, the links must go in both directions (from A towards B and from B to A). However, it is possible to define subgroups using indirect links. This is the case when one reveals an *n*-clique. In an *n*-clique, all the individuals are connected by a number of links that is less than *n*. This means that the link between two individuals in the *n*-clique passes at most by $(n-1)$ individuals. *N*-cliques enable researchers to find organizational subgroups using criteria that are less strict than those governing cliques. Another approach consists of disregarding the direction of a directed relationship, in which case weak components are obtained. However, neither the *n*-clique nor the clique of weak components are really satisfactory. They are rarely meaningful in organizational reality. The criteria used actually make it difficult to interpret the groups that are constituted. How, for example, can a researcher constitute a group while disregarding the direction of a supervision relationship? Or how can a group be defined around the concept of links that are longer than 1 (the length being defined by the number of links, or degrees, separating two units)?

Cliques, a Simple Grouping Criteria

The sociogram in Figure 14.2 shows a network in which there are two cliques, one comprising three individuals (A, B and C) and one of four individuals (D, E, F and G). The two cliques constitute collective actors within the network (A, B, C, D, E, F and G).

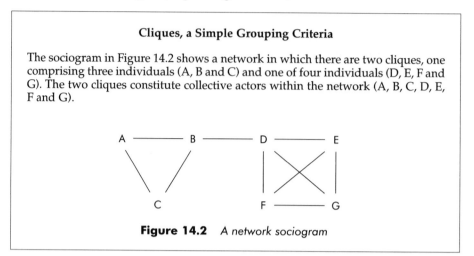

Figure 14.2   *A network sociogram*

However, there is a real need to find 'collective actors' within networks using more flexible criteria than those of the clique (direct and strong links) and without resorting to simplistic solutions like those of *n*-cliques or weak components (Frank, 1995).

The most commonly used software packages offer one solution to this, by either establishing criteria about the minimum number of interactions each actor must have with the other actors in the group, or by fixing a maximal value for the number of missing interactions. Another, similar, criterion involves establishing how many individuals must be removed from the group for its members to become disconnected (Borgatti et al., 1992). In this way the researcher isolates those blocs in the matrix that necessitate the removal of *n* individuals to become disconnected.

Other commonly used criteria include co-membership of cliques. The fact that two individuals belong to a significant number of the same cliques is considered to be an indication of their social closeness. The criterion of co-membership of cliques, or any other closeness criterion, can be applied systematically by means of ascendant algorithms (grouping begins from individual) or descendant algorithms (starting from the whole of the network which is then subdivided). These algorithms can vary in their degree of sophistication. Software packages offer solutions using these criteria and the appropriate algorithms in different ways. Some of the procedures enable this type of grouping to be effected for valued graphs.

When using this type of grouping method, a common problem is the frequent need to fix limits for the criteria used. Limits should be fixed according to the context, without referring to any objective criteria. Moreover, using limits does not always enable groups to be formed without overlap (Frank, 1995). It may be preferable to choose methods that involve fixing a limit that corresponds to the data used rather than those that require an arbitrary limit.

With all these methods, the principle is to maximize the intra-group interactions and minimize those that are intergroup. A vast range of possibilities is available to the researcher – it is not possible for us to describe here all the procedures that exist in the literature. However, it seems that, in practice, there are relatively few procedures that can be used for any particular type of data. In fact, restrictions are frequently made on the type of data that can be used for each of the procedures proposed by software packages. For example, the procedure presented below is suitable for a valued network, but not for a directed graph.

2.2 Equivalence classes

Researchers can also try to group together individuals that have the same kind of links with other members of the network. This is called equivalence. However, the members of an equivalence class are not necessarily linked to each other. The example below presents a study using the notion of structural equivalence.

**Reducing the Differences of Opinion among Members
of an Equivalence Class**

Friedkin and Johnsen (1997) were interested in how the effects of influence within a network lead to divergences in the opinions of its members. They grouped together individuals in an equivalence class and evaluated the way in which their opinions converged. The authors found that if the actors belonged to the same equivalence class, the differences in their opinions was reduced. However, while this phenomenon of reduced divergence may occur if the individuals are not in the same equivalence class, this was not always found to be the case.

Grouping by equivalence classes can be used to take into account the concept of social role and status. If we take the example of the different positions held within a company, we can suppose that each worker has similar relationships with individuals in other classes (executives, senior managers, floor managers, etc.). Grouping by equivalence classes allows us to identify classes of individuals who play the same role, independently of the one formally defined by their status and job description.

The main point of this process is to create classes that are defined not in themselves, but according to the relationship that links their members to other individuals. We can distinguish between structural, regular and automorphic equivalence.

Structural equivalence occurs when all the elements of one class have relationships with all the members of another class. In the army, for example, all the subordinates must show respect for their superiors.

Regular equivalence corresponds to the situation in which, if a member of class 1 is linked to a member of class 2, all the members of class 1 must have a

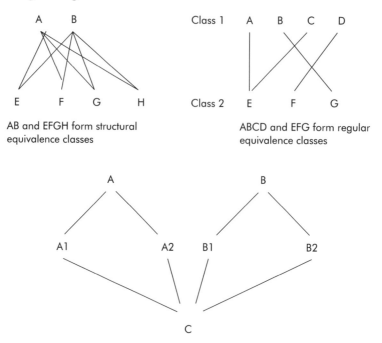

AB and EFGH form structural
equivalence classes

ABCD and EFG form regular
equivalence classes

(A, B), (A1, A2, B1, B2) and C form automorphic equivalence classes

Figure 14.3   *The three types of equivalence*

link with at least one member of class 2, and all the members of class 2 must have a link with at least one member of class 1. In a factory, for example, each supervisor is in charge of at least one worker and each worker is under the charge of at least one supervisor.

Two individuals belong to the same automorphic equivalence class if it is possible to switch their positions in the network around and reconstitute a network that is isomorphic to the original – that is, with exactly the same form as the initial network. This situation arises when the networks of two actors are exactly symmetrical. One can imagine, for example, two project managers in a company finding themselves in a situation of automorphic equivalence.

It seems clear that the type of equivalence sought depends directly on the problem being studied and the research question. Figure 14.3 illustrates structural, regular and automorphic equivalence.

In reality, it is rare to find classes that correspond precisely to any one of these three types of equivalence, and the strict application of one of the three definitions only rarely results in classes that can be interpreted in terms of social roles. It is generally more relevant to use one of the many statistical approximation procedures that software programs offer, and we will now give an overview of these.

A number of these procedures are designed to respect the logic of structural equivalence. This postulates that members of a single class within a network all have exactly the same links with the other actors in the network. This means that the adjacency matrix rows for these actors will be identical. The statistical approximation methods most often used in this case consist of grouping actors that resemble each other the most into one class. To do this, the closeness of the individuals is evaluated – by calculating, for example, a Euclidean distance, a correlation coefficient, or the number of common links shared by rows of the adjacency matrix. Once this has been achieved, the individuals are put into groups with the aid of a classification method (see Chapter 13 for a discussion of classification methods). This type of process can be applied to valued graphs or used when researching multiplex relationships.

Other algorithmic procedures aim to approach regular equivalence. They proceed by making successive comparisons of all the pairs of individuals. The researcher compares each pair of individuals with all the other pairs in the network and then evaluates whether they can be placed in the same equivalence class. These comparisons serve as a basis for calculating an index showing the closeness between pairs. A classification method can then be used.

There are also several ways of grouping together individuals according to the principles of automorphic equivalence. For example, it is possible to use geodesic equivalence to approximate automorphic equivalence. The geodesic path is the shortest path between two individuals. It is represented by its length (the number of links separating two units). Geodesic approximation involves calculating the length of the geodesic paths that link each individual to each of the other individuals in the network. Two individuals are considered to be equivalent if they present the same types of geodesic path; for example, if they are both linked to two individuals by a path of length 1, to three others by a path of length 2, etc.

Researchers are advised to be particularly careful when deciding upon the methods they will use to approach equivalence. While many methods can be used with valued graphs, these may not always be applicable to non-valued graphs.

3. Methods for Demonstrating the Notion of Centrality

Another aim of network analysis is to concentrate on particular actors and establish the role that their structural position permits them to play within the organization.

Literature on networks often focuses on individuals in central positions. We can generally suppose that the actors who play a key role within the network are able to draw a certain advantage from it. There are many ways of defining centrality and the corresponding algorithms vary in their degree of sophistication.

Freeman (1979) draws a distinction between centrality of degree, of closeness and of 'betweenness'.

Centrality of degree   Centrality of degree corresponds to the number of connections an individual has. Individuals are considered to be central if they are strongly connected to other members of the network. In other words, the centrality of degree index for each individual A is equal to the number of direct relationships he or she has. This index is purely local. It depends neither on the characteristics of the network as a whole, nor on the characteristics of the other individuals to which individual A is linked. However, an individual who has numerous links with marginal individuals is much less central than an individual whose links are with individuals who are themselves central. To resolve this difficulty, an index of relative or normed centrality is calculated for each individual, by dividing the absolute centrality scores by the maximal centrality possible for the graph. This concept is explained below.

Index of an Individual's Normed Centrality

In studying why certain forms of organizations have a capacity to react to environmental change, a researcher first determined each operational unit's position within the general organization. He found the organization to be made up of multiple related networks, and that certain units seemed to be protected from modifications to their environment. The researcher's aim was to understand whether the central position of these units within the network played a role in this. He decided to calculate the indicator of maximal centrality of degree, CDmax. The maximal centrality of degree of an entity corresponds to the situation best illustrate by the center of a star – it is the maximum number of entities to which it can possibly be connected. If n is the number of entities in the network, then CDmax $= n - 1$.

The index of centrality of normed degree of an entity i (CNDIi) is obtained by dividing the absolute centrality of degree of the entity CDi by the maximal

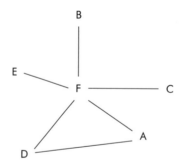

Figure 14.4   *The studied network*

centrality: CNDIi = CDi/CDmax. The result is a percentage, with 0 corresponding to an isolated point and 1 to the center of a star.

In the case of the studied network, represented in Figure 14.4, the index of normed centrality is 1 for individual F, 0.4 for A and D and 0.2 for the other actors: B, C and E.

F, which was one of the units sheltered from environmental variation, does, in fact, hold a central position, which confirms the researcher's intuition.

Centrality of closeness   Centrality of closeness is an assessment of an individual's centrality through an evaluation of their closeness to all the other individuals in a network. It is a more global measurement, which takes into account not only the connections individuals have with their immediate neighbors, but also their closeness to all the other members of the network.

One measurement used is the sum of the geodesic distances linking one point to all the other points of the graph. Geodesic distance is the shortest path linking two individuals on a graph. The centrality of an individual can be measured by comparing its total geodesic distance from other individuals with that of other actors in the network – the smaller the figure, the greater the individual's centrality. As we demonstrate below, other measurements based on the same principle have been also been proposed.

Measuring Centrality of Closeness

The index of centrality of closeness can be written in the following form:

$$C_{Api}^{-1} = \Sigma\, j = 1 ..n\ dij$$

where dij is the geodesic distance between individual i and individual j.

One can also use an index of relative closeness ($C - 1Npi$) by comparing the index of centrality relative to the maximal centrality, which is equal to $Cmax = n - 1$. This index is expressed as follows:

$$C_{Npi}^{-1} = C_{Api}^{-1} \Big/ n - 1$$

$$\text{or } C_{Npi} = n - 1 \Big/ C_{Api}^{-1}$$

where C_{NPi} is an index of normed relative closeness: i.e. a percentage that varies between 0 and 1.

If we return to the study into why certain forms of organizations have a capacity to react to environmental change, we can calculate a closeness index equal to 5 for F, 8 for A and D, and 9 for the other individuals. Calculation of the index of relative closeness gives 1 for F, 5/8 for A and D and 5/9 for the other individuals.

Centrality of 'betweenness'   Evaluation of centrality can also be based on the individual's role as a 'go-between'. Freeman (1979) proposed that an individual may be only slightly connected to others (weak centrality of degree), but prove to be an essential intermediary in exchanges. An individual's *'betweenness'* *vis-à-vis* two other people is defined by the frequency with which he or she appears on the geodesic path or paths (that is, of minimal length) linking the two others. The values of the centrality index of *'betweenness'* vary between 0 and 1, and can be compared between different networks.

Index of Centrality of *'Betweenness'*

If one assumes that two individuals, *j* and *k*, are indifferent to the geodesic used, the probability that they will use any particular one is equal to $1/gjk$ (gjk being the number of geodesics joining *j* and *k*). The capacity of an individual *i* to control communication between *j* and *k* can be defined by the probability bjk (*i*) that *i* will position himself or herself on this random geodesic between *j* and *k*.

This probability is dependant on how many of the geodesics linking j and k contain i, which we denote by gjk (i). This is equal to: bjk $(i) = gjk$ $(i)/gjk$. The absolute centrality of '*betweenness*' of individual i is calculated by adding up his or her intermediarities for all the pairs of points on the graph:

$$C_{A/i} = \sum_{nj} \sum_{nk} b_{jk} (i)$$

where $j \neq k \neq i$
and $n =$ the number of individuals.

Other measurements of centrality   As Hage and Harary (1995) have shown, models of centrality using the concepts of centrality of degree, closeness and '*betweenness*', have been used in many research works; studying power in informal exchange networks (Hage and Harary, 1983) and social stratification in commercial networks (Hunt, 1988; Irwin, 1983; Milicic, 1993). Nonetheless, the authors also proposed supplementary measures.

In the case of a network where each individual is linked to at least one other individual, Hage and Harary (1995) propose introducing the idea of eccentricity. By *eccentricity*, the two authors mean the maximal distance that separates a given individual from other individuals. Using the notion of eccentricity, one can calculate the diameter of a network, which is equal to the maximal *eccentricity* existing within it. Similarly, the notion of radius is understood as the minimal *eccentricity*. An individual is, therefore, central if his or her *eccentricity* is equal to the radius of the network. Another way of measuring centrality was proposed by Bonacich (1987).

For comparative purposes, the researcher needs to be in a position to judge the network's overall centralization. There is a marked difference between being a unit at the center of a decentralized network and one at the center of a centralized network. When judging the network as a whole, therefore, we talk about its centralization. This indicator always varies between 0 and 1, and indicates the degree to which the maximal centrality is greater than the centrality of all the other points. When it equals 0, all the centralities are equal. When it equals 1, one point dominates the centralization of the network. This situation corresponds to a star.

CONCLUSION

Network analysis groups together many different data processing methods. These methods have been refined since the early developments of sociometry, and they continue to be improved – with particular impetus coming from advances in graph theory. In the field of management, the small amount of research that does use network analysis is still far from exploiting all its possibilities. All network analysis methods (including cohesion, which comes within the structuralist paradigm) offer us a real opportunity to change our perspective. We can begin to consider reality in terms of the links between entities. Recent moves to take the dynamics of networks into account have further increased the potential of network analysis.

The fact that network analysis is rarely used in management when it is so widespread in sociology can no doubt be explained by the relative division that exists between these two disciplines, and by the complexity of some of the procedures and tools involved. Mathematical or statistical modeling is often complex, and choosing analysis tools can be equally complicated. However, methods continue to be developed both at the level of the collection and the analysis of data, and our mastery and understanding of the tools used is growing. All this helps to make network analysis a very rich ensemble of methods that can be used in many different types of research, whether the researcher is studying process or content, or is taking an inductive or hypothetico-deductive approach.

FURTHER READING

Ossowski, S., *Class Structure in the Social Consciousness*, London: Routledge and Kegan Paul, 1963.

Scott, J., *Social Network Analysis: A Handbook*, London: Sage, 1991.

Software Packages

Borgatti, S.P., Everett, M. and Freeman, L.C., 'Ucinet IV', Columbia: Analytic Technologies.

Burt, R.S., 'Structure', Center for Social Science, Columbia University.

Krackart, D., Blythe, J. and McGrath C., 'KrackPlot', Columbia: Analytic Technologies.

Richards, W.D., 'Negopy'. Information can be found at the following Internet address: http://www.sfu.ca/~richards

Richards, W.D., 'Multinet'. Information can be found at the following Internet address: http://www.sfu.ca/~richards

15

LONGITUDINAL ANALYSES

Bernard Forgues and Isabelle Vandangeon-Derumez

Outline

This chapter examines longitudinal analyses. The first section introduces these analyses, emphasizing the importance of the conception of time, and raising preliminary questions that must be considered by the researcher. The second and third sections present a number of quantitative and qualitative methods for dealing with longitudinal data.

Longitudinal analyses study the development of a phenomenon over the course of time. These developments can concern organizations, individuals, concepts or variables; they are the origin of the data to be analyzed. A number of quantitative methods – such as regressions over time – are included in this class of analyses, as are various qualitative methods – individual case studies, for example. However, while these analyses are numerous and diverse, they do share common characteristics, particularly in their objectives and the data collection methods they use.

Longitudinal analyses are becoming ever more common in management research (Bergh, 1993) and this trend is expected to continue (Hitt et al., 1998).

SECTION 1 FUNDAMENTALS OF LONGITUDINAL ANALYSES

1. Definition and Role of Time

Longitudinal analyses form a group of analyses focusing on the study of phenomena over the course of time. Longitudinal analyses are often contrasted with cross-sectional studies, by arguing that the data collected for longitudinal analyses relate to at least two distinct points in time, while for cross-sectional studies data are collected in relation to a distinct moment. This distinction, while ostensibly correct, does however raise some problems, and therefore needs to be refined.

First, it should be noted that this dichotomy is only a simplification of a more complex phenomenon. Thus, a *pure* cross-sectional analysis would require the data to be collected at one particular moment, or at least over a period sufficiently short to be considered as such. However, in management, data collection often extends over a relatively long period, frequently lasting for several months. We then must question whether this is still a cross-sectional collection. Similarly, this makes it necessary to explain how the time that has elapsed might have an impact on the study. Take, for example, a research study that seeks to investigate the perception two different managers in the same company have of a past investment. If a week passes between interviewing one manager and interviewing the second, we would wonder whether this time lapse had had an impact on the study or not – that is, whether the responses of the second manager would have been the same a week earlier. It is quite possible that during the week something might have happened to change her perception.

Drawing from Menard's (1991) definition, we can recognize the following three characteristics:

1   the data relate to at least two distinct periods;
2   the subjects are identical or at least comparable from one period to the next;
3   the analysis consists basically in comparing data between (or over the course of) two distinct time periods, or in retracing the observed evolution.

Depending on the research, time may be attributed an important role or it may be relegated to a secondary level. At the extremes of this continuum we would find studies strongly influenced by the time factor, and studies of the development of a phenomenon without particular reference to time. It is therefore essential that researchers consider the significance they wish to attribute to time in their project, to ensure that the research design will enable the research question to be answered.

When time is an important factor in the research, it might be considered in terms of either duration or chronology. Duration corresponds to an interval between two points in time, and is measured in terms of the subject at hand. According to the phenomenon being studied, duration may be expressed in seconds, hours, days, years, etc. For example, it could concern the duration of the development of an innovation, or the time lapse between a takeover bid and a restructuring. Chronology, however, is external to the subject of the study, existing outside the research. Chronology is used to determine the order of occurrence of events, and in management research it is generally expressed by dates.

Finally, another possible use of time is in terms of cohorts. The concept of cohorts is drawn from demographics, where a cohort refers to a group of individuals born at the same period (birth cohort). Generalizing from this we can define a cohort as a group of observations having experienced the same event on a particular date. Determining a cohort in a research project allows researchers to make multiple comparisons. We can measure the differences between cohorts, or the evolution of a cohort. Table 15.1 presents a summary of these different possibilities.

Table 15.1 *Time in longitudinal research*

Conception of time	Impact	Examples
Used only to classify observations	Time is of secondary importance. The researcher is carrying out a longitudinal study and therefore studies a phenomenon across time, but without attributing any special significance to time. Time passes, but that is all.	Brown and Eisenhardt (1997) study continuous change in six firms in the computer industry without focusing on the duration or time period concerned.
An important variable, operationalized in the form of duration	Time is a key element to the research. The period between different events has to be carefully measured.	Taylor et al. (1996) examine whether the length of general managers' tenure in their current job has an impact on their commitment and turnover.
An important variable operationalized in chronological form	Time is an important variable but has a starting point that is common to all the observations, this is generally the date.	Pelz (1985) studies the sequence of innovation processes, focusing on the order of occurrence of the different stages.
Used to classify individuals into cohorts for purposes of comparison	Time is an important variable used to classify observations into cohorts – i.e., groups having experienced a common event on a particular date.	Shaver et al. (1997) test the effect of experience on the survival of a foreign direct investment, comparing two cohorts of companies, established according to whether or not they had a presence in the USA in 1986.

2. Preliminary Questions

A researcher who decides to undertake longitudinal research is confronted with two major questions: what period of time should be covered by the study, and how many points in time should data be collected on over this time period? While the answer to the first question depends on the research question, the second question is linked to the importance the research places on time.

2.1 Analysis period

Determining the analysis period requires fixing the limits of the time interval in which data are to be gathered. In setting these limits several elements must be considered.

The first element is the research question. This provides us with the information needed to determine the phenomenon that is to be studied, and thus to determine the study period. It is always up to researchers themselves to set the time limits of their studies, while ensuring that the data they collect will enable them to answer their research question.

The researcher can also question the continuity of the phenomenon being studied: is it regarded as a permanent element in the life of an organization or is it only temporary? To fully understand this distinction let us look at the topic of change. In some studies, change is considered as forming an integral part of the life of an organization (a permanent phenomenon). Conversely, when change is seen as a particular event (a temporary phenomenon) it is studied over a limited period in the evolution of an organization. This period could be extended, depending on the research question, from the realization of the necessity for change to the stabilization of an organization after that change has been implemented.

2.2 Data collection points

Data collection points refer to moments in the life of the phenomenon for which data are to be collected. They do not necessarily coincide with the moments the researcher collects data. For example, the data may be collected on a single occasion, some time after the event, when the phenomenon has passed completely.

Given that a study qualifies as longitudinal on the basis of having two or more data collection points, the problem arises as to whether it must be limited to those two points, or whether this number should be increased. In the latter case, then the time interval separating them needs to be determined.

Limiting data collection to two points in time comes down to carrying out a study using a pre-test, post-test design. The choice of collection points can therefore have a strong impact on the results (Rogosa, 1988). Furthermore, this type of research does not enable the process of the phenomenon's evolution to be studied, that is, what happens between what we observe 'before' and what we observe 'after'? If one wants to focus on analyzing a process, it is therefore appropriate to increase the number of data collection points.

When researchers increase the number of data collection points, however, they are still confronted with the problem of how much time should separate these various points. To determine this time interval they once again need to consider the place of time in longitudinal research. There are three possible scenarios here:

- When time is not important, collection intervals depend on the evolution of the phenomenon being studied. In this case these intervals are irregular and vary according to the successive states of the phenomenon or the occurrence of events affecting this phenomenon.
- When time (in terms of duration) is a key element in the research, the period that elapses between two events is measured by predefined units: hours, days, years, etc. In this case data must be collected regularly, respecting this period.
- When time (in terms of chronology) is important, it has a starting point that is common to all the observations (usually a date). In theory, continuous data collection is necessary so as to be able to note the dates each event occurs (other dates correspond to non-occurrences). These occurrences can then be accurately positioned in the context of time. In practice this type of collection can be difficult to implement, in which case the researcher can gather information within the context of regular periods, and reconstitute the chronology of the events afterwards.

There is a fourth case, however, although this is transversal to the three preceding case scenarios. Time can be used to class individuals into cohorts – groups of individuals (or, more generally, of observations) that experienced a common event on a particular date. Once a cohort has been identified, the position of time can vary according to the research question, as before.

Table 15.2 summarizes longitudinal research designs according to the above case scenarios.

3. Problems Related to Data Collection

Researchers deciding to carry out longitudinal research can choose between:

- collecting data retrospectively, and therefore studying a past phenomenon
- collecting data in real time, on a phenomenon that may occur or on a phenomenon as it occurs.

3.1 Problems related to retrospective data collection

Retrospective studies (concerning a past phenomenon) draw upon archived secondary data and/or primary data retracing the evolution of a phenomenon after the events (mainly retrospective interviews).

Table 15.2   *The research question and longitudinal designs*

Research question	Issues in longitudinal design
Study of a permanent phenomenon in the life of an organization	Continuous data collection, going from the birth of an organization until its demise
Study of an isolated phenomenon that is independent of the life of an organization	Data collection over a relatively short period that is delimited in time
Study of the effect of an event on a phenomenon ('pre-test, post-test' research)	Two data collection points
Study of a process	Several data collection points
Research in which time is considered to be important in terms of chronology	Data collected continuously
Research in which time is considered to be important in terms of its duration	Data collected at regular intervals
Research in which time is not considered to be important	Data can be collected at irregular time intervals

The secondary data that is necessary for retrospective research raise two types of problems: accessibility and validity. In its most acute form, the problem of accessibility can make it absolutely impossible for the researcher to obtain the information required for the research. This information might not exist, not have been preserved, be impossible to find, or be refused (explicitly or implicitly). The question of the validity of documents, when they can be obtained, also arises. The original purpose of the document is one important initial consideration, as biases, intentional or not, might have been introduced into it by its author. Documents should also be considered in the context in which they were written. The organization of a company may have been different, the way in which certain indices were calculated could have changed – factors such as these make comparisons precarious.

Primary data is generally in the form of retrospective interviews, which can be influenced by two important biases: faulty memory and rationalization after the fact. By faulty memory we mean that the person questioned may not remember certain events, either intentionally (he or she does not want to remember) or unintentionally (the phenomenon relates to an unremarkable event which he or she has forgotten). Rationalization too may be either intentional (a desire to present things in a positive light) or not (an unconscious 'tidying up'). To add to the problem, these two biases are not mutually exclusive. Memory lapses and rationalization have created doubt about using retrospective interviews (Golden, 1992), although their supposed limitations have been hotly debated. Miller et al. (1997) argue that the validity of retrospective interviews relies above all on the instrument used to gather the data.

There are several ways researchers can limit the effects of these biases. To limit errors resulting from memory lapses the following methods are recommended:

- If the research question permits, interviews can focus on events that are relatively memorable for the people being questioned, or interviewees can be selected according to their degree of involvement in the phenomenon being studied (Glick et al., 1990).

- Information given in different interviews can be compared, or secondary data can be used to verify it (Yin, 1990).
- A non-directive interview method can be used, in which interviewees are not pushed to answer if they don't remember (Miller et al., 1997).
- Each interview can be transcribed or recorded, so that interviewees can add to their initial statements.

Several strategies can be employed to limit rationalization after the fact:

- Interviewees can be asked to list events chronologically before they are asked to establish causal connections between them.
- Information given in different interviews can be compared.
- Dates of events can be verified through secondary sources.

3.2 Problems related to collecting longitudinal data in real time

The collection of data in real time consists in studying a phenomenon at the same time as it is happening.

As the collection of data in real time extends over a given period, the problem arises of how to interpret any changes or developments that may be observed. Should they be attributed to the phenomenon itself or to the measuring instrument used (in collecting and analyzing the data)? When a measuring instrument is used on successive occasions there is a risk of it falsifying the observations. To avoid such a bias administration conditions must not vary from one period to another. It is incumbent on the researcher to control external variables that might influence responses to the questions. These variables include, for example, the person who administers the survey, external events that may occur between two collection points, and the context in which the survey is administered.

A second source of bias emerges when the first wave of data collection leads to the introduction of new hypotheses, or to the modification of existing ones. In extreme cases the original hypotheses may be brought into question between two successive rounds of data collection. In this situation the researcher has no choice but to take these new hypotheses into account, while ensuring that the data collected before the initial hypotheses were modified as appropriate to the new questions that have been raised. If this is not the case, the information will not be included in the study.

3.3 General problems related to collecting longitudinal data

Longitudinal research also presents the more general problem of the evolution of the variables used to explain the successive modifications of a phenomenon

(Menard, 1991). Explanatory variables are prone to variation between the time they are collected and the time the phenomenon occurs. If the impact of such an evolution might falsify the results of the study, the researcher will have to change the data collection strategies used or use an analysis taking this into account. For example, data collection could instead be spaced out over the period of the study.

Longitudinal studies that involve several organizations face the problem of having to take the life cycles of these organizations into consideration (Kimberly, 1976). Comparative studies, for instance, would be best carried out using data from comparable periods in the organizations' life cycles.

SECTION 2   QUANTITATIVE LONGITUDINAL ANALYSES

A large number of quantitative longitudinal methods are not specific to longitudinal analysis, and therefore will not be developed in detail here. An example of this is regression. Nevertheless, often additional conditions have to be respected when applying these methods to longitudinal analyses – notably concerning error terms, which should be homoscedastic, and free of autocorrelation. If this condition is not respected, either the model will need to be adjusted, or procedures that are not reliant on the variance-covariance assumptions must be used (for more details, see Bergh and Holbein, 1997).

1. Event Analysis Methods

Longitudinal analyses are often chosen because a researcher is particularly concerned with certain events that may affect the life of an organization. When the event itself is the object of study, the event history analysis method is used. If, however, the event is not the subject of the study, but the research seeks to discern the influence of a certain event on the actual subject, the event study method would be used.

1.1 Event history analysis

Any relatively sudden qualitative change that happens to an individual or to an organization can be classed as an event. Examples of events that may occur include an individual being promoted or dismissed, or an organization experiencing a strike or a takeover bid.

One could consider using regression for an event study. However, regression entails a risk of introducing a bias into the results, or of losing information. In fact, the data that is collected possesses two characteristics that violate the assumptions underlying 'classic' regression (Allison, 1984). The first of these characteristics appears when data have been collected on the possible causes of an event: explanatory variables can change over the observation period. Imagine, for example, a study trying to identify how much time will pass between when a company begins exporting and when it establishes a presence abroad. Those companies that began exporting in 1980 could be used as a sample, observing in each case whether they have established a presence abroad, and if so, when this occurred, along with possible explanations. For example, sales figures achieved overseas could possibly result in consolidating a company's position there. The problem we encounter here is that the explanatory variables could change radically during the study. A company that established itself overseas in 1982 could sustain a sharp increase in export sales figures because of this fact. Sales figures, from being a cause of the foreign development, then become a consequence of it.

The second characteristic of the collected data that prevents the use of classical regression is known as *censoring*: this refers to the situation when data collection has been interrupted by the end of the study. In our example, information is gathered on the establishment of companies overseas from 1980 to the present. At the end of the studied period, certain companies will not have established themselves overseas, which poses a major problem. We do not know the value of the explanatory variables for these companies (the period between beginning to export and establishing a presence). This value is then said to be 'censored'. The only possible solutions to such a situation could lead to serious biases: to eliminate these companies from the sample group would strongly bias it and make the results questionable; to replace the missing data with any particular value (including a maximum value – the time from 1980 to the end of the study), would minimize the real value and so once again falsify the results.

Another important concept when analyzing event history concerns the risk period (Yamaguchi, 1991). The time in which the event is not happening can generally be broken into two parts: the period in which there is a risk the event will happen, and the period in which occurrence of the event is not possible. For example, if the studied event is the dismissal of employees, the risk period corresponds to the time the studied employees have a job. When they do not have a job, they are at no risk of losing it. We can also speak in terms of a risk set to refer to those individuals who may experience the event.

Two groups of methods can be used to study transition rates: parametric and semi-parametric methods on the one hand, and non-parametric methods on the other. The first are used to develop hypotheses of specific distribution of time (generally of exponential distributions, such as Weibull or Gompertz), and aim to estimate the effects of explanatory variables on the hazard rate. Non-parametric methods, however, do not generate any hypotheses on the distribution of time, nor do they consider relationships between the hazard rate and the explanatory variables. Instead, they are used to assess the hazard rate specific to a group, formed according to a nominal explanatory variable that does not change over time.

1.2 Event study

The name 'event study' can be misleading: it does not refer to studying a particular event, but rather its impact on the object of the research. Event study methods measure how a dependent variable will evolve in the light of the occurrence of a particular event. The evolution of this variable is therefore measured both before and after the occurrence of the event. Through an OLS regression, the researcher tries to estimate what the value of the dependent variable would have been on the date the event occurred, had that event not taken place. The difference between the calculated value and the real value is called abnormal return, and it is considered to correspond to the effect of the event. This abnormal return is generally standardized by dividing it by its standard deviation. However, it can happen that the effect of the event takes place on a different date (before the event, if it was anticipated, or after it, if the event had a delayed impact). The impact might also be diluted over a somewhat longer period, called an event window – in which case we can calculate the sum of the differences between the estimated values and those observed in the event window. If the aggregate difference is not zero, the following test will be used to verify whether it is significant:

$$Z = ACAR_t \times \sqrt{n}$$

where $ACAR_t$ = average standardized cumulative
abnormal return
n = number of observations.

McWilliams and Siegel (1997) emphasize the precautions that must be taken with such types of analysis. First, the sample should be reasonably large, as the test statistics used are based on normality assumptions. Moreover, OLS regressions are very sensitive to outliers, which should therefore be identified, especially if the sample is small. Another major difficulty concerns the length of the event window. It should be as short as possible, to exclude disruptive elements, external to the study, while still remaining long enough to capture the impact of the event. Finally, the abnormal returns should be justified theoretically.

2. Sequence Methods

Sequence methods are used to study processes. One type of research that can be conducted using these methods consists in recognizing and comparing sequences. We could, for example, establish a list of the different positions held by CEOs (chief executive officers) of large companies over their careers, as well as the amount of time spent at each post. The sequences formed in this way could then be compared, and typical career paths could be determined.

Another type of research could aim at determining the order of occurrence of the different stages of a process. For example, the classic decision models indicate that in making decisions we move through phases of analyzing the problem, researching information, evaluating the consequences and making a choice. But in reality, a single decision can involve returning to these different steps many times over, and it would be difficult to determine the order in which these stages occur 'on average'.

2.1 Comparing sequences

Sequence comparison methods have to be chosen according to the type of data available. We can distinguish sequences according to the possibility of the recurrence or non-recurrence of the events they are composed of, and according to the necessity of knowing or not knowing the distance between these events. The distance between events can be assessed by averaging the temporal distance between them across all cases, or on the basis of a direct categorical resemblance, or by considering transition rates (Abbott, 1990).

The simplest case is a sequence in which every event is observed once and only once (non-recurrent sequence). In this case, two sequences can be compared using a simple correlation coefficient. Each sequence is arranged in order of occurrence of the events it is composed of, and the events are numbered according to their order of appearance. The sequences are then compared two by two, using a rank correlation coefficient. The higher the coefficient (approaching 1) the more similar the sequences are. A typical sequence can then be established: the sequence from which the others differ least. A typology of possible sequences could also be established, using a typological analysis (such as hierarchical or non-hierarchical classification, or multidimensional analysis of similarities). This procedure does not require measuring the distances between events.

The most frequently used measure of correlation is the Spearman rank correlation coefficient. It is calculated in the following manner:

$$\rho = 1 - \frac{6 \sum_i d_i^2}{n \, (n^2 - 1)}$$

where d_i = distance between the two classifications of event i
n = number of classified events.

This coefficient assumes that the ranks are equidistant – in other words, that the distance between ranks 3 and 4 is equal to the distance between ranks 15 and 16, for example. For cases in which it seems that this hypothesis is not appropriate, we can use the Kendall's tau, which is calculated as follows:

$$\tau = \frac{n_a - n_d}{N}$$

where n_a = number of agreements between two classifications
(any pair of objects classed in the same rank order
both times)
n_d = number of discrepancies between two classifications
(any pair of objects classed in different rank-order)
N = number of possible pairs.

Third, if the classifications reveal any tied events, an index such as Goodman and Kruskal's gamma should be used, with the following formula:

$$\Gamma = \frac{n_a - n_d}{n_a + n_d}$$

In the case of recurring sequences, the most popular approach is to use a Markov chain, or process, which postulates that the probability of an event occurring depends entirely on its immediate predecessor. A Markov chain is defined with the conditional probabilities that make up the matrix of transitions. This matrix groups estimations based on observed proportions (the percentage of times an event is followed by another – or by itself, on the matrix diagonal).

Another possibility for recurring sequences consists of a group of techniques called optimal matching. The optimal matching algorithm between two sequences begins with the first sequence and calculates the number of additions or suppressions necessary to produce the second sequence (Abbott and Forrest, 1986). The necessary transitions are weighted according to the distance between the events. We then obtain a matrix of distance between sequences, which can be used in sequence comparisons.

2.2 Determining order of occurrence

Other types of research can be used to determine the order of occurrence of events. In this case the researcher wants to identify a general pattern from a mass of events. One of these methods was proposed by Pelz (1985), who applied it to analyzing innovation processes. The method is based on Goodman and Kruskel's gamma, and allows the order of observed events to be established, as well as defining to what extent these events overlap.

The calculation method comprises the following steps:

1   The number P of times that event A happens before event B is counted.
2   The number Q of times that event B happens before event A is counted.
3   The gamma is calculated for each pair of events as follows:

$$\gamma = \frac{P - Q}{P + Q}$$

€ᵧ is between +1 and −1.

4   Repeating the process for each pair of events enables a squared gamma matrix to be established, with a number of lines equal to the total number of events.

From this gamma matrix the researcher can calculate a time sequence score, which determines in which order the events took place, and a separation score, which indicates whether the events are separated from one another or if they overlap.

The time sequence score is obtained by calculating the mean from the columns of gamma values. In this way, a score ranging from + 1 to − 1 is ascribed to each event. By reclassifying the events according to their score, in diminishing order, the events are ordered chronologically.

The separation score is obtained by calculating the mean from the columns of absolute gamma values. Each event is credited with a score of between 0 and 1. It is generally considered that an event for which the score is equal to or above 0.5 is clearly separated from those that surround it, whereas an event with a score lower than 0.5 cannot be separated from the events that surround it and therefore must be grouped with these events (Poole and Roth, 1989).

Interpretation of Pelz's gamma, in which a high gamma indicates that two events are separate, rather than associated, is opposite to the interpretation of Goodman and Kruskal's gamma, on which the method is based. This is because it is calculated using the two variables time and the passage of event A to an event B. A high gamma therefore, indicates that the passage from A to B is strongly associated with the passage of time. The interpretation that can be drawn is that A and B are strongly separated.

An important advantage of this method is that it is independent of the time elapsed between events: therefore it is not necessary for this information to be available. In fact, the results do not change if the interval of time between the two incidents differs. The only point that has to be observed in relation to time is chronological order.

3. Cohort Analysis

Cohorts represent groups of observations having in common the fact that they have experienced the same event within a given period of time. The event in question is frequently birth but could be any notable event. The period of this event may extend over a variable duration, often between one and ten years. But for very dramatic events it can be considerably reduced. Cohort analysis enables us to study changes in behavior or attitudes in these groups. We can observe three types of changes: changes in actual behavior, changes due to aging, or changes due to an event occurring during a particular period (Glenn, 1977). We can distinguish intra-cohort analysis, focusing on the evolution of a cohort, from intercohort analysis, in which the emphasis is on comparisons.

3.1 Intra-cohort analysis

Intra-cohort analysis consists in following a cohort through time to observe changes in the phenomenon being studied. Let us imagine that we want to study the relationship between the age of a firm and its profitability. We could select a cohort, say that of companies created between 1946 and 1950, and follow them over the course of time by recording a profitability measure once a year. This very simple study of a trend within a cohort does, however, raise several problems. First, a certain number of companies will inevitably drop out of the sample over time. It is, in fact, likely that this mortality in the sample will strongly bias the study, because the weakest companies (and therefore the least profitable) are the most likely to disappear. Another problem is that intra-cohort analyses generally use aggregated data, in which effects can counterbalance each other. For example, if half the companies record increased profits, while the other half record a decrease in their profits of equal proportions, the total effect is nullified. Methods originally developed for studying panel data can, however, be used to resolve this problem.

A third problem raised by intra-cohort studies is that our study will not enable us to ascertain the true impact of company age on profitability. Even if we observe a rise in profitability, we will not know if this is due to the age of the company or to an external event – an effect of history such as a particularly favorable economic situation. Other analyses are therefore necessary.

3.2 Inter-cohort analysis

Among the other analyses just mentioned, one method is to compare several cohorts at a given time. In our case, this could bring us to compare, for example, the profitability in 1990 of companies created at different periods. In this we are leaving the domain of longitudinal analysis, though, as such a study is typically cross-sectional. Second, this design on its own would not enable us to resolve our research question. In fact, any differences we might observe could be attributed to age, but also to a cohort effect: companies established in a certain era may have benefited from favorable economic circumstances and may continue to benefit from those favorable circumstances today.

3.3 Simultaneous analysis of different cohorts

The connection between age and profitability of companies can be established only by simultaneous intra- and inter-cohort analysis. Changes observed in the performance levels of companies could be due to three different types of effects: the effects of age (or that of aging, which is pertinent in this case), cohort effects (the fact of belonging to a particular cohort), and period effects (the time at which profitability is measured). To try to differentiate these effects, a table can be established with rows representing the cohorts and with the observation periods recorded in columns. Where it is possible to separate data into regular intervals this should always be preferred. The period between readings should also be used to delimit the cohorts. For example, if the data easily divides into ten-year intervals, ten-year cohorts are preferable – although this is not always possible, it does make for better analyses. The resulting table can be used to complete intra-cohort and inter-cohort analyses. If identical time intervals have been used for the rows and the columns (for example, ten-year intervals), the table presents the advantage that the diagonals will give the intra-cohort tendencies (Glenn, 1977).

All the same, the differences observed between the cells of the table have to be analyzed with caution. First, these differences should always be tested to see if they are statistically significant. Second, the findings may have been biased by the mortality of the sample, as we mentioned earlier. If the elements that have disappeared did not have the same distribution as those that remain, the structure of the sample will change. Finally, it is very difficult to differentiate the three possible effects (age, cohort, and period), because they are linearly dependent, which poses problems in analyses such as regression, where the explanatory variables must be independent. Here, in the case of a birth cohort, the three factors are linked by the relationship:

$$\text{cohort} = \text{period} - \text{age}$$

A final possibility consists in recording each age, each cohort, and each period as a dummy variable in a regression. However, this leads us to form the hypothesis that the effects do not interact: for example, that the effect of age is the same for all the cohorts and all the periods, which is usually unrealistic (Glenn, 1977).

SECTION 3   QUALITATIVE LONGITUDINAL ANALYSIS

The mass of information collected when doing qualitative research can be impressive. But this mass of data cannot simply be analyzed directly – it must first be manipulated and put into usable form.

1. Preliminary Processing of Qualitative Longitudinal Data

Very often the first question for researchers using qualitative longitudinal data is how to reduce the copious amount of information they have amassed. The risk of drowning in data is real, and a number of authors have proposed simple techniques for consolidating and summarizing qualitative data, or reducing the amount of data, before analysis.

1.1 Monograph

The first preliminary step in processing qualitative longitudinal data is to write a monograph. A monograph traces the development of the phenomenon being studied, over the analysis period defined by the researcher. It gives a transversal view of the phenomenon while reducing the amount of information that has been accumulated during the data collection phase. Often taking the form of a descriptive narrative, a monograph can be accompanied by an initial analysis of the data (Eisenhardt, 1989); perhaps in the form of a graph of relationships between the events, in which chronological order will be respected.

When research focuses on several organizations (or on several case studies), monographs also provide the basic elements for comparison. They enable individual development patterns to emerge which, when compared with each other, facilitate the identification of common characteristics.

1.2 Time-ordered matrices

The time-ordered matrix proposed by Miles and Huberman (1994), presents information relating to a phenomenon by establishing a temporal relationship between the variables it is composed of. The aim is to understand quickly and easily what has happened. Such a matrix has its columns arranged in sequence, so that one can see when a given phenomenon occurred. The basic principle is chronology (Miles and Huberman, 1994).

In constructing time-ordered matrices, researchers begin by determining the specific components or aspects of the phenomenon they are studying. These form the rows of the matrix. The columns represent successive periods – that is, the period of analysis divided into subperiods, or successive stages of development. The intersection between the line and the column shows the changes that have occurred to a component or to an aspect of the phenomenon over the course of a given period.

This chronological matrix enables the researcher to pinpoint shifts or important modifications that have been experienced by components of the phenomenon.

Miles and Huberman (1994) also propose longitudinal variants of the basic time-ordered matrix: the role-by-time matrix and the time-ordered meta-matrix. In the first, the lines represent individuals. This matrix allows us to determine at which moment an action was carried out by a protagonist occupying a particular role in relation to the phenomenon being studied. The time-ordered meta-matrix compares the evolution of a particular phenomenon for several cases at the same time. The different case studies make up the rows and the time intervals of the period of analysis form the columns. This matrix can be constructed in relation to the studied phenomenon as a whole, or one of its components alone.

The tools presented above pave the way for the analysis. In fact, it is difficult to determine which is an element of the preliminary processing of the data, and which forms part of the analysis itself.

2. Qualitative Analysis of Longitudinal Data

Qualitative longitudinal analysis methods are rarely formalized. However, certain authors have proposed general procedures that can be used to analyze the evolution of a phenomenon.

2.1 Analyzing a phenomenon in terms of time

Van de Ven and Poole (1989) proposed a method that can be broken into four steps:

1   Put together a chronological list of events that occurred during the course of the studied phenomenon. An 'event' is understood to mean a change experienced by one of the conceptual categories studied.

2   Rearrange this list according to the conceptual categories of the research, in order to establish, for each category, a chronological series of events – which is called a trajectory. The set of trajectories gives us a description of the process studied.
3   Carry out a phase analysis. This consists in identifying discrete phases of activity and analyzing their sequences and properties. A phase is defined as being a meaningful set of simultaneous activities within the trajectories established in the second stage. Thus, a phase is a set of changes undergone by a certain number of conceptual categories.
4   Examine the order of sequences in the series of connected events.

2.2 Concepts describing evolution: stages, cycles, phases, and sequences

Stages   We speak of a stage in the evolution of a phenomenon to characterize a moment in this evolution. The stage can sometimes signify a provisional stopping point. All evolution is essentially a succession of stages.

Cycles   This can have two different meanings. A cycle can be seen as a recurrent succession of steps giving cadence to the evolution of a system by always returning it to its original state, as in the cycle of the seasons. This is known as cyclical evolution. We can also describe as a cycle the evolution of a phenomenon that follows a fixed order without necessarily being recurrent – as in the life cycle, where every creature is born, grows and dies. This is called an evolution schema.

Both of these types of cycles have been identified in organizational theory. Cyclical evolution is found, for example, when successive periods of stability and change are observed. Evolution schema can be seen in the recognition of evolutionary constants in the life of organizations. The cycle then expresses a permanent organizational phenomenon. It can be broken up into phases that represent different stages of the evolution of the organization.

Phases   The concept of the phase is very close to that of the cycle as understood in its second meaning: that is to say, as a succession of stages which always occur in the same order. Phases are temporary phenomena in the life of the organization (for example, the phases in the development of a new product). They generally follow on from each other in a given, irreversible, order, but they can overlap. Phases are composed of fairly unified activities that carry out a function necessary for the evolution of the phenomenon (Poole, 1983). By working from an overview of the phenomenon, the researcher tries to determine a relatively limited number of phases that take place in a definite order.

Sequences   A sequence is defined as an ordered succession of events or objects. This order, as defined by Abbott (1990), may be temporal or spatial (although we are here only concerned with temporal order). A sequence may be either continuous or discrete.

When the objects observed are phases in the evolution of a phenomenon, the development model obtained using sequence methods is identical to that obtained by phase analysis. However, the order of the events (or phases) is not irreversible and shows more complex evolutions, such as retroactive looping, permutations, recurrent and non-recurrent events, etc.

2.3 Concepts describing dynamics: dynamic factors rupture points

The passage from one event to another or from one phase to another within an evolving phenomenon is not always stable and linear. Evolving phenomena are subject to interference, cycles, rupture points, etc. These factors of dynamics can create accelerations, slowdowns, reversals, or ruptures within the evolution of a single phenomenon.

In their research on decision processes, Mintzberg et al. (1976) identify six dynamic factors:

- interrupts, which are caused by environmental forces, and cause a suspension of the evolution of the phenomenon
- scheduling delays, which permit managers who are under strong time pressures to break complex processes down into manageable steps
- feedback delays. These characterize periods in which managers are waiting to see the results of actions that have already been engaged upon before undertaking other actions
- timing delays and speedups, which result from the intervention of managers wanting perhaps to seize an opportunity or to create a surprise effect, or to wait for more favorable conditions or gain time
- comprehension cycles, which enable a better understanding of a complex problem by going over it numerous times
- failure recycles, which lead the decision-maker to slow down the process while waiting for an acceptable solution when none have proved satisfactory so far, or to change the criteria relating to a problem to make one of the proposed solutions acceptable.

Rupture points, which represent transitions between the main trends in the development of a phenomenon, are also factors in the phenomenon's dynamics. Poole (1983) distinguishes three types of rupture points:

- Normal points, which result from a process that can be described as ordinary. These include, for example, adjournments of a decision process operating within a small group.
- Delays (or cycles of comprehension), which signify a period in which the observed phenomenon is suspended. These periods are important, as they can signal either the beginning of a difficult phase, or a time of great creativity. The actors involved in the evolution of the phenomenon are generally unable to anticipate these rupture points.

- Ruptures (or interruptions), which characterize an internal conflict, or the arrival of unexpected results. Ruptures result in a reorientation of the evolution of the observed phenomenon.

CONCLUSION

To conclude, two points must be emphasized. First, we must remember that longitudinal analysis methods are rarely specific. However, as supplementary assumptions are applied to longitudinal data, there is very often a need to verify such assumptions. Second, the quality of longitudinal research depends largely on the data collection process. It is therefore important that data collection should be well thought out, and that the advantages and disadvantages of the various possible collection methods are weighed up before going into the field. This takes on an even greater importance for data collected in real time. The design stage of the research is therefore absolutely fundamental.

FURTHER READING

Abbott, A., 'A Primer on Sequence Methods', *Organization Science*, 1 (4), 1990: 375–92.

Allison, P.D., *Event History Analysis: Regression for Longitudinal Event Data*, Sage University Paper Series on Quantitative Applications in the Social Sciences, no. 07–046, Beverly Hills, CA: Sage, 1984.

Bergh, D.D. and Holbein, G.F., 'Assessment and Redirection of Longitudinal Analysis: Demonstration with a Study of the Diversification and Divestiture Relationship', *Strategic Management Journal*, 18 (7), 1997: 557–71.

Glick, W.H., Huber, G.P., Miller, C.C., Doty, D.H. and Sutcliffe, K.M., 'Studying Changes in Organizational Design and Effectiveness: Retrospective Event Histories and Periodic Assessments', *Organization Science*, 1 (3), 1990: 293–312.

Kimberly, J.R., 'Issues in the Design of Longitudinal Organizational Research', *Sociological Methods & Research*, 4 (3), 1976: 321–47.

Menard, S., *Longitudinal Research*, Sage University Paper Series on Quantitative Applications in the Social Sciences, no. 07-076, Newbury Park, CA: Sage, 1991.

Miller, C.C., Cardinal, L.B. and Glick, W.H., 'Retrospective Reports in Organizational Research: A Reexamination of Recent Evidence', *Academy of Management Journal*, 40 (1), 1997: 189–204.

Van de Ven, A.H., Angle, H.L. and Poole, M.S. (eds), *Research on the Management of Innovation: The Minnesota Studies*, New York: Harper and Row, 1989.

Yin, R.K., *Case Study Research: Design and Methods*, Applied Social Research Methods Series, 5, Newbury Park, CA: Sage, 1990.

16

ANALYZING REPRESENTATIONS AND DISCOURSE

Florence Allard-Poesi, Carole Drucker-Godard and Sylvie Ehlinger

Outline

How can we scrutinize, classify, and analyze information contained in a document, a communication or an interview? This chapter sets out the methods for analyzing discourse and representations that are most applicable to the study of organizations. After a general presentation of these methods, it takes a closer look at content analysis and cognitive mapping.

Research in management and organizational science often relies on the analysis of communications, either oral (conversations, individual or group interviews) or written (annual reports, strategic plans, letters to shareholders, etc.). Researchers may simply want to analyze the content or the structure of these communications; or they may attempt to establish, through the text or discourse, the author's representations or thought processes. Inspired in particular by the cognitive approach to organizations, many researchers today are developing an interest in individuals', groups' or organizations' representations. In a very broad sense, by 'representation' we mean the structure composed of the beliefs, values and opinions concerning a specific object, and the interconnections between them. This structure is supposed to enable individuals to impose coherence on information received, and therefore to facilitate its comprehension and interpretation. From this point of view, in order to understand the decisions and actions taken by an organization, one first needs to apprehend the representations of the actors with whom they originate.

Thus, discourse and documents are believed to transmit some of the representations of organizational members, or their interests and concerns. Researchers can turn to different methods to enable them to reduce and analyze the mass of data contained in the discourse and documents. These methods were developed as an alternative to subjective interpretation, and to avoid running the risk of filtering or deforming the information.

We do not intend here to present all possible methods for analyzing representations and discourse. Indeed, these methods, which come from such varied domains as linguistics, social and cognitive psychology, statistics and artificial intelligence (Stubbs, 1983; Roberts, 1997) are particularly numerous. We will restrict ourselves to presenting those methods that are used the most in management research: content analysis and cognitive mapping.

Content analysis   Content analysis is based on the postulate that the repetition of units of analysis of discourse (words, expressions or similar signifiers, or sentences and paragraphs) reveal the interests and concerns of the authors of the discourse. The text (written document or transcription of an interview or speech) is broken down and rearranged in terms of the units of analysis that the researcher has decided to study, according to a precise coding methodology. The analyses will be based on the classification of the different units of analysis into a limited number of categories related to the objectives of the study. These analyses usually involve counting, statistical analysis or more qualitative analysis of the context in which the words appear in the discourse.

Content analysis can be used, among other things, to analyze responses to open-ended survey questions, to compare different organizations' strategies through their discourse and the documents which they distribute, or to discern the interests of different individuals, groups or organizations.

Cognitive mapping   This method, which stems from cognitive psychology, has been used frequently in management since the late 1970s (inspired in particular by the work of Axelrod, 1976). The objective of this method is to establish and analyze cognitive maps, that is the representation of a person or an organization's beliefs concerning a particular domain (Axelrod, 1976). A cognitive map is composed of two elements:

1   Concepts, also called constructs or variables; ideas that describe a problem or a particular domain.
2   The links between these concepts.

Once they are collected, these concepts and relations can be represented graphically in the form of knots and arrows: the knots standing for the concepts (or categories) and the arrows symbolizing the links between these elements.

A cognitive map is supposed to be precise enough to capture the person's perceptual filters and idiosyncratic vision (Langfeld-Smith, 1992). Although it is not aimed at representing the subject's thought processes, the beliefs it reveals are considered to be at the their root.

Cognitive mapping is principally used in management:

• To study the representations of individuals, especially managers, to explore their vision. These studies often attempt to compare different people's representations, or those of the same person over the course of time; to explain or predict behavior; or to assist executives in formulating strategic problems.
• To establish and study a group, organization or a sector's representation. In this case, the studies' goals are to understand either the evolution of

corporate strategy over a period of several years, or the interactions and influence of different groups of managers.

SECTION 1 METHODS OF DISCOURSE AND REPRESENTATION ANALYSIS

Discourse and representation analysis methods generally require three major steps: data collection (Subsection 1), coding (Subsection 2), and analysis (Subsection 3).

1. Collecting Discourse or Representations

There are two main types of methods for collecting representations or discourse: structured (or *a priori*) and non-structured methods.

1.1 Structured or a priori methods

The objective of structured methods is to directly generate a subject's representation concerning the problem or theme that the researcher is interested in. These representations are established graphically in the form of cognitive maps (for example, Figures 16.2 and 16.3 later in this chapter). Structured methods are not based on natural discourse data. They can not, therefore, be used for content analysis (method based on coding 'natural' textual or interview data).

With structured methods, the researcher establishes the subject's representation using a predefined framework (whence the term '*a priori*' for this type of method). Whatever type of representation the researcher wishes to generate, structured methods require two steps:

1   The researcher chooses a set of categories (to establish category schemes) or concepts – also known as constructs or variables – (to establish cognitive maps). A category is a class of objects that are supposed to share similar attributes. If we are concerned, for example, with an executive's representation of the competitive environment in the textile sector, the following categories might be selected: 'textile firms', 'firms selling trendy fabric', 'classics', 'firms with top-quality merchandise', 'lower-quality', 'successful firms', 'less successful', etc. A concept, a construct or a variable is an idea that is likely to describe a particular problem or domain, and that can acquire different values or represent the level, presence or absence of a phenomenon or an object (Axelrod, 1976), for example, 'corporate cost-effectiveness', 'the manager has a strategic mind', or 'the employees are highly adaptable'.

2   Once a certain number of elements have been selected (generally around ten), the researcher submits them to the respondent and asks what kind of link he or she sees between them: hierarchical (is Category A included in

Category B?); similarity or difference (used to establish category schemes); or influence or causal links (does A influence B? If so, how: positively or negatively), which are used to establish, for example, cognitive maps.

The advantage of structured methods is that they generate reliable data: researchers will obtain the same type of data if they use the same methods on other subjects or the same subjects on different occasions (stability), and if other researchers use these methods, they will also get the same results (replicability) Laukkanen, 1992: 22). These methods do not require data coding, they spare the researcher from a tremendous amount of pre-collection work and from the reliability problems related to this phase. They are therefore usable on a large scale. But the main advantage of these methods is that they generate representations emanating from the same set of initial concepts or categories. Representations established in this manner can thus be immediately compared to each other and are easily aggregated.

The major drawback in this type of method is that the elements of the representation do not originate from the subject. So we run the risk of dispossessing the subject of part of its representation or even of introducing elements that do not belong to it (Cossette and Audet, 1992).

1.2 Non-structured methods

The purpose of these methods is to generate data that is as natural as possible.
These methods dissociate the data collection phase from the coding and analysis phases.

Interview methods   If the researcher wishes to establish the representation of a subject concerning a particular domain, or if there is no existing data about the theme in question, the researcher will collect discourse data from a free or semi-structured interview. These interviews are generally recorded and then retranscribed in their entirety in order to then be coded (for more details about this step, see below).

The main advantage of these methods is the validity of the data produced. The data, having usually been generated spontaneously by the respondent or in response to open questions, is more likely to reflect what they really think (Cossette and Audet, 1992). In addition, these methods generate much richer data than do structured methods.

The logical counterpart to these advantages is that these methods reduce the reliability of the data produced. And, insofar as they demand a lot of work on the researcher's part before the data can be coded, they are not practicable on a large scale. In fact, they are mostly used for in-depth studies of discourse or representations of a small number of subjects (see Cossette and Audet, 1992).

Documentary methods   When the researcher has transcriptions of discourse or meetings, or else documents (for example, strategic plans, letters to shareholders, activity reports) at their disposal, they will use the documentary methods.

The main advantage of these methods is that they avoid data reliability problems, as the researcher does not intervene in the data-production process. In addition, these methods do not require any transcription work.

These methods are commonly used to establish the representation or to analyze the organization or group's discourse.

2. Coding

The coding process consists of breaking down the contents of a discourse or text into units of analysis (words, phrases, themes, etc.) and integrating them into categories which are determined by the purpose of the research.

2.1 Defining the unit of analysis

The unit of analysis is the basic unit for breaking down the discourse or text. Depending on the chosen method of analysis (content analysis or cognitive mapping) and the purpose of the research, the researcher usually opts for one of the six units of analysis below (Weber, 1990):

- a word – for example, proper or common nouns, verbs or pronouns
- the meaning of a word or group of words – certain computer programs can now identify different meanings for the same word or expression
- whole sentences
- parts of sentences of the subject/verb/object type. For example, the sentence, 'The price reduction attracts new customers and stymies the competition', will be divided into two units of analysis: first, 'The price reduction attracts new customers', and then, 'The price reduction stymies the competition'. Identifying this type of unit of analysis, which does not correspond to a precise unit of text (for example, word, sentence) can be relatively tricky
- one or more paragraphs, or even an entire text. Weber (1990) points out the disadvantages in choosing this type of unit of analysis, in terms of coding reliability. It is much more difficult to come to an agreement on the classification of a set of phrases than of a word.

2.2 Classifying units of analysis

Once the units of analysis have been pinpointed in the discourse or text, the next step is to place them in categories. A category is a set of units of text. All units of analysis belonging to the same category should have either similar meanings (synonyms like 'old' and 'elderly', or equivalent connotations like 'power' and 'wealth') or shared formal characteristics (for example, one category could be 'interrogative sentences', another 'affirmative sentences', a third 'silence', a fourth 'active verbs', another 'passive verbs').

The more clear and precise the definitions of the units of analysis and categories are, the more reliable the coding will be. For this reason, it is advisable to establish a protocol specifying the rules and definitions of these elements.

2.3 Coding reliability

The combination of the ambiguity of discourse and the lack of precision in the definitions of categories and coded units or other coding rules makes it necessary to check coding reliability.

Reliability can be declined into three more specific subcriteria (Weber, 1990):

1 *Stability*: this is the extent to which the coding results are the same when the same data is coded by the same coder more than once.
2 *Accuracy*: this dimension measures the proximity of a text's classifications to a standard or norm. It is possible to establish this when the standard coding for a text has been elaborated. This type of reliability is rarely evaluated. Nevertheless, it can be useful to establish it when a coding protocol created by another researcher is being used.
3 *Replicability (or inter-coder reliability)*: this criterion refers to the extent to which the coding produces the same results when the same data is coded by different coders. This is the most common method for evaluating coding reliability.

3. Analyzing Data

Analyzing data is equivalent to making inferences based on the characteristics of the message which appeared in the data-coding results. The researcher can decide to analyze more specifically the structure of the representations or their contents, using quantitative or qualitative methods, in order to compare, describe, explain or predict objectives which all require different methods of analysis.

3.1 Analyzing content or structure

Content analysis consists of inferring the signification of the discourse through detailed analysis of the words used, their frequency and their associations. The different modalities of analysis will be described in greater detail later on in this chapter, in relation to the methodology used (content analysis or cognitive mapping).

When analyzing the structure of a text, discourse or representation, the goal is to discover the rules of organization of the words, sentences and themes employed. Analysis of the structure of discourse or representations, although it does not enable us to perceive all of the thought or decision-making processes, does reveal certain cognitive characteristics, such as the subject's cognitive complexity. Structure analysis can be used in particular for explaining or predicting behavior.

3.2 Quantitative or qualitative analysis

After coding, interpreting the text or discourse data can be done with either quantitative or qualitative techniques. Quantitative analyses depend essentially on counting the units of analysis, or on more elaborate statistical analyses. These can be performed with the help of specialized software. Qualitative analyses allow us to interpret the arrangement of these units by placing them in a more global context. These analyses can be based on procedures which are not specific to discourse or text data analysis, such as, for example, seeking the opinions of experts. These judges, who could be the researcher himself or herself, members of the organization under study, the subject interrogated or outside experts, will evaluate the similarities or differences in the coded data in a more global manner.

These quantitative and qualitative analyses are complementary and should be used conjointly for a richer interpretation of the data.

3.3 Describing, comparing, explaining or predicting

Analyzing discourse or representation can be done solely for the purpose of description. In that case, the point is to describe, using the data collected, the contents or structure of a text or representation. The researcher can also attempt to describe the structure of a discourse's argumentation, or the state of beliefs of an active member of the organization (see Cossette and Audet, 1992).

If the researcher's goal is to compare the discourse or representations of several different individuals, groups of individuals, or organizations, or to evaluate their evolution over time, then they will have to reveal the similarities and differences in their contents or structure (see Laukkanen, 1994). The researcher can undertake quantitative[1] or qualitative comparative analyses. These methods will be presented further on in this chapter.

The researcher can also attempt to explain and, by extrapolation, predict, certain phenomena or behavior through discourse and representation analysis. For example, exposing important or antagonistic concepts within a representation can testify to their importance for an individual or organization, and therefore explain some of their behavior or decisions in situations where these concepts are activated (see Komokar, 1994).

After this overview of the general steps in representation and discourse analysis methods, we will present two of these methods more precisely here: content analysis and cognitive mapping.

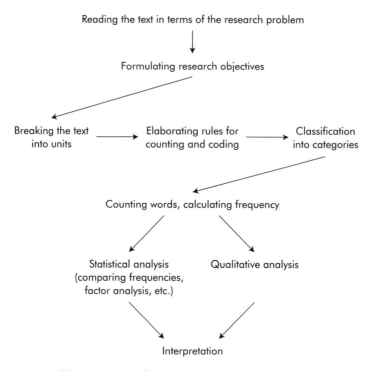

Figure 16.1   *The main steps in content analysis*
(Source: Bardin, 1993)

SECTION 2   CONTENT ANALYSIS

Content analyses were developed to study newspaper articles and political speeches in the USA in the 1920s. They are based on the theory that repeating certain elements of discourse (words, expression or similar meanings) revealed the interests or concerns of the persons involved. Their purpose is to analyze the manifest contents of a communication.

The 'content analysis' category, includes several different methods which, although they all follow the steps presented in Figure 16.1, differ in terms of the coding units selected and the methods used for analyzing the results.

We will restrict ourselves herein to presenting the most common methods in organizational research, while acknowledging nevertheless that many other methods, such as those applied to newspaper studies, non-verbal communication analysis and linguistic analyses do exist (see, for more details, Robert, 1997; Stubbs, 1983).

1. Collecting Data

Content analysis is performed on data that has been collected according to non-structured or semi-structured methods, such as (free or semi-directive) interviews.

Certain replies to questions in surveys can also be processed in this way. These are usually replies to simple open-ended questions, for example, 'How do you evaluate your staff's work?' More generally, any kind of verbal communication or written material can be processed by content analysis.

2. Coding Data

As for any coding process, the discourse or text is broken down into units of analysis, then classified into the categories defined according to the purpose of the research.

2.1 Defining the units of analysis

There are basically two types of content analyses which can be defined according to the units of analysis defined:

- Lexical analyses, which are the more frequently used, examine the nature and range of vocabulary used in the discourse or text and analyze the frequency with which words appear. In this case, words are the unit of analysis.
- Thematic analyses adopt sentences, portions or groups of sentences as their unit of analysis. This last type is more common in organizational studies (D'Aveni and MacMillan, 1990; Dougherty and Bowman, 1995).

2.2 Defining categories

Depending on the coding unit selected, categories are usually described:

- Either in the form of a concept that will include words with related meanings (for example, the category 'power' could include words like strength, force or power). Computer-aided content analyses and their associated dictionaries, which automatically assign words to categories, can be used here. They offer several advantages: they reduce the amount of time spent on defining and validating categories, they standardize the classification process, and they facilitate comparisons with other studies.
- Or in the form of broader themes (for example, competitive strategies) which include words, groups of words or even whole sentences or paragraphs (depending on the unit of analysis defined by the researcher). The main difficulty lies in defining the breadth of selected categories. For example, a category like 'organizational strategies' is broader than 'competitive strategies' or 'competitiveness factors'. Defining the breadth of the category must be related to both the researcher's objectives (narrow categories make comparative analysis more difficult) and the materials used (it is easier to

construct narrow categories based on rich, in-depth interviews than on letters to shareholders, which are generally more shallow).

- In certain cases, the categories may be assimilated to a single word. So there will be as many categories as there are different words that the researcher has decided to study (even if their meaning is similar). In this case, the words competitors and rivals, for example, will constitute two different categories.
- Finally, the categories can be characteristics of types of discourse, such as pauses, different intonations, grammatical forms or different types of syntax.

Defining categories before or after coding   In the *a priori* method, categories are defined prior to coding – on the basis of experience or the results of earlier research. This method is used when attempting to verify hypotheses arising from other studies. The organizational verbal behavior classification system used by Gioia and Sims (1986) is an excellent example of *a priori* classification in which the categories stem from earlier research. Boland and Pondy (1986) also relied on *a priori* classification to code transcriptions of budgetary meetings. The categories were defined in terms of the decision model used (fiscal, clinical, political or strategic) and the mode of analyzing the situation (instrumental or symbolic).

In the *ex post* method, the categories are defined during the coding process. The choice of categories springs from the contents themselves. The idea is usually to create an inventory of the different themes in the text or discourse being studied. The text must be read and reread several times in order to isolate the essential themes in relation to the purpose of the study. Themes whose importance is underlined by repetition should suggest ideas for categories.

3. Analyzing Data

3.1 Quantitative analysis

Content analysis sprang from a desire for quantification in reaction to literary analysis. The qualitative notion was therefore foreign to its original concerns. So in general, the first step of the analysis is to calculate, for each category, the number and frequency of the units of analysis. Therefore, for each document studied, the number of units of analysis in each category studied is counted in order to deduce the category's importance. The analyses performed in Boland and Pondy's (1986) work dealt essentially with word-frequency counts. However, frequency calculation runs into several problems. In the first place, when the categories correspond to single words, they may have different meanings depending on their context (whence the need to combine both quantitative and qualitative analysis). In addition, the use of pronouns, which often are not counted, can bias the frequency analysis if it involves nouns only.

Researchers performing content analysis also have at their disposal various statistical data-analysis techniques, of which factor analysis is the most commonly used. It enables us, for example, to associate the presence of a greater or lesser number of units in a given category to the presence of a greater or lesser number of units in another category. Other types of analysis, such as regressions, discriminant analyses, and cluster analysis, can also be performed. It is up to each researcher to determine the most appropriate analyses for the purposes of the research. Therefore, to study the relation between managerial attribution and verbal behavior in manager–subordinate interaction during a simulated performance appraisal, Gioia and Sims (1986) performed content analysis on verbal behavior. This analysis was based particularly on a set of statistical analyses: multivariate analysis of variance, t test and correlation analysis.

3.2 Qualitative analysis

A more qualitative analysis, aimed at judging, rather than measuring, the importance of the themes in the discourse, can also be performed. The difference between quantitative and qualitative analysis lies in the way they perceive the notion of importance for a category: 'how often' for quantitative analysis or 'theme value' for qualitative analysis. Qualitative analysis tries to interpret the presence or absence of a given category, taking into account the context in which the discourse was produced (which can explain the presence or absence of certain categories). Qualitative analysis also allows for a more refined approach, studying the units of analysis in their context in order to understand how they are used (with which other units of analysis do they appear or are they associated to in the text?).

Qualitative analysis enables the researcher to go beyond simple content analysis of a discourse or document. It enables us to formalize the relations between the different themes contained in a communication in order to reveal its structure. Thanks to content analysis, it is equally possible to study the contents or the structure of a discourse or document.

Finally, content analysis can be used for descriptive, comparative or explanatory ends. Content analysis allows us to go beyond plain description of the contents of a communication and to discover the reasons for certain strategies or behaviors. By revealing the importance of certain themes in the discourse, content analysis can lead to explanations for the behaviors or strategies of the authors of the discourse analyzed. It is also possible to make certain unrecognized variables or influence factors appear, or to reveal relations between different organizational behaviors and different concerns of the organization's leaders. By analyzing the contents of letters to shareholders, the work of D'Aveni and MacMillan (1990) succeeded in revealing the relation between the decision-makers' main points of interest (focused on the internal or external environment) and the companies' capacity to weather a crisis.

SECTION 3   COGNITIVE MAPPING

As stated earlier, cognitive mapping is aimed at establishing and analyzing cognitive maps, that is, representations of a person or organization's beliefs concerning a particular domain (Axelrod, 1976). A cognitive map is made up of two types of elements:

1 Concepts, also known as constructs or variables.
2 The links between these concepts. These links can be based on similarity (that is, category schemes; see Rosch, 1978), contiguity, resemblance, influence (that is, influence maps; see Cossette and Audet, 1992), causality between concepts (that is, causal maps; see Huff, 1990) or all of these at once (that is, cognitive maps, Bougon 1983, although certain authors use the term when referring to maps that indicate only causal or influence links between variables).

1. Collecting Data

1.1 Structured or a priori methods

The researcher chooses a set of variables (generally around ten) which he or she considers to be applicable to defining the domain that the map will represent, either based on existing research (Ford and Hegarty, 1984) or on preliminary interviews (Bougon, 1983). Then the links are collected from the respondents by having them consider each pair of variables. For example, does variable A influence variable B? If so, is the influence positive or negative? These links are collected by presenting the respondent with a matrix that cross-references all the variables (Ford and Hegarty, 1984), or pairs of cards with the variables to consider written on them (Bougon, 1983).

Because of the lack of validity of such methods, researchers may prefer to use more natural methods.

1.2 Non-structured methods

When dealing with non-structured methods, as we have seen, data is collected through documents or more open interviews.

Interview methods   Researchers collect discourse data through in-depth interviews which are recorded and then entirely transcribed before coding (see, for example, Cossette, 1994). Because of the amount of pre-collection work that these methods entail, some researchers have developed semi-directive methods for cognitive mapping (Ackermann et al., 1992; Eden et al., 1983; Laukkanen, 1989; 1992). The subject is asked about the causes, effects and consequences of the chosen theme for the interview (which will be the central variable on the map). This reveals new variables which are noted down and which can then be submitted to a similar set of questions, and so on and so forth until the person reaches saturation point – that is, has nothing more to say. Thus the map is built interactively with the respondents, who can see it and therefore reflect on their own vision. This method is commonly used to help managers make decisions and formulate strategic problems (Ackermann et al., 1992; Cossette and Audet, 1992). The COPE software developed by Eden (1988; 1990) was in fact conceived essentially with this goal in mind. The main advantage of this method is that it eliminates the need for the researcher to do a lot of coding work. On the other hand, it reduces the possibility of comparing different subjects maps, as they are no longer structured by the researcher beforehand. In addition, since this method implies showing the map to the respondents as they go along, it restricts the validity of the collected data.

Documentary methods   The other method available to the researcher is to establish a map based on written documents or interview transcriptions. These methods are mainly used in management for establishing representations of organizations or groups of managers. In these methods, the interview transcriptions or documents collected must be coded by the researcher.

2. Coding Data

2.1 Defining units of analysis

As a cognitive map is a representation composed of concepts and the links that relate them to each other, all of the statements that contain this type of relation should be identified in the text. The type of statement a researcher is looking for will depend on the type of map he wishes to make. We may seek:

- statements containing links of influence (of the 'A affects, encourages, prevents B' kind); to construct an influence map
- statements containing causal links (of the 'A causes B, if A then B' kind); to establish a causal map
- statements containing similarity links (A is like or unlike B), or hierarchy links (A is included in B, A is an example of B); to construct category schemes
- or all of these links; to construct a cognitive map (Bougon, 1983).

The unit of analysis in cognitive mapping is, therefore, a statement of the 'concept A/link/concept B' type (Axelrod, 1976). These statements generally correspond to a sentence like 'cost-effectiveness encourages corporate growth' (influence relationship), 'if cost-effectiveness increases, then corporate growth is encouraged' (causal relationship), 'quality concerns are often similar to job-safety problems' (similarity relationship). Some statements, however, can be spread out over several sentences: 'The employees are on strike. We won't be able to deliver to our customers on schedule' (causal relationship between the two sentences). Since units of analysis do not necessarily correspond to a precise unit of text (for example, sentences), evaluating the reliability of their definition is highly recommended (Axelrod, 1976). The agreement rate between two coders will be calculated in terms of which elements they both consider to be codable in the text (see Robinson, 1957).

2.2 Defining categories

Identifying concepts Once all the statements have been identified, the researcher will attempt to locate within these statements the elements that the speaker considers to be links or influencing or influenced concepts (causes and effects, means and consequences). To facilitate identification of cause and effect elements (or influencing and influenced factors), Wrightson (1976) and Huff (1990) advise asking the following questions:

- 'Which came first, A or B?'
- 'Does A logically precede B?'
- 'Does A necessarily precede B?'

A being the supposed causal concept and B being the supposed effect.

When coding statements in a text, the general rule is not to modify their meaning. Variables are generally preserved in their literal form. However, in order to give the map a more dynamic aspect, it is advisable to transform nominal propositions expressing actions into the corresponding verb (Ackermann et al., 1992). So the variable 'Increase in the promotional budget' would be transformed into 'Increasing the promotional budget'. In addition, concepts should be expressed in the form of a variable, which can require modifying them slightly. For example, the variable 'product listing' should be expressed as 'quality or degree of product listing'.

Identifying links The next step is to search for the nature of the link relating the concepts that have been identified. These links can usually be identified by verbs (such as implies, leads to, prevents, etc.). For causal or influence maps, we generally look for the following links:

- Positive influence or causal links, (graded /+/): leads to, causes, has as a consequence, increases, enables ...
- Negative influence or causal links, (graded /−/): prevents, harms, damages, reduces, is harmful to, gets in the way of, decreases, diminishes, restricts ...
- Non-influence links, (graded /0/): has no effect on, is not tied to ...
- Positive non-implication influence links, (graded /0 +/): does not entail, does not increase, does not allow/enable, does not lead to ...
- Negative non-implication influence links, (graded /0 −/): does not prevent, does not harm ...

Besides these categories for qualifying relations of influence between identified variables precisely, Huff (1990) adds a certain number of coding rules which, although their goal is not to code relations of influence per se, do facilitate a later merging of the variables involved in different relations. These rules enable us, in fact, to identify the relations of 'definition' – in the broadest sense – expressed by subjects between different variables: particularly relations between examples illustrating a variable's level (for example, 'Machine X is a dangerous machine'), and relations of equality (for example, 'Competition means rivalry between conductors'). These categories allow us to detect connotative links between variables, thereby facilitating their later merging. However, taking these links into account makes data coding more complicated and weighs down the graphic representation that will be established.

The ambiguity of data discourse makes these coding operations difficult. Identifying variables and the links between them is no easy task, and certain links of influence (for example, contingent, interactive or reversible causal relations) have proven themselves to be extremely difficult to handle using the classic rules of coding (Cossette and Audet, 1992). Processing choices made in these cases (not coding them, creating specific coding rules, assimilating them to other relationships) must be specified.

Once the concepts and links in the statements that are considered codable have been identified, we have a list of relationships at our disposal. The next step is to combine the synonymous and redundant variables and influence links.

2.3 Merging similar concepts and variables

This phase involves deciding which variables the researcher considers as similar or synonymous. While the general rule is, when in doubt, leave the variables the way the interviewee expressed them, several guidelines can be of help during this phase (Wrightson, 1976):

1 If a variable is mentioned several times by a single respondent, then it is very likely that a modified expression of this variable is nothing more than a stylistic variation. We can then merge the variable and its modified expression, unless the respondent had explicitly specified a distinction between the two.
2 If a variable appears to be an example or a part of a more general one, then the two can be merged, as long as they are both expressed by the same person.
3 The basic rule underlying this operation is to ask oneself if the respondent's comments would be fundamentally modified if the merging were carried out.

By combining similar concepts and variables, links can be made between seemingly unrelated variables, which is of great assistance in drawing the interviewee's cognitive map. In order to facilitate data coding, it is a good idea to make a list of concepts and their corresponding merged terms.

Example: Coding data to establish an influence map

Say we seek to code the following paragraph:
'Increasing our publicity budget and the efforts on the part of our salesforce enabled us to improve our product listing in mass distribution. So our market share improved considerably, moving us from fifth to second place in our market.'
1. Identify codable statements
The paragraph contains four codable statements: two in the first sentence (increasing our publicity budget enabled us to improve our product listing in mass distribution; the efforts on the part of our sales force enabled us to improve our product listing in mass distribution), one connecting the first and the second sentences (improving

our product listing in mass distribution lead to a considerable improvement in our market share), and one in the last sentence (our market share improved considerably, going from fifth to second place in our market).

2. Specify the influencing factors/link/influenced factors

The statement 'increasing our publicity budget enabled us to improve our product listing in mass distribution' includes an influencing variable (increasing our publicity budget), an influenced variable (our product listing in mass distribution), and a positive influence relationship (enabled us to improve). The following example shows how the statement is coded:

    Publicity budget   /+/ (Quality or degree of) product listing

This is how the other statements are coded:

    Our salesforce's efforts /+/ (Quality or degree of) product listing
    (towards distributors)
    (Quality or degree of) /+/ Market share
    product listing
    Market share   /+/ Going from fifth to second place in our market

3. Merging synonymous variables

As the coded variables are different from each other, there are no merging operations to do. If, instead of the second sentence, we had had, 'Better store placement enabled us to improve our market share considerably, going from fifth to second place', we would undoubtedly have merged the variables 'degree of product listing' and 'store placement' and kept only one of them.

2.4 Coding reliability

Coding then follows the procedure described above (see Subsection 1.2). Intercoder reliability must be established: (1) for the units identified as codable, (2) for the classification of these units, (3) for merging decisions (see Axelrod, 1976, for calculating reliability rates).

Once the set of relations has been identified and merged, they can be represented graphically (with knots representing the concepts, and arrows the links between them).

2.5 Graphic representations of cognitive maps

Graphic representations can be arranged in different ways. Axelrod (1976) put the factual variables (environmental data, political options) on the left and the goals and consequences on the right (see Figure 16.2). Bougon et al. (1977) draw a map with the variables in a circle, so the final representation looks like a spider web. Eden et al. (1992) arrange them from bottom to top (from the means to the goals). Cossette (1994), using the COPE software, arranges the map in such a way that the distance separating variables that are linked through direct influence is as small as possible.

For someone using *a priori* methods, a graphic representation is less useful since the maps are subjected essentially to quantitative analysis. They are, therefore, generally left in the form of a matrix.

The matrix in Figure 16.3 corresponds to the map in Figure 16.2. This matrix cross-references the set of *n* variables included in the map with themselves. Cell

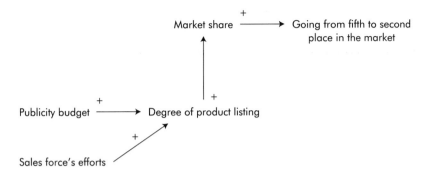

Figure 16.2 *Graphic representation of a cognitive map*

Variables/ influence	Publicity budget	Sales force's efforts	Degree of product listing	Market share	Company's market rank
Publicity budget	0	0	+1	0	0
Sales force's efforts	0	0	+1	0	0
Degree of product listing	0	0	0	+1	0
Market share	0	0	0	0	+1
Company's market rank	0	0	0	0	0

Figure 16.3 *An example of matrix representation of a cognitive map*

ij indicates the absence – value 0 – or presence – non-0 value – of a direct-influence link of the variable in line i on the variable in column j, as well as the polarity of this influence (positive, + 1; or negative, –1).

3. Analyzing the Data

3.1 Analyzing the structure of cognitive maps

Two main types of methods can be distinguished here: (1) methods which evaluate the subjects' cognitive complexity via general quantitative indicators, and (2) methods which reveal the structural dimensions upon which the subjects have organized their representations.

Complexity indicators   In order to apprehend the structure of a cognitive map, one can calculate a set of general complexity indicators:

- The number of variables (Weick and Bougon, 1986) and clusters (Cossette and Audet, 1992; Eden et al., 1992) included in the maps, which are indicators of the degree of differentiation between their constitutive elements.
- The number of links (Eden et al., 1992) and loops (Axelrod, 1976; Cossette and Audet, 1992; Eden et al., 1992; Weick and Bougon, 1986), which are indicators of their degree of interconnection.

These indicators depend largely on the method of establishing influence maps, and particularly on the degree of merging operated between synonymous variables and influence links.

Methods for analyzing the organization of cognitive maps   Along with these measurements, there is a set of methods that are more specifically intended to apprehend the organization of the subjects' representations. We can start by looking for the 'central' concepts in the map, that is, the concepts which are either strongly influenced (in which case they are taken as goals to achieve or consequences) or strongly influencing (seen as reasons for the phenomena described in the map or means of acting upon them; Cossette and Audet, 1992). A concept's centrality is generally defined by the number of direct links which it influences or is influenced by (Hart, 1976), or else by the total number of direct and indirect links influencing or influenced by it, weighted by the average length of the paths linking the factor under consideration to the others (Eden et al., 1992).

The general organization of a map can also be apprehended through cluster analysis. The particular dimensions around which subjects organize their representations are determined in this manner.

Eden's COPE software enables us to do all of these analyses. The advantage of these methods is that they do not require *a priori* structuring of the maps or standardization of the variables and links found within them (Daniels et al., 1993), while still enabling comparison between maps from different subjects or from the same subject at different times. On the other hand, they only examine the maps' organization, and not their content.

3.2 Analyzing the content of cognitive maps

The main purpose of the different methods for analyzing the contents of representations is to compare representations collected from a single subject at different times or from a group of subjects at the same time.

Global methods of comparing the content of cognitive maps   Global methods for comparing the contents of individual representations establish general indicators of content similarity based on the complete set of variables and links the representations contain. Within these methods, we generally distinguish between measures of distance and of similarity.

Distance measures   Distance measures are generally based on the Euclidean notion of distance. Nevertheless, due to a desire to compare the measurements obtained and to apply these ratios to different types of maps, these measurements quickly became more complex – through weighting, taking into account the strength of the links, the possible number of polarities in the influence links, the nature of the variables – receptive or transmitting – the unique nature of certain types of variables, the strength of the beliefs relative to the existence of links and so on (Langfield-Smith and Wirth, 1992; Markoczy and Goldberg, 1993). Despite the increase in the formulae's complexity and adaptability, these methods still require some structuring of the maps by the researcher: either through *a priori* collection methods or through *ex post* merging of the variables and links used by the subjects (Daniels et al., 1993). They thus reduce the validity of the individual maps; and are not very well-adapted to maps generated by non-structured methods.

Similarity measures   To establish similarity measurements, we first need to find the number of points in common between the different spaces to be compared in terms of links or variables, which can be weighted by the number of common and different points available (see, for example, the Jaccard or Dice indices; see Jaccard et al., 1990). Like distance measures, these ratios require a certain amount of standardization of the links and variables. However, unlike distance measures, the researcher can perform these operations *ex post*. These measures also have the advantage of being founded on dimensions shared by the maps that are being compared – the results obtained are then easier to interpret.

Aside from these mathematical evaluations, Daniels et al. (1993) suggest asking independent judges to evaluate the degree of similarity of pairs of maps. The average evaluation established in this manner will be retained as an indicator of their similarity. Unlike the preceding mathematical methods, turning to qualitative methods has the following advantages:

- It enables comparison between entirely idiosyncratic maps. Neither *a priori* nor *ex post* structuring is required.
- It is not contingent to a particular type of map.

These characteristics undoubtedly endow these methods with greater validity than mathematical measurements. Unfortunately, the size of the maps to be compared poses serious problems. Although it is easy to use qualitative evaluation for maps containing 10 to 50 variables, it becomes much less so when evaluating similarity for idiosyncratic maps that can contain 100 to 200 concepts. It can, therefore, be useful to focus analysis on a part of a cognitive map, rather than on the whole.

Local methods for analyzing the content of cognitive maps   This is one of the purposes of domain analysis. Domain analysis was developed by Laukkanen (1989; 1994) for comparing maps from different subjects or groups thereof. These analyses bear on sub-maps made up of factors that are to some extent directly influenced by, or influence, a variable that particularly interests the researcher. The CMAP2++ software developed by Laukkanen automatically generates to this effect databases made up of all the links and variables included in the sub-maps in which that variable is inserted. These lists of links and variables are easy to represent graphically and to analyze qualitatively (see Laukkanen, 1994) by, for example, collating the chains of factors influencing or influenced by a variable included in different subjects' sub-maps.

These analyses, bearing on the structure and contents of cognitive maps, can serve different research purposes. Up until now, most research concerned map analysis as such (see Cossette and Audet, 1992) or the elaboration of analysis methods (see Laukkanen, 1992; Eden et al., 1979; 1983). But cognitive maps can also serve to explain or to predict other behavioral variables or organizational phenomena (Komokar, 1994; Axelrod, 1976) and to assist in decision making (Eden et al., 1983; Eden, 1988; 1990; Eden and Banville, 1994).

CONCLUSION

To provide readers with a better idea of how they could use content analysis and cognitive mapping as part of their research, we will conclude with a presentation of the respective advantages and drawbacks of these two techniques.

Although content analysis's full potential is as yet rarely used in management research, it does offer researchers several advantages. In the first place, it can be used in a wide variety of cases. This methodology can be used for both quantitative and qualitative research. It can be applied to different types of discourse and documents and at various levels of analysis (individual, group, unit, organization or branch of industry).

In addition, it offers the advantage of being able to operate directly on data produced by organizational members, independently from the researcher and his or her objectives. The measurements it provides can be considered non-intrusive. The multiplication of computer-aided content-analysis programs makes this methodology even more attractive. Their coding is reliable, and they save a considerable amount of time, particularly in terms of coding procedures and statistical analysis.

However, certain drawbacks cannot be denied. Weber (1990) presents a fairly complete enumeration of these disadvantages; we will discuss only the main ones here. The first type of drawback is related to the classification process, which engenders certain problems related to the breadth or narrowness of the classification. Certain units of analysis which are classified in the same category may not reflect the category in the same way, but will be counted at the same value. We have described the difficulties encountered during the categorization process above. Another drawback is related to the fact that content analysis can really only capture a communication's manifest contents. A semiotic analysis would be necessary to reach the discourse's deeper, latent structure. In addition, although on the one hand content analysis does enable us to reduce and analyze a large quantity of diversified data, on the other, it can not grasp all of language's richness and subtleties. When assigning words to categories, some nuances and connotations are sure to be missed.

And finally, as relatively easy as quantitative data analysis now is, thanks to data analysis software and earlier research which has led the way, it is still difficult to offer precise methodologies for qualitative analysis, for which researchers must define their own rules depending on the purposes and context of their research.

Cognitive mapping it reveals a thought's complexity more precisely than simple content analysis can. This particularity of the cognitive mapping method is what makes it one of the most popular methods of analyzing discourse and representations in management today. There is a wide variety of data collection and analysis methods available for different research purposes. These range from quantitative comparison of the representations of a large number of individuals to in-depth analysis of free-interview or document data. Audet (1994) speaks of the 'plasticity' of cognitive mapping. Besides this advantage, relatively well-documented – and therefore practically usable as is – data coding methods for cognitive mapping are available to the researcher. As the graphic representation that this method enables us to achieve is relatively compact, it is an excellent communication and analysis tool for both consultants and researchers.

Nevertheless, this method does present a certain number of drawbacks. First, as we emphasized above, while cognitive mapping's *a priori* collection techniques can be used on a large scale, they pose certain validity problems for the data collected. Conversely, more natural methods generate representations that are likely to be closer to the subjects' thinking, but they pose data collection and coding reliability problems. In addition, these methods entail a tremendous amount of fastidious work for the researcher during the collection and coding processes, and therefore cannot be considered for large-scale studies. Second, unlike content analysis methods, the cognitive mapping method does not let us study processes (although we can study the evolution of static data collected over several occasions). Cognitive mapping is therefore not really appropriate for a detailed analysis of interaction data (for example, collected during meetings or discussions). For this, we are more likely to choose content analysis.

Finally, cognitive mapping, undoubtedly a victim of its own success, has become the object of a certain amount of criticism (for example, Schneider and Angelmar, 1993). This criticism must certainly be taken into account by the researcher, but, in our opinion, it depends more on the theoretical current on which the method relies (the cognitive approach to organizations) than on the method itself. The recent debate surrounding the cognitive mapping method encourages researchers to be vigilant in their use of it, which can only improve the quality of their work.

NOTE

1 For more details refer to Donada and M'Bengue, Chapter 13 in the present work.

FURTHER READING

Axelrod, R., *Structure of the Decision: The Cognitive Maps of Political Elites*, Princeton, NJ: Princeton University Press, 1976.

Cossette, P., Audet, M., 'Mapping an Idiosyncrasic Schema', *Journal of Management Studies*, 1992, 29 (3).

Huff, A.S., *Mapping Strategic Thought*, New York: Wiley, 1990.

Krippendorf, K., *Content Analysis: An Introduction to Its Methodology*, Beverly Hills, CA: Sage, 1980.

Roberts, C.W., 'Text Analysis for the Social Sciences: Methods for Drawing Statistical Inference from Texts and Transcripts', *Lea's Communication Series*, Mahwah, NJ: Lawrence Erlbaum Associates, 1997.

Stubbs, M., *Discourse Analysis*, Chicago: University of Chicago Press, 1983.

Weber, R.P., *Basic Content Analysis*, Sage University Papers, Newbury Park, CA: Sage, 1990.

PART IV

PUBLICATION
AND COMMUNICATION

The fourth and last part of this work brings us to the area of promoting the research results. Once we have completed our research, we must then communicate it, disseminate our results and transmit the fruits of our labor to the scientific community. To do this, the researcher has to prepare a report, a communication or an article. But for such writing to reach the broadest possible audience, and to have any hope of being published, it has to conform to conventions of style and form. Diffusion of our research depends also on the networks through which we can communicate it. Here too, there are forms and customs that researchers should be familiar with if they want their work to benefit from the broad dissemination they are entitled to expect.

17

WRITING UP THE RESEARCH

Bernard Forgues

Outline

Writing is a fundamental part of the research process. Not only does the communication of a researcher's work give meaning to research as a social phenomenon, but the quality of a study is almost inevitably judged on the evidence of its final presentation. This chapter outlines the different ways a work can be communicated to others, and then focuses on the primary medium: the research article. The final section of the chapter looks closely at the writing process itself, from the planning stage through to seeking feedback and revising your work.

> There's nothing to writing. All you do is sit down at a typewriter and open a vein.
>
> (Red Smith, cited by Wolcott, 1990: 24)

The writing up of research work is a subject that is raised comparatively rarely in manuals dealing with research methodology. However, it is a fundamental aspect of the process, for three reasons:

- Research, in so much as it is a social phenomenon, takes on meaning only when it is communicated to its audience, whoever this audience may be (peers, members of the organization studied, etc.). Research is of no use, from the point of view of advancing knowledge or from a practical point of view, if it remains confidential. It must be made public.
- Publication is an integral part of the work of researchers, and often serves as a criterion for their evaluation. Therefore, it plays an important role in their careers.
- Content is often indistinguishable from form. The final product (the article or thesis) is generally the only contact that readers have with the research that has been carried out. Readers confronted with a poor quality manuscript (for example, containing faults or calculation errors, or missing references) will naturally tend to think that the project as a whole was poorly conducted (Meyer, 1995).

In this chapter I review the factors that should be taken into account when writing up research work. The advice I give is intended to guide researchers, but it should be considered in context. Many researchers call for diversity in research, which includes allowing considerable liberty of form to writers. On this point, which goes beyond the scope of this chapter, I refer you to Daft and Lewin (1990) or Van Mannen (1995a). Moreover, the emphasis here is primarily on the writing of documents intended for a readership of researchers, and particularly on the writing of articles, the quintessential research vehicle.

SECTION 1   COMMUNICATION MEDIA

Communication of research work can be directed towards various readers. Research on organizations may be of interest to three particular kinds of readers: researchers, managers and other members of the organization, and, to a lesser extent, the general public. The same research project may then need to be adapted to different target audiences – and for this the text will need to be encoded. This encoding is the subject of the first part of this section, while the second part identifies the requirements of different audiences. The third and final part will examine the particular case of communication media destined for a readership made up of other researchers.

1. Encoding

Encoding is the process of producing a message according to an appropriate system of signs – a code. This message will then be decoded by the recipients, as long as they share, or know, the code used. If the message is to be understood, it is important it conforms strictly to the code.

What concerns us particularly is that the code has a bearing on the form of the text, and indicates to the readers what type of message it is: research, summary, popularization, etc. For this reason, in encoding a text for a scientific purpose researchers generally include a section on methodology, direct the reader to appropriate references and avoid what Daft (1995) calls an amateur style and tone – such as exaggerating the importance of the project, over-insistence (for example by using exclamation marks) or expressing an overly negative attitude towards previous studies.

Such encoding might seem constraining to the writer of the text, in so far as the form of the text is to a large degree imposed from above. If one considers, however, the 'Instructions to Contributors' provided by all academic journals, the importance of encoding is tangible. A text that disregards this encoding will be seen as deviating from the norm, and it will be more difficult to have it accepted for publication. In some cases an article can be rejected without thorough evaluation, simply because its form betrays the fact that the author has not tried to adapt the work to the journal's editorial policy. However, the strictness to which certain criteria are applied depends very much on the people at the top of the system: the gatekeepers (the publication's editor and reviewers).

Table 17.1   *Publication media and their readerships*

Media	Researchers	Managers
Research articles	Very strong use	Weak use
Management articles	Strong	Strong
Books	Strong	Strong
Oral communication	Very strong	Weak
Reports	None	Very strong

Although the code is generally shared across different publication media within the scientific genre, particular publications often have their own lesser conventions that should also be respected. For example, *Administrative Science Quarterly* and the *Academy of Management Journal* share the same scientific code, but one can easily tell, on reading an article, from which of these journals it has been taken.

2. Target Readerships

The three kinds of possible readerships can be classified according to their exposure to different forms of communication. First, researchers form the principal audience. Managers may be interested, to a lesser degree, in accordance with the theme of the study or the industry being studied, and particularly in the application aspects of the research. Finally, it is only rarely that the general public has any contact with research. For these reasons, we will not broach here the question of adapting research to a very large readership. Richardson (1990), however, provides a good analysis of an example of adaptation for the general public.

Research can be communicated through five general types of publications: research articles, managerial articles, books, conference papers and reports. To these can be added, although generally only once in the life of a researcher, a doctoral dissertation. There is an amount of consistency between the two principal readerships – researchers and managers – and the different publication media, as is shown in Table 17.1.

Other researchers are interested in most publication media, but their expectations can vary in line with the medium in which they are seeking information. They may look for specific results in an academic journal, but use a management journal to find examples to use in illustrating a course. Unfortunately, managers are less concerned with research, apart from, of course, applied studies they have commissioned, and which are to be the subject of a report. Managers can, however, ensure the success of some books as far as sales are concerned, or turn to practitioner-oriented journals to keep themselves informed.

As these different readerships have different expectations, the content of the text must be adapted accordingly, keeping within the encoding norms

Table 17.2   *Encoding according to readership*

Encoding	Researchers	Managers
References	Numerous	Limited number
Methodology	Important: must be able to be evaluated	Non-existent, or placed in an appendix
Status of data	Synecdoche*	Illustration
Results	Discovery, theory	Practical application
Style	Impersonal, 'scientific'**	Lively, oriented towards practice

* Figure of speech in which a part comes to stand for the whole (such as 'roof' standing for 'house'). For example, the use of samples (Richardson, 1990).
** This style implies the neutrality of the researcher, which is debatable. Because of this its legitimacy is vigorously challenged (see Van Mannen, 1995b, or Kilduff and Mehra, 1997).

appropriate for the intended medium. Table 17.2 presents encoding rules as a function of the intended readership.

It is sometimes difficult to apply these encoding rules, as the same text can have various readerships.

As an example of the adaptation of research articles for a public consisting of managers, The *Academy of Management Executive* has since 1993 provided 'research translations' – presentations of research articles that have appeared in other journals. These presentations are often much (two pages) shorter than the original article, are not referenced and are written in a direct style, with emphasis on the implications of the research.

3. Media for Researchers

Before we look at research articles, the principal medium in which research work is written, let us look briefly at the various possible means of communicating with colleagues in the field.

We can distinguish between oral communication methods, such as conference presentations, and written methods, such as articles. Within these two groups we can also distinguish works based on data from those that are purely conceptual.

Conference presentations generally do not go beyond 20 minutes. It is important to observe this time limit, so as to leave room for discussion with the audience. Speakers must therefore plan their presentation carefully beforehand, and select the points to develop. One recommends a quick presentation of the fundamental theoretical concepts and the main lines of development of the research. The accent should always be placed on the results and on their contributions to the field, both practical and theoretical.

As for written media, the differences between them depend more on the presence of data than on the type of document. A conceptual article or a literature review will necessarily be presented differently than an empirical article. Methodology and results will be absent, with the emphasis placed on theoretical implications and on future research. To see the differences between empirical and non-empirical articles, I refer you to the *Academy of Management Journal*, which publishes only empirical articles, and to the *Academy of Management Review*, which publishes only conceptual articles.

SECTION 2   RESEARCH ARTICLES

1. Structure

The principal medium by which studies reach other researchers is the research article, published in an academic journal. The structure of these articles is very often identical, even where guidelines are not precisely defined. The structure that I outline below, which is almost universal for quantitative research, is equally well adapted to qualitative research. For example, the article presenting the quantitative research of Zajac and Westphal (1996) adopts the same structure as that of Barley's (1996) qualitative research published in the same issue of *Administrative Science Quarterly*.

This structure usually consists, after the abstract, of an introduction, an analysis of existing literature, presentation of the methodology, presentation of the results and discussion of the results. A fundamental point in writing an article is that a logical sequence is essential, through which the reader can understand the argument and follow its development. This is achieved by concentrating on research aims, avoiding digressions and taking care to clearly explain transitions.

The *abstract* is a difficult exercise, all too often replaced by a paragraph taken from the introduction. A good abstract must present in a few words the context of the study and its principal results.

The *introduction* is generally fairly short. The interest the topic holds, theoretically and/or practically, should be made clear.

The *literature analysis* enables the study to be situated in relation to previous research. The author should underline any divergences, and may establish links between related fields. One must, however, stress the importance of staying focused on the research question, and so guiding the reader. This analysis may, where appropriate, lead to the formulation of hypotheses.

The *methodology presentation* explains the different stages of the research, and the order followed. Here we find descriptions of any samples used or of the case or cases studied, operationalization of the concepts, and discussion of the analyses conducted. It is important to recount exactly what was done, without any rationalization after the fact (Daft, 1995).

Results are limited to the main findings. As this part is usually fairly short, the results can be presented in a summarized form, as in the case of quantitative analyses, where tables are frequently used.

A *discussion of research results* puts them in the perspective of existing studies. Agreements and discrepancies are pointed out, and explanations for these are explored. In this section, the author will also talk about the implications of his or her research, in both theoretical and practical terms. We will also find here an analysis of the limits of the study, and often propositions are made for future research arising from these new results.

2. Form: Figures, Tables, References and Footnotes

2.1 Figures

It is very difficult to produce an interesting diagram that will have a real impact on the reader. A too-complex diagram will be illegible, and a too-simple diagram will not provide any information. Two essential types of diagrams are used: those presenting relationships (I will refer to these as models), and those presenting data (graphs). Models allow us to illustrate a process that would be too cumbersome to describe, or visually represent a group of relationships among variables. Similarly, graphs are visual representations of quantitative data. Graphs are an effective way of drawing attention to aspects considered to be important.

As Daft (1995: 178) points out diagrams can be adapted to every type of research. 'For traditional hypothesis-testing studies, a visual representation strengthens the early part of the manuscript and can be revised in the conclusion section. For qualitative studies, a visual representation at the end of the manuscript is an ideal way to crystallize the theory developed from personal observations.' As regards presentation, figures should be referred to in the text, and should be self-explanatory.

2.2 Tables

Tables, which are used very often, offer readers a visual summary of a discussion. They can present a synthesis of a literature review or of research data, whether quantitative or qualitative. As with diagrams, tables should be referred to in the text, and must be comprehensible in their own right.

2.3 References

References are important in that they situate the research within a body of theory and give credibility to the results. They must therefore be selected with care. For this, three basic criteria should be used: relevance, credibility, and accessibility.

A reference will be relevant if it gives something to the reader. It has to be strongly linked to the problem concerned. An article should be cited as a reference only because of its results, and not for some minor point that it may only mention in passing.

The credibility of a reference depends essentially on its medium. A top-ranking journal will be regarded as very credible. It is important that references have the same level of credibility. Credibility also demands that authors follow up their sources: it is preferable to cite an article in which an idea originated, rather than a more recent work which has only reworked this idea. This can, however, pose a problem in the case of a work which is out of print.

In this regard, accessibility relates to the ease with which readers will be able to obtain the references cited. It is preferable to make use of works published in journals with a wide distribution.

A common error is to introduce too many references. In some manuscripts every phrase, or nearly every one, is backed up with one or several references, even when it treats only a minor aspect. Such a superabundance causes the force of the main argument to be lost, drowned under a mass of minor information. Campion (1997) conducted an inquiry among reviewers to determine criteria with which to select references to use in research articles (see Table 17.3).

2.4 Footnotes

Most journals recommend limiting as much as possible the use of footnotes, which break up the reading. Some journals simply forbid them, on the basis of the following principle: if the point is important, it should be in the body of the text, if it is not important, it should be removed.

3. Style and Qualitative Research

The style of writing to use for qualitative research articles has been addressed in numerous articles and books. The form of such writing too is crucial, particularly for two quite different reasons: the difficulty of presenting qualitative research and the realization that 'data' is already very strongly a matter of interpretation.

On the first point, Richardson (1990: 53–4) remarks:

> Shaping qualitative material for mainline journals requires telling your research story in a way that meets the expectations of the editors/reviewers of those journals. Quantitative writers have an easier time with this, for their work is already strongly encoded as positivist-empiricist (through such rhetorical devices as tables and path diagrams) and because the criteria for judging the work is more precise and shared among the community of believers. Qualitative writers have a more difficult time, I think, because their papers have fewer strong encodings, and their reviewers have fewer and less precise agreements about significance and other such matters …

In a somewhat provocative article, Sutton (1997) presses the argument, and identifies four situations in which it can be preferable to hide or at least minimize the role of qualitative data in the development of a study: 'when weak qualitative data lead to good insights, when describing the qualitative research reduces the quality of the writing, when an outlet does not publish "empirical" papers, and when writing for an audience that remains biased against qualitative research' (Sutton 1997: 97–8).

Table 17.3   *Use of references in research articles (after Campion, 1997)**

Is it necessary to give references?

- Yes, to indicate a source (of a theory, a result, a method).
- Yes, to point out similar or contradictory results.
- Possibly, to justify the subject or the use of a particular technique.
- Possibly, to support a concept or an assertion.
- No, for assertions that are evident, or commonly accepted techniques.

What determines the quality of a reference?

- First of all, the fact that it is appropriate to the context.
- It draws on original results or results of meta-analyses.
- It draws on research or theories.
- Some references do not, however, constitute solid support. These are references to assertions that are not results, to textbooks, and to non-refereed publications.

What references should be given?

- Preferably, those at the origin of the field of research.
- Those that are the most rigorous in their methodological or conceptual design.
- The most recent and easiest to find.
- Avoid those chosen only because they are often cited or are better known.
- Avoid those that have not been evaluated or are difficult to find (research notebooks, theses).

How many references should be given?

- A lot, for synthesis articles.
- Several to show that a point is controversial.
- Several to indicate different types of support (theoretical and empirical).
- Several to show the scope of the literature, or to retrace its history.
- Less in fields that are new and have been little explored.
- In no case to show that one has read a lot, or to enable readers to develop their knowledge.
- Avoid giving an excessive number of references, and avoid references on marginal topics.

Can the writer cite himself or herself?

- Yes, if the study cited is pertinent.
- Yes, to indicate other studies that have used the same data.
- No, if other more pertinent references exist.
- No, if simply to prove his or her expertise in the field.
- In general, avoid giving too many self-references.

How do we monitor references?

- By assuring their pertinence in relation to the topic at hand.
- By verifying the accuracy of the information provided (date, publication, page numbers, etc.).

* Based on the responses of around 300 reviewers from *Personnel Psychology, Academy of Management Journal, Academy of Management Review* and *Journal of Applied Psychology.*

The second point stresses the fact that no description can be neutral, that all texts have their biases (Denzin, 1994; Mitroff, 1972). This takes on special importance in a qualitative project. As Geertz (1973: 9) points out in ethnography, a description is thick with the interpretations of the researcher: 'what we call our data are really our own constructions of other people's constructions'.

Consequently, the distinction between data and analysis becomes at best difficult, perhaps impossible. The whole chain of evidence of a positivist approach is put into question. To convince the reader of the sound basis for the study, one can, as Johanson (1996) advises, set up a network of presumptions.

Drawing an analogy with the judicial process, she advises authors to try to convince the reviewers in the way that a prosecutor tries to convince the jury. In the absence of formal 'proof', it is a question of winning over the jury by a body of elements that mutually reinforce one another.

3.1 Case studies

A case study can be presented in different ways, each of which have advantages and drawbacks, and each of which favor one or another purpose. The first possibility is to set out an account which is as neutral as possible, so that readers are left to form their own opinion. To achieve this a chronological account may be adopted. However, we should be aware that the apparent neutrality of the account is deceptive: certain aspects have been chosen for discussion, and others not, the structure of the text implies a particular logic, and so on. The difficulty of this choice lies in its structure, which does not allow for the topics covered to be grouped according to type. This makes comprehension difficult, and weakens the arguments. The solution most often adopted is to follow the account with a discussion of the analyses according to themes, which necessitates repetition and lengthens the document. By contrast, another possibility is that of breaking the case study up into the topics discussed. Here the advantage is in having an article that is more structured, more focused, but the elements of the context are minimized. This kind of structure can also invite criticism as it can seem that the author chooses to describe examples that support his or her theory. Glaser and Strauss (1967) call this *exampling* and rightly condemn it.

All the same, if several cases are to be presented, one can arrange a presentation in a case-by-case order of priority, or transversely, in order of topics. The presentation of individual cases has the advantage of giving an overview, but to the detriment of comparisons, which can mean that the argument is less convincing. The transverse presentation is, on the contrary, more analytical, but makes it very difficult to give an overall picture.

3.2 Style

The style of writing that is adopted takes on a special importance in qualitative research. The writer has to convince readers without using figures. An ethnographic text involves three dimensions (Golden-Biddle and Locke, 1993): *authenticity* (assurance that the researcher was there and was genuine about the experience in writing up the account), *plausibility* (does this have meaning; does it contribute to our knowledge?) and *criticality* (does the text impel readers to reconsider ideas and beliefs they have taken for granted?). Authenticity is obtained by particularizing everyday life, by delineating the relationship of the researcher to the field, by describing the methods used in collecting and analyzing data, and by qualifying personal biases. As for plausibility, meaning is gained by encoding the text so that unorthodox methodologies are normalized, by legitimating the atypical and smoothing the contestable, and by presenting oneself as an expert. The contribution the work makes is emphasized by pointing out gaps in existing studies, and in leading readers to feel that something new has been presented.[1] Finally, criticality is obtained by challenging readers to reconsider the assumptions that underlie their own work.

Still in the area of ethnography, Van Maanen (1988) distinguishes three principal styles, and illustrates them by examples drawn from his own work:

- The realistic style aims to be neutral and impersonal. It is characterized by the absence of the author in the final text, by relying on precise details arranged redundantly into categories, by the point of view of the subject being presented through quotations, and by the interpretative omnipotence by which the researcher assumes the right to interpret and describe reality.
- The confessional style, by contrast, is very personal. Here the researcher recounts in detail any difficulties that arose, and incidents that occurred in the field. The three conventions that characterize this style are: the researcher is brought to the fore; the researcher is strongly involved in the field, and his or her point of view is taken into account; and a final distancing of the researcher helps to return a degree of objectivity to the account.
- The impressionist style focuses on the process, rather than on the results of fieldwork or on the researcher. This style is characterized by: a raw account that aims to make the experience come alive to the reader; by the fragmentation of the results because of this linear narration; by the personal way in which the subjects and the researcher are described, which makes the story more lively; and by its dramatic flavor, which imposes standards of literature rather than standards of the appropriate discipline, that is, of ethnography.

It is clear that the choice of style is not a neutral decision. It reflects the epistemological position of the researcher, his or her conception of research itself. This link between epistemology and writing style explains the homogeneity in tone observed in any given journal. Given this, authors are wise to identify the journal whose style best corresponds to their own, or otherwise to conform to the style of the journal in which they seek to be published.

SECTION 3   THE WRITING PROCESS

I examine here the questions of when to write, how to improve a text (by soliciting feedback on the manuscript) and the revision process used by refereed journals.

1. When to Write

On the issue of when to write, the principal advice we find repeatedly given is, begin as soon as possible (Richardson, 1990; Wolcott, 1990; Yin, 1990). To fully understand this argument, it is important to remember that the writing up of a research project is not done in one sitting. It is a long process, a labor to which one returns many times in order to improve the text. Commencing writing early in the project brings several advantages. The most trivial is purely practical: the early stages of the research are relatively less demanding, and there is time to collect the required documentation. By writing in advance in this way researchers can free up their time, allowing them, when the time comes, to devote their full attention to analysis and results (Yin, 1990).

Wolcott (1990) highlights another advantage. He points out that writing is a form of reflection, and therefore that writing enables us to clarify our thoughts and to expose weaknesses in our reasoning. So, he explains, the process of writing can reveal how the work is unfolding: if the writing is going badly, it is surely because one has nothing to say, or more correctly, that one is not yet able to explain the research. Wolcott (1990) also points out that authors who postpone writing, arguing that they have not yet clarified their ideas perfectly, run the risk of never commencing.

2. Feedback

A text will be revised many times during the writing phase, which is a long and delicate process. Numerous questions arise as this process unfolds, including the degree of exposure to give to a paper in progress, and when to start looking for comments and feedback. First, it must be noted that there is unanimous agreement on encouraging writers to seek comments on their manuscripts before formally submitting them to a journal. It is important to have the manuscript read by colleagues, friends, and students who may be able to give advice relating to the research, but equally well to the way in which the article is written. As Daft (1995: 180) advises: 'Allow the paper to ripen naturally with the passage of time, lots of sunshine, and many revisions …'.

An article should undergo at least two or three major revisions before it is submitted to a journal (Meyer, 1992; 1995). These revisions should relate to both content and form, (Wolcott, 1990). We must also bear in mind that comments and modifications can be endless: there will always be something in a paper that can be improved, whether as a result of comments from a reviewer, or the writer's own development on the subject. It is important then to know when to stop. Comments are more often related to form than to content (Richardson, 1990), as it is easier to criticize a phrase than a general process, and because readers are there to help writers to convey their ideas, and not to impose their own (Wolcott, 1990). Hence it is important to provide them with a paper that is already well advanced. A manuscript that is full of errors and approximations, or is incomplete, distracts the readers' attention from its most important points, and prevents them from making a worthwhile contribution: it is much easier to help improve a good manuscript than a really poor paper.

Comments are generally negative. It is well to be aware of this beforehand, so as not to be surprised or discouraged. We are more inclined to pick up on imperfections, problems or difficulties, than to stop at an excellent passage to congratulate the author on it. This is, first, because a precise, meticulous reading renounces a general impression in favor of a detailed examination of each point. The second reason is the fact that, in doing this, the reader is fulfilling the expectations of the writer. In order to help improve the text, it is necessary to pick up on all its imperfections. So, whatever the quality of the text, comments are always disproportionately on the negative side. Submitting an article to a refereed journal will provide ample demonstration of this.

3. The Reviewing Process

The major academic journals have an extremely rigorous process of selecting articles. Each article is evaluated anonymously by specialists in the field, called *reviewers*, and returned to the author for revision. This process is repeated until the article is rejected or, less often, accepted for publication.

The Reviewing Process

Articles are submitted by authors to the editor of the journal, who then nominates reviewers, chosen for their expertise in the field. Reviewers are usually members of the editorial board, but this is not always the case. The evaluation is generally anonymous: the reviewers do not know who wrote the paper, neither does the author know who the reviewers are (double-blind review process). This is to guarantee that the evaluation is neutral.

The reviewers make their recommendation to the editor as to whether to reject, accept or modify the article, and they suggest modifications to the author.

The editor, on the basis of two or three evaluations and his or her own judgement, informs the author as to the decision on the paper. Whatever the decision, the editor sends the author all the reviewers' comments.

The rate of acceptance of articles in the major journals is very low (for example, 11 per cent for the *Academy of Management Review* (Jackson, 1996)). It almost never happens that an article is accepted without having to be revised.

From first writing up the results to publication of the article can take up to three years (writing + submission + two or three revisions + delay in publication).

The reviewing process is a strongly emotional issue that is often poorly understood. To appreciate the various aspects of this – the development of the research, publishing of its results, maintaining the required minimum level of quality, the power relationships involved, etc. – *Publishing in the Organizational Sciences*, edited by Cummings and Frost (1995), is a good source of perceptive advice.

The reviewing process should be seen as a social activity, with interaction between the author, the editor, and the reviewers (Pondy 1995). This interaction should be constructive. As Meyer says (1995: 265) in reference to reviewers, the process should 'turn umpires into coaches'. It is therefore strongly advised to attach a personal reply to each of the reviewers when returning the revised article, explaining point by point which of their comments have been incorporated and why the others have not.

It is important to maintain a positive attitude during the review process. Certainly, it is often difficult to accept criticism of a labor into which one has put so much of oneself, but objectivity is essential. As Rousseau (1995) points out, even the most provocative commentaries may have been written by reviewers who appreciate the research. And in the contrary situation, seemingly negative reviewers can eventually change their mind, or have their opinion rejected by the editor. A reviewer is there to improve the article: if a point has not been understood, this is surely because it was not expressed clearly enough (Daft, 1995; Meyer, 1995). The importance of feedback in improving an article is shown clearly in the examples given by Frost and Stablein (1992). Each of the research projects they discuss benefited greatly from feedback, as much informally through the views of colleagues, as formally through the reviewing processes of the journals to which these articles were submitted.

Often, however, the process does not lead to the desired result and the article is rejected. Faced with this situation, the researcher has to resist several impulses: arguing that the reviewers are stupid, giving up on the article entirely or sending it straight off to another journal. The first solution is not constructive and stops an author from reflecting on the weaknesses of the article. The second is unproductive and comes down to obliterating all the effort that went into the research. And the third brings with it the risk of suffering a new rejection. It is better to allow some time to pass so as to be able to take a step back from the manuscript. The researcher is then in a position to study the reviewers' comments, discuss them with colleagues, and thoroughly rework the article before submitting it to another journal. Here it is important to note that, almost universally, journals have a policy against the same article being sent to several of them at the same time. Authors must wait for the decision of one journal before soliciting another.

CONCLUSION

In conclusion, it can be said that trial and error is the best apprenticeship in writing articles. Writing can be improved in purely technical ways, and by a thorough attention to detail on the part of authors. It is always surprising to see, when managing a journal, how often authors submit papers that could have been greatly improved simply by rereading them with an eye towards copy-editing. Aspects of form should not be neglected either, as to some extent they are seen as indicating the quality of the research presented, and of the author's motivation. An author who submits a paper without having compared it to other articles published by that same journal, or without respecting the publication's presentation norms, will greatly reduce its chances of being accepted.

Research projects are judged on the quality of the final product – the research article. Above all else, this article requires of the researcher both persistence and diligence.

NOTE

1 The rhetorical construction of the contribution has been analyzed by Locke and Golden-Biddle (1997).

FURTHER READING

Cummings, L.L. and Frost, P.J. (eds), *Publishing in the Organizational Sciences*, 2nd edn., Thousand Oaks, CA: Sage, 1995.

Golden-Biddle, K. and Locke, K.D., *Composing Qualitative Research*, Thousand Oaks: Sage, 1997.

Richardson, Laurel, *Writing Strategies: Reaching Diverse Audiences*, Qualitative Research Methods Series, 21, Newbury Park, CA: Sage, 1990.

Thyer, B.A., *Successful Publishing in Scholarly Journals*, Survival Skills for Scholars Series, 11, Thousand Oaks, CA: Sage, 1994.

Van Maanen, J., *Tales of the Field: On Writing Ethnography*, Chicago: University of Chicago Press, 1988.

18

THE RESEARCH ENVIRONMENT

Jean-Marc Xuereb

Outline

The traditional, stereotypical image of the academic researcher, tucked away in an obscure office, surrounded by piles of papers and making new discoveries through the fruit of solitary endeavor, is far from modern reality. Connected to the scientific and academic community by e-mail, Internet, telephone and fax, and with conferences and symposiums providing regular opportunities to meet with peers, researchers today find themselves at the center of a vast network of contacts from which they can draw inspiration, knowledge and recognition.

This chapter outlines the various elements of the researcher's environment. It describes how researchers can create and develop their network of contacts and broaden their knowledge, and explains how they can profit from the possibilities of the current academic world.

Traditionally, a career in academic research begins by writing a dissertation and obtaining a PhD. However, this initial research work should be seen as a stage rather than an achievement in itself. Beyond the realization of the dissertation, this stage is vital for planning and building a future career.

Writing a dissertation is a personal task, but the researcher's environment plays an important role in its realization. The aim is not only to write the dissertation, but also to build a network, to participate in conferences and to start publishing. The thesis advisor will have a considerable influence during this phase. But the nature, quality and intensity of the exchanges with the thesis advisor will also have a tangible influence on for the postgraduate student's entire future career. A great deal of the following is therefore dedicated to the role and functions of the thesis advisor in guiding the postgraduate student at the beginning of his or her career. The environment of the researcher is then examined in further detail.

SECTION 1   THE THESIS ADVISOR

One day, a fox met a rabbit in the woods. The rabbit was preoccupied with a small laptop computer, which he wore hanging from a strap across his shoulders.

Fox: 'Rabbit, what are you doing with that computer?'

Rabbit: 'I'm working on a dissertation, about rabbit predation of the fox and wolf populations.'

Fox, bursting out laughing, replies: 'But, my dear rabbit, everyone knows that the fox hunts the rabbit, not the other way around!'

Rabbit: 'I know, that's what people think, but I've already carried out a literature review proving the opposite. Would you like to see it?'

Fox: 'With pleasure, but if this literature review of yours isn't convincing, you'll be the first to suffer the consequences.'

The fox and the rabbit walked over to the rabbit's burrow, and both went inside. Twenty minutes later, the rabbit came out again, with the laptop still slung across his shoulders, and set off towards the woods.

Two hours later, the rabbit returned to his burrow, this time followed by a wolf. The rabbit invited the wolf inside. After a moment, the rabbit entered, and hopped over to a small workstation, framed by two piles of bones, labeled 'Wolf Bones' and 'Fox bones' respectively. After entering some data into his computer, the rabbit turned to an impressive desk, where a lion sat enthroned. The rabbit spoke with deep respect:

'Venerable Thesis Advisor, I believe we have collected enough data to start the statistic analysis and verify our hypothesis.'

This story, which is probably as old as the academic world it comes from, partly illustrates the three main roles of a thesis advisor. The thesis advisor is first of all a guide. The researcher will profit from his or her greater experience, especially in defining the subject of the dissertation. The thesis advisor should provide guidance towards research domains that have been rarely or never explored, but also present a real interest over the long term. The advisor is to be a problem-solver, helping the researcher to identify and solve epistemological, methodological and ethical problems that appear during the writing process. A thesis advisor will often become a mentor. A master–disciple relationship can develop between these two people, sharing the same interests inside an intellectual community. A mentorship is commonly maintained throughout the researcher's academic career.

Choosing the thesis advisor is thus a decision of great consequence, having an influence on the final quality and outcome of the dissertation and on the launch of a researcher's career. The researcher should therefore pay close attention to the choice of thesis advisor. Several criteria may help making this decision.

Intellectual proximity to the considered research problem   This is vital. No matter how brilliant his or her academic qualities, a thesis advisor who is not interested in the envisaged research domain will be of very limited use to the postgraduate student. He or she will not be familiar with the literature, and may not be able to help define the problem in a precise manner, not knowing if the subject is truly innovative or if it has already been explored elsewhere. Furthermore, an uninterested advisor will probably not have established a contact network in the specific field – a network from which the doctoral student can benefit greatly. The differing interests of the thesis advisor and the student provides no ground for the emergence of an intellectual community.

Academic achievements (including publications, participation in national and international conferences, editorial responsibilities) A thesis advisor generally holds a PhD. It is important to look beyond accreditations, however, and consider a potential thesis advisor's publications, involvement in the academic community, and participation in national and international academic events. An advisor who has not published many articles in the international press or who only takes part in statewide (regional) or national activities will not be of much help to a graduate aiming for an international career.

Availability Writing a dissertation requires frequent meetings with the thesis advisor – to keep the advisor up to date as to the state of the work, to exchange new ideas, and to identify and resolve problems as they arise. It is therefore important to ensure that the potential advisor will be available for such regular meetings for the course of the research. This is not to suggest that the advisor must be immediately available at all times, but if a serious problem arises, his or her presence may be needed at short notice. One useful way to assess in advance the availability of a particular thesis advisor is to find out how many postgraduate students he or she is already responsible for. The more students an advisor has, the less time he or she can commit to each one. Beyond the question of the number of postgraduate students a thesis advisor has, information can also be obtained from other students who have already worked with him or her.

Of course, it is difficult to find a thesis advisor fulfilling all these criteria, even more so because some of them can seem mutually incompatible. For instance, a potential thesis advisor who is highly involved in international academic circles and who frequently publishes articles in the best reviews will probably have limited time for students. Also, the academic quality of potential advisors should be evaluated according to the length of their career: one could not expect someone who has only recently obtained a doctorate to have published the same volume of articles as an experienced professor.

Each PhD candidate should take these criteria into consideration and seek the best balance possible in accordance with his or her individual needs. Some postgraduate students need a lot of back-up and regular meetings with their thesis advisor. Such students should make availability their primary criteria. Others may be more independent, and attach more importance to academic accreditation or experience when choosing an advisor.

A French academic, Pierre-Gilles de Gennes, who won the Nobel Prize for Physics in 1991, gives this practical advice to young researchers-to-be:

> Above all, chose a good thesis advisor for your dissertation: don't go for the first one, but take time in choosing, and talk to a number of possible candidates. As to the subject, it should be connected to a future national need. Some [advisors] suggest subjects of interest to themselves, but which will clearly not be of interest to any employer.[1]

Once an advisor for the research has been selected, the dissertation student must in turn gain his or her acceptance. It is important to submit an abstract of a dozen or so pages, clearly setting out the proposed research question, so that the advisor has a basis from which to come to a decision.

When both parties have agreed to the project, the postgraduate student should take care to respect the thesis advisor's demands in terms of the research schedule. A lack of involvement on the part of the dissertation student may well provoke a corresponding lassitude on the part of a thesis advisor, who will direct more attention to students who show more commitment to their projects.

Along with consideration of the aptitude and the personality of the thesis advisor, the research department and the university or college of which it is a part must be chosen with great forethought, as this will influence the quality of any research project. Here are some points to take into account.

Reputation   The reputation of management schools varies greatly, and is often directly associated to the quality of the research projects hosted. While there are no objective criteria for measuring the reputation of a research center, examining career paths and the articles published by doctors from different centers can give an indication as to the reputation of the school.

Facilities   The presence of workspace reserved for research, free access to computers and necessary software, a well-stocked and up to date library, and the availability of funds to finance conference participation are among the facilities that are useful in writing a dissertation and in founding a contact network.

Academic activities   Some research centers organize research symposiums, conferences and international gatherings, all of which can be intellectually rewarding for the student. Such intellectual stimulation can have a very positive effect on the quality of graduate work carried out at the school.

The criteria detailed above, both for the thesis advisor and for the center, may seem a little demanding. They should, however, be considered in context. A postgraduate student who decides to write a PhD dissertation is taking on a project that will take an average of four years to complete. At the end of these long years, competition is strong for a limited number of positions available. The quality of the dissertation becomes then an important factor in embarking upon an academic career. In addition to the personal investment involved, it is important to have as many factors as possible working for you: such as the support of a good thesis advisor and the advantages of a high-quality working structure. Too many researchers abandon their dissertation at an early stage, or write a paper that can handicap them throughout their career, primarily because they did not place enough weight on these considerations, or they overestimated their own capacities or desire to complete the postgraduate work.

SECTION 2   RESEARCH CONSORTIUMS

At conferences held by research associations, researchers of different origins come together to discuss subjects connected to the writing of a dissertation and how to embark upon and construct an academic career. Because of the diversity of research questions, methodologies and experiences, participants often find these meetings very rewarding.

2.1 The Academy of Management

The Academy of Management (AoM) comprises 15 different divisions, each dealing with one specific field of research. Each division generally holds a doctoral consortium the weekend before the annual conference of the Academy of Management. The level of these conferences tends to be highly specialized, due to the presence of researchers and students from one specifically defined research domain (technology and innovation management, organizational behavior, strategy). The doctoral consortium is generally organized by the 'Program Chair Elect' of the division, who is accompanied in leading the conference by three to five researchers recognized within the domain.

Over two days, the participants of the doctoral consortium are given the opportunity to discuss:

- current and future research
- how to carry out a research project
- publication issues
- teaching at different levels and to different audiences
- managing an academic career.

These discussions are generally fairly informal, and a sizeable amount of time is reserved for presenting participants' research projects.

As well as organizing doctoral consortiums, a number of divisions of the Academy of Management also hold a 'Junior Faculty Consortium'. These two-day conferences are reserved for researchers who have just begun their academic career. Typical issues covered during these consortiums include:

- how to obtain tenure
- how to have articles published
- how to choose a mentor;

An invitation is required to take part in the consortiums of the Academy of Management. Further information can be found on the web site of the Academy of Management (http://www.aom.pace.edu/).

SECTION 3   ACADEMIC CONFERENCES

By taking part in academic conferences, a researcher has the opportunity to:

- present the results of research work and receive feedback from the academic community
- constructively integrate suggestions and critiques made by academic peers into the final work

- keep up with current developments in a specific research domain by becoming familiar with projects before they have been published
- become an active member of national or international research networks and maintain contacts with other researchers in a specific field of expertise
- meet the editors of the principal academic reviews, who are usually present at conferences and often organize informal get-togethers
- consult and buy books and research publications at considerable price reductions (20 per cent to 50 per cent depending on the editor; prices often drop further towards the end of a conference).

In addition to these general considerations, which could apply to any conference or seminar, the specific characteristics of each individual conference should be considered before submitting a research project to any particular one.

Proposition format   Certain conferences require a full scientific article of 20 pages or more presenting the research project (Academy of Management, European Institute for Advanced Studies in Management), while others will accept an abstract of two or three pages (Strategic Management Society, Institute for Operations Research and Management Science, European Group of Organization Studies).

Along with individual propositions, some academic societies (Academy of Management, Strategic Management Society, Institute for Operations Research and Management Science) accept and even encourage group initiatives, taking the form of a symposium presenting four or five research projects treating a single subject or theme. This kind of proposition should contain a two-page general presentation of the symposium, and a two- or three-page abstract for each project. The title page should state the names and affiliations of all writers, and indicate the session chairperson and the participants in each presentation.

Project status   Some associations will only admit completed research projects (Academy of Management, European Institute for Advanced Studies in Management), while to others it may be possible to submit on-going work or even didactic cases.

Type of research   While it is difficult to generalize, some academic societies do seem to have a preference for research projects that take a quantitative approach (Academy of Management), whereas qualitative methods are more likely to be presented at certain conferences (Strategic Management Society, European Group of Organization Studies). Econometric models are predominant in some organizations (Institute for Operations Research and Management Science). To avoid rejection of a project on the basis of choice of methods, it can be rewarding to consult archives from past conferences. The predominant methodological approach, and any core theories, will quickly stand out among the projects that have been presented, and the current proposition can then be submitted to those organizations more likely to accept it.

Below, some of the major academic conferences in the field of management are presented in further detail.

3.1 The Academy of Management (AoM)

http://www.aom.pace.edu/

The Academy of Management is an American-based association for researchers in management, with more than 10,000 members world-wide.

The AoM generally organizes an annual conference in the USA at the beginning of August, gathering between 3,000 and 4,000 researchers and PhD students from all over the world. The proportion of contributions from outside the USA and Canada has been constantly increasing over the last ten years, and represents up to 25 per cent in some divisions. In order to further encourage this internationalization, some divisions, such as Technology and Innovation Management, have purposefully established a network of international correspondents.

The conference is held over five days, with the opening weekend reserved for pre-conference activities (including a Doctoral Consortium, a Junior Faculty Consortium, a Teaching Seminar, an All Academy Symposium and a Distinguished Speaker); the actual conference covers the remaining three days.

Some thousand presentations are given in the 15 different AoM divisions (Business Policy and Strategy, Careers, Conflict Management, Entrepreneurship, Health Care Administration, Human Resource Management, Management History, Managerial Consultation, Managerial and Organizational Cognition, Organization and Management Theory, Organizational Communication and Information Systems, Organizations and the Natural Environment, Public and Non-Profit Sector, Research Methods, Social Issues in Management, Technology and Innovation Management).

Each division has its own program, organized according to the propositions that have been submitted directly by authors. Propositions should be transmitted to the Program Chair of the division concerned (postal and e-mail addresses can be found on the AoM web site). In general, the deadline is the Friday of the first complete week of January. Deadlines must be stringently observed – a proposition received Saturday morning will not be considered. Each proposition is examined by two readers, and returned to the author in April, accompanied with the readers' comments and notification of their acceptance or rejection of the proposition.

Approximately one-third of the propositions submitted are accepted for presentation at the conference, but regardless of the final outcome, all authors will receive a detailed evaluation of their work from the readers, which is itself invaluable in improving the quality of the project. The two or three most interesting articles submitted to each division are published in the *Academy of Management Proceedings*, as well as abstracts of all the presentations accepted.

A job placement market is set up during the AoM annual conference, bringing together universities and professors from all over the world. A specific page on the AoM web site is also dedicated to placement services.

The AoM publishes the *Academy of Management Review*, the *Academy of Management Journal* and the *Academy of Management Executive*. The registration fee for the conference is a little under US$100.

3.2 The Strategic Management Society (SMS)

http://www.smsweb.org

The SMS is an international academic association that holds an annual congress in North America, Asia or Europe. The conference is referred to as 'ABC' – Academic, Business, Consultant – and gathers participants from different professional categories, with a majority being researchers.

There are approximately 400 presentations over the three days of the conference. The deadline for submitting propositions is in March, for a conference held in September/October. Propositions should be presented as two- or three-page abstracts outlining the research project, or as joint symposiums similar to those described above for the AoM. The final decision is made by a committee of 15 research experts after examining the abstracts, and is announced in June. About 50 per cent of the propositions are accepted for presentation during the conference.

Every year, SMS selects 20 or so of the presentations given during the conference to be published in book form. The series, published by John Wiley and Sons under title 'SMS Collection' is generally co-edited by Howard Thomas and the organizer of the conference.

The registration fee for the conference is approximately US$500. The SMS publishes *Strategic Management Journal*.

3.3 The Institute for Operations Research and Management Science (INFORMS)

http://www.informs.org/

INFORMS is the result of a merger in 1995 of the Operations Research Society of America (ORSA) and The Institute of Management Sciences (TIMS). Informs is principally a conference on operations research, statistics and information technology. Nevertheless, several sections are dedicated to management. This conference can be a good opportunity to encounter an academic audience of varying origins. INFORMS is a four-day conference, in which around 1,000 presentations are made.

INFORMS is unique in accepting all presentation propositions submitted to it (propositions are submitted in the form of an abstract). This policy represents an attempt to provide an audience for all types of research projects, regardless of the methodology used or the research question. Organizers often need to use the full resources of their creativity when finding titles for sessions that may group presentations with strong variations in field, method and approach. In an attempt to encourage greater homogeneity within sessions, INFORMS recently decided to accept symposiums.

INFORMS edits *Management Science and Organization Science*. The registration fee for the conference is approximately US$300.

3.4 The European Group of Organization Studies (EGOS)

EGOS was created in 1973 as an informal research network. It rapidly grew to be the principal European association for researchers in the organizational field, and became an official association in 1997. Although essentially European, quite a number of members are of other nationalities.

The annual conference is held in July in Europe. Abstracts are to be submitted at the beginning of February, to the person responsible for that particular area of research. If accepted, the author must send a copy of the research project to all other researchers whose proposals have been accepted in the same section. At the conference, participants are put into workshops of approximately 30 per group, according to their area of research. This method strongly encourages participants to attend all presentations by members of their group, to develop common references in the course of the conference.

EGOS also organizes doctoral consortiums similar to those held by the Academy of Management during its annual conference.

EGOS edits *Organization Studies*. The registration fee for the conference is approximately US$150.

3.5 The European Institute for Advanced Studies in Management (EIASM)

http://www.eiasm.be/

EIASM is a European group that organizes annual or bi-annual symposiums and seminars in different fields of management science. Each event gathers between 30 and 100 research professors specialized in a given domain. These conferences are usually appreciated for their more 'human' size, favoring personal contacts and the development of networks. Meetings are generally held in collaboration with other academic associations or universities, in Europe or elsewhere, and are open to non-European researchers.

Research projects presented at EIASM events are generally published in the form of conference proceedings.

The registration fee varies between meetings, averaging approximately US$200.

In addition to these 'major' conferences, symposiums on clearly defined subjects are regularly organized by universities and informal groups. At these meetings of varying duration, researchers get together and discuss a common question. Calls for papers are often more 'confidential', and may even be replaced by personal invitations. It may seem difficult to find a way into these informal networks, but taking part in bigger conferences normally helps – a researcher may also be invited to give a presentation on the basis of a published article. Such exposure enables the researcher to be recognized by a member of the network as having the potential to add to their discussions.

SECTION 4   THE RESEARCHER'S RELATIONSHIP
WITH THE NON-ACADEMIC WORLD

In 1991, Fortune published a three-page article on the 'third generation idiot'. By this provocative term, the review described a 28-year-old MBA student reporting to a 30-year-old assistant professor, himself supervised by a 35-year-old associate professor. None of the three had ever worked outside the academic world, or only for a very short period of time. Beyond the obvious provocation, this picture revealed a serious problem.

How can one teach enterprise management, let alone initiate research projects of interest to anyone outside the academic microcosm, without having any experience of working within a company? How could one link together theories, concepts and models to real organizational problems, without having any kind of professional relationships outside the academic world?

All researchers must work on finding a solution to this problem, and build networks that enable them to maintain strong academic links to their field of expertise without losing contact with the corporate world. An individual balance should be established between different possible means of contact with organizational reality. Here are some examples.

Internships   This is probably the most effective way to experience the non-academic world. The researcher works full-time inside an organization, and for a period long enough to become fully integrated. Many academics take a sabbatical year or unpaid leave to broaden their knowledge with such hands-on experience.

Consulting   When a researcher is taken on by an organization as a consultant, he or she is contracted to solve a particular, predefined, problem. However, in focusing on one single question, the global view and directions of the organization may be lost. The consultant often remains an outsider.

Fieldwork and case studies   Based on observation, interviews, or historical analysis, fieldwork and case studies force researchers out of the academic cocoon and confronts them with real organizational problems. There is, however, a risk that the researcher may have preconceived notions of the phenomenon that is to be studied, which can influence the process of data collection and the accuracy of the study.

Continuing education   Teaching an audience of organizational executives obliges a researcher to take a fresh look at the theories and concepts covered in the class. In such a case, the researcher-teacher will benefit greatly from the comments and hands-on experience of his or her executive students.

If researchers in strategic management neglect to use one or more of the methods cited above to maintain contact with the organizational world, they quickly become isolated in an 'ivory tower'. Their research then only rarely has any impact outside academia. If they are ever obliged to leave the academic world, such researchers will find it extremely difficult to integrate into a corporate world of which they have no practical knowledge.

The problem of academic alienation from the day to day reality of working within a company is often expressed in social small-talk. The following situations will be familiar to all professor-researchers:

'So, what do you do for a living?'
'I'm a professor and a researcher, in management.'
'Oh really? What sort of research is there to do in management?'

Or:

'So, what do you do for a living?'
'I'm a professor-researcher in management.'
'What exactly does that mean?'
'There are two parts to it: I teach at the university and I'm writing my dissertation.'

'Oh, I see, so you're a student.'
'Yes and no, because I'm already working.'
'So, what are you going to do when you've finished?'
'Same thing.'
'Yes, but I mean, when you start working in a company.'
'No, I'm planning to stay at the university.'
'So you'll be a student forever?'
'No, I'm getting paid, it's a job.'
'What? I've never heard of students being paid!'

Whereas a negative response to such an attitude will only reinforce the walls of the 'ivory tower', these remarks could lead a researcher to question the role a professor-researcher should have in society. Research, methodology, epistemology and theory are seen by many as esoteric concepts that are of no utility in dealing with actual everyday problems that arise within an organization. Consequently, researchers may decide that only research that is relevant to the academic and to the non-academic world will justify their social utility. Such pertinent research can only result from the researcher maintaining a real knowledge of professional reality by developing frequent and fruitful contacts with the non-academic environment.

In considering the relationship between academia and the outside world, we do not mean to establish an opposition between fieldwork and theoretic research. Retaining close ties to organizational reality is no guarantee for a successful research project, or for a successful research career. In some cases, a lack of distance may even present an obstacle to critical or conceptual reasoning, by influencing the perception of the researcher. On the other hand, a purely theoretical work can very well prove to be a fertile source of practical applications for organizations, and stimulate invaluable reflection.

If we are to assess the social utility of professor-researchers we must consider two separate domains, and it is up to each teacher-researcher to find his or her own balance between them. The first is the academic, where 'usefulness' is measured in terms of academic value: of the material taught and any publications and other research work carried out. The second domain is the non-academic, where 'usefulness' is measured by the relevance of the professor-researcher's work to the corporate world – by the actual impact the material taught and the research undertaken has on everyday life within organizations.

NOTE

1 Interviewed in the French publication, *Figaro Grands Ecoles et Universités* in November 1997.

FURTHER READING

Gmelch, W.H., *Coping with Faculty Stress*, Newbury Park, CA: Sage, 1993.
Metzger, R.O., *Developing a Consulting Practice*, Newbury Park, CA: Sage, 1993.
Rudestan, K.E. and Newton, R.R., *Surviving your Dissertation*, Newbury Park, CA: Sage, 1992.

BIBLIOGRAPHY

Aaker, D. and Day, G., *Marketing Research*, New York: Wiley, 1990.

Aaker, D.A. and Bagozzi, R.P., 'Unobservable Variables in Structural Equation Models with an Application in Industrial Selling', *Journal of Marketing Research*, 16, 1979: 147–58.

Abbott, A., 'A Primer on Sequence Methods', *Organization Science*, 1 (4), 1990: 375–92.

Abbott, A. and Forrest, J., 'Optimal Matching Methods for Historical Sequences', *Journal of Interdisciplinary History*, 16 (3), 1986: 471–94.

Abrahamson, E. and Rosenkopf, L., 'Social Network Effects on the Extent of Innovation Diffusion: A Computer Simulation, *Organization Science*, 8 (3), 1997: 289–309.

Ackermann, F., Cropper, S. and Eden, C., 'Getting Started with Cognitive Mapping', *The 7th Young Operational Conference Tutorial Papers*, 1992, pp. 65–81.

Ackroyd, S., 'The Quality of Qualitative Methods: Qualitative or Quality Methodology for Organization Studies', *Organization*, 3 (3), 1996: 439–51.

Adlfinger, A.C., 'Sequential Sampling Technique Reduces the Fixed-Size Sampling Number and Corresponding Labor', *Industrial Engineering*, 13 (5), 1981: 74–80.

Albreck, P. and Settle, B. *The Survey Research Handbook*, Boston: Irwin, 1989.

Aldenderfer, M.-S. and Blashfield, R.-K., *Cluster Analysis*, Newbury Park, CA: Sage, 1984.

Allard-Poesi, F., 'Representations and Influence Processes in Groups: Towards a Socio-cognitive Perspective on Cognition in Organizations', *Scandinavian Journal of Management*, 14 (4), 1998: 395–420.

Allison, G.T., *Essence of Decision: Explaining the Cuban Missile Crisis*, Boston, MA: Little, Brown, 1971.

Allison, P.D., *Event History Analysis: Regression for Longitudinal Event Data*, Sage University Paper Series on Quantitative Applications in the Social Sciences, no. 07–046, Beverly Hills, CA: Sage, 1984.

Altheide, and Johnson, 'Criteria for Addressing Interpretive Validity in Qualitative Research', in N.K. Denzin and Y.S. Lincoln (eds), *Handbook of Qualitative Research*, Thousand Oaks, CA: Sage, 1994, pp. 485–99.

Anderson, P.F., 'Marketing, Scientific Progress and Scientific Method', *Journal of Marketing*, Fall, 1983: 18–31.

Arbuckle, J.L., *AMOS Users' Guide: Version 3.6*, Chicago: SPSS, 1997.

Argyris, C. and Schön, D.A., *Organizational Learning: A Theory of Action Perspective*, Reading MA: Addison Wesley, 1978.

Atkinson, P. and Hammersley, M., 'Ethnography and Participant Observation', in N.K. Denzin and Y.S. Lincoln (eds), *Handbook of Qualitative Research*, Thousand Oaks, CA: Sage, 1994, pp. 248–61.

Audet, M., 'Plasticité, instrumentalité et réflexivité', in P. Cossette (ed.), *Cartes Cognitives et Organisations*, Québec: Les Presses de l'Université de Laval et les Editions Eska, 1994, pp. 187–98.

Axelrod, R., *Structure of the Decision: The Cognitive Maps of Political Elites*, Princeton, NJ: Princeton University Press, 1976.

Bailyn, L., Fletcher, J.K. and Kolb, D., 'Unexpected Connections: Considering Employees' Personal Lives can Revitalize Your Business', *Sloan Management Review*, Summer, 1997: 11–19.

Bardin, L., *L'analyse de contenu*, Paris: PUF, 1993.

Barley, S.R., 'Images of Imaging: Notes on Doing Longitudinal Field Work', *Organization Science*, 1 (3), 1990: 220–66.

Barley, S.R., 'Technicians in the Workplace: Ethnographic Evidence for Bringing Work into Organization Studies', *Administrative Science Quarterly*, 41 (3), 1996: 404–41.

Barney, J.-B. and Hoskisson, R.-E., 'Strategic Groups: Untested Assertions and Research Proposals', *Managerial and Decision Economics*, 11, 1990: 187–98.

Baron, R.M. and Kenny, A., 'The Moderator-Mediator Distinction in Social Psychological Research: Conceptual, Strategic, and Statistical Considerations', *Journal of Personality and Social Psychology*, 51, 1986: 1173–82.

Barr, P.S., Stimpert, J.L. and Huff, A.S., 'Cognitive Change, Strategic Action and Organizational Renewal', *Strategic Management Journal*, 13, 1992: 15–36.

Bartlett, C.A. and Ghoshal, S., *Managing Across Borders*, Boston: Harvard Business School Press, 1989.

Bartunek, J.M., Bobko, P. and Venkatraman, N., (guest co-editors' Introduction) 'Toward Innovation and Diversity in Management Research Methods', *Academy of Management Journal*, 36 (6), 1993: 1362–73.

Bearden, W.O., Netmeyer, R.T. and Mobley, M.F., *Handbook of Marketing Scales*, Thousand Oaks, CA: Sage, 1993.

Bentler, P.M., *EQS: Structural Equation Manual*, Los Angeles: BMDP Statistical Software, 1989.

Bentler, P.M. and Chou, C.P., 'Practical Issues in Structural Modeling', *Sociological Methods and Research*, 16 (1), 1987: 78–117.

Benzécri, J.-P., *Analyses des données, tome 1: la taxinomie, tome 2: analyses des correspondances*, 3rd edn, Paris: Dunod, 1980.

Benzécri, J.-P, *Correspondence Analysis Handbook*, New York: Marcel Dekker, 1992.

Berger, P. and Luckmann, T., *The Social Construction of Reality*, New York: Doubleday, 1966.

Bergh, D.D., 'Watch the Time Carefully: The Use and Misuse of Time Effects in Management Research', *Journal of Management*, 19 (3), 1993: 683–705.

Bergh, D.D. and Holbein, G.F., 'Assessment and Redirection of Longitudinal Analysis: Demonstration with a Study of the Diversification and Divestiture Relationship', *Strategic Management Journal*, 18 (7), 1997: 557–71.

Black, J. and Champion, D., *Methods and Issues in Social Research*, New York: Wiley, 1976.

Blaug, M., *The Methodology of Economics: Or How Economics Explain*, Cambridge: Cambridge Surveys of Economic Literature, 1992.

Boland, B.J. and Pondy, L.R., 'The Micro-Dynamics of a Budget-Cutting Process: Modes, Models and Structure', *Accounting, Organizations and Society*, 11 (4: 5), 1986: 402–22.

Bonacich, P., 'Power and Centrality: A Family of Measures, *American Journal of Sociology*, 92 (5), 1987: 1170–82.

Borgatti, S.P., Everett, M. and Freeman, L.C., *Ucinet IV version 1.0, Reference Manual*, Columbia: Analytic Technologies, 1992.

Bouchard, T.J., 'Field Research Methods: Interviewing, Questionnaires, Participant Observation, Systematic Observation, Unobstrusive Measures', in: M.D. Dunette (ed.), *Handbook of Industrial and Organizational Psychology*, Chicago: Rand McNally, 1976, pp. 363–413.

Bougon, M.G., 'Uncovering Cognitive Maps', in G. Morgan (ed.), *Beyond Method, Strategies for Social Research*, 4th edn, Beverly Hills, CA: Sage, 1983, pp. 173–87.

Bourque, L.B. and Fielder, E.P., *How to Conduct Self Administered and Mail Surveys*, Thousand Oaks, CA: Sage, 1995.

Bovasso, G., 'A Structural Analysis of the Formation of a Network Organization', *Group and Organization Management*, 17 (1), 1992: 115–35.

Boyd, B., 'Corporate Linkages and Organizational Environment: A Test of the Resource Dependence Model', *Strategic Management Journal*, 11, 1990: 419–30.

Brewer, D. 'No Associative Biases in the First Name Cued Recall Procedure for Eliciting Personal Networks', *Social Networks*, 19, 1997: 345–53.

Brown, S.L. and Eisenhardt, K.M., 'The Art of Continuous Change: Linking Complexity Theory and Time-paced Evolution in Relentlessly Shifting Organizations', *Administrative Science Quarterly*, 42 (1), 1997: 1–34.

Brown, W., 'Some Experimental Results in the Correlation of Mental Abilities', *British Journal of Psychology*, 3, 1910: 296–322.

Bunge, M., *Scientific Research*, Berlin: Springer-Verlag, 1967.

Burgelman, R., 'Fading Memories: A Process Theory of Strategic Business Exit in Dynamic Environments', *Administrative Science Quarterly*, 39, 1994: 24–56.

Burrell, G. and Morgan, G., *Sociological Paradigms and Organizational Analysis*, London: Heinemann, 1979.

Burt, R.S. 'A Note on Social Capital and Network Content, *Social Networks*, 19, 1997: 355–73.

Camerer, C., 'Redirecting Research in Business Policy and Strategy', *Strategic Management Journal*, 6, 1985: 1–15.

Campbell, D.T. and Fiske, D.W., 'Convergent and Discriminant Validation by the Multitrait-Multimethod Matrix', *Psychological Bulletin*, 56, 1959: 81–105.

Campbell, D.T. and Stanley, J.C., *Experimental and Quasi-Experimental Designs for Research*, Chicago: Rand McNally, 1966.

Campion, M.A., 'Rules for References: Suggested Guidelines for Choosing Literary Citations for Research Articles in Applied Psychology', *Personnel Psychology*, 50, 1997: 165–7.

Carley, K. and Krackhardt, D., 'Cognitive Inconsistencies and Non Symmetric Friendship', *Social Networks*, 18, 1996: 1–27.

Carmines, E. and Zeller, R., *Reliability and Validity Assessment*, London: Sage, 1990.

Carnap, R., 'Statistical and Inductive Probability', in E.H. Madden (ed.), *The Structure of Scientific Thought*, Boston: Houghton Mifflin, 1960.

Carnap, R., *Logical Foundations of Probability*, Chicago: University of Chicago Press, 1962.

Chakavarthy, B. and Doz, Y., 'Strategy Process Research: Focusing on Corporate Self-Renewal', *Strategic Management Journal*, 13, Summer special issue, 1992: 5–14.

Chalmers, A., *What is this Thing Called Science? An Assessment of the Nature and Status of Science and its Methods*, St Lucia: University of Queensland Press, 1976.

Chandler, A., *Strategy and Structure*, Cambridge, MA: MIT Press, 1962.

Cheng, Y.-T. and Van De Ven, A., 'Learning the Innovation Journey: Order out of Chaos', *Organisation Science*, 7 (6), 1996: 593–614.

Childers, T.L. and Skinner, S.J., 'Gaining Respondent Cooperation in Mail Surveys Through Prior Commitment', *Public Opinion Quarterly*, 43, 1979: 558–61.

Chow, G.C., 'Tests for Equality Between Sets of Coefficients in two Linear Regressions,' *Econometrica*, 28 (3), 1960: 591–605.

Churchill, G.A., *Marketing Research: Methodological Foundations*, 5th edn, Hinsdale, IL: Dryden Press, 1991.

Cohen, J., 'A Coefficient of Agreement for Nominal Scales', *Education and Psychological Measurement*, 20 (1), 1960: 37–46.

Cohen, J., *Statistical Power Analysis for the Behavioral Sciences*, 2nd edn, Hillsdale, NJ: Lawrence Erlbaum, 1988.

Comte, A., *Introduction to Positive Philosophy*, Paris: Carillian-Gœury and Dalmont, 1988.

Converse, J.M. and Presser, S., *Survey Questions: Handcrafting the Standardized Questionnaire*, Beverly Hills, CA: Sage, 1986.

Cook, T.D. and Campbell, D.T., *Quasi-Experimentation: Design and Analysis Issues for Field Settings*, Chicago, IL: Rand McNally College Publishing Company, 1979.

Cortina, J.M., 'What is Coefficient Alpha? An Examination of Theory and Applications', *Journal of Applied Psychology*, 78 (1), 1993: 98–104.

Cossette, P. and Audet, M., 'Mapping an Idiosyncrasic Schema', *Journal of Management Studies*, 29 (3), 1992: 325–47.

Cronbach, L.J., 'Coefficient Alpha and the Internal Structure of Tests', *Psychometrika*, 16, 1951: 297–334.

Crozier, M. and Friedberg, E., *L'acteur et le système*, Paris: Seuil, 1977.

Cummings, L.L. and Frost, P.J. (eds), *Publishing in the Organizational Sciences*, 2nd edn, Thousand Oaks, CA: Sage, 1995.

Cutcher-Gershenfeld, J., Nitta, M., Barrett, B., Belhedi, N., Bullard, J., Coutchie, C., Inaba, T., Ishino, I., Lee, S., Lin, W., Mothersell, W., Rabine, S., Ramanand, S., Strolle, M. and Wheaton, A., 'Japanese Team-Based Work Systems in North America: Explaining the Diversity', *California Management Review*, 37 (1), Fall, 1994: 42–64.

D'Aveni, R.A. and MacMillan, I.C., 'Crisis and the Content of Managerial Communications: A Study of the Focus of Attention of Top Managers in Surviving and Failing Firms', *Administrative Science Quarterly*, 35, 1990: 634–57.

Daft, R.L., 'Why I Recommended That Your Manuscript Be Rejected and What You Can Do About It', in L.L. Cummings and P.J. Frost (eds), *Publishing in the Organizational Sciences*, 2nd edition, Thousand Oaks, CA: Sage, 1995, pp. 164–82.

Daft, R.L., 'Learning the Craft of Organizational Research', *Academy of Management Review*, 8 (4), 1983: 539–46.

Daft, R.L. and Lewin, A.Y., 'Can Organization Studies Begin to Break Out of the Normal Science Straitjacket? An Editorial Essay', *Organization Science*, 1 (1), 1990: 1–9.

Daniels, K., Markoczy, L., Goldberg, J. and Chernaton, L., 'Comparing Cognitive Maps', paper presented at the International Workshop on Managerial and Organizational Cognition, Brussels, Belgium, 1993.

Davis, J.A., *The Logic of Causal Order*, Sage University Paper Series on Quantitative Applications in the Social Sciences, Beverly Hills, CA: Sage, 1985.

De Groot, A., *Methodology, Foundations of Inference and Research in the Behavioral Sciences*, The Hague: Mouton, 1969.

Denzin, N.K. and Lincoln, Y.S. (eds), *Handbook of Qualitative Research*, Thousand Oaks, CA: Sage, 1994.

Denzin, N.K., 'The Art and Politics of Interpretation', in N.K. Denzin and Y.S. Lincoln (eds), *Handbook of Qualitative Research*, Thousand Oaks, CA: Sage, 1994, pp. 500–15.

Denzin, N.K. and Lincoln, Y.S. (Introduction) 'Entering the Field of Qualitative Research', in N.K. Denzin and Y.S. Lincoln (eds), *Handbook of Qualitative Research*, Thousand Oaks, CA: Sage, 1994, pp. 1–17.

Dess, G.G. and Davis, P.S., 'Porter's (1980) Generic Strategies as Determinants of Strategic Group Membership and Organizational Performance', *Academy of Management Journal*, 27, 1984: 467–88.

Dess, G., Lumpkin, G.T. and Covin, J.G.S., 'Entrepreneurial Strategy Making Firm Performance', *Strategic Management Journal*, 18, 1997: 677–95.

Devellis, R.F., 'Scale Development: Theory and Applications', *Applied Social Research Methods*, 26, 1991.

Dillman, D.A., *Mail and Telephone Surveys: The Total Design Method*, New York: Wiley-Interscience, 1978.

Dillman, D.A., *Mail and Internet Survey: The Tailored Design Method*, New York: Wiley, 1999.

DiRenzo, G., *Concepts, Theory and Explanation in the Behavioral Sciences*, New York: Random House, 1966.

Dodd, S.C., 'Introducing "Systemmetrics" for Evaluating Symbolic Systems: 24 Criteria for the Excellence of Scientific Theories', *Systematics*, 6 (1), 1968: 29–51.

Donaldson, L., 'A Positivist Alternative to the Structure-Action Approach', *Organization Studies*, 18 (1), 1997: 77–92.

Doreian, P. and Woodward, K., 'Defining and Locating Cores and Boundaries of Social Networks', *Social Networks*, 16, 1994: 267–93.

Dougherty, D. and Bowman, E.H., 'The Effects of Organizational Downsizing on Product Innovation', *California Management Review*, 37 (4), 1995: 28–44.

Douglas, J.D., *Investigative Social Research*, Beverly Hills, CA: Sage, 1976.

Douglas, J.D., *Creative Interviewing*, Beverly Hills, CA: Sage, 1985.

Downey, K.H. and Ireland, D.R., 'Quantitative versus Qualitative: Environment Assessment in Organizational Studies', *Administrative Science Quarterly*, 24, 1979: 630–7.

Durkheim, E., *Rules of Sociological Method*, New York: Free Press, 1982.

Dyer, W. and Wilkins, A., 'Better Stories Not Better Constructs, to Generate Better Theory: A Rejoinder to Einsenhardt', *Academy of Management Review*, 16 (3), 1991: 613–19.

Eco, U., *The Limits of Interpretation (Advances in Semiotics)*, Bloomington, IN: Indiana University Press, 1990.

Eden, C., 'Cognitive Mapping', *European Journal of Operational Research*, 36, 1988: 1–13.

Eden, C., 'Strategic Thinking with Computers', *Long Range Planning*, 23 (6), 1990: 35–43.

Eden, C. and Banville, C., 'Construction d'une vision stratégique au moyen de la cartographie cognitive assistée par ordinateur', in P. Cossette (ed.), *Cartes Cognitives et Organisations*, Québec: Les Presses Universitaires de Laval and Les Editions Eska, 1994, pp. 57–80.

Eden, C., Ackermann, F. and Cropper, S., 'The Analysis of Causal Maps', *Journal of Management Studies*, 29 (3), 1992: 309–24.

Eden, C., Jones, S. and Sims, D., *Thinking in Organization*, London: Macmillan, 1979.

Eden, C., Jones, S. and Sims, D., *Messing about in Problems: An Informal Structured Approach to their Identification and Management*, Oxford: Pergamon Press, 1983.

Eisenhardt, K.M., 'Building Theories from Case Study Research', *Academy of Management Review*, 14 (4), 1989: 532–50.

Erickson, F., 'Qualitative Methods in Research on Teaching', in M. Wittrock (ed.), *Handbook of Research on Teaching*, New York: Macmillan, 1986, pp. 119–61.

Everitt, B., *Cluster Analysis*, 3rd edn, New York: Halsted, 1993.

Evrard, Y., Pras, B. and Roux, E., *Market. Études et recherches en marketing*, Paris: Nathan, 1993.

Fink, A., *The Survey Kit*, Thousand Oaks, CA: Sage, 1995.

Fink, A. and Kosecoff, J., *How to Conduct Surveys*, 2nd edn, Thousand Oaks, CA: Sage, 1998.

Fontana, A. and Frey, J.H., 'Interviewing: The Art of Science', in N.K. Denzin and Y.S. Lincoln (eds), *Handbook of Qualitative Research*, Beverly Hills, CA: Sage, 1994, pp. 361–73.

Ford, J.D. and Hegarty, W.H., 'Decision Maker's Beliefs about Causes and Effects of Structure', *Academy of Management Journal*, 27 (2), 1984: 271–91.

Frank, K., 'Identifying Cohesive Subgroups', *Social Networks*, 17, 1995: 27–56.

Freeman, L.C., 'Centrality in Social Networks I. Conceptual Clarification', *Social Networks*, 1, 1979: 215–39.

Friedkin, N.E. and Johnsen, E.C., 'Social Positions in Influence Networks', *Social Networks*, 19, 1997: 209–22.

Frost, P.J. and Stablein, R.E., 'Themes and Variations: An Examination of the Exemplars', in P.J. Frost and R.E. Stablein (eds), *Doing Exemplary Research*, Newbury Park, CA: Sage, 1992, pp. 243–69.

Galbraith, C. and Schendel, D.E., 'An Empirical Analysis of Strategy Types', *Strategic Management Journal*, 4 (2), 1983: 153–73.

Garrette, B. and Dussauge, P., 'Determinants of Success in International Strategic Aliances: Evidence from the Global Aerospace Industry', *Journal of International Business Studies*, 26, 1995: 505–30.

Geertz, C., 'Thick Description: Toward an Interpretive Theory of Culture', in *The Interpretation of Culture*, New York: Basic Books, 1973, pp. 3–30.

Geertz, C., *Works and Lives: The Anthropologist as Author*, Stanford, CA: Stanford University Press, 1988.

Giddens, A., *The Constitution of Society*, Cambridge: Polity Press, 1984.

Gioia, D.A. and Chittipeddi, K., 'Sensemaking and Sensegiving in Strategic Change Initiation', *Strategic Management Journal*, 12, 1991: 443–8.

Gioia, D.A. and Sims, H.P., 'Cognition-Behavior Connections: Attributions and Verbal Behavior in Leader–Subordinates Interactions', *Organizational Behavior and Human Decision Processes*, 37, 1986: 197–229.

Gioia, D.A. and Thomas, J., 'Identity, Image and Issue Interpretation: Sensemaking During Strategic Change in Academia', *Administrative Science Quarterly*, 41 (3), 1996: 370–403.

Girod-Séville, M., *La mémoire des organisations*, Paris: L'Harmattan, 1996.

Glaser, B., *Theoretical Sensitivity*, Mill Valley, CA: Sociology Press, 1978.

Glaser, B.G. and Strauss, A.L., *The Discovery of Grounded Theory: Strategies for Qualitative Research*, New York: Aldine De Gruyter, 1967.

Glenn, N.D., *Cohort Analysis*, Sage University Paper Series on Quantitative Applications in the Social Sciences, no. 07–005, Beverly Hills, CA: Sage, 1977.

Glick, W.H., Huber, G.P., Miller, C.C., Doty, D.H. and Sutcliffe, K.M., 'Studying Changes in Organizational Design and Effectiveness: Retrospective Event Histories and Periodic Assessments', *Organization Science*, 1 (3), 1990: 293–312.

Gmelch, W.H., *Coping with Faculty Stress*, Newbury Park, CA: Sage, 1993.

Goetz, J.P. and LeCompte, M.D., 'Ethnographic Research and the Problem of Data Reduction', *Anthropology and Education Quarterly*, 12, 1981: 51–70.

Gold, R.L., 'Roles in Sociological Field Work', in N.K. Denzin (ed.), *Sociological Methods*, Chicago: Aldine, 1970, pp. 370–80.

Golden, B.R., 'The Pat Is the Past – Or Is It? The Use of Retrospective Accounts as Indicators of Past Strategy', *Academy of Management Journal*, 35 (4), 1992: 848–60.

Golden-Biddle, K. and Locke, K., 'Appealing Work: An Investigation of How Ethnographic Texts Convince', *Organization Science*, 4 (4), 1993: 595–616.

Golden-Biddle, K. and Locke, K.D., *Composing Qualitative Research*, Thousand Oaks, CA: Sage, 1997.

Goodman, J.S. and Blum, T.C., 'Assessing the Non-Random Sampling Effects of Subject Attrition in Longitudinal Research', *Journal of Management*, 22 (4), 1996: 627–52.

Goold, M. and Campbell, A., *Strategies and Styles*, London: Blackwell, 1987.

Govindarajan, V.A., 'Contingency Approach to Strategy Implementation at the Business Unit Level: Integrating Administrative Mechanisms with Strategy', *Academy of Management Journal*, 31 (4), 1988: 828–53.

Greenacre, M., *Correspondence Analysis in Practice*, London: Academic Press, 1993.

Greenacre, M. and Blasius, J., *Correspondence Analysis in the Social Sciences*, London: Academic Press, 1994.

Grunow, D., 'The Research Design in Organization Studies', *Organization Science*, 6 (1), 1995: 93–103.

Guba, E. and Lincoln, Y., 'Competing Paradigms in Qualitative Research', in *Handbook of Qualitative Research*, N.K. Denzin and Y.S. Lincoln (eds), Thousand Oaks, CA: Sage, 1994, pp. 105–17.

Guetzkow, H., 'Unitizing and Categorizing Problem in Coding Qualitative Data', *Journal of Clinical Psychology*, 6, 1950: 47–8.

Hage, P. and Harary, F., *Structural Models in Antropology*, Cambridge: Cambridge University Press, 1983.

Hage, P. and Harary, F., 'Eccentricity and Centrality in Networks', *Social Networks*, 17, 1995: 57–63.

Hair, J.-F., Anderson, R.-E., Tatham, R.-L. and Black, W.-C., *Multivariate Data Analysis*, 3rd edn, New York: Macmillan, 1992.

Hambrick, D.-C., 'An Empirical Typology of Mature Industrial-Product Environments', *Academy of Management Journal*, 26, 1983: 213–30.

Hannan, M.T. and Freeman, J., 'Structural Inertia and Organizational Change', *American Sociological Review*, 49, 1984: 149–64.

Hannan, T. and Freeman, J., 'The Population Ecology of Organizations', *American Journal of Sociology*, 82 (5), 1977: 929–64.

Hardy, A., 'An Examination of Procedures Determining the Number of Clusters in a Data Set', in E. Diday et al. (eds), *New Approaches in Classification and Data Analysis*, Berlin: Springer-Verlag, 1994.

Hart, J., 'Comparative Cognition: Politics of International Control of the Oceans', in R. Axelrod (ed.), *Structure of Decision: The Cognitive Maps of Political Elites*, Princeton, NJ: Princeton University Press, 1976.

Hassard, J., 'Multiple Paradigms and Organizational Analysis, a Case Study', *Organization Studies*, 12, 1991: 275–99.

Hatten, K.J. and Schendel, D.E., 'Heterogeneity within an Industry: Firm Conduct in the U.S. Brewing Industry', *Journal of Industrial Economics*, 26, 1977: 97–113.

Hayduk, L.A., *LISREL Issues, Debates, and Strategies*, Baltimore, MD: Johns Hopkins University Press, 1996.

Hempel, C., *Aspects of Scientific Explanation*, New York: Free Press, 1964.

Hempel, C., *Philosophy of Natural Science*, Englewood Cliffs, NJ: Prentice Hall, 1966.

Henry, G.T., *Practical Sampling*, Newbury Park, CA: Sage, 1990.

Hickson, D., Butler, R., Gray, G., Mallory, G. and Wilson, D., *Top Decisions: Strategic Decision Making in Organizations*, San Francisco: Blackwell, 1986.

Hirschman, E.C., 'Humanistic Inquiry in Marketing Research: Philosophy, Method and Criteria', *Journal of Marketing Research*, 23, 1986: 237–49.

Hitt, M.A., Gimeno, J. and Hoskisson, R.E., 'Current and Future Research Methods in Strategic Management', *Organizational Research Methods*, 1 (1), 1998: 6–44.

Holstein, J.A. and Gubrium, J.F., *The Active Interview*, Thousand Oaks, CA: Sage, 1995.

Horwitch, M. and Thiétart, R.A., 'The Effect of Business Interdependencies on Product R&D Intensive Business Performance', *Management Science*, 33 (2), 1987: 178–97.

Hoskisson, R.-M., Johnson, H.-R. and Moesel, D., 'Construct Validity of an Objective (Entropy) Measure of Diversification Strategy', *Strategic Management Journal*, 14, 1993: 215–35.

Hoyle, R.H. (ed.), *Structural Equation Modeling: Concepts, Issues, and Applications*, Thousand Oaks, CA: Sage, 1995.

Hudson, L. and Ozanne, J.L., 'Alternative Ways of seeking Knowledge in Consumer Research', *Journal of Consumer Research*, 14, 1988: 508–21.

Huff, A.S., *Mapping Strategic Thought*, New York: Wiley, 1990.

Hunt, S., Sparkman, R.D. and Wilcox, J.R.B., 'The Pretest in Survey Research: Issues and Preliminary Findings', *Journal of Marketing Research*, 19, 1982: 267–73.

Hunt, T., 'Graph Theoretic Network Models for Lapita Exchange: A Trial Application', in P.V. Kirch and T.L. Hunt (eds), *Archaeology of the Lapita Cultural Complex: A Critical Review*, Seattle, WA: Burke Museum Research Reports, 5, 1988.

Irwin, G., 'Chieftainship, Kula and Trade in Massim Prehistory', in J.W. Leach and E.R. Leach (eds), *The Kula: New Perspectives on Massim Exchange*, Cambridge: Cambridge University Press, 1983.

Itami, H. and Numagami, T., 'Dynamic Interaction Between Strategy and Technology', *Strategic Management Journal*, 13, Winter special issue, 1992: 119–35.

Jaccard, J., Turrisi, R. and Wan, K., *Interaction Effects in Multiple Regression*, Thousand Oaks, CA: Sage, 1990.

Jackson, S.E., 'Editorial Comments', *Academy of Management Review*, 21 (4), 1996: 907–11.

Jackson, N. and Carter, P., 'In Defense of Paradigm Incommensurability', *Organization Studies*, 12 (1), 1991: 109–27.

Jauch, L., 'An Inventory of Selected Academic Research on Strategic Management', *Advances in Strategic Management*, 2, 1983: 141–75.

Jemison, D., 'The Importance of an Integrative Approach to Strategic Management Research', *Academy of Management Review*, 6, 1981: 601–8.

Jick, T.D., 'Mixing Qualitative and Quantitative Methods: Triangulation in Action', *Administrative Science Quarterly*, 24, 1979: 602–11.

Johanson, L., 'Convincing the Jury', *Academy of Management Workshop: Writing Up Qualitative Research: Practical Insights from Authors and Editors*, Academy of Management Conference, Cincinnati, August 1996.

Johansson, J.K. and Yip, G.S., 'Exploiting Globalization Potential: U.S. and Japanese Strategies', *Strategic Management Journal*, 15, 1994: 579–601.

Joreskog, K.G., 'Testing Structural Equation Models', in K.A. Bollen and J.S. Long (eds), *Testing Structural Equation Models*, Newbury Park, CA: Sage, 1993.

Joreskog, K.G. and Sorbom, D., 'Recent Developments in Structural Equation Modeling', *Journal of Marketing Research*, 19 (4), 1982: 404–16.

Jorgensen, D.L., *Participant Observation: A Methodology for Human Studies*, Newbury Park, CA: Sage, 1989.

Junker, B.H., *Field Work: An Introduction to the Social Science*, Chicago, IL: University of Chicago Press, 1960.

Kalton, G., *Introduction to Survey Sampling*, Newbury Park, CA: Sage, 1983.

Kanji, G.K., *100 Structural Tests*, Thousand Oaks, CA: Sage, 1993.

Kanuk, L. and Berenson, C., 'Mail Survey and Response Rates: A Literature Review', *Journal of Marketing Research*, 12, 1975: 440–53.

Kaplan, A., *The Conduct of Inquiry: Methodology of Behavioral Science*, New York: Chandler, 1964.

Kerlinger, F.N., *The Foundation of Behavioral Research*, New York: Holt. Rinehart and Winston, 1973.

Ketchen, D.J. and Shook, C.L., 'The Application of Cluster Analysis in Strategic Management Research: An Analysis and Critique', *Strategic Management Journal*, 17, 1996: 441–58.

Ketchen, D.J., Thomas, J.B. and Snow, C.C., 'Organizational Configurations and Performance: A Comparison of Theoretical Approaches', *Academy of Management Journal*, 36 (6), 1993: 1278–313.

Kilduff, M. and Mehra, A., 'Postmodernism and Organizational Research', *Academy of Management Review*, 22 (2), 1997: 453–81.

Kim, J.-O. and Mueller, C.W., *Factor Analysis: Statistical Methods and Practical Issues*, Newbury Park, CA: Sage, 1978.

Kimberly, J.R., 'Issues in the Design of Longitudinal Organizational Research', *Sociological Methods and Research*, 4 (3), 1976: 321–47.

Kirk, J. and Miller, M., *Reliability and Validity in Qualitative Research*, London: Sage, 1986.

Knorr-Cetina, K.D., *The Manufacture of Knowledge: An Essay on the Constructivist and Contextual Nature of Science*, New York: Pergamon, 1981.

Komokar, J.M., 'Cartes Causales d'un milieu de travail', in P. Cossette (ed.), *Cartes Cognitives et Organisations*, Québec: Les Presses de l'Université de Laval et les Editions Eska, 1994, pp. 155–84.

Kopalle, P.K. and Lehman, D.R., 'Alpha Inflation? The Impact of Eliminating Scale Items on Cronbach's Alpha', *Organizational Behavior and Human Decision Processes*, 70 (3), 1997: 189–97.

Krippendorf, K., *Content Analysis: An Introduction to Its Methodology*, Beverly Hills, CA: Sage, 1980.

Kuhn, T., *The Structure of Scientific Revolutions*, Chicago: University of Chicago Press, 1962.

LaGarce, R. and Kuhn, L.D., 'The Effect of Visual Stimuli on Mail Survey Response Rates', *Industrial Marketing Management*, 24, 1995: 11–19.

Lakatos, I., 'Falsification and the Methodology of Scientific Research Programs', in: I. Lakatos and A. Musgrove (eds), *Criticism and the Growth of Knowledge*, Cambridge: Cambridge University Press, 1974: 91–196.

Lakatos, I. and Musgrave, A., *Criticism and the Growth of Knowledge*, Cambridge: Cambridge University Press, 1974.

Lambin, J.-J., *La recherche marketing*, Paris: McGraw-Hill, 1990.

Lambin, J.-J., *La recherche marketing: analyser, mesurer, prévoir*, Paris: Ediscience, 1993.

Landry, M., 'A Note on the Concept of "Problem"', *Organization Studies*, 16 (2), 1995: 315–43.

Langfield-Smith, K., 'Exploring the Need for a Shared Cognitive Map', *Journal of Management Studies*, 29 (3), 1992: 349–68.

Langfield-Smith, K. and Wirth, A., 'Measuring Differences Between Cognitive Maps', *Journal of Operational Research Society*, 43 (12), 1992: 1135–50.

Langley, A., Mintzberg, H., Pitcher, P., Posala, E. and Saint Macary, J., 'Opening Up Decision Making: the View from the Black Stool', *Organization Science*, 6 (3), 1995: 260–79.

Laukkanen, M., 'Understanding the Formation of Managers' Cognitive Maps: A Comparative Case Study of Context Traces in Two Business Firm Clusters', Helsinki School of Economics and Business Administration, Helsinki, Finland, 1989.

Laukkanen, M., 'Comparative Cause Mapping of Management Cognitions: A Computer Data Base Method for Natural Data', Helsinki School of Economics and Business Administration, Publications D-154, Helsinki, Finland, 1992.

Laukkanen, M., 'Comparative Cause Mapping of Organizational Cognitions', *Organization Science*, 5 (3), 1994: 322–43.

Laumann, O.E., Marsden, P.V. and Prensky, D., *The Boundary Specification Problem in Network Analysis*, London: Sage, 1983, pp. 18–34.

Lazarsfeld, P., 'Des concepts aux indices empiriques', in R. Boudon and P. Lazarsfeld (eds), *Le vocabulaire des sciences sociales*, Paris: Mouton, 1967.

Lazega, E., 'Analyse de réseaux d'une organisation collégiale: les avocats d'affaires', *Revue Française de Sociologie*, 23, 1992: 85–95.

Lazega, E., 'Analyse de réseaux et sociologie des organisations, *Revue Française de Sociologie*, 35, 1994: 55–78.

Le Moigne, J.L., *Les épistémologies constructivistes*, Collection Que Sais-je?, 2969, Paris: Presses Universitaires de France, 1995.

Lebart, L. and Mirkin, B., 'Correspondence Analysis and Classification', in C.M. Cuadras and C.M. Rao (eds), *Multivariate Analysis: Future Directions 2*, Amsterdam: North Holland, 1993.

Lebart, L., Morineau, A. and Warwick, K., *Multivariate Descriptive Statistical Analysis*, New York: Wiley, 1984 .

Lee, A., 'Integrating Positivist and Interpretative Approaches to Organizational Research', *Organization Science*, 2 (4), 1991: 342–65.

Lee, R.M., *Doing Research on Sensitive Topics*, Thousand Oaks, CA: Sage, 1993.

Lehmann, E.L., *Testing Statistical Hypotheses*, Pacific Grove, CA: Wadsworth and Brooks, 1991.

Leik, R. and Chalkey, M., 'On the Stability of Network Relations Under Stress', *Social Networks*, 19, 1997: 63–74.

Lessler, J.T. and Kalsbeek, W.D., *Nonsampling Error in Surveys*, New York: Wiley, 1992.

Levy, P.S. and Lemeshow, S., *Sampling of Populations: Methods and Applications*, New York: Wiley, 1991.

Lewis, P. and Thomas, H., 'The Linkage Between Strategy, Strategic Groups and Performance in the UK Retail Grocery Industry', *Strategic Management Journal*, 11, 1990: 385–97.

Lincoln, Y.S. and Guba, E.G., *Naturalistic Inquiry*, Beverly Hills, CA: Sage, 1985.

Linsky, A.S., 'Stimulating Responses to Mailed Questionnaires: A Review', *Public Opinion Quarterly*, 39, 1975: 82–101.

Locke, K. and Golden-Biddle, K., 'Constructing Opportunities for Contribution: Structuring Intertextual Coherence and "Problematizing" in Organizational Studies', *Academy of Management Journal*, 40 (5), 1997: 1023–62.

MacCallum, R.C., Browne, M.W. and Sugawara, H.M., 'Power Analysis and Determination of Sample Size for Covariance Structure Modeling', *Psychological Methods*, 1 (2), 1996: 130–49.

Maclean, N., *Young Men and Fire*, Chicago: University of Chicago Press, 1992.

Markoczy, L. and Goldberg, J., 'A Method for Eliciting and Comparing Causal Maps', Working Paper, Budapest University of Economics, 1993: 5.

Marshall, C. and Rossman, G.B., *Designing Qualitative Research*, Beverly Hills, CA: Sage, 1989.

Maruyama, G.M., *Basics of Structural Equation Modeling*, Thousand Oaks, CA: Sage, 1998.

Mazen, A.M., Lee, A.G., Kellogg, C.E. and Hemmasi, M., 'Statistical Power in Contemporary Management Research', *Academy of Management Journal*, 30 (2), 1987: 369–80.

McCall, M. and Bobko, P., 'Research Methods and Discovery in Industrial/Organizational Psychology', in M. Dunnette and L. Hough (eds), *Handbook of Industrial and Organizational Psychology*, Palo Alto, CA: Consulting Psychologists Press, vol. 1, 1990, pp. 381–418.

McKinley, W. and Mone, M., 'The Re-construction of Organization Studies: Wrestling with Incommensurability', *Organization*, 5 (2), 1998: 169–90.

McWilliams, A. and Siegel, D., 'Event Studies in Management Research: Theoretical and Empirical Issues', *Academy of Management Journal*, 40 (3), 1997: 626–57.

Menard, S., *Longitudinal Research*, Sage University Paper Series on Quantitative Applications in the Social Sciences, no. 07–076, Newbury Park, CA: Sage, 1991.

Merton, R.K., Fiske, M. and Kendall, P.L., *Focused Interviews: A Manual of Problems and Procedures*, 2nd edn, New York: Free Press, 1990.

Metzger, R.O. (1993), *Developing a Consulting Practice*, Newbury Park, CA: Sage.

Meyer, A., Tsui, A. and Hinings, C., 'Configurational Approaches to Organizational Analysis', *Academy of Management Journal*, 36 (6), 1993: 1175–95.

Meyer, A.D., 'From Loose Coupling to Environmental Jolts', in P. J. Frost and R.E. Stablein (eds), *Doing Exemplary Research*, Newbury Park, CA: Sage, 1992, pp. 82–98.

Meyer, A.D., 'Balls, Strikes, and Collisions on the Base Path: Ruminations of a Veteran Reviewer', in L.L. Cummings and P.J. Frost (eds), *Publishing in the Organizational Sciences*, 2nd edn, Thousand Oaks, CA: Sage, 1995, pp. 257–68.

Miles, G. and Snow, C.C., *Organizational Strategy, Structure, and Process*, New York: McGraw-Hill, 1978.

Miles, M.B., 'Qualitative Data as an Attractive Nuisance: The Problem of Analysis', *Administrative Science Quarterly*, 24, 1979: 590–601.

Miles, M.B. and Huberman, A.M., *Analysing Qualitative Data: A Source Book for New Methods*, Beverly Hills, CA: Sage, 1984a.

Miles, M.B. and Huberman, A.M., *Qualitative Data Analysis*, London: Sage, 1984b.

Miles, M.B. and Huberman, A.M., *Qualitative Data Analysis: An Expanded Sourcebook*, Newbury Park, CA: Sage, 1994.

Milicic, B., 'Exchange and Social Stratification in the Eastern Adriatic: A Graph Theoretic Model', *Ethnology*, 32, 1993: 375–95.

Mill, J.S., *System of Logic*, London: Classworks, 1843.

Miller, C.C., Cardinal, L.B. and Glick, W.H., 'Retrospective Reports in Organizational Research: A Reexamination of Recent Evidence', *Academy of Management Journal*, 40 (1), 1997: 189–204.

Miller, D. and Friesen, P., 'Momentum and Revolution in Organizational Adaptation', *Academy of Management Journal*, 23 (4), 1980: 551–614.

Miller, D. and Friesen, P., 'The Longitudinal Analysis of Organizations: A Methodological Perspective', *Management Science*, 28 (9), 1982: 1013–34.

Miller, D. and Friesen, P., 'Strategy-Making and Environment: The Third Link', *Strategic Management Journal*, 4, 1983: 221–35.

Miller, D. and Friesen, P.H., 'Archetypes of Strategy Formulation', *Management Science*, 24, 1978: 921–33.

Miller, D.C., *Handbook of Research Design and Social Measurement*, 5th edn, Newbury Park, CA: Sage, 1991.

Miller, J.G., *Living Systems*, New York: McGraw-Hill, 1978.

Milton, J.S., 'A Sample Size Formula for Multiple Regression Studies', *Public Opinion Quarterly*, 50, Spring, 1986: 112–18.

Miner, S., Amburgey, L. and Stearns, T., 'Interorganizational Linkages and Population Dynamics: Buffering and Transformational Shields', *Administrative Science Quarterly*, 35, December, 1990: 689–713.

Mintzberg, H., 'Structure in 5's: A Synthesis of Research on Organization Design', *Management Science*, 26 (3), 1980: 322–41.

Mintzberg, H., *The Nature of Managerial Work*, New York: Harper and Row, 1973.

Mintzberg, H., *Mintzberg on Management: Inside our Strange World of Organizations*, New York: Free Press, 1989.

Mintzberg, H., Pascale, R., Goold, M. and Rumelt, R., 'The Honda Effect Revisited', *California Management Review*, 38 (4), 1996: 78–117.

Mintzberg, H., Raisinghani, D. and Théorêt, A., 'The Structure of "Unstructured" Decision Processes', *Administrative Science Quarterly*, 21 (2), 1976: 246–75.

Mitchell, R.G., *Mountain Experience: The Psychology and Sociology of Adventure*, Chicago: University of Chicago Press, 1983.

Mitchell, R.G., *Secrecy and Fieldwork*, Newbury Park, CA: Sage, 1993.

Mitroff, I.I., 'The Myth of Objectivity, or, Why Science Needs a New Psychology of Science', *Management Science*, 18, 1972: B613–B618.

Mizruchi, M.S. and Stearns, L.B., 'A Longitudinal Study of Borrowing by Large American Corporations', *Administrative Science Quarterly*, 39 (1), 1994: 118–40.

Molière, J.L., 'What's the Real Number of Clusters?' in W. Gaul and M. Schader (eds), *Classification as Tool of Research*, Amsterdam: North Holland, 1986.

Monge, P., 'Theoretical and Analytical Issues in Studying Organizational Processes', *Organization Science*, 1 (4), 1990: 406–30.

Mooney, C.Z. and Duval, R.D., *Bootstrapping: A Nonparametric Approach to Statistical Inference*, Newbury Park, CA: Sage, 1993.

Morgan, G., *Images of Organization*, Beverly Hills, CA: Sage, 1986.

Morse, J.M., 'Designing Founded Qualitative Research', in N.K. Denzin and Y.S. Lincoln (eds), *Handbook of Qualitative Research*, Thousand Oaks, CA: Sage, 1994, pp. 220–35.

Northrop, F.S., *The Logic of the Sciences and the Humanities*, Cleveland, OH: World, 1959.

Nutt, P., 'Types of Organizational Decision Processes', *Administrative Science Quarterly*, 29 (3), 1984: 414–50.

Ohsumi, N., 'The Role of Computer Graphics in Interpretation of Clustering Results', in E. Diday et al. (eds), *Recent Developement in Clustering and Data Analysis*, Boston: Academic Press, 1988.

Osborn, N. and Baughn, C., 'Forms of Interorganizational Governance for Multinational Alliances', *Academy of Management Journal*, 33 (3), 1990: 503–19.

Ossowski, S., *Class Structure in the Social Consciousness*, London: Routledge and Kegan Paul, 1963.

Otley, D.T. and Berry, A.J., 'Case Study Research in Management Accounting and Control', *Management Accounting Research*, 5, 1994: 45–65.

Parker, M., 'Life after Jean-Francois' in J. Hassard and M. Parker (eds), *Postmodernism and Organization*, London: Sage, 1993: 204–13.

Parker, M., 'Critique in the Name of What? Postmodernism and Critical Approaches to Organization', *Organization Studies*, 16 (4), 1995: 553–64.

Patton, M.Q., *Qualitative Evaluation Methods*, Beverly Hills, CA: Sage, 1980.

Pelz, D.C., 'Innovation Complexity and the Sequence of Innovating Stages', *Knowledge: Creation, Diffusion, Utilization*, 6 (3), 1985: 261–91.

Pentland, T.B., 'Grammatical Models of Organizational Processes', *Organization Science*, 6 (5), 1995: 541–55.

Peterson, R.A., 'A Meta-analysis of Cronbach's Coefficient Alpha', *Journal of Consumer Research*, 21, 1994: 381–91.

Pettigrew, A., 'The Character and Significance of Strategy Process Research', *Strategic Management Journal*, Special Issue, 13, 1992: 5–16.

Pfeffer, J., 'Barriers to the Advance of Organizational Science: Paradigm Development as a Dependent Variable', *Academy of Management Review*, 18 (4), 1993: 599–620.

Podsakoff, P.M. and Dalton, D.R., 'Research Methodology in Organization Studies', *Journal of Management*, 13, 1987: 419–41.

Pondy, L.R., 'The Reviewer as Defense Attorney', in L.L. Cummings and P.J. Frost (eds), *Publishing in the Organizational Sciences*, 2nd edn, Thousand Oaks, CA: Sage, 1995: 183–94.

Pondy, L.R. and Mitroff, I.I., 'Beyond Open System Models of Organization,' in B.M. Staw (ed.), *Research in Organizational Behavior*, Greenwich, CT: Jai Press, 1, 1979: 3–39.

Poole, M.S., 'Decision Development in Small Groups III: A Multiple Sequence Model of Group Decision Development', *Communication Monographs*, 50 (4), 1983: 321–41.

Poole, M.S. and Roth, J., 'Decision Development in Small Groups IV: A Typology of Group Decision Paths', *Human Communication Research*, 15 (3), 1989: 323–56.

Popper, K.R., *Objective Knowledge*, London: Oxford University Press, 1972.

Popper, K.R., *The Logic of Scientific Discovery*, London: Hutchinson, 1977.

Porter, M.E., *Competitive Strategy*, New York: Free Press, 1980.

Porter, M., 'Towards a Dynamic Theory of Strategy', *Strategic Management Journal*, Special Issue, 12, 1991: 95–117.

Pounds, W., 'The Process of Problem Finding', *Industrial Management Review*, 11 (1), 1969: 1–19.

Punch, M., *The Politics and Ethics of Fieldwork*, Beverly Hills, CA: Sage, 1986.

Punj, G. and Steward, D.-W., 'Cluster Analysis in Marketing Research: Review and Suggestions for Application', *Journal of Marketing Research*, 20, 1983: 134–48.

Quinn, R.E. and Cameron, K.S., 'A Dynamic Theory of Organization and Management', in B.E. Quinn and K.S. Cameron (eds), *Paradox and Transformation Toward a Theory of Change in Organization and Management*, Cambridge, MA: Ballinger Publications, 1988: 289–308.

Quivy, R. and Van Campenhoudt, L., *Manuel de recherches en sciences sociales*, Paris: Dunod, 1988.

Reeves Sanday, P., 'The Ethnographic Paradigm(s)', in J. Van Maanen (ed.), *Qualitative Methodology*, Newbury Park, CA: Sage, 1983, pp. 19–36.

Richardson, L., *Writing Strategies: Reaching Diverse Audiences*, Qualitative Research Methods Series, 21, Newbury Park, CA: Sage, 1990.

Roberts, C.W., *Text Analysis for the Social Sciences: Methods for Drawing Statistical Inferences from Texts and Transcripts*, Mahwah, NJ: Lawrence Erlbaum Associates, 1997.

Roberts, K.H. and O'Reilly, C.A. III, 'Some Correlations of Communication Roles in Organizations', *Academy of Management Journal*, 22 (1), 1979: 12–35.

Robinson, J.P., Shaver, P.R. and Wrightsman, L.S., *Measures of Personality and Social Psychological Attitudes*, New York: Academy Press, 1991.

Robinson, R.B. and Pearce, J.A., 'The Impact of Formalized Strategic Planning on Financial Performance in Small Organizations', *Strategic Management Journal*, 4, 1983: 197–207.

Robinson, W.S., 'The Statistical Measurement of Agreement', *American Sociological Review*, 22, 1957: 17–25.

Rogosa, D., 'Myths about Longitudinal Research', in K.W. Schaie, R.T. Campbell, W. Meredith, and S.C. Rawlings (eds), *Methodological Issues in Aging Research*, New York: Springer, 1988, pp. 171–209.

Romanelli, E. and Tushman, M.L., 'Inertia, Environments, and Strategic Choice: A Quasi-experimental Design for Comparative-Longitudinal Research', *Management Science*, 32 (5), 1986: 608–21.

Rosch, E., 'Principles of Categorization', in E. Rosch, and B.B. Lloyd (eds), *Cognition and Categorization*, Hillsdale, NJ: Lawrence Erbaum, 1978, pp. 27–48.

Ross, J. and Straw, B.M., 'Organizational Escalation and Exit: Lessons from the Shoreham Nuclear Power Plant', *Academy of Management Journal*, 36 (4), 1993: 701–32.

Rossi, P.H., Wright, J.D. and Anderson, A.B., *Handbook of Survey Research*, San Diego: Academic Press, 1985.

Rousseau, D.M., 'Publishing From a Reviewer's Perspective', in L.L. Cummings and P.J. Frost (eds), *Publishing in the Organizational Sciences*, 2nd edn, Thousand Oaks, CA: Sage, 1995, pp. 151–63.

Rubin, H.J., 'There Aren't Going to be Any Bakeries Here if There is no Money to Afford Jellyrolls: The Organic Theory of Community Based Development', *Social Problems*, 41 (3), 1994: 401–24.

Rubin, H.J. and Rubin, I.S., *Qualitative Interviewing: The Art of Hearing Data*, Thousand Oaks, CA: Sage, 1995.

Rudestan, K.E. and Newton, R.R., *Surviving your Dissertation*, Newbury Park, CA: Sage, 1992.

Ryan, B., Scapens, R.W. and Theobald, M., *Research Method and Methodology in Finance and Accounting*, London: Academic Press, 1991.

Salant, P. and Dillman, D.A., *How to Conduct your Own Survey*, New York: Wiley, 1994.

Sanday, P., 'The Ethnographic Paradigms', *Administrative Science Quarterly*, 24, December, 1979: 527–38.

Sarason, I.G., Smith, R.E. and Diener, E., 'Personality Research: Components of Variance Attributable to the Person and the Situation', *Journal of Personality and Social Psychology*, 32, 1975: 199–204.

SAS Institute, Inc., *SAS Users Guide: Statistics, Version 6 Edition*, Cary, NC: SAS Institute, 1989.

Sawyer, A.G. and Ball, A.D., 'Statistical Power and Effect Size in Marketing Research,' *Journal of Marketing Research*, 18 (3), 1981: 275–90.

Schatzman, L. and Strauss, A.L., *Field Research, Strategies for a Natural Sociology*, Englewood Cliffs, NJ: Prentice-Hall, 1973.

Scherer, A., 'Pluralism and Incommensurability in Strategic Management and Organization Theory: A Problem in Search of a Solution', *Organization*, 5 (2), 1998: 147–68.

Schneider, S.C. and Angelmar, R., 'Cognition in Organizational Analysis: Who's Minding the Store?', *Organization Studies*, 14 (3), 1993: 347–74.

Schultz, M. and Hatch, M., 'Living with Multiple Paradigms: The Case of Paradigm Interplay in Organizational Culture Studies', *Academy of Management Review*, 21 (2), 1996: 529–57.

Schuman, H. and Presser, S., *Questions and Answers in Attitude Surveys: Experiments on Question Form, Wording and Context*, Thousand Oaks: Sage, 1996.

Schwandt, T.A., 'Constructivist, Interpretivist Approaches to Human Inquiry', in N.K. Denzin and Y.S. Lincoln (eds), *Handbook of Qualitative Research*, Thousand Oaks: Sage, 1994: 118–37.

Schwenk, C., 'Why Sacrifice Rigor for Relevance? A Proposal for Combining Laboratory and Field Research in Strategic Management', *Strategic Management Journal*, 3, 1982: 213–25.

Scott, J., *Social Network Analysis: A Handbook*, London: Sage, 1991.

Segal, L., *Le rêve de la réalité*, Paris: Seuil, 1990 (Original title: *The Dream of Reality*, New York: Norton, 1986).

Selltiz, C., Wrightsman, L.S. and Cook, S.W., in collaboration with Balch, G.I., Hofstetter, R. and Bickman, L., *Research Methods in Social Relations*, New York: Holt, Rinehart and Winston, 1976.

Seungwha, A.C., 'Performance Effects of Cooperative Strategies among Investment Banking Firms: A Loglinear Analysis of Organizational Exchange Networks', *Social Networks*, 18 (2), 1996: 121–48.

Sharma, S., Durand, R.M. and Gur-Arie, O., 'Identification and Analysis of Moderator Variables', *Journal of Marketing Research*, 18, 1981: 291–300.

Shaver, J.M., Mitchell, W. and Yeung, B., 'The Effect of Own-Firm and Other Firm Experience on Foreign Direct Investment Survival in the United States, 1987–92', *Strategic Management Journal*, 18 (10), 1997: 811–24.

Silverman, D., *Interpreting Qualitative Data: Methods for Analysing Talk, Text, and Interaction*, London: Sage, 1993.

Sincich, T., *Business Statistics by Example*, 5th edn, Upper Saddle River, NJ: Prentice-Hall, 1996.

Smircich, L., 'Concepts of Culture and Organizational Analysis', *Administrative Science Quarterly*, 28, 1983: 339–58.

Snow, C.C. and Thomas, J.B., 'Field Research Methods in Strategic Management: Contributions to Theory Building and Testing', *Journal of Management Studies*, 31, 1994: 457–79.

Sosdian, C.P. and Sharp, L.M., 'Non Response in Mail Surveys: Access Failure or Respondent Resistance', *Public Opinion Quarterly*, 44, 1980: 396–402.

Spearman, C., 'Correlation Calculated with Faulty Data', *British Journal of Psychology*, 3, 1910: 271–95.

Spector, P.E., *Research Designs*, Sage University Papers series Quantitative Applications in the Social Sciences, Beverly Hills, CA: Sage, 1981.

Stablein, R., 'Data in Organization Studies', in S.R. Clegg, C. Hardy and W.R. Nord (eds), *Handbook of Organization Studies*, London: Sage, 1996.

Stake, R.E., *The Art of Case Study Research*, Thousand Oaks, CA: Sage, 1995.

Starbuck, W.H. and Miliken, F.J., 'Executive Perceptual Filters: What They Notice and How They Make Sense', in D. Hambrick (ed.), *The Executive Effect: Concepts and Methods for Studying Top Managers*, Greenwich, CT: JAI Press, 1988, pp. 35–65.

Steers, R.M., 'Problems in the Measurement of Organizational Effectiveness', *Administrative Science Quarterly*, 20, 1975: 546–58.

Stewart, D.W., 'The Application and Misapplication of Factor Analysis in Marketing Research', *Journal of Marketing Research*, 18, 1981: 51–62.

Strauss, A. and Corbin, J., *Basics of Qualitative Research. Grounded Theory, Procedures and Techniques*, Newbury Park, CA: Sage, 1990.

Strauss, A. and Corbin, J., 'Grounded Theory Methodology: An Overview', in N.K. Denzin and Y.S. Lincoln (eds), *Handbook of Qualitative Research*, Thousand Oaks, CA: Sage, 1994, pp. 274–85.

Stubbs, M., *Discourse Analysis*, Chicago: University of Chicago Press, 1983.

Sudman, S., *Applied Sampling*, New York: Academic Press, 1976.

Suitor, J., Wellman, B. and Morgan, D., 'It's About Time: How, Why and When Networks Change', *Social Networks*, 19 (1), 1997: 1–7.

Sutton, R.I., 'The Virtues of Closet Qualitative Research', *Organization Science*, 8 (1), 1997: 97–106.

Taylor, M.S., Audia, G. and Gupta, A.K., 'The Effect of Lengthening Job Tenure on Managers' Organizational Commitment and Turnover', *Organization Science*, 7 (6), 1996: 632–48.

Tellis, G.J. and Golder, P.N., 'First to Market, First to Fail? Real Causes for Enduring Market Leadership', *Sloan Management Review*, 37 (2), Winter, 1996: 65–75.

Thomas, H. and Venkatraman, N., 'Research on Strategic Groups: Progress and Prognosis', *Journal of Management Studies*, 25 (6), 1988: 537–55.

Thomas, J.B., Clark, S.M. and Gioia, D.A., 'Strategic Sensemaking and Organizational Performance: Linkages among Scanning, Interpretation, Action, and Outcomes', *Academy of Management Journal*, 36 (2), 1993: 239–70.

Thompson, J.D. and Demerath, N.J., 'Some Experiences with the Group Interview', *Social Forces*, 31, 1952: 148–54.

Thompson, S.K., *Sampling*, New York: Wiley, 1992.

Thyer, B.A., *Successful Publishing in Scholarly Journals*, Survival Skills for Scholars Series, 11 Thousand Oaks, CA: Sage, 1994.

Tichy, N.M., Tushman, M.L. and Fombrun, C., 'Social Network Analysis for Organizations', *Academy of Management Review*, 4 (4), 1979: 86–105.

Tomaskovic-Devey, D., Leiter, J. and Thompson, S., 'Organizational Survey Nonresponse', *Administrative Science Quarterly*, 39 (3), 1994: 439–57.

Toyoda, T., 'Use of the Chow Test under Heteroscedasticity', *Econometrica*, 42 (3), 1974: 601.

Tracy, L., 'Applications of Living Systems Theory to the Study of Management and Organizational Behavior', *Behavioral Science*, 38, 1993: 218–30.

Tull, D. and Hawkins, D., *Marketing Research, Meaning, Measurement and Method*, 4th edn, New York: Macmillan, 1987.

Van de Ven, A., 'Suggestions for Studying Strategy Process: A Research Note', *Strategic Management Journal*, 1 (3), 1992: 169–88.

Van de Ven, A. and Poole, M., 'Explaining Development and Change in Organizations', *Academy of Management Review*, 20 (3), 1995: 510–40.

Van de Ven, A.H. and Poole, M.S., 'Methods for Studying Innovation Processes', in A.H. Van de Ven H.L. Angle and M.S. Poole (eds), *Research on the Management of Innovation: The Minnesota Studies*, New York: Harper and Row, 1989, pp. 31–54.

Van de Ven, A.H., Angle, H.L. and Poole, M.S. (eds), *Research on the Management of Innovation: The Minnesota Studies*, New York: Harper and Row, 1989.

Van Maanen, J., 'Reclaiming Qualitative Methods for Organizational Research: A Preface', *Administrative Science Quarterly*, 24, 1979: 520–6.

Van Maanen, J., 'Reclaiming Qualitative Methods for Organizational Research: A Preface', in J. Van Maanen (ed.), *Qualitative Methodology*, Newbury Park, CA: Sage, 1983a, pp. 9–18.

Van Maanen, J., 'The Fact of Fiction in Organizational Ethnography in Qualitative Methodology', in J. Van Maanen (ed.), *Qualitative Methodology*, Newbury Park, CA: Sage, 1983b, pp. 37–55.

Van Maanen, J., *Tales of the Field: On Writing Ethnography*, Chicago: University of Chicago Press, 1988.

Van Maanen, J., 'Fear and Loathing in Organization Studies', *Organization Science*, 6 (6), 1995a: 687–92.

Van Maanen, J., 'Style as Theory', *Organization Science*, 6 (1), 1995b: 133–43.

Vaughan, D., 'Autonomy, Interdependence, and Social Control: NASA and the Space Shuttle Challenger', *Administrative Science Quarterly*, 35 (2), 1990: 225–57.

Venkatraman, N., 'Strategic Orientation of Business Entreprises: The Construct, Dimensionality, and Measurement', *Management Science*, 35 (8), 1989: 942–63.

Venkatraman, N. and Grant, J., 'Construct Measurement in Organization Strategy Research: A Critique and Proposal', *Academy of Management Review*, 11 (1), 1986: 71–87.

Von Glasersfeld, E., in P.D. Watzlawick (ed.), 'Introduction to Practical Constructivism', *Invented Reality: How We Know What We Believe We Know?* New York: W.W. Norton, 1984.

Von Glasersfeld, E., *The Construction of Knowledge*, Salinas, CA: Intersystem Publications, 1987.

Von Glasersfeld, E., 'Introduction à un constructivisme radical', in P. Watzlawick (ed.), *L'invention de la Réalité*, Paris: Seuil, 1988, pp. 19–43 (Original title: *Die Erfundene Wirklichkeit Wie Wissen Wir, was wir zu wissen glauben? Beiträge zur Konstructivismus*, München: Piper, 1981, 1985).

Walker, R., 'An Introduction to Applied Qualitative Research', in R. Walker (ed.), *Applied Qualitative Research*, Brookfield, VT: Gower, 1985, pp. 3–26.

Warwick, D.P., *The Teaching of Ethics in the Social Sciences*, New York: Hasting Center, 1982.

Watzlawick, P. (ed.), *Invented Reality: How We Know What we Believe We Know?* W.W. Norton, 1984.

Weaver, G. and Gioia, D., 'Paradigms Lost: Incommensurability vs Structurationist Inquiry', *Organization Studies*, 15 (4), 1994: 565–90.

Webb, E. and Weick, K.E., 'Unobstrusive Measures in Organizational Theory: A Reminder', *Administrative Science Quarterly*, 24, 1979: 651–9.

Webb, E.J., Campbell, D.T., Schwartz, R.D. and Sechrest, L., *Unobstrusive Measures: Non-Reactive Research in the Social Sciences*, Chicago: Rand McNally, 1966.

Weber, R.P., *Basic Content Analysis*, Sage University Papers, Newbury Park, CA: Sage, 1990.

Weick, K.E., 'Systematic Observational Methods', in G. Lindzey and E. Aronson (eds), *Handbook of Social Psychology*, vol. 4, Reading, MA: Addison Wesley, 1968.

Weick, K.E., *The Social Psychology of Organization*; Reading, MA: Addison Wesley, 1979.

Weick, K., 'Theory Construction as Disciplined Imagination', *Academy of Management Review*, 14 (4), 1989: 551–61.

Weick, K.E., 'The collapse of sense-making in organizations: the Mann Gulch disaster', *Administrative Science Quarterly*, 38, 1993: 628–52.

Weick, K. and Bougon, M., 'Organizations as Cognitive Maps: Charting Ways to Success and Failure', in D. Sims and D.A. Gioia (eds), *The Thinking Organization*, San Francisco: Jossey Bass, 1986.

Welman, B., Wong, R., Tindall, D. and Nazer, N., 'A Decade of Network Change: Turnover, Persistence and Stability in Personal Communities', *Social Networks*, 19, 1997: 27–50.

Whyte, W.F., *Street Corner Society: The Social Structure of an Italian Slum*, Chicago: University of Chicago Press, 1944.

Whyte, W.F., *Street Corner Society: The Social Structure of an Italian Slum*, 4th edn, Chicago: University of Chicago Press, 1993.

Wolcott, H.F., *Writing Up Qualitative Research*, Qualitative Research Methods Series, 20, Newbury Park, CA: Sage, 1990.

Wold, H., 'Systems Under Indirect Observation Using PLS', in C. Fornell (ed.), *A Second Generation of Multivariate Analysis*, New York: Praeger, 1982.

Wrightson, M.T., 'The Documentary Coding Method', in R. Axelrod (ed.), *Structure of the Decision: The Cognitive Maps of Political Elites*, Princeton, NJ: Princeton University Press, 1976.

Yamaguchi, K., *Event History Analysis*, Applied Social Research Methods Series, 28, Newbury Park, CA: Sage, 1991.

Yammarino, F.J., Skinner, S.J. and Childers, T.L., 'Understanding Mail Survey Response Behavior', *Public Opinion Quarterly*, 55, 1991: 613–39.

Yin, R., *Case Study Research, Design and Methods*, Newbury Park, CA: Sage, 1984, reprinted 1989.

Yin, R.K., *Case Study Research: Design and Methods*, Applied Social Research Methods Series, 5, Newbury Park, CA: Sage, 1990.

Zajac, E.J. and Westphal, J.D., 'Director Reputation, CEO-Board Power, and the Dynamics of Board Interlocks', *Administrative Science Quarterly*, 41 (3), 1996: 507–29.

Zaltman, C., Pinson, C. and Angelmar, R., *Metatheory and Consumer Research*, New York: Holt, Reinhart and Winston, 1973.

Zeller, R. and Carmines, E., *Measurement in the Social Sciences: The Link Between Theory and Data*, Cambridge: Cambridge University Press, 1980.

Zikmund, W.G., *Business Research Methods*, 4th edn, Orlando, FL: Dryden Press, 1994.

INDEX